1982

PERSONAL RELATIONSHIPS

AN APPROACH TO MARRIAGE AND FAMILY

PERSONAL RELATIONSHIPS

AN APPROACH TO MARRIAGE AND FAMILY

Ernest J. Green

Prince George's Community College

With Case Studies by

Sharon Davis Massey and Robert F. Massey

McGraw-Hill Book Company

New York   St. Louis   San Francisco   Auckland   Bogotá   Düsseldorf   Johannesburg
London   Madrid   Mexico   Montreal   New Delhi   Panama
Paris   São Paulo   Singapore   Sydney   Tokyo   Toronto

This is a Leogryph book.
The editors were Susan Hajjar, Rodie Siegler, and Ruth Zaslavsky.

The book was set in Optima by Black Dot, Inc.,
under the editorial supervision of Donald W. Burden, Lyle Linder, and Laura D. Warner;
the designer was Joan E. O'Connor;
the production supervisor was Charles Hess.
The drawings were done by J & R Services, Inc.
Von Hoffmann Press, Inc., was printer and binder.

See Acknowledgements and Permissions on pages 453–456.
Copyrights included on this page by reference.

PERSONAL RELATIONSHIPS: An Approach to Marriage and Family

1234567890VHVH 783210987

Library of Congress Cataloging in Publication Data

Green, Ernest J
Personal relationships.

Bibliography: p.
Includes index.
1.   Family life education.   I.   Title.
HQ10.G716   301.42   77-14208
ISBN 0-07-024270-4

CONTENTS

vii

CONTENTS

viii

CONTENTS

ix

CONTENTS

CONTENTS

PREFACE

Designed for a college-level course in marriage and the family, this book is intended to give the student an integrated, functional, and informative overview of intimate personal relationships between adults and between parents and children. It is unique among texts in the field, in that each chapter concludes with a study guide containing questions and other material to supplement the topics presented. In addition, each chapter includes a case study presenting problems typical of those faced by many people in the course of their lives. We believe that students do not need yet another package of facts and figures about marriage and family relationships and that they will not respond deeply to a mass of theories unattached to the mainland of their private experience. Our primary goal, and challenge, is nothing less than to provide a unifying theme that will serve as a bridge between sociological research and the events and problems which students confront in their daily lives.

The approach to personal relationships we have chosen is based on a profoundly deep regard for human worth and growth. It is an approach which deals most cogently and sympathetically with the problems of realizing human potential while encouraging others, especially those whom we love, to realize the full potential of their own lives.

The first five chapters of the text explore the nature of personal interactions and describe how relationships are formed with friends, lovers, and potential marital partners. These chapters orient students to the often confusing terrain of their own feelings and attitudes about commitment, communication, and intimacy with others. They clarify changing ideas about sex roles, which even now are altering the ways in which men and women perceive themselves and relate to one another.

Chapters 6 to 9 give an insight into the dynamics of marital adjustment and methods for both enriching married life and dealing with the conflicts which are a part of living intimately with another person. Students will gain an understanding of the social pressures which have shaped attitudes toward work, money, and marriage. The practical tools for coping with the financial aspects of a marital partnership are also discussed.

Interpersonal relationships in the context of the family life cycle, from planning for children to planning for retirement, are examined in Chapters 10 to 13. Considerable attention is given to understanding how children grow and, in effect, to understanding how the student's own life has been influenced by the parent-child relationship. Emphasis is placed on achieving the kinds of interaction which develop the creative potential of both parent and child. Chapter 14 deals with various life stresses, including death, which can strain and alter family relationships.

In Chapter 15 the student becomes acquainted with different aspects of the divorce experience and the effects of divorce on the wife, husband, and children. Chapter 16 explores a variety of lifestyles which are outside the traditional social structures of marriage and the family.

Mastery of the text material is aided by end-of-chapter summaries and an extensive glossary at the end of the book. The innovative end-of-chapter study guides provide a list of important terms; a review quiz (with answers given at the end of the guide); personal applications and miniprojects; paper-and-pencil exercises; opinionnaires, which encourage students to formulate and compare their attitudes toward various issues and problems; and suggestions for further reading, which include a range of material—popular literature, professional research, and fiction—relevant to the content of a given chapter.

The case studies serve to concretize the text discussion and enhance student identification with the material. Each study reflects one or several aspects of the chapter to which it is appended and provides a view of real-life situations illustrating the multifaceted nature of personal relationships. The questions at the end of each case study enable students to clarify their interpretation of the issues at hand, and suggest that there are always several possible views on interpersonal problems and more than one way of solving them.

In writing a sociological text exploring human relations from the humanist perspective, we have avoided the dogmatic and the judgmental. Throughout the text, the student is encouraged and helped to make individual decisions regarding issues and problems. Sociological theory and the latest research concerning social trends and developments are used to illuminate personal experience and, in some cases, to anchor it within the shared life of our modern society.

No attempt at organizing and developing a major college textbook can succeed at all its levels without the involvement and counsel of dedicated professionals—people who have a sophisticated understanding of their field and a personal commitment to their students. Special thanks must first be extended to Lyle Linder and Laura Warner at McGraw-Hill for their care and attention from the onset of the project. Our own effort to combine a humanist approach with an up-to-date presentation of sociological phenomena was monitored by several specialists in marriage and the family who were especially sensitive to the format employed and its usefulness and relevance to students. We extend our deepest thanks to Professor Betsy Bergen of Kansas State University, Professor Michael Goslin of Tallahassee Community College, Professor S. L. Harris of Terrant Community College, Professor Sharon Price-Bonhom of the University of Georgia, and Professor Tommie M. Lawhon of North Texas State University. Their insight and scrupulous attention to content and style have made the writing of this textbook a fulfilling experience. A special note of thanks is due to Zena Green for her assistance in the preparation of the study guides.

Ernest J. Green

PERSONAL RELATIONSHIPS
AN APPROACH TO MARRIAGE AND FAMILY

1

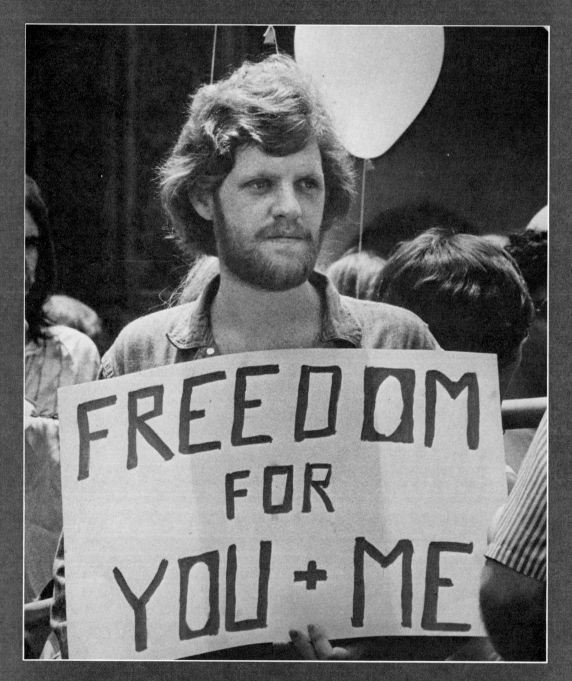

INTIMACY AND SOCIETY

We are living in an increasingly *self*-conscious society with a greater number of men and women than ever before seeking to explore their private selves. People are joining rap groups, entering analysis, and trying meditation; they are turning to play therapy, transactional therapy, and a host of other programs which have been developed to help them find out who they are and express how they really feel.

One message which is clear from these struggles for self-knowledge and self-liberation is that many people feel out of touch both with themselves and with others. They sense that their personal growth is at a standstill; they feel that they are not living up to their potential. What is also clear, however, is that human beings will never become all they *could* be unless they can first be what they *are*. And for this to happen, people need other people.

Personal relationships—with marriage partners, friends, lovers, and family members—are important because they have the potential for allowing a person to be his or her real self. Such relationships, at their best, can put human beings in touch with the profoundest pleasures in life and can help bring their individual identities into focus.

This does not mean that all relationships, or any single one, invariably benefit the persons involved. Marriage and all the other formal or informal contexts within which people establish their relationships can, in fact, be a part of the problem of out-of-touchness and alienation. In the process of conforming to expectations of how one *should* behave within a framework such as marriage, individuals may lose track of their true personal needs and feelings. Consider the experience of Eric, a young man who explained that:

> . . . the first part of our marriage was one in which most of our behavior, most of our expectations, our ways of relating to one another were determined by sets of predetermined social rules. I mean, we went into marriage with whole ideas about how we ought to act toward each other, how we ought to feel toward each other, how we ought to act toward each other sexually, how often we ought to make love. You know, we'd been taught, not only by parents, but by the whole culture . . . all the ways you relate to others. And we lived within that structure of social rules as a kind of template for our marriage for about five or six years, until it absolutely collapsed for us. . . . Denise ended up with a breakdown, and I ended up agonizing and miserable (Rogers, 1972, p. 166).

It seems that at any given period in nearly every society, human relationships have been burdened by expectations and standards of one sort or another. To meet basic needs, major social institutions—the sets of relationships, roles and values such as family—have emerged to provide guidelines for human relationships. It has been variously thought that personal relationships were good when they contributed to the health and harmony of the cosmos, fulfilled a divine plan, contributed to the hedonistic pleasure of the individual, or served to stabilize and strengthen society. Some also have claimed that relationships should be maintained for the sake of perpetuating institutions, such as marriage and the family. Thus, a marriage would be considered good simply if it lasted, no matter what the cost to the individual partners.

In this book, however, we shall observe another standard. It is our contention that personal relationships exist for the sake of the persons involved and that they are good when they benefit personal growth and contribute to personal satisfaction. The usual term for this standpoint is *humanism*, since it holds that human values—rather than cosmic, divine, social, or institutional values—are always paramount.

Implicit in this framework for examining human relationships is a particular attitude regarding human nature. If people were fundamentally selfish and egocentric, then marriages and most other relationships always would be at the mercy of individual desires and whims. But like the humanist psychologists, especially Carl Rogers and Abraham Maslow, we believe that people are basically good, giving, and trustworthy. In seeking personal growth and satisfaction, they will experience a natural desire to enhance the growth and satisfaction of others. And when permitted to act without restraint, from their own true nature, they will behave responsibly and constructively in their relationships.

Freeing Relationships

The psychoanalyst Erich Fromm has said, "The whole life of the individual is nothing but the process of giving birth to himself; indeed, we should be fully born when we die" (1955, p. 26). A major goal of humanist psychology is that of helping people give birth to themselves—helping them be self-actualizers, as Maslow would say—and become what they truly are. But this process does not take place only in a formal therapeutic setting. All the relationships people have in a lifetime affect the evolution of selfhood. Interactions with parents, teachers, employers and fellow workers, husbands, wives, friends, and lovers—all these help to shape the individual life.

Of course, as we noted, not all relationships live up to their potential for freeing people to become all they can be. Even in love relationships and friendships, people can feel obliged to adopt certain poses or masks without ever finding out whether this is what their partners really want, much less whether such poses correspond to who they "really" are. What, then, is a genuinely freeing relationship? How can a person build one or recognize one if ever it should be found?

First let it be said that the totally, constantly freeing relationship is an ideal, never to be achieved in practice. In all lasting relationships there are some good times and some that are not good. All people have their moods, and so do their friends, lovers, and spouses.

Furthermore, a relationship does not become truly freeing overnight or merely by chance. Rather, one creates a freeing relationship by actively trying to be oneself with another person and by encouraging that person to do the same. This is rarely an easy or rapid process.

OPENNESS

For one thing, there often is a tendency to hold back or conceal one's true feelings. This may seem a wise policy when those feelings are negative. Suppose, for example, Arnold said to his wife Vicky, "I can't stand the way you leave the lights on all the time!" Vicky would probably feel offended or hurt, and she might even retaliate with a criticism of her own. However, when he says what is on his mind, Arnold is at least letting his wife know the cause of his irritation. She would almost certainly feel it sooner or later, in one way or another, no matter how he might try to disguise it. And when she did, she would probably retaliate, giving Arnold no idea why. Her aggression would seem gratuitous and uncalled-for—just as his did to her.

The only way a person can hope to understand another person is to express and explain unfavorable reactions openly. To continue the example, Arnold's outburst—"I can't stand your leaving the lights on all the time!"—might prompt the reply, "Well, I can't stand those ragged old Levis of yours any longer!" Now, this might come as a hard (though not unexpected) blow, for Arnold's old Levis have been through a lot with him, and he loves them. But suppose he nevertheless takes them off, throws them out, and puts on a more respectable-looking pair. Abashed at this sacrifice, Vicky might feel encouraged to explain more about her own feelings and behavior: "It just seems so gloomy when I walk into a dark room, especially if I have to grope for the switch." This is a feeling Arnold can sympathize with, and one that can be measured against a disagreeably high electricity bill.

Now suppose that paying the high electricity bill turns out to be more depressing than walking into dark rooms. Vicky has resolved to switch off the lights when she does not need them, and Arnold has noticed some improvement. But tonight he suddenly finds all the lights blazing. "Why are all the lights on?" he might ask. "Trying to get me for something?"

"No," she might say, "I just forgot. Sorry." On the other hand, she might reply, "Yes, you left the car out last night, and I almost couldn't get it started this morning." Arnold might prefer the former response, but in either case both he and Vicky are benefiting; they are gradually gaining the courage to be open and honest about their feelings.

Carl Rogers has observed that when people start doing this, they find to their amazement that they have many positive feelings hiding along with the negative ones. It is a sad fact that individuals often feel admiration for someone, real gratitude, or sheer joy at being with another person and yet keep this to themselves. Sometimes they actually succeed in hiding these feelings from their own consciousness, which is sadder even than the meanness of being stingy with praise. When people fearfully deny the very existence of their desires and feelings, the tender and constructive along with the angry and hostile, they never realize how many good feelings they have.

Sometimes, too, feelings are mixed. Persons commonly feel envious when they feel admiring; they may feel timid or even frightened at the same time that they feel joyful. In a friendly argument—over politics or philosophy, for example—let us say that Ellen makes a very penetrating observation. However, her opponent, Carol, quickly dismisses Ellen's remark as immaterial. It is likely that Carol's behavior at this point reflects only a small part of a rather complex set of emotions. She may agree with Ellen but be jealous of her insight. She may even wish to compliment Ellen, but at the same time she may feel a need to defend her own argument and, in effect, protect her self-esteem. Perhaps the only way Carol could respond simply and honestly would be to say, "Very true—damn it!"

These illustrations are intended to give only a general idea of what openness is. They cannot convey how much time and work it takes to achieve. Probably one can never achieve complete openness with anyone, not even oneself. (In fact, being open *about* one's feelings often precedes being open *to* them.) The best people can hope for is to become gradually, tentatively more open than they were. And they cannot hope even for that, except with someone they trust.

ACCEPTANCE

Trust is a simple word, but in practice it becomes a thing of fine shadings and variations. If two strangers are sitting opposite each other on the train, it is highly doubtful that one would say to the other, "Excuse me sir, but to be perfectly open with you, I find your necktie atrocious." Instead, neither would say anything at all. In fact, they probably would avoid each other's gaze. After all, they are total strangers. Yet it is quite likely that both individuals are almost as reserved with people they have known for years. The reason for this is not very mysterious. Despite a long acquaintance, two people can still lack mutual trust.

Trust, in the context of a personal relationship, implies a feeling of security. One must feel safe about disclosing private thoughts and emotions and not fear betrayal or ridicule. One must believe that confidences will be kept and that the other person in the relationship will be equally candid about personal matters. But how does this sense of security develop? What is the underlying experience that generates a feeling of trust? The answer seems to be that when someone feels secure about being open with another person, he or she feels accepted. Carl Rogers describes acceptance as "a warm regard for [the individual] as a person of unconditional self-worth—of value no matter what his condition, his behavior, his feelings. It means a respect and liking for him as a separate person, a willingness for him to possess his own feelings in his own way" (1961, p. 34).

The act of acceptance, then, involves distinguishing between the person's behavior and feelings, on the one hand, and his or her inner self, on the other. In practice it includes learning how to criticize the behavior of another person without attacking that person's intrinsic worth. For instance, when Tom's son Allen leaves his room in a mess, Tom could say, "You're an inconsiderate slob, Allen," *or* "I think that leaving your room like this is a sloppy habit, and I want you to try not to do it anymore." In the former statement Tom is labeling Allen himself. In effect, he is saying that Allen is a slob for all time and that anyone else would share this judgment. But consider the latter statement: here Allen is labeling just one aspect of Allen's *actions* and, in effect, is acknowledging that Allen is and *can be* a number of things. Moreover, Tom is making it clear that in this case even the label for Allen's actions is a relative one—"I think. . . . "

To earn someone's trust, then, one must learn to communicate in a way that reflects acceptance and a respectful recognition of the other person's potential self. Some might feel that such care and concern can occur only between people who already like or love each other. This may often be true, but it is unfortunate; it narrows the scope of one's attachments and places limits on one's opportunities for growth. In trying to be accepting even of people for whom one has no special feelings— and who sometimes might even seem to behave reprehensibly or to be just plain boring—one gives others a chance to develop and express aspects of themselves which actually could prove interesting and appealing. Even if this does not result in a bond of friendship or love, it at least provides an opportunity for some degree of mutual enrichment.

By now it may be apparent that acceptance frequently starts as a one-sided enterprise. Some people are further along than others in their growth and find it easier to reach out and be open about their feelings. The fact is that they are better able to convey an attitude of acceptance because they have developed a deeper understanding of themselves and others.

UNDERSTANDING

Understanding involves being able to take another person's point of view and see things through that person's eyes. One learns how others view their own thoughts and emotions, accomplishments and failures, mistakes and good deeds. Understanding does not necessarily change how one regards another person's habits and attitudes, but it can make one feel more sympathetic toward, and accepting of, that person.

The ideal limit of understanding is complete empathy, an ability to feel just as the other person feels in a particular situation. But complete empathy is rare. Usually our own feelings obtrude into the process of understanding, making us think that the other person ought to feel as we do about something. Also, before we can be deeply empathetic, we need a great deal of information about the other person's inner world, information which that person might assume we already have and therefore not reveal unless specifically asked to do so.

Thus, progress toward understanding is very gradual—just like progress toward openness and acceptance, the other qualities of a freeing relationship. But it is now a little easier to see how these three qualities work together and reinforce one another as a relationship becomes more and more freeing. If one can only be a little more accepting and understanding, other people will feel safe enough to be a little more open with their feelings. And when they become more open with their feelings, one can begin to understand them better. The process eventually becomes two-sided: Openness begets openness, and trust begets trust. A feeling of acceptance develops as mutual understanding deepens.

It all begins to sound quite wonderful, and perhaps it should, since there are great rewards in a freeing relationship. But it must be emphasized that the development of a freeing relationship also requires effort and patience. One does not just stand there and watch the openness fuel the understanding and the understanding win the acceptance, which in turn allows for greater openness, and so on. The resistance of habit, convention, fear, and pain must be overcome for every little gain in openness. A single failure to understand on one person's part may cause

RATHER THAN acting as final authority and disciplinarian, this mother chooses to be involved with her child at a playful and intimate level.

the other person to withdraw some of his or her trust, and that, in turn, may make the relationship a little less open.

Personal Growth

This book is not about all the relationships an individual may enter into. It is not about relationships with United States senators from one's state or with one's faculty adviser. These are impersonal or casual relationships, and those who enter into them play certain prescribed roles: senator and constituent, adviser and student. The relationships we are examining in this book are personal relationships, and their distinguishing feature is that in principle they do not require people to play roles but, rather, allow them to be themselves. We have also seen that to be truly what one is can be quite an undertaking. But to a considerable extent it is possible, and personal relationships, though perhaps not the only way to approach self-fulfillment, are certainly one of the best means of doing so.

The full promise, however, is even greater. Being truly what one *is* can be a first step toward becoming all one *can* be. And exactly what is this "all we can be"? Abraham Maslow has studied several people who he believes are becoming all they can be. Sometimes he calls them *self-actualizing* individuals, and sometimes he refers to them as "just plain healthy." He writes:

> For self-actualizing people, there is a strong tendency for selfishness and unselfishness to fuse into a higher . . . unity. Work tends to be the same as play; vocation and avocation become the same thing. When duty is pleasant and pleasure is fulfillment of duty, then they lose their separateness and oppositeness. The highest maturity is discovered to include a childlike quality, and we discover healthy children to have some of the qualities of mature self-actualization. The inner-outer split, between self and all else, gets fuzzy . . . (1968, p. 207).

This is not to say that self-actualizing people are free of all problems. They suffer conflict, frustration, guilt, and sadness like everyone else. The difference is that they become upset for real, unavoidable reasons, not for imagined reasons. In a situation that is really troubling, they are troubled; but rather than becoming totally preoccupied with their own reactions to a problem, they are able to focus on ways of solving it.

It is worth noting that Maslow always uses the "-ing"; evidently, he never found a single person who was totally and finally self-actualized. Self-actualization, then, seems to be a process, an activity, not a state or attribute. Carl Rogers believes that life itself is by its nature "a flowing, changing process." This, he admits, can be a little frightening, but:

> I find I am at my best when I can let the flow of my experience carry me, in a direction which appears to be forward, toward goals of which I am but dimly

aware. In thus floating with the complex stream of my experiencing, and in trying to understand its ever-changing complexity . . . there can be no closed system of beliefs . . . Life is guided by a changing understanding of and interpretation of my experience. It is always in process of becoming (1961, p. 27).

Although this process does not lead to a final goal, to any point of completion, it does have a definite direction. People who are growing become more and more realistic in their view of themselves, with the perhaps surprising result that they value themselves more highly. This is partly because they are gradually becoming more like what they really want to be. They grow more self-confident, more self-directing. Thanks to their improved understanding of themselves, such people become more open to their experience and deny less and less of it. In their attitudes toward others, they grow more accepting and see others as being like themselves. They become less defensive, more adaptive, and better able to meet situations creatively and constructively (Rogers, 1961, p. 36). And, very important, people who are really involved in the process of actualizing their own potential are also deeply concerned about contributing to the development of others—their children and spouses, their friends, and all other significant persons in their lives. In other words, such people are increasingly able to *love*, if, as Erich Fromm says, one means by this term "a capacity for the experience of concern, responsibility, respect, and understanding of another person and the intense desire for that other person's growth" (1950, p. 87).

It would seem that a person does not have to worry, then, about the *direction* growth will take. He or she will naturally grow toward becoming a more constructive, responsible, and loving person. But the growth process itself is never effortless, and it rarely feels comfortable.

FINDING YOUR OWN WAY

"Each step forward," Maslow warns, "is a step into the unfamiliar and is possibly dangerous" (1968, p. 204). The fear of taking such a step helps to explain, for instance, why a person may remain for years in a relationship which is obviously a very unhappy one. It also helps to explain why people become upset when *other* people change. If a marital partner returns to school or begins to develop interests outside the marriage, it is not uncommon for the spouse to be anxious about the effects of this new behavior on accustomed patterns of living and relating. He or she may wonder, "Will my partner lose interest in me?" and "Will I have to change too?"

Growth often involves giving up some satisfying things; it may cost a parting or separation. In growing, one forfeits a familiar and perhaps easier life in quest of a life that is more difficult, more demanding, and more responsible, and to do this takes will power, courage, and strength.

It is not surprising, therefore, that many people develop only a small part of their capacity for growth. Fear of changing and of braving the unknown cannot be overestimated, and certainly it is not possible always to be courageous and strong.

This, however, is just part of the story. The full answer to the question of why people stumble and lose their way on the path toward self-fulfillment is perhaps as complex as the diversity of social influences and experiences which can affect people in the course of their lives. Here we refer back to the very beginning of our discussion and the description of how Eric and Denise spent the first years of their marriage. Eric spoke of social expectations and the dramatic and painful realization that he and Denise had confused these expectations with self-fulfillment. This is not an unusual story.

From the time of childhood, people begin to learn the roles and rules which are part of functioning in a society, and they become knowledgeable about the ways to win approval and other, more tangible, rewards— whether from parents or peers, teachers or employers. The problem is that a great many people are "overachievers." They learn their roles too well and submit to a variety of social pressures. In time, the guidelines for their behavior nearly all seem to derive from the outside, and they slowly grow to distrust any personal thoughts or feelings which do not correspond to the expectations of others. A vivid example of this situation is provided by Joan, a young woman whose marriage ended in divorce:

> . . . A very good friend of mine had gotten engaged and she had a very pretty ring, and was making all these wedding plans. My friends were saying, "God, Joan, when are you and Max getting married? You've been going together for three years now. You better not let him get away. If you let *him* get away, you're stupid!" My mother said, "Oh, Joan, when are you going to find another person like Max? He's so outstanding and responsible and mature and secure." I felt, "This is the one I should marry because my close friends, my roommate, my mother all say it," and although I had these doubts going on inside me, I thought . . . "They know what's best for you and you don't, so you had better follow their advice" (Rogers, 1972, pp. 12–13).

To a greater or lesser extent, social customs, traditions, and the opinions of other people color one's decisions and influence one's attitudes toward a broad range of topics. Sex roles, physical intimacy, work, marriage, childrearing—these are just a few areas of human interest and concern which are weighted with standards, stereotypes, and the opinions of professionals and lay people alike. It understandably becomes very difficult to exercise one's own creative potential in life, to carve one's way through the mass of possibilities and make choices which are personally satisfying.

But with effort it *is* possible to find one's own way, even within a context such as marriage, which is complicated by so many social expectations. Eric and Denise were themselves able to transform their marriage into a freeing relationship. For almost six years, they had stumbled through their life together, alienated from their own needs and blind to the influences which had shaped their lives. But as they worked toward greater understanding and acceptance of the people they themselves were, rather than the roles they had been playing, their relationship provided them with the freedom to grow beyond their social conditioning. In Eric's words:

> Both of us are pretty unconventional in sort of social and intellectual terms. . . . And the reason we have the freedom to be that way is because we have so much strength in our home. The power, the strength, the refuge of our marriage has given us a kind of core to operate from which has allowed both of us to be very much mavericks in most social terms. And my hunch is that that's far more important than most people generally think (Rogers, 1972, pp. 191–192).

Compromise is a necessary aspect of living together in a society, and playing roles and fulfilling social expectations form a part of that compromise. But people do not have to subject themselves blindly to the evaluations and expectations of others. They can choose when and how they will compromise, once they have the knowledge that there *are* choices to be made.

This book cannot tell you how to build a freeing relationship or hand you a passport to personal growth, nor can it tell you what your decisions or choices ought to be. Rather, it will describe the processes through which intimate relationships with friends and lovers are formed, and it will try to provide some of the knowledge which can assist you in the quest for a fulfilling life.

SUMMARY

Personal relationships have the potential for freeing a person to be his or her real self. But forming such relationships can be a slow and difficult process. It requires that people be open to their own feelings and those of the other person. This openness becomes possible as two people develop a greater trust of each other and feel secure about disclosing private thoughts and emotions. The basis of this trust is a feeling of acceptance, or the knowledge that one is regarded as a worthy individual above and beyond one's behavior or feelings at the moment. The ability to convey acceptance is enhanced as one grows in an understanding of the other person's point of view and motives.

Becoming all one is can be a first step toward becoming all that one is potentially capable of being. This never-ending process is termed *self-*

actualization and is reflected in a growing self-confidence and acceptance of oneself and others, an increasing ability to behave spontaneously and to approach problems constructively, and an increasing concern for the growth and welfare of others.

Growth is often thwarted because of a fear of changing and embarking on the unknown. But self-fulfillment is difficult to achieve also because of social pressures and expectations. Many people allow the roles they learn to play in different social situations to alienate them from their personal selves. They grow to distrust their own feelings and thoughts and receive nearly all their direction from other people. Though it is impossible to escape the influence of society and the necessity of making some compromises for the sake of harmonious interactions with others, people can achieve a greater objectivity, and hence greater freedom, regarding their personal selves and social roles. And freeing relationships—with husband or wife, friends, lovers, and family members—can help people discover and utilize this freedom.

CASE STUDY

Cathy and Bill Fowler were both working toward university degrees when they met. Each had a few years of work experience. They fell in love quickly, but were engaged for eighteen months before their wedding. They used this period to begin working on the relationship they wished to build together.

Bill's mother is a lawyer who gave up her practice when Bill was born. Cathy's mother is a housewife. During Cathy's and Bill's early years both their fathers assumed the traditional role of breadwinner and of final authority in matters of discipline. Their mothers assumed the major responsibility for homemaking and child care. Both Bill and Cathy expect Cathy to pursue her career, and they also wish to have one or more children. They hope to accent their personal interests and skills in developing their own unique marital relationship rather than roles, as they feel their parents have done.

Last month, after celebrating their fifth wedding anniversary with a quiet meal at home, Cathy and Bill were reminiscing about their seven-year relationship.

Her View

Cathy remembers that on her first date with Bill the conversation was somehow more immediate, more personal than she usually experienced. "I had always felt pretty unique. It was as though all the other guys I had dated carried around an invisible box that represented their expectations for me. To the extent that I fit into their mold they liked me. But they disliked or ignored the parts of me that didn't fit in. Either Bill didn't have a box or the one he had was a perfect fit.

"After the second date I came home feeling a warmth inside like someone had lighted a candle inside of me that had never been lit before, but I was painfully aware of Bill's 'otherness.' I realized that he could walk out of my life just as quickly and as surely as he had entered it. So I decided to take a little risk.

When Bill invited me to go with him to a friend's December wedding the following weekend, I took off my mitten and reached into the pocket of his heavy overcoat to squeeze his hand. Was I ever happy when he squeezed me back and held on!"

Something else which impressed Cathy was that "with Bill and me our minds and hearts met before our bodies. I was more than just an attractive face or body to Bill. It sounds funny, but for the first time I felt like I knew what it was to be appreciated as a person. With the exception of a soft good-night kiss, the first time Bill reached out spontaneously to touch me was after I had made an observation about the role of the United States in foreign policy that he agreed with. That really made my heart skip a couple of beats!

"We fell in love so quickly that Bill proposed to me, and I accepted, after only six weeks. But as soon as Bill slipped an engagement ring on my finger, I began to have doubts. I felt confused and was a little afraid of losing my sense of being a separate person.

"I began to think about those old cultural stereotypes of the perfect husband. I wasn't sure that Bill was assertive enough for my taste, and when he cried as I took off my ring and put it on the other hand to indicate that we were no longer engaged, I decided that he was possibly too weak for me. And when he kept pursuing me, I thought I was discovering what a dependent person he was. Of course I was encouraging him to come over every evening. As I look back, what I think was happening was that I really was afraid that anyone would have to be a little bit crazy to love me.

"Fortunately for me, Bill is a very patient person. He just hung in there. And his continuing love actually helped me to begin to love myself and to trust my original evaluation of him. Within six months we were engaged again, and we married the following year in June, three months after he defended his dissertation and six weeks before my defense.

"I think our wedding ceremony was beautiful. The minister let us write our own vows. And everything from my dress to the invitations was done by hand. Our families and friends helped with every detail. It was truly a community celebration.

"But you know," Cathy pauses, "the memory I cherish most now is a discussion Bill and I had a few months before the wedding. We both agreed that ideally for us marriage was a lifetime commitment. But while we were content with each other for the moment, we both expected ourselves and each other to grow a lot over the years. And we decided that if either of us did not, the other would likely become unhappy in the relationship and might wish to end it.

"The only thing that scares me is this—I firmly believe that the number of issues that a couple feel they can't talk about is a pretty good measure of the distance they have built up between them. That gives me the courage to be honest. And so far it has been working."

His View

Bill recalls how surprised he was, when he first met Cathy, to learn that someone so attractive as she had no romantic attachments. When Cathy began making statements about the future which involved him, like "I would like to learn to play tennis, if you would be willing to teach me," or "Maybe we can see that exhibit of Russian folk art next month," he was delighted.

"When I was with Cathy, I felt somehow more complete than I had ever felt before. I was enjoying working on my degree and teaching, but before I met Cathy there was just an empty spot somewhere deep in me that work or friends couldn't fill. I liked how she really appreciated me for being myself."

Bill recalls that he longed to tell Cathy how deeply he felt for her, but that he was hesitant, since he did not want to risk losing her by pressuring her into a commitment before she was ready. But her statements concerning things they might do in the future were so encouraging that he decided, after six weeks, to take the risk.

Bill was at Cathy's apartment, and Cathy had suggested that they play a competitive party game that evening. Bill won a couple of rounds easily, and reluctantly he played and won a third time, at Cathy's insistence. He then gathered up his courage and said, "I really don't want to play anymore." He found himself pouring out his feelings of love for Cathy and then telling her about his past loneliness, describing a long illness he suffered as a child, and sharing with her his hopes and his fears for the future. Strangely, he thought, as he was pouring himself out, he felt himself being filled by Cathy's joyous smile as he told her of his love, her tears when he spoke of his childhood illness, and her quiet attention as he shared his fears and hopes.

Bill was hurt when Cathy broke their engagement, but he feels that the painful six months that followed were a period of growth for them both: "I had to face the possibility of continuing life without Cathy. While I wanted with all my being to live the rest of my life with her, I came to grips with the reality that I could, if necessary, go on living without her.

"Another thing the six months did for us is this: It gave us some experience in challenging each other, which has proved valuable in our marriage. I used to be a terrible grouch in the morning, but I wanted Cathy to wake me up. About three weeks after we were married, Cathy refused to wake me if I didn't stop grousing at her. It wasn't easy, but I quit. And Cathy very often needs some strong encouragement to advance herself professionally. She will start an article for a journal. Then months will go by until I get her to set a deadline and make her stick to it. She complains, but she thanks me later. That means, of course, that we do argue. But I think it's good. My parents just kind of settled into their own ways. I sense that they are unhappy about a lot of things, but they never square off with each other. I personally hope that we are still arguing when we are eighty because to me that will mean we are still caring about each other."

Interpretation and Questions

Cathy and Bill want to develop a relationship which stresses persons rather than roles. Do you think they have succeeded in doing so? How did their families and cultural norms influence their developing relationship? Cathy once feared "losing her self" in her relationship to Bill, and Bill was surprised to feel that he was "being filled" as he "poured himself out" to her. Is it important for each partner to maintain a separate sense of self in a love relationship? Do you agree with Bill and Cathy that arguing can help build and maintain a close relationship?

STUDY GUIDE

Important Terms

hedonism
humanism
commitment
social institution
self-actualization

acceptance
openness
understanding
personal growth

Review Quiz

1 The sets of relations, roles, and values which meet the basic needs of society are called:
   a roles
   b social institutions
   c functions
   d social structure

2 Someone who believes that relationships should exist for the good of the persons involved and that each individual strives to maximize his or her pleasure is:
   a a cosmologist
   b a hedonist
   c a humanist
   d a functionalist

3 The values espoused in this book are based upon the underlying philosophy of:
   a Sigmund Freud
   b hedonism
   c humanism
   d sociological functionalism

4 Which of the following relationships generally allows one greater freedom to be oneself?
   a husband-wife
   b parent-child
   c teacher-student
   d boss-employee

5 People who attempt to be open in their relationships often discover that:

   a others become more open with them
   b positive feelings about others have been hidden along with negative ones
   c their feelings about others are mixed
   d all the above

6 According to Carl Rogers, acceptance consists in:
   a tolerance of all the other person's attitudes and behaviors
   b a warm regard for the other individual as a person of unconditional self-worth
   c a willingness to criticize another person without attacking that person's intrinsic worth
   d all the above

7 Understanding is most closely related to the concept of:
   a freedom
   b judging
   c empathy
   d acceptance

8 According to Maslow, a self-actualizing person is:
   a able to separate work and play
   b adult rather than childlike
   c someone for whom the split between self and all else is fuzzy

d all the above

9 The psychologist who developed the concept of self-actualization is:

   a Abraham Maslow

   b Carl Rogers

   c Rollo May

   d none of the above

10 A major goal of this textbook is:

   a to encourage everyone to marry

   b to teach people which relationships are most important

   c to show how social expectations affect intimate relationships

   d to encourage everyone to become self-actualized

Opinionnaire

Agree	No opinion	Disagree		
_____	_____	_____	1	The family is a dying institution in modern society.
_____	_____	_____	2	People were actually happier in their marriages two generations ago.
_____	_____	_____	3	There really is no such thing as altruism in human relationships.
_____	_____	_____	4	The most important characteristic in a relationship is honesty.
_____	_____	_____	5	People should be able to be themselves in any relationship.
_____	_____	_____	6	Being really open and honest with people is a good way to lose friends.
_____	_____	_____	7	Trust is a quality that should be reserved for only a very few persons in one's life.
_____	_____	_____	8	Empathy, or seeing things from another person's point of view, is something most people cannot manage.
_____	_____	_____	9	A relationship with another person should be enjoyed, not analyzed.
_____	_____	_____	10	A commitment to another person necessarily puts restrictions on one's freedom and growth.

Exercise

DESIGN YOUR OWN SOCIETY

This book is about intimate relationships, especially those which develop in the context of marriage and family. Personal relationships cannot be considered apart from the overall social structure, however. The structure of the family as a social institution can be analyzed as one of a number of other institutions. As an aid to understanding the interdependence of institutions in a society, list the functions and check the structural characteristics you believe should exist in an ideal society as they pertain to the institutions below:

A Family:

_____ Monogamous (one man married to one woman)

_____ Polygamous (multiple partners)

Functions

1 _____ 2 _____ 3 _____ 4 _____

B Government:

_____ Democratic

_____ Autocratic or plutocratic

Functions

1 _____ 2 _____ 3 _____ 4 _____

C Economy:

_____ Capitalist

_____ Socialist

Functions

1 _____ 2 _____ 3 _____ 4 _____

D Education:

_____ Open to everyone

_____ Available only to the elite

Functions

1 _____ 2 _____ 3 _____ 4 _____

E Religion:

_____ No religion

_____ State religion (ecclesia)

_____ Religious freedom

Functions

1 _____ 2 _____ 3 _____ 4 _____

Now examine your society. While a real society is infinitely more complex, certain interdependencies may reveal that simplistic solutions to social problems as they relate to the family will not work. Is the government capable of making all the decisions and carrying out the functions you assigned? See whether any major inconsistencies occur in the responsibilities across social institutions. Have you made provision for the fact that others may not agree with your vision of an ideal society? What will you do about them?

Projects for Class or Home Study

1   Observation of others, and often an evaluation of your own responses, is the key to an understanding of the concepts in this book. For example, look around you at others in the classroom. Are any of the students involved in *primary* relationships with each other? What tells you whether they are or not?

2   Try experimenting with the idea of openness. Express yourself with several persons in a slightly more open fashion than you usually do. Note carefully their reactions and responses. Do the responses depend upon the intimacy of the relationship?

3   Think about someone of whom you are very fond. List what you like about the person. Did you list attributes? If someone else possessed the same attributes, would you be equally fond of that person?

4   Marriage generally implies mutual commitments. Do you believe that the exact nature of the commitments should be written out, and the document signed by both parties, before marriage?

5   Make up a brief checklist for self-actualization (see the text). Evaluate yourself against this ideal. Be honest! Is the ideal possible?

Suggestions for Further Reading

Hardy, Thomas. *Tess of the d'Urbervilles*. (First published in 1891) New York: Airmont, 1965.
 Hardy's classic concerns marriage in nineteenth-century Victorian England. The heroine presents a model of emotional growth attained after a seduction and an unpleasant marriage.

Maslow, Abraham H. *Toward a psychology of being*. (2nd ed.) New York: Van Nostrand, 1968.
 The classic in which psychologist Maslow explains his theory of emotional needs and growth. It is here that the self-actualizer is described and explained. The book is clear and well written.

Mousseau, Jacques. The family, prison of love. *Psychology Today*, August 1975, **9**, 52–53.
 The author interviews historian Philippe Ariès, who believes that families are confining to the individual. Ariès predicts a future in which monogamy will exist for only a short period in each person's life.

Oates, Joyce Carol. *Marriages and infidelities*. Greenwich, Conn.: Fawcett, 1972.
 An award-winning collection of short stories by a master storyteller. The stories are bound together by the theme of marriage and a sense of the tragic.

Putney, Snell, and Putney, Gail. *The adjusted American*. New York, Harper & Row, 1965.

The authors develop a sophisticated and controversial explanation of human needs. They contend that Americans behave in a neurotic fashion in their quest for fulfillment.

Rogers, Carl R. *On becoming a person: A therapist's view of psychotherapy*. Boston: Houghton Mifflin, 1961.

The father of nondirective counseling discusses personal fulfillment through emotional, intellectual, and behavioral growth. Part of the book is concerned with the application of growth principles to life in the family.

Stolte-Heiskanen, Veronica. Family needs and societal institutions: Potential empirical linkage mechanisms. *Journal of Marriage and the Family*, November 1975, **37**, 903–916.

A scholarly article showing the connection of the family to other institutions. The author tests hypotheses with data from twenty-four European countries.

Answers to Review Quiz

1-*b*　2-*b*　3-*c*　4-*a*　5-*d*　6-*d*　7-*c*　8-*c*　9-*a*　10-*c*

2

FRIENDS
AND LOVERS

> Human life and humanity come into being in genuine meetings. There man learns not merely that he is limited by man, cast upon his own finitude, partialness, need of completion, but his own relation to truth is heightened by the other's different relations to the same truth—different in accordance with his individuation, and destined to take seed and grow differently (Buber, 1966, p. 47).

This observation, made by the great philosopher Martin Buber, emphasizes a fundamental truth of human existence: People need one another. They need one another physically and psychologically as friends and, more important, as lovers. Our friends and lovers offer us companionship against the tyranny of solitude. They offer us solace in the face of our own mortality and in time of need. They offer us wholeness in the face of our own incompleteness. They offer us enlightenment in the face of our own ignorance. And they offer us the opportunity to grow so that we may be richer, fuller human beings. In short, our friends and lovers help us confirm our oneness not only with others of our kind but also with the rest of nature as well.

Friends

"One friend in a lifetime is much," wrote historian Henry Adams, "two are many; three are hardly possible." Adams's words have a sad ring about them; nevertheless, they are true. Few of us have many really close friends because close friends demand complete honesty and openness; a friend is a person in whose company one can drop social masks and be oneself. Indeed, a friend has been defined as "one who knows all about you, but likes you just the same" (Davis, 1973, p. 128).

What does friendship mean? It means, first of all, mutual understanding and shared activities. It means support—both emotional and economic—in the course of everyday life and especially in times of crisis. It means companionship and something that psychologists Howard Miller and Paul Siegel (1972) call "mutual mirroring." This phenomenon enables both partners in an intimate relationship to see themselves as others see them. Through the eyes of our friends, we perceive the importance of our activities, thus sensing our errors and experiencing the world outside ourselves. Friends not only protect us from the world when necessary but also remind us of its harsh realities and demands.

Friendship can be based on the need for love; on a mutual interest in

sports, money, or politics; or even on the hatred of a common enemy. The great majority of friendships involve aspects of all these characteristics. An individual brings unique things to a friendship: his or her own special perspective of human relationships and of the world. The degree to which perceptions of the other's views are distorted affects the quality of the friendship (Rubin, 1975).

COMMUNITY, SOCIETY, AND FRIENDSHIP

An individual looking at interpersonal relationships in the world today might conclude that the nature of friendship is a constant—changeless over time. However, as sociologist Ferdinand Tönnies pointed out more than seventy-five years ago, such is not the case. Tönnies used the terms *Gemeinschaft* and *Gesellschaft* to refer to social relations in the small, relatively isolated community (*Gemeinschaft*) and in the city (*Gesellschaft*), where life is more organized.

   Gemeinschaft still exists in many nonindustrial communities today, in the villages and backwaters of an urbanized world. These communities are small, unchanging, isolated, and so tightly knit that everyone knows virtually all there is to know about everyone else from birth to death. The organization of interpersonal relations is well defined; through the kinship system all individuals know the exact nature of their relationship to all others in the community. They know who can claim their loyalties and to whom they can turn in times of need (Haviland, 1974).

   Social roles among such peoples are said to be inclusive rather than segmental because they include many aspects of behavior rather than merely some limited segment of a person's activities. Since life is confined to the village, the tribe, or the encampment, one's relationships with others are permanent and highly personal. As people from small communities thronged into cities, each person became not only an individual but also a stranger to most other people. Each had to find out about another all those things that are known in a *Gemeinschaft* community by everyone. Moreover, each individual in urban society began to relate to most others only through one or two of their segmented social roles. An automobile mechanic, for example, is a different person to different people. To his employer he is a valued employee; to customers he is a silent, scarcely noticed man in the shop; to his doctor he is a diabetic patient; and to his banker he is a man with a solid credit rating who makes his mortgage payments faithfully on the first of each month. Most social relations, then, are likely to be compartmentalized and transitory because few individuals in mass society are wholly and entirely known by all others.

   The two opposing pressures—to be many people and to be unique at the same time—create stress. To relieve this stress, we all seek to create our own sense of community by forming personal relations with those who will relate to us as individuals and as whole persons, rather than as segmented entities. Such personal relations—with friends, lovers, and family members—bestow on us a psychological integrity which helps us pull ourselves together, so counterbalancing the social-role relations which are acting to pull us apart. In short, whereas the community presented individuals with their own ready-made friends and intimates, mass society challenges them to find their own (Davis, 1973).

And these challenges have been demanding. The roadblocks to friendship in modern industrial society are many, creating impersonality and what David Riesman has called "the lonely crowd." For one thing, people are segregated from one another throughout life—from the time they are in grade school, when children are separated by age (and in some cases, by sex), to the time when they are senior citizens, perhaps living in separate housing communities or nursing homes. Then, too, our highly competitive society interferes with close friendships by its very nature; in school and on our jobs we are encouraged to do better than others. Finally, our great mobility impedes friendship; individuals who have lived in the same neighborhood for ten or more years are rare. With family ties and the sense of community growing weaker, the need for sustained friendships is greater than ever (R. Winter, 1975).

The impact of the city on interpersonal relations was noticed as early as the Golden Age in Greece. Psychologist Henry Winthrop (1972) notes that Aristotle classified friendship into three types. First, there is the friendship that is based on profit. This is particularly evident in market-oriented societies, where success is measured by one's ability to manipulate others. Such friends are in reality merely "contacts" who are to be used as stepping-stones in the attainment of one's objectives. When these friends are no longer useful, they are dropped for others who may be more useful.

Aristotle's second type of friendship is based on mutual pleasure and distraction. Such friendships, as Winthrop points out, are as easily dissolved and as superficial as those based on profit: "When a more charming, more amusing, more charismatic, more widely experienced or more knowledgeable person comes along, we are very likely to adopt him as a friend—while simultaneously gradually or suddenly dropping our interests in another friend of long standing" (1972).

Finally, there is the kind of friendship based on that which is permanent in us, on our own true inner selves. This rare type of friendship is very close to love, which will be discussed later in this chapter.

MAKING FRIENDS

The change from *Gemeinschaft* to *Gesellschaft* also changed the ways people make friends. In a village, each adult usually has known his or her friends from childhood and makes few new friends in later years. In urban society, by contrast, one generally forgets childhood friends and during adulthood spends much time seeking to make friends of strangers.

As Davis (1973) indicates, strangers become acquaintances, and later possibly friends, for a variety of reasons. First, the individual seeks out others because of a need for some external stimulation—not readily available in the environment—which others can provide. Second, the individual needs to release surplus emotional residue that has built up inside. By opening his or her emotional reservoirs to friends, the individual can increase the enjoyment of pleasurable experiences and decrease the pain of unpleasurable ones. A third reason we seek friends is to prove ourselves, to maintain our sense of self by pitting it against other selves. Interacting with friends, in short, exercises the muscles of the self, giving it a workout in the social world. Finally, a person seeks friends in order to participate in activities that are more enjoyable when shared with others. Going to a concert, a film, or a play with someone

FRIENDSHIPS MADE during the school years, if sustained over a lifetime, become the most precious and irreplaceable.

else, for example, heightens our enjoyment of the activity. One young man observes: "There seems to be no substitute for time together—relaxed—free to be defined in the moment—unpressed by work agendas—to share the same events, e.g., music, a movie, to dance together, to free our bodies—to explore our feelings, wishes, and fantasies together" (Rogers, 1972, p. 63).

SHARING SECRETS

As might be expected, people meeting each other for the first time reveal only a tiny part of themselves at both the verbal and nonverbal levels. First meetings have been called *orientations* (Altman and Taylor, 1973). At such times, people tend to create an image of accepting and understanding each other, and they are quite superficial in giving and probing for information about the other person.

As acquaintances become friends, they tend to become open and to reveal more and more about themselves. Davis (1973) suggests that it is the depth of the revelation which determines whether the two individuals will interact in terms of *familiarity* (the public knowledge that two acquaintances acquire about each other as they interact over time) or in terms of *confidentiality* (the secret knowledge which two close friends have of each other and which they conceal from the outside world). On the basis of the depth of information received from an acquaintance or friend, one gradually builds up an image of the other person and orients oneself toward this image.

The true mark of close friends is their willingness to drop their social masks and to allow each other to see the kinds of people they really are. Close friends, in other words, reveal their inner secrets—including their weaknesses and vulnerable points—to each other because they trust each other: "You become more honest. You tell more of the truth about yourself; you don't find it as important to act a part or pretend to be something other than your real self. And you find that you can love someone else even when that person is less than perfect" (Hunt, 1976, p. 128).

Intimates establish their bonds by revealing crucial secrets to each other—secrets that make each vulnerable to the other, secrets that involve important weaknesses: "It is only to someone who we feel is loyal to us that we can confide comfortably. We do so with the unspoken assumption that our confidence will not be betrayed or the information used against us" (Segal, 1975, p. 112). If we know another person's crucial secrets, we know the best place to attack that person; such secrets are what Davis (1973) calls "psychological hostages" that two people hold. When two friends exchange such psychological hostages, a state of mutual trust (or mutual deterrence) is reached in which neither can hurt the other without the possibility of being hurt in return.

When two intimates have shared everything and have revealed all their crucial secrets to each other, they have achieved the ideal relationship, in which they are completely open. Under such conditions, they will be able to render critical opinions of each other. Expressions of hurt or anger can be brought out into the open between close friends without fear of terminating the relationship. Writer Judith Viorst, for example, observes: "Love is agreeing with him completely when he needs you to agree with him completely, and telling him the plain unvarnished truth when he needs you to tell him the plain, unvarnished truth, and knowing when he needs which" (1975, p. 16). Of course, it is very hard for many of us to be completely honest and to share our own innermost secrets because we find it difficult to understand how another person could accept us with all our weaknesses and faults. But once we discover that another person knows our secret weaknesses and still likes us, the feelings of happiness that we derive from being with that person are deeply rewarding. Indeed, the weaknesses we perceive in ourselves are not necessarily perceived as such by others. Often, in fact, we are our own worst critics.

Many of our secrets involve feelings—feelings of love, hate, pity, or disgust in relation to other people or objects in our environment. When a woman tells her friend about her emotions, she is telling her friend who she really is; she is, in effect, giving herself to her friend:

> My feelings are like my fingerprints, the color of my eyes and the sound of my voice: unique to me and unrepeatable in anyone else. To know me you must know my feelings. And only when you know *me* through dialogue, at any

moment in my life, will you be able to understand my ideas, preferences, and intentions, shared in discussion (Powell, 1974, p. 76).

Sidney Jourard, one of the foremost theorists of the value of self-disclosure in intimate relationships, calls secrets one's "mysteries" and observes that before one person can truly know another, that person must disclose his or her mysteries to the other: "But for me to know, she must show. And for her to show her mysteries to me, she must be assured that I will respect them, take delight in them" (1972, p. 44).

FAVORS: PHYSICAL AND PSYCHOLOGICAL

One reason intimates reveal important secrets to friends is to obtain favors—both physical and psychological. Indeed, most requests for significant favors are accompanied by the revelation of important secrets because such favors involve a friend's doing what the asker cannot do or cannot ask mere acquaintances to do. In such cases, the asker must often tell the friend why he or she needs the favor.

In terms of physical favors, a friend offers a "third hand" for the purpose of obtaining or fetching things that are out of reach (a glass of Scotch or a theater ticket, for example). The most common physical favor is the lending of money. Other physical favors include sex, protection from danger, and help in times of illness.

Perhaps more important are the psychological favors that one friend can do for another. A person can help revitalize the self of a friend who is sagging by propping up the friend's spirits and offering support and encouragement. One teenage girl, for example, who had just broken up with her boy friend observes:

> So there I was, angry, depressed, and alone. Except for Barbara. Right now, I think Barbara saved my life. She didn't give me advice on what to do next, and she didn't try to tell me everything was going to be great tomorrow when we both knew it wasn't going to be. What she did do was listen for as long as I wanted to talk or cry, and she decided to stay over with me for a few weekends. Barbara was just there, she was available (Segal, 1975, p. 112).

A friend can also buttress our self-esteem. Our self-esteem is normally upheld when others whom we consider important or attractive think us worthy enough to share their secrets (Davis, 1973). At other times, such as when we are being attacked by enemies, a friend can bolster our self-esteem by filtering out the bad things others are saying behind our back and conveying only positive feelings and statements.

Third, a close friend can help to strengthen one's concept of self. A friend will reflect back one's own behavior and attitudes. A study by Roger Bailey, Phillip Finney, and Bob Helm (1975) supports this idea. These social psychologists found that support of each other's self-concept is a more reliable indicator of friendship than similarity of the friends' self-concepts.

The idea of self-esteem is important in interpersonal relations, especially in close friendships and love relationships. Virtually all researchers point to the fact that a person can neither love others nor have close friends without a clear idea of who he or she is and without a certain degree of self-respect or self-esteem. As psychiatrist Erich Fromm (1956) points out, a person who can love productively loves himself or herself too; a person who can love only other people cannot love at all. Furthermore, the making of friends involves self-trust; if we do not trust ourselves first, we will have difficulty trusting others (Rubin, 1975). Psychiatrists Thomas Verny and Ari Kiev note that only those who have a good understanding of themselves "can have a deep kind of friendship. . . . You must be in touch with your feelings. You must be able to risk yourself a little bit and be vulnerable to rejection" (quoted in R. Winter, 1975, p. 65).

Lovers

For thousands of years, men and women have wondered, written, and debated about love. Poets and philosophers, kings and fools, have attempted to define, explain, categorize, and describe this powerful human experience. Both St. Paul and Erich Fromm, for example, wrote that love was an altruistic attitude toward all human beings. The French novelist Stendhal thought love was ecstasy and passion. The German poet Rainier Maria Rilke defined love as two solitudes that protect, greet, and touch each other. Freud thought that love was sex, pure and simple. Psychiatrist Harry Stack Sullivan saw love in these terms: "When the satisfaction, security, and development of another person becomes as significant to you as your own satisfaction, security, and development, love exists." Philosopher Martin Buber defined love as the responsibility of an I for a Thou. And psychologists Stanton Peele and Archie Brodsky think love is an addiction in which an individual becomes psychically dependent on another (1974).

LOVE

Is love an emotion, a feeling, as Stendhal held? Is it sex, as Freud believed? Or is it an altruistic attitude toward another person that holds the humanness in this person sacred, as St. Paul and Fromm posited? Novelists and poets usually have much to say about this subject, and so we might start with one of them:

> But if you think about him the first thing in the morning and the last thing at night . . . if you walk to the sound of his name . . . and wait for the sound of his voice . . . if you earmark the best of everything to share with him—the best wisecracks, the best cartoons, newspaper clippings, columns and books—if the town goes grey when he is out of it . . . and conversations are brilliant only when he is part of them . . . if your heart almost stops with

fright when you see strain in his face . . . if you figure time backwards from the last time you saw him . . . and forward to the day he comes back . . . if you never grow tired of hearing him talk and even retell his jokes . . . if you are dashed by his failures and glow with his success. . . . Possibly it is romantic. Maybe it is hero worship. It is also love (Cannon, 1956, pp. 40–41).

This passage describes one kind of love—romantic love, the intense emotional involvement of one person with another. Romantic love is what one ordinarily means when he or she speaks of being or falling in love. Some individuals think romantic love is a cure-all—a panacea that will solve all their personal problems. Such people often believe that love will bring them companionship, security, fulfillment, satisfaction, joy, ecstasy, growth, completion, and more (Gillies, 1974).

Other tenets in the credo of romantic love include the ideas that there is only one "right" person, who must be found; that one unwittingly "falls in love" and becomes a victim of some supreme cosmic force; that lovers are blind to each other's imperfections and weaknesses; and that love conquers all—nothing can stand in its way, not even parents, in-laws, or basic personality and attitude differences (Hunt, 1959).

But there are other kinds of love, as psychiatrist Rollo May (1969) suggests. In May's eyes, human beings have lost the ability to will and to love, two vital faculties that they possessed in the intimacy of *Gemeinschaft*. However, with depersonalized *Gesellschaft*, we have become machines which lack the basic human qualities of feeling and commitment. Instead, industrialization has numbed us into a state of apathy in which no person is important. As a result, we are lonely, lacking in identity, and anonymous. To overcome this anomie, we must learn how to exercise love and will once again.

May identifies five kinds of love. The first is *sex*, often referred to as *lust* or *libido*, which is the mere physical attraction that one person feels for another. This is what Freud meant by love. The second kind of love is *eros*, the drive to create: "the drive toward union with what we belong to—union with our own possibilities, union with significant other persons in our world in relation to whom we discover our own self-fulfillment" (May, 1969, p. 317). The third is *philia*, which is friendship, or brotherly love. "Philia is the relaxation in the presence of the beloved which accepts the other's being as being; it is simply liking the rhythm of the walk, the voice, the whole being of the other" (May, 1969, p. 317). The fourth kind of love is *agape*, sometimes referred to as *charity*, which is altruism, a concern for the welfare of the other. The most basic form of agape is the love of God for human beings. Finally, there is what May calls *authentic love*, which is a combination of the other four types.

THE NATURE OF LOVE

The conception of love put forth in this book is virtually identical to May's fifth type. But what exactly is the nature of this kind of love? A composite definition of love might read something like this: Love is an attitude which is the same toward all objects; it includes a sense of care, giving, responsibility, respect, and knowledge of other people, as well as the active striving for their development and happiness (Fromm, 1956).

First, let us examine the element of care. Care is an active concern for the growth and life of the love object. It is best seen in the love of a parent for a child: the mother or father feeds and bathes the baby and sees to its overall physical comfort. The parent actually labors at caring for the child. The same effort is required of all those who love another person. A young husband, for example, notes: "The other side to this is that community takes work. . . . No lasting sharing and feeling of emotional depth comes from simply moving from one relationship to another—from what feels good to what feels good. Depth comes from commitment to working through even the most painful feelings" (Rogers, 1972, p. 64).

Second, one voluntarily takes responsibility for the love object by responding to his or her needs, expressed and unexpressed. In the case of mother and child, responsibility means attending to physical needs. In the case of love between adults, responsibility means responding to the other's psychic needs by supporting and bolstering self-esteem.

The element of respect assures that responsibility will not degenerate into possessiveness or dependency. Fromm's component of respect is the ability to see a person just as he or she is and to be aware of that

CARING AND TOUCHING, respect and commitment, are some of the components of loving relationships.

person's uniqueness. Respect means the absence of exploitation—the use of another to gain some profit for oneself—as a result of being concerned that the loved one will grow according to his or her natural components, for his or her own sake. "If I love the other person I feel one with him or her, but with him *as he is*, not as I need him to be as an object for my use" (Fromm, 1956, p. 24).

Moreover, one cannot respect an individual about whom one lacks a deep knowledge. One must know the core of the other person; one must know his or her strengths and weaknesses—all the other person's secrets, in other words. This enables the lover to see the beloved in the beloved's own terms. "In the act of loving, of giving myself, in the act of penetrating the other person, I find myself, I discover myself, I discover us both, I discover man" (Fromm, 1956, p. 26).

Finally, for Fromm love is not merely a feeling or an experience. Instead, it is an attitude, an orientation of character that determines the way the person relates to the world, not toward any particular person. This important idea rules out the romantic preoccupation that many people have with finding the right person to love. If we are true lovers, there is no need to wait for the right person: " 'I love you,' I must be able to say, 'I love in you everybody, I love through you the world, I love in you also myself' " (Fromm, 1956, p. 39). Or, as French actress Stephane Audran observes: "You can't separate love between a man and a woman and love for your fellow human beings. Love if you can't love other people—which means you can't love yourself—is possessive, destructive" (1976, p. 65).

It is easy to see that a person who can love in this manner must be mature. In Abraham Maslow's terms, he or she must be a *self-actualizing* human being (Maslow, 1968). Swensen (1972) put the theories of Maslow and Fromm to the test by comparing a group of self-actualizing people with ordinary people. (He obtained data on the former from their biographies.) Swensen found that the self-actualizing individuals differed from ordinary ones in that they attempted to help other people develop to the fullest. Specifically, the self-actualizing people were eager to give others useful advice, to teach them values and standards, and to persuade them to achieve their own goals. Love "provides the kind of relationship that induces the other to develop toward the best that is within him" (Swensen, 1972, p. 99).

How does one know whether one is a self-actualizing person and a mature lover? Of course, there is no litmus test that will make a positive identification. But as Powell (1974) suggests, one can start by asking oneself certain questions and answering them honestly. For example, with regard to one's lover, a person might ask, "Is it more important to me that you are pleased with yourself or that I am pleased with you?" "Is it more important to me that you reach the objectives you have set for yourself, or that you achieve the goals I want for you?" "Do I want you to love other people (of both sexes) and others to love you?"

Giving the "correct" answers to Powell's questions indicates that the love of the lover affirms and liberates the beloved to live fully, to be alive in all his or her physical and psychological components, and to experience the world completely.

LOVE AND SEX

For many people today, love and sex are the same; most people opening a book entitled *A Manual of Love*, for example, do not expect to find a philosophical or sociological discourse on love, but a practical guide to lovemaking, or sex. But love and sex are entirely different entities (Reik, 1949).

Part of the confusion about the two concepts derives from the influence of Freud, who advanced the notion that love springs from sex, that love consists of the tender feelings experienced after sex. As Reik points out, sex differs from love in that it is an instinct, a biological need, a drive which can be localized in the erogenous zones of the body. Love, by contrast, is an emotional relationship between an I and a Thou; it cannot be pinpointed in any particular part of the body.

Moreover, the aim of sex is discharge, the release of physical tension, whereas the aim of love is psychic release. Sex seeks satisfaction; love seeks happiness. Furthermore, sex occurs among all animals and is a phenomenon of nature. Love is a cultural entity which is not experienced by every human being. At its extreme, sex is selfish—it uses its object solely for satisfaction. Love, as we have seen, is altruistic; it involves being happy because one's beloved is happy: "Real lovers get a reward not only from their own satisfactions, but from seeing the other respond and become satisfied" (Comfort, 1972, p. 14). In brief, sex is passionate interest in another's body, whereas love is passionate interest in another's life.

How are love and sex related? What is sexual love? As Alexander Lowen (1972) notes, strong feelings of love enable the lover to be involved in both a physical and a spiritual fusion with his or her beloved. The result of the fusion is orgasm, an experience of intense pleasure. During sexual intercourse, the complete surrender of the lovers to love and sex fills their heads with a uniquely pleasurable sensation. The consciousness of the two individuals is completely overwhelmed with the ecstasy of this surrender. One woman describes the experience in these terms: "When Roy and I were making love, waves began to overpower my body—and I let it happen—I let go—and I will never be the same. What a powerful thing! This orgasm seemed to last forever. I had no control over what was happening to me—I just let it happen. I gave up control and this overpowering experience flooded my body" (Rogers, 1972, p. 61).

The feelings of love experienced by the couple actually constitute a commitment that enables them to yield themselves fully to the experience of the sexual act and so ensures the pleasure that goes beyond all bounds, the joy of complete sexual fusion and release. "Our hearts yearn for love," writes Lowen, "because our bodies long for joy. It must be that the advocacy of sex without love expresses the desperation of an individual who has not known the joy and is willing, therefore, to settle for the lesser pleasure derived from the release of genital tension" (1972, p. 20).

As Rollo May (1969) points out, humans are the only animals that make love face-to-face, who look at each other during the sex act. This means that the front portions of both lovers are completely exposed—the breasts, chests, stomachs, and other vulnerable areas. In such a position, each partner is open to the kindness or cruelty of the other. In this respect, the act of sexual love involves revealing one's most crucial secret, one's most profound weaknesses.

Finally, as May notes, during the sexual act, "there is an accelerating experience of touch, contact, union to the point where, for a moment, the awareness of separateness is lost, blotted out in a cosmic feeling of oneness with nature" (1969, p. 316). This, of course, is what Erich Fromm meant when he wrote that the ultimate goal of love is the reunion of the individual with the rest of the natural world.

LOVE AND MARRIAGE

Love may result in marriage, an institution that places the lovers in a new situation which demands many adjustments. Marriage frequently alters the way the two lovers respond to each other. During courtship, each lover yearned intensely for the other's presence. Since there was no certainty that the two would always be in love, a permanent state of tension existed between them—a state that kept them oriented toward each other. In this state, the two were forever trying to please each other. With marriage, the chase ends, the tension is relaxed, and attention deteriorates. Married couples tend to take each other for granted (H. Miller and Siegel, 1972).

Another difficulty with love and marriage in modern America, suggested by Snell Putney and Gail Putney (1964), is that the great majority of us marry for the wrong reason—we marry for love. This statement may seem false, even absurd, at first glance. But an examination of the Putneys' idea of love will help our understanding. For these researchers, love is an attraction based on the projection of alienated but desired characteristics onto the love object. Thus, the lover alienates some qualities which he or she would like to possess, but does not, and projects these onto someone else, whom the lover then adores.

What is meant by "the projection of alienated but desired characteristics"? Let us explore this question from the male point of view. In the eyes of the Putneys, American males are taught from early childhood that it is unmasculine to cry, to want to be cuddled, to be clean, to be dainty, or to be pretty. Even though the male may desire to be all these things, he must disdain them if he is to become a "real" man. But the cultural mold from which he has been poured does not entirely banish these desires from his mind. Deep down inside, he might still want to be cuddled and fussed over, but he dare not exhibit such desires. Instead, he must be reserved, virile, tough, and masculine. Females, of course, are encouraged to express the same qualities that are discouraged in males.

When a man looks for a wife, say the Putneys, he projects onto her those qualities which he would like to possess but for which he is forbidden to express his desire. Thus, he projects his idealized image onto a young woman and is attracted to it. Such, say the Putneys, is the nature of romance and love in America.

But falling in love with one's projected images leads away from the knowledge of self, which, as we saw, is crucial to being able to form any kind of meaningful friendship or love relationship. Lovers can avoid this mistake by looking for honesty, warmth, and the development of the self—a task which is made much easier with the cooperation of a partner who is trying to achieve the same goal. As the Putneys conclude: "The person who sees marriage as an opportunity for experiencing the warm, demonstrative potential in himself, and for satisfying needs in a candid and stable association, usually finds what he seeks" (1964, p. 142).

BANISHING BOREDOM After the married couple have had sufficient time to make their initial adjustments to their new state, their relationship begins to seem routine, and their interest in each other starts to wane. Like rigor mortis, "the stale death of passion" sets in. Under such circumstances, sexual love in marriage can become the first victim of boredom. One way to eliminate sexual boredom is variety: "Dietetic breakfasts of passion instead of pancakes, surprise lunch visits, the room upstairs at your favorite motel-restaurant after dinner out, a quick feel in the car, and experimentation with technique, will all help maintain this level of excitement, expectation, and arousal" (H. Miller and Siegel, 1972, p. 98).

The elimination of monotony in other areas of marriage is also important for keeping love alive. The couple should seek new acquaintances, new learning, and new experiences so that they can continuously change themselves and the routines they have settled into. Such modifications require effort and work. Making new and stimulating friends, returning to school, and seeking self-growth, for example, bring new life to marriage. As one young husband observes:

> Increasingly sameness is boring and boredom is less tolerable. Change is becoming the rule rather than the exception. In fact, continually doing new things together is so stimulating that old patterns are boring. For example, we've discovered that changing time and place of being together, being with each other in different situations, adds dimensions to our perceptions of each other—shit—this is too abstract—we move furniture—change our bedroom—spend time together in the morning—have lunch together—the point is that sameness becomes background. If we're always together at the same time in the same place perceptions tend to get fixed (Rogers, 1972, p. 63).

Happily married couples have managed to balance the sameness with the novelty so that the needs of both partners are met. The sameness imparts stability and continuity to the love, and the novelty imparts freshness (Fromme, 1965).

THE USES OF LOVE IN MARRIAGE Allan Fromme (1965) suggests that love can be employed to enrich marriage in a variety of ways. First, as love in marriage matures, it can increase understanding, a faculty that helps one partner fill the needs of the other. A husband who understands his wife's needs, for example, will not give her a gold brooch when what she really needs is someone to make dinner two or three times a week so that she can complete her studies at college.

Love in marriage also eliminates the need for constantly having a good time—for "living it up" by making every day spent together a special occasion, as many young lovers do before marriage. Married love enables the couple to enjoy themselves in themselves: "They can enjoy a warm sense of each other's presence even though their activities demand little or no response from each other. They can read, listen to music, pursue their own interests freely" (Fromme, 1965, p. 286).

Unlike premarital love, married love is an integral part of life, rather than an isolated entity. The quality of the marriage, as well as the quality of the love that keeps it going, depends greatly on how well the love component is orchestrated with the other parts of the couple's lives. The two must be able to deal with all the other aspects of life—children, friends, work, money problems, and so forth—if they are able to keep their love alive.

Love within marriage also must be durable; an argument over some petty matter will not tear a good marriage apart—as it well might tear apart a premarital relationship—because the couple have been through such battles before. Marital love, in short, must enable the couple to live with the daily frictions that inevitably arise as two people share the same intimate space.

Finally, love allows the two people to grow into fuller, richer human beings: "They grow as a result of what they live through together. They grow on each other's strengths and the strengths they develop to meet each other's weaknesses" (Fromme, 1965, p. 288).

SUMMARY

People need one another as casual acquaintances, as friends, and as lovers. In small, isolated communities social relationships are based on *Gemeinschaft*—each member knows everything about every other member. There are no strangers. City life (*Gesellschaft*) is otherwise; most other people are strangers, and we may know about only one aspect of their lives. Social roles are segmented and compartmentalized.

In urban society we do not have our friends from birth. We must make friends. We have many acquaintances, a few of whom gradually become friends. Part of the process of making friends involves dropping our social masks and sharing our secrets with another person. We make ourselves vulnerable to another person by exchanging what Murray Davis calls "psychological hostages." For this to happen, each friend must trust the other.

Friends perform favors for each other, both physical and psychological. Chief among physical favors is lending or offering money or obtaining other objects. Psychological favors involve listening, supporting, and encouraging. Friends bolster one's self-esteem. Most important, friends share one's own view of oneself.

Lovers are friends with whom one is physically intimate. Romantic love, however, does not have much in common with friendship. It is surrounded by a mystique involving an intense emotional attachment to another person. People "fall" in love, as in "fall down" or "fall over." For a time love and one's beloved become the major force in one's life. One believes that love will solve every problem, bring fulfillment, and conquer all.

Love, fortunately, takes other forms. Erich Fromm writes of love as care, giving, responsibility, respect, and knowledge in relationship to another person. Depth of feeling involves commitment and working through a relationship. Love, like friendship, is predicated on a sense of self-worth; one cannot accept the love of another if one does not feel worthy. Love of another includes the desire not to change that person to conform to one's own requirements; but rather to love the person for his or her own qualities. Love is the desire to help the other person grow and be fulfilled according to the needs of his or her own psyche.

Sex is not love, but it is the physical manifestation of love. During the sex act, each lover is most open to the kindness or cruelty of the other. In sex one is reunited with the physical world.

In America marriage is predicated upon love. The lovers then have the task of transforming romantic love into an enduring relationship. As passion wanes, the qualities of caring, respect, and openness become more important.

CASE STUDY

Jo Ann Jackson met Leonard Davis at a party given by a coworker one Friday evening in the art studio where she works. Finding themselves drawn to each other and involved in conversation which was becoming more personally meaningful as the evening passed, they decided to leave the party and continued their animated discussion until two o'clock in the morning at a McDonald's drive-in restaurant. Leonard drove Jo Ann home and called the following morning to ask whether he could spend the day with her.

On Sunday they enjoyed a trip to the zoo with Laura, Jo Ann's seven-year-old daughter. Before a month had passed, Leonard suggested that he move his clothing and personal belongings into Jo Ann's apartment, and Jo Ann agreed.

Her View

When she was eighteen, Jo Ann married her high school sweetheart, James. Their romance soon dissolved into disillusion for Jo Ann when she slowly began to realize that her young husband was becoming a regular user and finally an addict of hard drugs. During the six years of their marriage, Jo Ann completed two years of work toward a bachelor's degree in elementary education, a career she had chosen for practical reasons, although she would have preferred to study art. She was loyal to James until the end, which occurred two weeks before Laura's fifth birthday, when she and her sister returned from shopping and found James sprawled on the bathroom floor, dead from an overdose of heroin.

Jo Ann recalls the six years of her marriage to James as being extremely lonely. She avoided friendships out of embarrassment. She protected James's family and her own parents from the truth about James's addiction for as long as she could. She confided only in her sister and swore her to silence. Laura seemed the one bright spot in those six dismal years, and Jo Ann spent every free moment after work with her daughter.

After James's death, Jo Ann moved into a small apartment not far from her sister and her parents. Laura lived with Jo Ann's parents, and Jo Ann immersed herself in her work and her family. In looking back, Jo Ann says, "For a whole year grocery shopping for my mother and worrying about every detail of my parents' lives and my sister's marital squabbles took up 100 percent of my time. I didn't think about myself. I don't think I even had a self."

Jo Ann was respected at work as an efficient and dependable assistant bookkeeper. She became friendly with a couple of young artists at the studio. One of her new friends encouraged her to get back into art. Jo Ann did some charcoal sketches and a couple of paintings at home. Soon her family and friends were offering to pay for certain paintings and were delighted with their charcoal portraits. She was encouraged to take evening courses at the Art Institute, a suggestion that Jo Ann hesitantly followed. A friendship with a studio artist resulted in his instructing her in the basics of animation. Jo Ann's work was better than average, and she was thrilled when the studio hired her to work on an animation project.

When Jo Ann met Leonard, she was as pleased with his interest in her as an artist as she was with his gentleness. As she grew to know him, she reveled in his generosity and his growing relationship with her daughter. She was shocked, however, to learn that Leonard had a temper. She fears becoming locked into the role of wife, as she was in her marriage to James. For example, once when Leonard complained because she stayed after class to talk with friends at the Institute, she chafed at what she felt to be unreasonable limitations on her personal freedom and stayed even longer the next night. Then when he complained about her lack of attention to household chores, she suggested that he move out. He did, for six weeks, but he came back when Jo Ann called him after her cousin had been killed in an automobile accident. That evening Jo Ann discussed her fears about aging and death with Leonard and was moved when he revealed that a few years earlier he had been so discouraged by his failure to produce anything of artistic value that he had made an abortive attempt at suicide.

His View

Leonard graduated from a high school which prepares students for careers in art, and then he took two years of further professional training. He has been able to find work most of the time; however, some projects are of short duration, and he has to look for new opportunities rather frequently.

Leonard is aware that he sets high standards for himself and finds that he is often less pleased with his work than other people are. He dislikes the commercial aspect of working as an artist and questions the good taste of the people who purchase what he considers to be his less satisfactory works.

Leonard has a number of women friends, but he rarely allows himself to become really close to anyone. This is true of his friendships with men also. His expectations of others are high, and he is often disappointed. His close friendships are usually intense but often last only a short time. He is pleased with his developing relationship with Jo Ann, but he fears that one of them may say or do something that will cause their friendship to end. Thus, he was not surprised when Jo Ann asked him to move out, but he was pleased when she asked him to return.

Since Leonard is quick to anger, he expects Jo Ann to return his fireworks. However, Jo Ann learned from her mother to "hold her tongue" when she is criticized. Her silence makes Leonard even angrier, and his rage builds until he loses control. When Jo Ann finally threw a plastic bag filled with garbage at him last month after he had ended a long list of complaints with "and you haven't even taken out the garbage," he was first shocked and then pleased. His first impulse was to hit her; his second was to laugh uncontrollably, which he did. He then fell back on the couch weakly, pulling Jo Ann down with him, and said, in tones that originated somewhere in the deepest part of him, "You know, honey, I love you."

Leonard has noticed that although he is proud of Jo Ann's artistic ability, he is somewhat more irritable when she is working and less so when she is at home between jobs. When Jo Ann is working and Leonard is not, he feels very uncomfortable being around the house all day and finds doing household chores under these circumstances very abrasive. He says, "Intellectually I tell myself that I shouldn't feel that way. But so far it doesn't seem to make any difference. I hope Jo Ann can put up with me. I really want to build something solid with her."

Interpretation and Questions

Is Jo Ann's relationship with Leonard different from her relationship with James? Has Jo Ann grown in her ability to relate intimately to others? Does their self-confidence or lack of it affect Jo Ann's and Leonard's developing relationship? How close does their relationship come to your ideal for an intimate relationship? In what ways does it fall short? If Leonard should ask Jo Ann to marry him now, would you advise her to say "yes"?

STUDY GUIDE

Important Terms

mutual mirroring	romantic love
Gemeinschaft	eros
Gesellschaft	philia
orientations	agape

familiarity
confidentiality
self-esteem
altruism

caring
projection
alienation

Review Quiz

1 One function of friendship is that of allowing each party to see himself or herself through the eyes of another. This is called:
   a shared activities
   b emotional support
   c companionship
   d mutual mirroring

2 In a community characterized by a *Gemeinschaft*, relationships between people tend to be:
   a all-inclusive
   b segmented
   c based upon roles
   d means rather than ends

3 An example of *Gesellschaft* is:
   a Rome during the Roman Empire
   b Florence during the Renaissance
   c Houston, Texas, today
   d all the above

4 In modern industrialized societies, friendships are important because:
   a most social relations are deep and meaningful
   b most persons relate to others as individual, whole persons
   c the individual needs the opportunity to cast aside all segmented roles and act as a whole and unique individual
   d all the above

5 The type of friendship based upon profit, and noted first by the philosopher Aristotle, would be more common in a _____ -type society.
   a *Gemeinschaft*
   b *Gesellschaft*
   c village
   d rural

6 Among the important functions of friendship is:
   a the provision of external stimulation
   b the provision of emotional release
   c the provision of opportunities to participate in activities which are more enjoyable when shared by others
   d all the above

7 A study of the significance of self-esteem in interpersonal relationships has shown that:
   a similarity of self-concepts is the best indicator of friendship
   b difference in self-esteem is the most reliable indicator of friendship
   c support of the other's self-concept is the most reliable indicator of friendship
   d all the above

8 The Freudian definition of love emphasizes:
   a sexual desire
   b altruism
   c addiction
   d emotion

9 The myths of romantic love include the beliefs that:
   a there is only one right person
   b love conquers all
   c love is blind
   d all the above

10 According to Rollo May, one type of love, called _____ , is the drive to create.
   a sex
   b eros
   c philia
   d agape

11 Erich Fromm believes that human beings need love because:
   a we are like all other animals
   b we need to counteract a basic drive toward aloneness
   c only through love can separate individuals be fused with all mankind
   d only through love can we establish our separateness from the rest of nature

12 A study by Swensen shows that, in contrast to ordinary persons, self-actualizing persons are:
   a less in need of love
   b eager to give help to other persons
   c more independent of others
   d all the above

13 Sex and love are different because:
   a sex is partly biological; love is emotional
   b love is psychic release; sex is release of physical tension
   c sex occurs among all animals; love occurs only among humans
   d all the above

14 If a woman loves a man who has characteristics she possesses but will not recognize, the Freudian mechanism of _____ is involved.
   a repression
   b rationalization
   c sexualization
   d projection

15 Unlike premarital love, married love is:
   a a more isolated, or separate, part of life
   b more casual
   c more intense
   d all the above

Opinionnaire

Agree	No opinion	Disagree		
_____	_____	_____	1	Although infatuation may occur a number of times, true love comes only once.
_____	_____	_____	2	Love is too mysterious to be studied like other types of behavior.
_____	_____	_____	3	Persons of the same sex can experience the same feelings of love toward each other as two persons of the opposite sex.
_____	_____	_____	4	Women can express their love for others more easily than men can.
_____	_____	_____	5	It is possible to love someone who feels very negative toward you.
_____	_____	_____	6	Love is the same regardless of whether the love object is a child, an adult, or God.
_____	_____	_____	7	Love is no different from a deep friendship.
_____	_____	_____	8	Someone who lacks love for himself or herself cannot love another.
_____	_____	_____	9	It is possible for a couple to be deeply in love and yet not be able to stay married.
_____	_____	_____	10	One can be "in love" with only one person at a time.

Exercise

Many psychological tests are called *projective* because they are ambiguous and allow the respondent to project aspects of his or her personality into the interpretation of some stimulus.

Read the short story below and answer the questions which follow it. There are no right or wrong answers.

A ROMANTIC TRAGEDY

Once upon a time a young and poor college student fell in love with a pretty, rich co-ed and won her heart. He proposed marriage, and she eagerly accepted. However, his parents opposed the marriage because they wanted the youth to study and become a doctor. Eventually they prevailed, and the young man asked his beloved to wait. Angered, she retaliated by going out with a football player. She became pregnant by the athlete. Distraught, she called up her former fiancé and confessed all. Overcome with jealousy, grief, and pain, the young man committed suicide.

Who was responsible for the young man's death?
1 _____ The co-ed
2 _____ The young man's parents
3 _____ The football player
4 _____ The young man himself
5 _____ Fate

What should the young man have done?
1 _____ Just what he did
2 _____ Opposed his parents and married
3 _____ Become a doctor and not committed suicide
4 _____ Forgiven the co-ed, married her, and raised the child
5 _____ Forgiven the co-ed and suggested an immediate appointment at the abortion clinic

With whom did you identify most strongly?
1 _____ The young man
2 _____ The co-ed
3 _____ The parents
4 _____ The football player

Now examine your responses. Did you become involved in the romantic, tragic aspects of the story, or did you answer from a rational and practical viewpoint? Try the story on your friends.

Projects for Class or Home Study

1 Love has recently been compared to an addiction. List the "symptoms" you experienced the last time you were in love. Are they similar to those which accompany addiction to drugs?

2 A number of myths about romantic love are discussed in this chapter. How many of them are repeated during one evening's television viewing?

3 List your best friends in order of preference. Next to each name estimate the percentage of time in that person's company that you can be truly yourself. Do the percentages decrease as you move down the list?

4 Ask several persons to define love. Do the answers fit the concepts of love presented in this chapter?

5 Many writers have remarked on the ways in which lovers communicate nonverbally. Watch couples closely and note the amount of eye contact which occurs. Can you tell which couples are in love?

Suggestions for Further Reading

Clanton, Gordon, and Smith, Lynn G. The self-inflicted pain of jealousy. *Psychology Today*, March 1977, **11**, 44–49.

We often assume that jealousy is a natural by-product of love. The authors offer some practical advice on how to cope with this painful emotion.

Crane, Stephen. The pace of youth. In Stephen Crane, *Maggie and other stories*. New York: Airmont, 1968.

A delightful short story about young love. Crane describes the language of love through the nonverbal interaction between a boy and girl at a carnival.

Herrigan, Jackie, and Herrigan, Jeff. *Loving free*. New York, Grosset & Dunlap, 1973.

A husband and wife discuss the meaning of love and intimacy in their marriage. Interesting and easy to read.

Otto, Herbert A. (Ed.). *Love today: A new exploration*. New York: Association Press, 1972.

A collection of readings covering topics such as love at different ages and taboos on spiritual and homosexual love. The book also contains a list of human growth centers.

Slater, Philip. *The pursuit of loneliness*. Boston: Beacon Press, 1971.

A thoughtful social analyst discusses the conditions in American society which prevent the attainment of true love and intimacy.

Wilkinson, Melvin. Romantic love: The great equalizer? Sexism in popular music. *Family Coordinator*, April 1976, **25**, 161–166.

Our values show up in our popular culture. This author analyzed 200 songs which were popular between 1954 and 1968 and found that men could express love in songs in ways not allowed in real life.

Answers to Review Quiz

1-*d* 2-*a* 3-*d* 4-*c* 5-*b* 6-*d* 7-*c* 8-*a* 9-*d* 10-*b* 11-*c*
12-*b* 13-*d* 14-*d* 15-*b*

3

SEX ROLES

Perhaps the one moment in life that has the greatest impact on the future development of any human being occurs at birth with the announcement, "It's a boy," or "It's a girl." The events that follow range from the choice of a name and the color of the receiving blanket to the decision concerning the kind of work the person will do in a lifetime. The development of that person's perceptions and feelings about himself or herself and about other people as well is strongly influenced by gender.

Which is more important—the sex of the child at birth or the way the child is reared? Is it nature or nurture—biology or culture—that causes men and women to come close to what we consider the "normal" way of behaving and of viewing themselves?

Current research indicates that neither genetics nor socialization alone can totally explain human behavior. *Socialization* is the process of learning to behave in the way in which other members of the society expect one to behave. If one grows up in Houston, for example, one learns to speak with what other Americans hear as a Texas drawl, and, like other Americans, one learns to get to school on time, use a telephone, drive a car, and manage a checking account. If one grows up in Marrakesh, however, one learns how to speak the Berber language and perhaps how to ride a camel, weave a rug, and drive a hard bargain at the market. An important component of socialization is learning the behavior that is appropriate to one's sexual assignment and learning the meaning of one's role and one's identity as male or female. Socialization begins at the moment of birth. It continues in the nursery, with its pink or blue wallpaper, and in the playroom, which may be strewn with dolls or trucks. Later, there are ballet lessons or baseball games, and one may learn to sew one's own clothes or fix one's own car.

Many of the differences between boys and girls develop while they are quite young, but that does not necessarily mean that these differences are genetically determined. "The passivity that is the essential characteristic of the 'feminine' woman is a trait that develops in her from the earliest years. But it is wrong to assert a biological datum is concerned; it is in fact a destiny imposed upon her by her teachers and by society" (de Beauvoir, 1953).

Schools tend to reinforce and perpetuate sexual stereotypes through their administrative setup, through their selection of educational materials, through the segregation of boys and girls in certain classes such as shop and home economics, and through the biases of teachers which reflect those of the society. Any child can see who is boss in the elementary school. A study made in 1971 showed that 85 percent of all elementary school teachers were women and that 78 percent of all elementary school principals were men. Children do not have to be taught the comparative power of sex roles in the schools. They learn about status from what they see around them (Women on Words and Images, 1972).

Sex Differences

Anatomy is destiny, according to Freud. He meant that biology determines not only one's behavior but also one's place; that because of their bodies, men and women develop different needs and abilities and perform different roles in society. To some extent, Freud was right; anatomical differences between men and women have an important bearing on behavior. But it is also true that much so-called masculine and feminine behavior is learned. Men are generally bigger, stronger, and more aggressive than women. But these are generalizations that have little meaning in individual cases. Men and women are more alike than different, and there is a great variety among individuals of the same sex.

PHYSICAL DIFFERENCES

For every 100 females born, about 106 males are born, but more male babies than female babies die at birth or are stillborn. The sex of the infant is determined at the moment of conception and depends on a pair of chromosomes, the structures in the cell that carry the hereditary-bearing material in the genes. Each human cell contains twenty-three pairs of chromosomes, one chromosome in each pair coming from the maternal side, and the other coming from the paternal side. There are two kinds of chromosomes that determine sex—X and Y. The female egg cell always contributes an X chromosome; the male sperm cell can contribute either an X or a Y, which determines the sex of the embryo. If the configuration of the fertilized egg cell is XX, the embryo will develop as a female; if it is XY, the embryo will develop as a male (Swerdloff, 1975).

In addition to sex, there are other characteristics, such as color blindness, which are determined by the sex chromosomes and thus are said to be sex-linked. Most of the genes for these traits are carried on the X chromosome. Females possess two X chromosomes, and if one of them carries a gene for a defect, the same gene is not likely to be present in the

AN AMERICAN BOY who does not like to play baseball is not going to have an easy time with his peers.

matching X chromosome, which is capable of actually masking the defect. Males, however, have no matching X chromosome, and their Y chromosome cannot mask an X-linked defective gene. Thus, nearly all sex-linked defects are "carried" by females but appear only in males. For a female to display an X-linked defect, she would have to be the child of a carrier mother and a father who displayed the defect. Hemophilia, a disease that impairs the clotting of the blood, is sex-linked. Queen Victoria was apparently a carrier of the disease, but she did not have the illness and neither did her daughters or granddaughters. One of her sons suffered from hemophilia, and several of her great-grandsons also inherited it.

Once the embryo is formed, its sexual development depends on the presence or absence of male hormones, or chemical substances in the blood called *androgens*. If androgens are present, a small embryonic protuberance will develop as a penis. If androgens are not present, it will develop as a clitoris. If something goes wrong before birth in an embryo with an XY chromosome pattern, the baby will be born with female sexual characteristics but will not become a fully developed female without the aid of estrogens or female hormones (Swerdloff, 1975).

The distinctiveness in the reproductive system is responsible for what Money and Ehrhardt call the "four imperatives"—differences between men and women: Men impregnate, while women menstruate, gestate, and lactate. Beyond these anatomical differences are the many social, cultural, and psychological factors that determine an individual's gender identity or socialized sex role. Occasionally, embryos develop abnormalities and an infant may be born who is not immediately identifiable as belonging to one sex or the other. Called *hermaphrodites*, such infants must be assigned a sexual identity, and the sexual identity they are assigned strongly influences their lives. A study of matched pairs of hermaphrodites revealed wide contrasts between those brought up as girls and those brought up as boys. In many cases it was impossible to determine their previous medical history, and it was concluded that for children whose sexual identity is ambiguous, upbringing is more important than anatomy (Money and Ehrhardt, 1972). It should be noted, however, that current genetics techniques enable the chromosomes of such a baby to be examined immediately after birth. Once it has been determined whether the infant is XX or XY, the appropriate sex hormones are administered to promote proper development of the correct sex characteristics.

MENTAL DIFFERENCES

It is hard to determine mental differences between the sexes from intelligence tests because these tests are designed to eliminate questions that depend on sex differences for a response. As a result there is not much difference between the overall IQ scores of boys and girls, but there is a large variability in certain areas, notably counting, mathematical reasoning, memory, abstract reasoning, and perceptual speed. These differences have been used to support the hypothesis that men and women differ in their cognitive style. While this appears to be true in some respects, however, many questions about sex differences in intelligence are unanswerable because there are no tests which measure native ability. Performance always reflects the experience the individual has undergone (Hacker, 1975).

One area in which boys and girls have been demonstrated to differ is that of spatial reasoning and analytic ability—the capacity to pay attention to visual details and discard the irrelevant while abstracting a single element that will help solve a particular spatial problem. Kagan and Moss illustrated the difference in an experiment in which subjects were given pictures of objects and also pictures of people in a variety of postures and dress and engaged in different activities. They were asked to group the pictures that belonged together. Girls were more likely to form functional groups, such as a nurse, a doctor, and a wheelchair, whereas boys were more likely to form analytic groups based on a common detail, such as the position of an arm or a leg (Kagan and Moss, 1962).

The fact that, on the average, girls score higher in math in the elementary grades, where the main concern is with arithmetic problems, is also often cited as evidence of differing mental characteristics of the two sexes. By the time the college aptitude tests are administered, boys score an average of 50 points higher in the math portion. Eleanor Maccoby (1963) suggests several explanations for the lower scores of girls. One is that mathematics and science are often considered preparation for engineering and other professions generally considered masculine. In addition, she says, girls, on the average, are less analytic and tend to view subjects in a more global manner, which is not conducive to productivity in high-level mathematics. She cites the importance of encouraging initiative and independence as a way to encourage the analytic mode of thought. However, she leaves unanswered the question of whether parents treat daughters differently from the way they treat sons with respect to training in independence, and the question of whether that accounts for the difference in the modes of perceiving and performing other analytic tasks (E. E. Maccoby and Jacklin, 1974).

EMOTIONAL DIFFERENCES

Are the apparent differences between men and women, then, based mostly on emotional characteristics deriving from physical differences and stereotyped sex roles? Eleanor Maccoby and Carol Jacklin (1974) made a study of some of the popular views about the emotional differences between boys and girls and men and women. They found that some of our beliefs are true, some are false, and some are in that gray area in which there is inadequate research to warrant a conclusion. They found no evidence to support the myth that girls are more social, are more suggestible, have a lower sense of self-esteem, or are less motivated to achieve than boys. One area in which they found a consistent pattern of difference was aggression. Boys are more likely to fight, engage in mock fighting, and harbor aggressive fantasies than girls, a sex difference the researchers say is present in all cultures in which aggressive behavior has been studied.

Many traditional anthropologists disagree with these findings. In general, such anthropologists say that many of the roles men and women play in society are derived from the biological function of preserving the species. The female striving is to procreate and guarantee the survival of the family. The male must be unencumbered by childbearing and childrearing because he is the protector of the family. As a result of these biological roles, each sex developed certain qualities. The male, who fathered the child, became the hunter and developed fighting skills to protect the family. The female, who had to bear and nurture children, became passive and dependent.

FOR A pretty girl there is always reinforcement of the feminine—the charm of ruffles and fluff, the dropped glance, the half smile.

But in a groundbreaking study, anthropologist Margaret Mead (1935) examined the variety of patterns based on differences in sex and temperament of three primitive tribes living in New Guinea. She found that sex roles in the three tribes differed widely not only from our own but also from one another. Among the Arapesh, a mountain people, the behavior of both sexes was similar. Both were gentle, noncompetitive, passive, and, above all, nurturing. "To the Arapesh, the world is a garden that must be tilled . . . that the yams and the dogs and the pigs and most of all the children may grow" (M. Mead, 1935). Among the neighboring Mundugumor, both sexes were aggressive and hostile. Children received only minimal attention and had to learn to fend for themselves. The Tchambuli tribe displayed an image opposite to our own in regard to sex-role assignments. The women did most of the hunting and fishing and took the initiative in economic and social matters. The men were gentle and unaggressive and given to self-adornment. "The material suggests that we may say that many, if not all, of the personality traits which we have called masculine or feminine are as lightly linked to sex, as are the clothing, the manners, and the form of headdress that a society at a given period assigns to either sex" (M. Mead, 1935).

The study indicates that the temperament of men and women is not so deeply rooted in anatomy as Freud would have it. Mead highlights the malleability and variety of human nature, as a result of which men and women can develop their full human potential in many different ways.

The Feminine Mystique

"I love the kids and Bob and my home. There's no problem you can even put a name to. But I'm desperate. I begin to feel that I have no personality. I'm a server of food and a putter-on of pants and a bed maker, somebody who can be called on when you want something. But who am I?"

The problem had no name until Betty Friedan came along in 1963 and put a label on it. Her book, *The Feminine Mystique*, was an attempt to define the aching feeling of dissatisfaction that troubled many American women, particularly middle-class housewives. Never before had women enjoyed so many privileges, owned so many cars or television sets, and had so many appliances to help them with the housework. And never before had they felt such a great malaise and such anger.

Novelist Doris Lessing describes that anger and the need to avoid taking it out on the people near you. The leading character in *The Golden Notebook* wakes up in bed with her lover and expresses her resentment: "It must be six o'clock. . . . I realize the 'housewife disease' has taken hold of me. . . . I must dress Janet, get her breakfast, and don't forget to buy tea, etc., etc. With all this useless tension a resentment is also switched on against unfairness . . . that I should have to spend so much of my time worrying over details.'' She goes on to say that she resents her lover because he will spend his day being served by women in all kinds of capacities—secretaries, waitresses, laundresses. ''The anger is the disease of women in our time'' (Lessing, 1962).

Why were American women unable to accept the housewife role gracefully, *Newsweek* magazine asked in 1960, at the very time Ms. Friedan was formulating her theory about ''the feminine mystique''? ''A young mother with a beautiful family, charm, talent, and brains is apt to dismiss her role apologetically. 'What do I do?' you hear her say. 'Why

nothing. I'm just a housewife.' " A good education, the article concluded, had given the American woman everything except a feeling of her own worth (Friedan, 1963). The fact is that these American women wanted to be someone more than Jack's daughter, Robert's wife, Johnny's mother, or Billy's grandmother. They wanted an identity of their own.

The feminine mystique is a syndrome consisting of all the dissatisfactions of women with their place in society. Not all, or perhaps not even most, women are unhappy with their lives as women. However, a bias in society against achievement by women does exist. In the following section we shall examine some of the ways in which it operates against women as they are growing up and forming their identities. In the chapter on making money there will be a further examination of discrimination against women in the workplace.

SEXISM: A SUBTLE BIAS

Textbooks at all levels, from elementary school to college, exhibit a sexual bias ranging from mathematics problems that refer to inept woman drivers to history books which all but ignore the contributions of women to the arts, science, government, and the professions. Sexism, a bias against equality for women, has been documented in elementary school readers, which abound with examples showing Dick doing adventurous, active, and creative things while Jane watches, appreciates, or cries. The message beamed to young readers is that boys achieve active mastery, whereas nice girls finish last. A study of sex stereotyping in 2,760

ARE YOU SEXIST?

1. Do you believe in the natural superiority of men?
2. Do you believe in the natural superiority of women?
3. Do you believe that since men are responsible for the support of their wives and children, it's only fair that they should earn more money?
4. Do you believe that there is "men's work" and "women's work" and never the twain should meet?
5. Do you believe raising children is primarily a woman's job?
6. Do you believe fathers have the primary responsibility for disciplining the children?
7. Do you believe women are naturally too emotional to be leaders in business or government?
8. Do you believe that no "real man" would want to be an interior decorator, a nurse, a hairdresser?
9. Would you let a woman surgeon perform your operation?
10. Do you believe politics is a man's game too dirty for women to play?
11. Do you believe housework is a woman's job and yardwork is a man's?
12. Do you believe women are naturally more caring and compassionate than men?
13. If you are religious, are you certain God is male?

Source: Women's Lib: The Case against Chauvinism. *Human Behavior*, May/June 1972, p. 49.

stories in 134 children's readers uncovered some startling ratios. The ratio of boy-centered to girl-centered stories was 5 to 2. Biographies of males outnumbered those of females 6 to 1. Even in animal stories, the ratio of male animals to female animals was 2 to 1. There was a wide selection of role models on the basis of which boys were encouraged to choose a trade or learn a skill. Boys skated all day to avoid capture by Indians, rescued adults and girls from fires, and saved planes and spaceships. Girls who acted bravely were more likely to carry warnings on horseback or go to the rescue of small animals. Wives and mothers were almost the only role models presented for girls. The entire study unearthed only three working mothers, even though about 40 percent of all working women have children under eighteen. The report criticized the children's readers for "placing the pressure of official expectation on children at such a susceptible age" and for failing to prepare girls for the roles that they would be expected to play in society. "More women than ever will find fulfillment outside the traditional mother role for the greater part of their lives. By narrowing the role models, the books are crippling both sexes" (Women on Words and Images, 1972).

Partly because of the pressure of women's groups and the raised consciousness of many people in the publishing field, women are now being portrayed in more egalitarian roles. The following quotation is from a set of guidelines that McGraw-Hill issued to its editorial staff in 1974:

> Women as well as men have been leaders and heroes, explorers and pioneers, and have made notable contributions to science, medicine, law, business, politics, civics, economics, literature, the arts, sports, and other areas of endeavor. Books dealing with subjects like these, as well as general histories, should acknowledge the achievements of women. The fact that women's rights, opportunities, and accomplishments have been limited by the social customs and conditions of their time should be openly discussed (*Guidelines for Equal Treatment of the Sexes*, 1974, p. 1).

As shown in the table on page 57, there have been sizable advances in women's professional training. However, with the Ph.D. as a measure, men still dominate the scientific fields.

KEEPING GIRLS OUT

In 1970, Irving Anker, acting chancellor of the New York City Board of Education, acknowledged that discrimination against women exists in our society, but, he added, "our public schools are hardly party to the practice in any large degree." The following year, at a hearing on sex bias in public schools, Laura Edelhart and her daughter Bonnie presented the following public testimony in a lawsuit contesting segregated classes in junior high school:

I asked Miss Jonas if my daughter could take metal working or mechanics, and she said there is no freedom of choice. That is what she said.

THE COURT: That is it?

THE WITNESS: I also asked her whose decision this was, that there was no freedom of choice. And she told me it was the decision of the Board of Education.

I didn't ask her anything else because she clearly showed me that it was against the school policy for girls to be in the class. She said it was a Board of Education decision. . . .

Q. Did she use that phrase, "no freedom of choice"?

A. Exactly that phrase; no freedom of choice. That is what made me so angry that I wanted to start this whole thing.

[THE COURT]: Now, after this lawsuit was filed, they then permitted you to take the course; is that correct?

[BONNIE]: No, we had to fight about it for quite a while.

[THE COURT]: But eventually, they did let you in the second semester?

[WITNESS]: They only let me in there.

[THE COURT]: You are the only girl?

[WITNESS]: Yes.

[THE COURT]: How did you do in the course?

[WITNESS]: I got the medal for it from all the boys there.

[THE COURT]: Will you show the court?

[WITNESS]: Yes (indicating).

[THE COURT]: What does the medal say?

[WITNESS]: Metal 1970 Van Wyck.

[THE COURT]: And why did they give you that medal?

[WITNESS]: Because I was the best out of all the boys (National Organization of Women, 1972).

Teachers and guidance counselors have an important influence on students. An experiment with sixty-two high school guidance counselors—eighteen women and forty-four men—indicated that counselors often steer girls into female-dominated professions, such as teaching or nursing, while they steer boys into medicine or law. Each counselor listened to a tape on which a girl with a traditional vocational

PERCENTAGE OF WOMEN AMONG TOTAL SCIENCE AND ENGINEERING DOCTORATE RECIPIENTS, BY FIELD

	1965	1969	1974
Total	7	9	14
Physical sciences	4	5	7
Engineering	Z*	Z*	1
Mathematical sciences	10	14	18
Social sciences	13	17	24

*Z-less than 0.5 percent.
Source: U.S. Bureau of the Census, 1976c, p. 75.

goal and a girl with a more "masculine" goal talked about their ambitions. The counselors gave the girls scores indicating acceptance of each goal. A large majority of the counselors found the more traditional goals more appropriate than the less traditional ones, and they also recommended further counseling for the more ambitious girls (Women's Lib: The Case against Chauvinism, 1972). Nor are classroom teachers immune to sexism. On March 19, 1971, Marcy Silverman, a student at Jamaica High School in New York City, testified in court that her physics teacher had told girls to put down their hands when he asked for a volunteer lab assistant. She said he was interested in working only with boys. At the same hearing, Gigi Gordon, from Van Wyck High School, told how the teacher in charge of the school's audio-visual equipment squad at first refused to accept girl applicants. He relented under pressure, but did not allow the girls to serve in the classrooms (National Organization of Women, 1972).

THE DOUBLE MESSAGE: FEMININITY VERSUS ACHIEVEMENT

On the face of it, it is hard to believe that girls actually get off to a better start in school than boys. Girls generally start speaking, reading, and counting earlier than boys; girls do better in math for the first several years of school (Freeman, 1973). But at the onset of puberty, girls are faced with a major crisis. They must come to terms with their emerging femininity, and they must conform to new socialization standards which emphasize beauty and charm as a way to attract men. In elementary school and junior high, girls are encouraged to do well in school, but toward the end of high school the message changes. Competition is aggressive and unfeminine, they are told. Their most rewarding achievement will come through marriage. Many girls are made to feel that they must choose between marriage and a serious career, and the correct choice is always made explicit (Sheehy, 1976).

Those women who go on to college are faced with what seem to be mutually exclusive goals—that of becoming a homemaker and that of having a career. The personality traits of self-reliance and achievement necessary for a career—not just a job to mark time until marriage—are interpreted as aggression in the context of finding a mate and relating in a feminine fashion to a man.

In a classic study by Mirra Komarovsky (1946), a group of college women were asked to submit autobiographical documents on the nature of the sex roles imposed on them by society. From the data, Komarovsky characterized one of the roles as the "feminine" role and the other as the "modern" role, a role which demands the same behavior patterns and attitudes that are demanded of college men. For college women, the conflict between these two roles centers on academic and social life, vocational plans, and a number of personality traits.

More than one-fourth of the college women expressed some grievance against their families for failing to present them with consistent goals. One girl wrote:

> I get a letter from my mother at least three times a week. One week her letters will say, "Remember that this is your last year at college. Subordinate everything to your studies. You must have a good record and secure a job." The next week her letters are full of wedding news. This friend of mine got married; that one is engaged; my young cousin's wedding is only a week off. When, my mother wonders, will I make up my mind? Surely, I wouldn't want to be the only unmarried one in my group. It is high time, she feels, that I give some thought to it (Komarovsky, 1946, p. 183).

It seemed to many of the young women that their world had been turned upside down: what had previously evoked praise now evoked criticism. Forty percent of the women said they occasionally "played dumb" on dates and concealed their intelligence. At the same time, social pressures were being exerted for them to compete to the best of their abilities.

> Society confronts the girl with powerful challenges and strong pressure to excel in certain competitive lines of endeavor and to develop certain techniques of adaptations very similar to those expected of her brothers. But then, quite suddenly, as it appears to these girls, the very success in meeting these challenges begins to cause anxiety. It is precisely those most successful in the earlier role who are now penalized (Komarovsky, 1946, p. 186).

Komarovsky's conclusion is that the problems will persist until "the adult roles of women are redefined in greater harmony with the socioeconomic and ideological character of modern society" (Komarovsky, 1946).

Many studies have indicated a high level of anxiety among college-educated women. But Matina Horner (1969), now president of Radcliffe College, tried to pinpoint why many bright college women fail to achieve success. Horner postulated a psychological barrier to achievement in college women who found success threatening. Many college women, the study showed, consider success and femininity mutually exclusive and pay a price in anxiety for defying the conventional sex norms. In an experiment, women undergraduates were asked to complete a story about Anne, who found herself after first-term finals at the top of her medical school class. Over 65 percent wrote stories about Anne losing her friends or feeling guilty and unhappy. In a similar test about John administered to undergraduate men, only 9 percent wrote negative stories. Horner concluded that the prospect of success raised a fear concerning the consequences of success in 65 percent of the women but in only 9 percent of the men. She pointed to fear of social rejection and role conflict as a motive for avoiding success (Horner, 1969).

With the women's movement, some people are beginning to look at men's and women's roles differently. A continuing effort is being made to create more options for women and men to develop careers without regard to sexual stereotypes. More men are becoming aware that they must share the responsibility for household duties and child care if their wives work. Remaining single is less stigmatized, and single people who want children have in some cases been able to adopt them. But in spite of all the changes in the family, in the home, in schools, on campuses, and in business and industry, masculine privilege to a great extent still prevails. Many women, too, still struggle with the burden of the dream that somewhere there is an ideal mate who will make their lives complete. "Until recently, most men and women spent a good deal of time living with one of two illusions: That career success would make them immortal and that a mate would complete them. Each sex had half the loaf" (Sheehy, 1976). Men's half of the loaf included power and prestige, but it also entailed heavy financial responsibilities and restrictions on emotions. Middle-class women were freed of the necessity to work, but they were trapped in the housewife syndrome, which wore them down spiritually and stripped them of their sense of self-worth.

The Masculine Role

> It's just so . . . hard to keep this . . . posture of manliness, this strength you're supposed to have all the time, this getting things done efficiently, and planning for the future, and fearing that you might fail or that you're not as good as someone, or that you're not getting the rewards. I mean, I don't understand sometimes why women want anything we have. I mean, I understand, only sometimes it sure seems to me that it's a curse to be a man (Cottle, 1974, p. 5).

The Bible says God created woman out of Adam's rib. Whether one takes the Scriptures literally or not, the fates of the two sexes have been irrevocably intertwined since the beginning of the human race. If there is a woman's problem, there is a man's problem; if women are inferior, men are superior; if women are subservient, men are dominant; if women are caught in the homemaker trap, men are imprisoned in their roles as husbands, fathers, and sons. At first glance, it seems that men get all the rewards—they are at the top of the power structure in business, government, politics, the arts, and the professions. Even in the home, which is traditionally woman's domain, the man is the head of the household. By providing the goods and services, he maintains control of the economic life of the family. Work is his burden and his salvation. Without it he feels emasculated, and through it he sustains and perpetuates his power.

THE *MACHO* IMAGE

Anthropologist Ruth Benedict noted a long time ago that cultures can be described in terms of certain characteristic patterns. Our culture was created by men and has been described as *macho*. *Macho* is derived from a Spanish word which connotes pride bordering on arrogance, hypersensitivity to insult, stubbornness, aggressiveness, and lust characterized by amorous conquest (Stevens, 1973).

The *macho* cult in our society is characterized by Marc Feigen Fasteau as the "male machine":

> The male machine is a special kind of being, different from women, children, and men who don't measure up. He is functional, designed mainly for work. He is programmed to tackle jobs, override obstacles, attack problems, overcome difficulties, and always seize the offensive. He will take on any task that can be presented to him in a competitive framework, and his most

important positive reinforcement is victory. He has armor plating which is virtually impregnable. His circuits are never scrambled or overrun by irrelevant personal signals. He dominates and outperforms his fellows, although without excessive flashing of lights or clashing of gears. His relationship with other male machines is one of respect but not intimacy; it is difficult for him to connect his internal circuits to those of others. In fact, his internal circuitry is something of a mystery to him and is maintained primarily by humans of the opposite sex (1974, p. 7).

"Be a man," the father tells the boy, meaning that he should be brave, hardworking, and strong and—above all—that he should not be a sissy. Masculinity is traditionally expressed through courage, toughness, competitiveness, and aggression. When a young boy cries, his parents are quick to assert, "You're a big boy, and big boys don't cry." What the parents are really telling their son is that real men do not express their emotions and that if he is a real man, he will not allow his to show. Outward expressions of emotion are viewed as a sign of femininity and as undesirable in a male (Balswick and Peek, 1971).

However, a problem that young boys who are forming their concept of maleness often face is that of having no role model to relate to. The father bears the chief responsibility for the guardianship of the children, but in practice he often plays a subordinate role (Hacker, 1957). Since most fathers do not spend much time with their children, boys must learn about the male role from their peers. Their exaggerated version of the strength, bravery, and toughness that constitutes manliness is really a caricature of the male role.

Boys also learn from the media, from which two clear-cut images emerge: the inexpressive male as "cowboy" or as "playboy." The cowboy is the strong, silent type epitomized in the movies by John Wayne. He is protective and even chivalrous toward women, but he cannot show tenderness or affection because that would be unmanly. The playboy image is reflected in the James Bond character; he is a great lover but is incapable of *being* in love or even of caring deeply for the woman he is with. An incapacity for emotional expression is characteristic of both types. It can be highly destructive in marriage—where communication and companionship are so vital to the success of the relationship—unless the man is able to drop the facade in the privacy of his own home (Balswick and Peek, 1971).

If the emotional life of men is impoverished in comparison with that of women, men's intellectual life is more rewarding and less characterized by conflict. Men and women may sit side by side in the same classroom, but the implicit and explicit messages they receive are different. Men are told to work hard, persevere, and plan for a career. Women may be told, "I know you're competent and your thesis adviser knows you're competent. The question in our minds is are you really serious about what you're doing?" (Women's Caucus, University of Chicago, 1970).

Men *are* serious about their ambitions, particularly middle-class men, partly because their ambitions are taken seriously. They know they have to earn a living, follow in their fathers' footsteps, and, if they are intellectually oriented, compete for admission to a prestigious school and continue competing for admission to the right law, medical, or graduate school. The fear of failing to carry out these responsibilities causes much stress and anxiety among men.

THE *MACHO* IMAGE VERSUS THE ACHIEVING WOMAN

Today, a new factor confronts the male *macho* image on the college campus. The traditional concept of male intellectual superiority conflicts with an increasing freedom and intellectualism among women on campus. Mirra Komarovsky (1973) studied the extent of strain induced by the new style of collegiate companionship between the sexes. Of the sixty-two college males from an Ivy League senior class that she interviewed, 30 percent reported intellectual insecurity or strain in their relationships with bright women. One man said, "I enjoy talking to more intelligent girls, but I have no desire for a deep relationship with them. I guess I still believe that the man should be more intelligent." Of the thirty-seven students who said that intellectual relationships with dates were not a problem, eight said that their women friends were intellectually superior. In seven of the eight cases, however, the female friend had some weakness such as emotional instability or lack of beauty to offset her intellectual superiority. Overall, the young men did not seem to regard intellectualism as inherently unfeminine, and, in fact, most of them hoped to share their intellectual life with their female friends. Such an attitude could serve as a buffer against the undue pressure on men to achieve at college and later in the work world. But these same young men were ambivalent in their attitudes toward working women. Although they thought that being a full-time housekeeper seemed dull, a career woman could become an occupational rival. "A woman should want her husband's success more than he should want hers. Her work shouldn't interfere with or hurt his career in any way," one young man said (Komarovsky, 1973).

The masculine mystique, with its heavy emphasis on competition and achievement, is not without enormous human cost. It takes its toll not only on women but also on men who have refused to adopt the characteristics that seem to be essential for success in the system or who have been denied access to many of the avenues of success. In the words of a forty-eight-year-old black man who was fired from three jobs:

And now, you take a good look at me, young man. Look at me and see failure. Not just unemployed, not just scrapping after dollars in the streets, but a failed man. . . . All those years I was growing up they taught me that a man brings in money for his family, and that's what I did. Quit school in the fourth grade and went to work. If you want to work and you can't work, they might as well be killing you. That's the long and short of it (Cottle, 1974, p. 6).

BEYOND *MACHO*

Men and women are becoming increasingly aware of the limits of the *macho* cult, but new criteria for manhood are still largely undefined. Certainly many more men are now sharing housekeeping and child-rearing responsibilities than was the case years ago. These are outward manifestations of a change, but there are other indications that the John Wayne–James Bond male image may be disappearing from the scene among certain segments of the population.

According to 28,000 readers of *Psychology Today* who responded to a questionnaire (Tavris, 1977), the *macho* male who is tough and aggressive and makes many sexual conquests is not admired by either sex. Both sexes want men to be more warm and loving and emotionally expressive. Masculinity today, the study indicated, is a set of qualities that can be possessed as easily by women as by men. Almost all readers felt that both men and women should be willing to stand up for their beliefs and fight to defend their families. Fewer than 10 percent of the men said that a man would lose his masculinity if he were in a traditionally female occupation such as that of nurse or elementary school teacher. In short, most people who responded to the questionnaire supported the women's liberation movement, but they felt that men could use some liberating to become freer with their emotions and less obsessed by their work. One man wrote: "I'm tired of American male stereotypes! I have a beard, two biceps, a penis AND I'm capable of showing warmth, sharing housework, and shedding a tear. Why are so many men threatened by that combination of characteristics?" (Tavris, 1977).

Though there are both men *and* women who feel threatened by anything which challenges traditional sex roles, it seems that behavior patterns nonetheless are becoming more flexible. In the past we may have emphasized the differences between men and women, but today we are beginning to stress the similarities. In fact, some envision a future society in which more and more individuals will lead an androgynous lifestyle. *Androgyny* is defined by Joy Osofsky and Howard Osofsky (1972) as a "society in which there are no stereotyped behavioral differences between the roles of males and females on the basis of their sex alone." Various activities, from building bridges to child rearing, would not be viewed as either masculine or feminine—that is, there would be no "sex-appropriate" choices. Individuals would feel free to develop their skills in accordance with their desires and abilities without self-

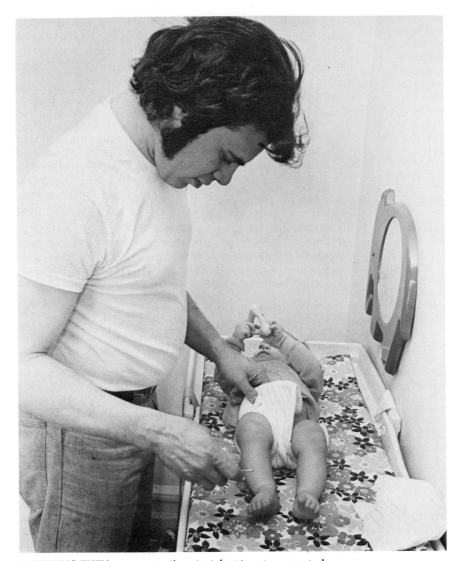

DIAPERING EVEN a momentarily quiet infant is not an easy task.

consciousness about their sexual identities. And they would express their emotions without being fettered by conventional expectations of "manliness" or "femininity."

In many ways this vision seems to describe a world of self-actualizing individuals who are open to exploring the full range of human possibilities, both for their own satisfaction and for the good of the society in which they live. As Maslow has said of such people: "They live more in the real world of nature than in the man-made mass of concepts, abstractions, expectations, beliefs, and stereotypes that most people confuse with the world" (1954, p. 205).

SUMMARY

Socialization involves learning the behavior appropriate to one's sexual assignment and the meaning of one's role as male or female. Since the process begins at birth, it is difficult to determine whether there are innate differences between men and women. Male and female reproductive systems are distinctive. But when sexual identity is ambiguous, upbringing appears more important than anatomy. It is hard to determine differences in general intelligence, since performance on IQ tests always reflects the experience of the person tested. Boys and girls have been found to differ in spatial reasoning and analytic ability. In math, girls usually test higher in the lower grades, and boys generally score higher at the college level. Reasons suggested for this difference relate to the socialization process. A recent study found no evidence to support the assumption that there are many emotional differences between men and women. And Mead's cross-cultural study suggests that many or all "masculine" and "feminine" personality traits may actually have little relation to the sex of the individual.

The feminine mystique is a syndrome of all the dissatisfactions of women with their role in society. From childhood on, females have been exposed to sexism. They have confronted biased instructors, segregated classes, and sex stereotyping in children's readers and textbooks. They have received double messages about femininity and achievement which have undermined motivation and generated conflict and guilt. And they continue to face discrimination in all areas which have been dominated by men.

Men have also been exposed to messages in the home, at school, and via the media which bolster sex stereotypes. They are pressured to conform to the *macho* image, which is traditionally prized in our culture; to act aggressively; to be emotionally inexpressive; and to succeed at whatever they are doing. The cost of sustaining the male mystique has been the oppression of women as well as the oppression of those men who fail or who are prevented from fulfilling their role expectations. Studies indicate, however, that attitudes and behavior are changing, that the *macho* image is being rejected by a growing number of men and women, and that sexism is becoming somewhat less virulent. Some have suggested the possibility of a future society in which neither men nor women will be limited to sex-appropriate choices, and will be more free to develop their abilities and interests than they are now.

CASE STUDY

Ted Janoff and Ellen Rossi both work for the same university, she as a division secretary and he as assistant director of a pool of computer operators. The area where Ellen works is not far from Ted and his coworkers. Ellen and Ted have been dating steadily for five months, and they like each other very much. Ellen, however, is very wary about making any kind of long-term commitment to Ted, and Ted sometimes wonders whether he is fighting a losing battle.

Her View

Ellen, aged twenty-eight, attended a nearby secretarial school after she graduated from high school. Until recently she lived at home with her parents and younger sister. Six months ago Ellen moved into a small apartment in a township that is near her parents' hometown and close to the university where she works. Ellen feels that she has always been active and assertive, but that these qualities have usually gotten her into trouble. As a child, Ellen remembers talking out loud to a classmate in the first grade and being severely reprimanded for it by her first-grade nun. She attributes her shyness in the area of academics to this incident. She remembers jumping over a fence and tearing the skirt of an expensive new Easter frock her mother had bought her. In her happiest memory Ellen remembers playing beside her father with scraps of wood, a hammer, and nails as he built a bookshelf. She imagined herself building also.

Ellen's mother wanted her to be a teacher, but Ellen did not feel drawn toward academics and was afraid that committing herself to a four-year college program might deflect her from her goal of marrying and having children. Her father wanted her to be a secretary, like his own mother. Ellen liked the idea of earning her own salary, and so she entered a two-year professional training program.

Ellen's present position is her second since graduating from the secretarial program. In the first position she worked for a small firm with a pool of three secretaries. She quickly found herself making suggestions for using the secretarial staff more efficiently. Her boss noticed Ellen's organizational ability and made her his personal secretary, with responsibility for overseeing the work of the other two women. Ellen feels that she performed well in this situation, perhaps too well. "An executive secretary is something like an office wife," she says. "There is a lot of responsibility involved. Before long I was organizing this man's whole life: airline tickets, hotel reservations. . . . " Ellen found herself working long hours and clashing more and more frequently with her boss over things such as efficient ways to organize his day's schedule. After a particularly heated argument over a small incident, Ellen resigned. Somewhat startled by her own action, she was quick to find another position, this time at the local university. Not wanting to repeat what she considered to be her experience of overworking, she began working part time, three mornings a week. Because he likes her accurate and efficient work, her present boss asked Ellen to extend her working schedule to five mornings a week. She has done this; however, again she finds herself called upon to assist in coordinating the work of the secretarial pool, and she worries that she may be getting into a situation similar to the one she left.

Ellen has really dated only one person besides Ted. She broke up with her high school steady, Don Adams, when she discovered that she was making all the decisions about where they would go and what they would do. "He was really dependent on me. He didn't seem to have much ambition either. And he was too

68
CHAPTER 3

quiet. He would never tell me when he was upset about anything. I'm an emotional person. I need somebody who's more like me."

Ellen sees Ted as being different from Don in some important ways. "He always knows if I'm upset. And he wants me to be happy. He is the most considerate person I have ever met. He tells me when he's bugged about something, too." However, she also reports: "I don't think Ted is assertive enough. He is twenty-seven years old and has been working here for five years. He has been promoted once, but he should be a director by now. I've told him I think he should press for that. And another thing bothers me, too. Ted is still living at home with his parents. They and his older sister, who is married, are running his life. But it doesn't seem to bother him. I don't like that."

His View

Ted lived at home and attended a local community college after graduating from high school. He studied electrical engineering. He feels close to his family, and his childhood memories focus on interpersonal relationships. He remembers how his family and friends cared for him tenderly after he was struck by an automobile. And he recalls how devastated he felt when his first girl friend jilted him. Although being close to people has opened him to being hurt, Ted describes himself today as being happiest when he is making someone else happy.

Ted has quite a bit of dating experience but has never felt until recently that he was ready for marriage. He says he has never met anyone else as nice or as beautiful as Ellen. He especially likes her expressiveness. Ted is puzzled, though, that Ellen has been pushing him away lately. "She says that she thinks we're seeing each other too much and that she needs some time to herself. Then she goes off shopping with her sister and her mother. Now, I don't mind her seeing them sometimes, but Ellen has been burning my ear about how I shouldn't let my folks run *my* life. I can't see where she is any different."

Ted likes the way Ellen encourages him to assert himself. He spoke with his superior about a promotion and was surprised when he got a favorable hearing. "You know, I really should be working in my own field. I'm trained as an electrical engineer. But when I finished community college, this job was open and I took it. It pays well, but I'm really bored here. Maybe Ellen will help me get up the courage to look for something in my field—that is, if she doesn't give up on me."

Ted is considering moving out of his parents' home, but he was puzzled that Ellen was upset recently when he asked her to clip advertisements for apartments near hers from the local newspaper. Ted now lives outside the area of its circulation. "She said I should do that for myself. I'm helping her put up wallpaper in her new place. I don't see why she can't do me a favor. You know, I wonder what direction this relationship is really moving in."

Interpretation and Questions

How do you think Ellen and Ted have been affected by traditional sex roles? Do you think they are fulfilling their potential? If not, how do you think this affects their attitudes toward marriage and marital partners? Do Ted and Ellen have the same expectations of themselves that they do of each other? Are Ted and Ellen likely to be happy if they marry with their present expectations of each other? If you foresee possible difficulties, in what areas might these arise?

STUDY GUIDE

Important Terms

socialization
X and Y chromosomes
androgens
hermaphrodite
sex roles

sexual stereotypes
sexism
macho
androgyny
feminine mystique

Review Quiz

1 Whether the fertilized egg cell will develop as a female is determined by the chromosomes:
   a XYY
   b XX
   c XY
   d XXY

2 Which of the following reproductive characteristics biologically differentiates men and women?
   a the ability to impregnate
   b the ability to menstruate
   c the ability to lactate
   d all the above

3 Differences in the average mental performance of males and females have been found in:
   a overall IQ
   b vocabularies of preschoolers
   c spatial reasoning and analytical ability
   d all the above

4 Margaret Mead's study of sex and temperament in New Guinea showed that in some societies:
   a both sexes may be passive and nonaggressive

   b both sexes may be aggressive and hostile
   c females may be aggressive, and males passive
   d all the above

5 Studies of sex-role learning in preschoolers show that:
   a boys are made to feel ashamed if they cry
   b mothers talk to boy infants more than to girl infants
   c much kicking activity by unborn fetuses leads mothers to the conclusion that a female will be born
   d boys are more likely to conform to parents' expectations than girls are

6 The "feminine mystique" refers to:
   a women's emotional nature and the mystery that has always surrounded them
   b the syndrome consisting of the dissatisfactions of women with their role in society
   c the unknown ways in which

women are able to "work their wills"

d the allure of sophisticated, upper-class women

7 Studies of sex stereotyping show that elementary school text-books:

a contain more girl-centered than boy-centered stories

b present more role models for boys than for girls

c contain more stories about female than male animals

d typically present examples of girls using more initiative in solving problems than boys

8 A study of high school counse-lors showed that female students with _____ goals are more likely to gain acceptance and ap-proval.

a traditional

b ambitious

c unrealistic

d unclear

9 Many college women, but few men, find success anxiety-provoking. Women may avoid success because of:

a fear of social rejection

b lack of real ability

c stronger desires for sexual gratification

d lack of innate aggression

10 In the United States, the stereo-type of the traditional male sex role has included the characteris-tics of:

a pride

b hypersensitivity to insult

c aggressive competitiveness

d all the above

11 Compared with that of women, men's _____ life seems impov-erished.

a intellectual

b emotional

c occupational

d all the above

12 A study of male college students shows that the majority want:

a serious relationships in which the man is intellectually su-perior to the woman

b all women to be nonintellec-tual

c their wives' careers to be as important as their own

d surface relationships with women who are emotionally unstable

13 Current research indicates that the image of the *macho* male is now admired by:

a men

b women

c neither sex

d both sexes

14 A society with no sex-role differ-entiation would be called:

a androgynous

b sexist

c feminist

d *macho*

15 In respect to discrimination against women in American soci-ety today, one would say that:

a discrimination still exists

b our institutions still reflect sexist biases

c people are increasingly free from sex-role restrictions based upon stereotypes

d all the above

Opinionnaire

Agree	No opinion	Disagree	
———	———	———	1 It is primarily mothers who are responsible for providing nurturance for children.
———	———	———	2 God is male.
———	———	———	3 Male hairdressers are as masculine as other men.
———	———	———	4 Women are naturally more emotional than men.
———	———	———	5 Most people would be perfectly willing to allow a woman surgeon to perform an operation on them.
———	———	———	6 There is no difference between taking orders from a woman and taking orders from a man.
———	———	———	7 A society without some sex-role differentiation could not exist.
———	———	———	8 Even if two opposite-sex children are treated exactly alike, the boy will still become more aggressive.
———	———	———	9 Women are harder to understand than men.
———	———	———	10 Fathers could never be quite as good at child rearing as mothers.

Exercise

Read the following passage to several persons, substituting the word *boy* for *girl* in the first line half the time you read it. Then have the people to whom you read the passage fill out the rating scales below.

> Terry, a four-year-old (*girl*), was having a very active morning. Terry's first altercation was with an older brother. When the brother refused to lend a shirt, Terry stomped on his toe with enough force to hurt. Breakfast was oatmeal, a cereal which Terry despises. The dish was cleaned by the family dog while Terry's mother was out of the room. After breakfast, Terry was denied permission to play in the yard. As soon as the telephone occupied Terry's mother's attention, however, Terry ran outside.

Rate Terry's behavior on the following dimensions:

Obedient	1	2	3	4	5	Disobedient
Mature	1	2	3	4	5	Immature
Passive	1	2	3	4	5	Aggressive
Little initiative	1	2	3	4	5	Great initiative
Controlled	1	2	3	4	5	Uncontrolled

Average the results. Are the averages different if your respondents think Terry is male rather than female? What does this mean?

Projects for Class or Home Study

1   There is some concern that if couples could choose the sex of their children by means of genetic engineering, an overabundance of males would result. Ask some of your friends which sex they would prefer and why.
2   Look through some of your college textbooks. Count the number of pictures of males and females. Note the occupations portrayed for each sex. Also note the activities men and women are engaged in. Are the books sexist?
3   Much writing still uses masculine pronouns for the general case ("Each pupil should open *his* book . . . ") and is liberally sprinkled with such terms as *man*kind. What effect do you believe this usage has? Can you eliminate such terms from your writing?
4   Thumb through a few issues of a typical "women's" magazine and a few issues of a "men's" magazine. How do the images of men and women differ in the two? Which magazines do you think present the more realistic images?

5   Ask a group of preschoolers who their best friends are. Then ask the same question of children between the ages of six and nine. Which group made more cross-sex choices? Do boys or girls choose the opposite sex more often? Can you explain your results?

Suggestions for Further Reading

Balswick, Jack O., and Peek, Charles W. The inexpressive male: A tragedy of American society. *Family Coordinator*, October 1971, 20, 363–368.
    The authors argue that American men have been encouraged by society to disregard and suppress their feelings.
Fasteau, Marc Feigen. *The male machine*. New York: McGraw-Hill, 1974.
    Fasteau describes the competitive male in American business. Most interesting are his accounts of the ways in which men relate to one another according to their bureaucratic level.
Maccoby, Eleanor E., and Jacklin, Carol N. *The psychology of sex differences*. Stanford, Calif.; Stanford University Press, 1974.
    Hundreds of studies of psychological sex differences have been evaluated by these authors, including those on intelligence and character and on emotional traits. The authors found consistently that men are more aggressive than women, but they found less support for other differences.
Morgan, Robin (Ed.). *Sisterhood is powerful*. New York: Random House, 1970.
    This anthology is a good introduction to the feminist philosophy.
Olsen, Tillie. *Tell me a riddle*. New York: Dell, 1971.
    Olsen, perhaps better than any other living author, is able to catch the quality of a woman's life. The title story is heartbreaking in its honesty and faithfulness to detail.
Piercy, Marge. *Small changes*. Garden City, N.Y.: Doubleday, 1973.
    This novel concerns the lives of two women, one of the working class and the other of the upper middle class, who found that the woman's role appropriate to their station was inappropriate to their own lives. In recounting their struggles, Piercy covers, in almost encyclopedic detail, a history of the women's movement.

Roper, Brent S., and Labeff, Emily. Sex roles and feminism revisited: An intergenerational attitude comparison. *Journal of Marriage and the Family*, February 1977, 39, 113–119.

This study duplicated questionnaires on sex roles which were collected by the sociologist Kirkpatrick in 1934. The comparison shows how sex-role attitudes have changed in thirty years.

Answers to Review Quiz

1-*b* 2-*d* 3-*c* 4-*d* 5-*a* 6-*b* 7-*b* 8-*a* 9-*a* 10-*d* 11-*b* 12-*a* 13-*c* 14-*a* 15-*d*

4

PHYSICAL INTIMACY

. . . the power of the sexual impulse. It was there before we arrived on the scene and will be there after we leave it. It is as much a part of the universe we inhabit as the sun and the rain and the lightning, and the force of gravity (Hemming and Maxwell, 1974, p. 26).

The sexual impulse is virtually a universal biological phenomenon. Yet, throughout the history of diverse human societies, few other aspects of the natural world have created as much hope and despair; generated as much fear, guilt, and repression; or inspired as many elaborate fantasies and eloquent idealizations. Sex has been invested with magical and mystical properties; it has been made part of the rituals and ceremonies of a number of religions; and it has been celebrated and venerated as the ultimate source of human pleasure and satisfaction. It has also been invested with the power to corrupt and defile; it has been used to exploit and subjugate both men and women; and it has been regarded as the ultimate effector of human misery and damnation.

Making Sense of Sex

Attitudes toward sex in the Western world have varied between the extremes of an almost total suppression of sexuality—at least on the surface—and a public tolerance of all varieties of sexual expression. Today, we feel we are in a period of enlightened sexual attitudes; in the view of most people, sex is an enduring and abiding part of life. Indeed, sex has surfaced as an activity which can be practiced justifiably without a marriage contract or the goal of procreation. Contraceptives have enhanced the possibilities for sex outside marriage, at least for some part of the population. The mass media have given sex the hard sell, processing and packaging it for a variety of tastes and styles. And during the past several decades the first systematic, large-scale studies of sexual behavior in our own post-Victorian society were carried out. But as two of the people responsible for these studies pointed out only a few years ago, " . . . even to this date our culture has not permitted clear exploration of human sexual functioning. We're still on the fringes . . . " (Masters and Johnson, 1974, p. 86).

Apparently many people are also "on the fringes" in the search for their own personal expression of sexuality. One can thumb through magazine articles for information about how celebrities regard sex, turn to orthodox standards of morality perpetuated by various religious communities, conform to the apparent norms of peers or close friends, model one's sexual behavior on the basis of parental norms and prescriptions, or attempt to bypass any and all standards and try to do what feels right at the moment. It seems that even in this period of changed and changing attitudes, each of us must set his or her own course through these well-charted waters. "The message has already gotten across that life is sexual. . . . The proper question is . . . how to respond" (Hofmann, 1967, p. 16).

An approach to sexuality can start with a knowledge and acceptance of certain sexual realities (Katchadourian and Lunde, 1972). People need to be acquainted with the facts about the male and female sexual organs and the way they function. It is important to understand and accept certain facts of behavior—that people express themselves in a variety of ways. To dismiss these variations as deviant or to deny that they exist is a refusal to face reality. Finally, people must realize that to bypass or ignore their own sexual needs is not a solution. Each must face his or her sexuality openly and honestly.

After we understand our own physiology and become familiar with varieties of sexual behavior, we still must find the meaning and content of the sexual experience as it shapes itself in an individual life. In its fullest potential, sex is not simply the discharging of physical urges or a pleasant distraction from the mental and emotional pressures of daily life. "Sex is not just an appetite like the appetite for food. . . . Sex, at any stage above the physical, becomes, inescapably, a personal involvement'' (Hemming and Maxwell, 1974, p. 46).

It is in this personal involvement that the sexual experience has its broadest and deepest potential. As reasoning creatures, we can relate to others verbally, and through self-disclosures we can learn something about another person and about our own identities as well. But as sexual creatures, we have the ability to express ourselves—our feelings, thoughts, and fantasies—through our bodies. Sex, from this viewpoint, is not seen as a goal or a segregated aspect of human reality. Rather, it becomes an ongoing process of relating, sharing, and communicating.

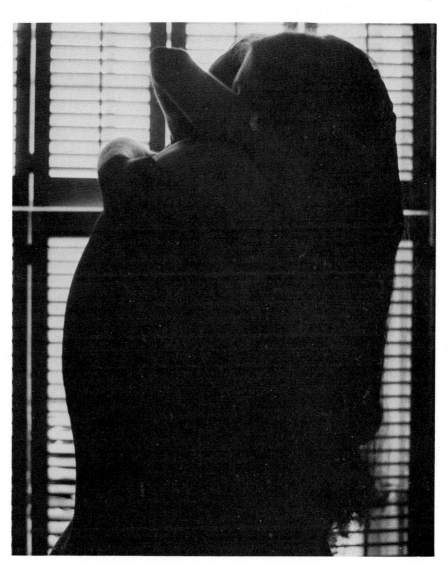

Like verbal self-disclosures, sexual expression can make one feel vulnerable. Being open with another person can involve the risk of betrayal, misunderstandings, feelings of embarrassment, and fears of losing oneself in the identity of the other person. But any attempt to breach the barrier of solitude and communicate with another human being inevitably involves risk. Sexual expression, like other forms of communication, provides a means of testing and shaping one's attitudes and aspirations and of building a sense of identity on the solid basis of interactions with another human being:

> No man is an island to himself. . . . Sexuality explodes the dangerous illusion of any such one-sidedness by being at once the most personal and intensively interpersonal human experience. Who one is can be determined only by interaction between the self and others. . . . Sexuality forces each person to assess his personal identity by appraising how able he is to share himself with others without losing his sense of independence. . . . Indeed, sexuality does not relent until a human has dealt with his ability to be intimately at ease with another human (Hofmann, 1967, p. 5).

NAMING THE PARTS

The orgasm has been likened to a sneeze—it is an involuntary muscular spasm. Yet no one thinks of the sneeze as mysterious; people sneeze in public, and the face is usually covered only at the moment of sneezing in order to prevent the spread of germs. With the orgasm it is otherwise. We have surrounded sex with secrecy and mystery, particularly as it relates to women. Little girls are not likely to show each other their private parts or masturbate in a group, as little boys do. Many little girls, cautioned as they are against touching themselves, are scarcely aware of the exact nature of their private parts. They do know that there is something down there "between their legs" which they can't see directly. Indeed, one woman recalls: "The first month I was at college some of my friends were twittering about a girl down the hall. She was having a painful time trying to learn to put in a tampon. Finally someone helped her and found she was trying to put it in her anus" (Boston Women's Health Book Collective, 1971).

Ruth Herschberger, writing almost thirty years ago, asked, "Why is woman so persistently regarded as a mystery?" And she answers her own question: "It is not that she has labored to conceal the organic and psychological facts of her constitution, but that men have shown no interest in exploring them" (1970). Perhaps it is not unfair, then, to begin a description of genital anatomy as it relates to the female of the species.

FEMALE GENITAL ANATOMY The *vulva* is the area of the female anatomy which includes all external genitalia—the *clitoris*, the *labia minora* and *labia majora* (major and minor lips), the opening to the vagina, and the *mons veneris* (mound of Venus), which becomes covered with hair during puberty. Beneath the two layers of the labia, and positioned between the clitoris and the vagina, is the opening of the urethra, the pathway to the bladder. The opening of the anus, which leads to the rectum, is located behind the vaginal entrance.

The clitoris is usually considered to be the homologue of the penis. But whereas the penis is as visible as a finger or a toe, the shaft of its female counterpart is often concealed under the fleshy layers of the labia, available to the touch but with only its head (glans) usually visible. "The mystery of the clitoris, if one wishes to speak of mysteries, is its ability to accommodate the same quantity, as well as quality, of nerve endings that the penis accommodates" (Herschberger, 1970, p. 32). In fact, the nerve branches running to the glans are larger than their counterparts in the penis, and the nerve endings are concentrated in a much smaller area. In view of this and because the clitoris serves no apparent function other than that of giving pleasure to its owner, it has been referred to as the "ecstasy organ" (or, to call it by its more romantic-sounding German equivalent, the *Wollustorgan*).

Also very sensitive because of nerve endings are the labia minora, the pink folds of skin which unite in the upper part of the genital area to form a hood (partially or completely covering the head of the clitoris) and

FEMALE GENITAL ANATOMY

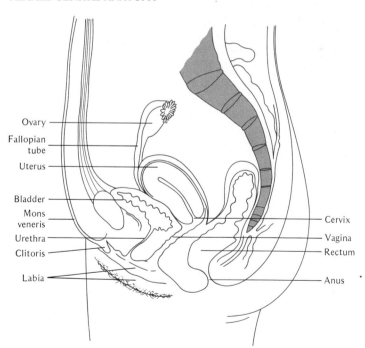

which also enclose the *vestibule*, the funnel-shaped area in which the vaginal opening is located. The nerve endings in the labia minora and the vestibule make them almost as sensitive to touch—and therefore as significant in terms of female sexual arousal—as the clitoris. The elongated folds of the labia majora, which form the outermost genital boundaries in the adult female, are responsive to manipulation but are not of great importance as an area of arousal (Kinsey, Pomeroy, Martin, and Gebhard, 1953, pp. 578–579).

The vagina itself is a muscular cavity which runs upward and back from the external genitalia. At its upper end is the cervical canal, a tiny opening that leads to the uterus, or womb. Its lower end, as noted, opens into the genital area known as the vestibule. The ring of muscle tissue just inside the vaginal opening is responsive to stimulation, and the part of the vaginal opening near the base of the clitoris is richly supplied with nerves; however, the walls of the vagina generally lack nerve endings and are therefore usually quite insensitive—so insensitive, in fact, that minor surgical procedures within the vagina are performed without anesthetic.

> It is difficult . . . in the light of our present understanding of the anatomy and physiology of sexual response, to understand what can be meant by a "vaginal orgasm." The literature usually implies that the vagina itself should be the center of sensory stimulation, and this . . . is a physical and physiologic impossibility for nearly all females (Kinsey et al., 1953, p. 582).

MALE GENITAL ANATOMY In the male, the external genitalia consist of the *penis* and *scrotum*. The *testes*—glands within the scrotum which produce sperm and male sex hormones—are not usually considered part of the external genitalia.

The penis is constructed of three masses of tissue which form a shaft and which swell at the tip to form the head, or *glans*. Within each of these tissue masses are several cavities which, during sexual arousal, fill with an extraordinary amount of blood, causing the tissues to swell and resulting in an erection of the penis. When these cavities are empty, the penis is flaccid; it hangs loosely from the area at which it is attached to the pelvis.

The *urethra* runs through the shaft and opens at the head, serving as a channel for the release of either semen or urine. A thin layer of skin envelops the scrotum and the penis, folding over the head to form a *foreskin*. Since glandular secretions accumulate in the folds of the foreskin, thus necessitating continual hygienic care, the foreskin is often surgically removed (circumcised) soon after birth.

The glans, especially on its undersurface, is the most sensitive and erotically responsive area of the penis because of the large number of nerves it contains. However, the shaft appears to have much less sensitivity. The subject of penis dimensions has inspired an abundance of spurious claims:

The size and shape of the penis, contrary to popular belief, are not related to a man's body, build, race, virility, or ability to give and receive sexual satisfaction. Furthermore, variations in size tend to decrease in erection: The smaller the flaccid penis, the proportionately larger it tends to become when erect. The penis does not grow larger through further use (Katchadourian and Lunde, 1972, p. 26).

What was noted earlier about the insensitivity of the vaginal walls further substantiates the relative unimportance of penis size, at least in terms of female sexual arousal. A woman may experience a sense of satisfaction from penetration, but her physiological sensitivity to erotic stimulation ends a few inches within the vaginal cavity.

The scrotum is a sacklike, multilayered structure. It is covered with a layer of dark skin, and at puberty, a light mass of fine hairs appears. The muscle fibers in its layered structure enable it to contract in cold weather and expand in warmer weather in order to give off heat. This is important to the protection of the testes, which require the proper temperature in order to produce viable sperm. As an area of erotic response, the scrotum appears to have very limited significance:

> There are quite a few males who react erotically, and a small number who may respond to the point of orgasm when there is some stimulation or more

MALE GENITAL ANATOMY

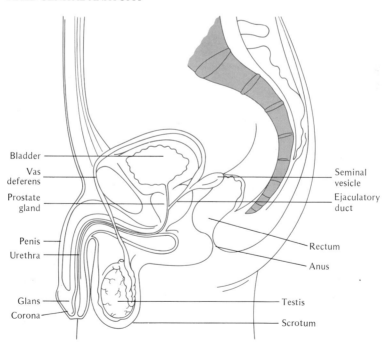

active manipulation of the testes; but this response is not due to the stimulation of the skin of the scrotum (Kinsey et al., 1953, pp. 578–579).

Exploring Sexuality

There is no denying the role of biological factors, genetic and hormonal, in the development of sexual behavior. However, especially among humans, biological factors are not sufficient to explain sexual behavior. As in all other aspects of human behavior, learning is a major factor—learning through experiences within the family in peer groups, and in the larger context of the society and culture in which one lives. The importance of learning is underscored by cross-cultural studies (Ford and Beach, 1951) which indicate that cultural traditions and mores have a great deal of influence on sexual behavior—what we do and how we do it. Except for incest, which is universally tabooed, forms of sexual behavior unacceptable to one culture or society are often openly expressed in another.

MASTURBATION

One of the ways in which sexual behavior can be learned is through masturbation, the manipulation and stimulation of one's own genitals to experience pleasurable sensations and to induce orgasm:

> Masturbation is one of the best means we have of learning about our bodies and about sex directly—without fear, hesitancy, guilt, or shyness. Since all of the genital area is an erogenous zone, through masturbation one can discover the specific areas of greatest sensitivity and the means and mechanisms of sexual responsiveness (Eisner, 1970, p. 222).

In contrast to this glowing contemporary appraisal of masturbation is the list of symptoms and ailments once attributed to the practice (Katchadourian and Lunde, 1972). Included are insanity, epilepsy, asthma, hallucinations, and acne. There is also a curious and tragic history of threats and punishments used to curtail masturbation (or cure its alleged symptoms), including removal of the clitoris. The unfortunate aspect for us today is that the topic of masturbation is still shadowed by prejudice, misinformation, and guilt. If given its proper evaluation, however, it may be that the only detrimental aspect of masturbation is a psychological and social one—specifically, the continual use of masturbation and masturbatory fantasies as a substitute for, or way of avoiding, sexual exploration with another human being.

TOUCHING AND PLEASURING

In their book *The Pleasure Bond*, Masters and Johnson (1975) discuss an activity which can be an important way of pleasuring and of working toward mutuality of sexual and emotional response. It is *touching*—a simple word, but, as the authors point out, something which we are virtually conditioned to fear and avoid: "The lesson is taught early in life and remains deeply ingrained. 'Don't touch!' is a childhood litany. Don't touch yourself, it's naughty; don't touch her, that's nasty; don't touch him, nice girls don't do such things" (Masters and Johnson, 1975, p. 245).

In the transition to adolescence, as the double standard comes into full effect, young women are expected to be passive or resistant and to restrain their natural vitality, and young men are encouraged and pressured in a number of ways to be sexually aggressive. In this context touching becomes sharply reduced to a sexual come-on. A young woman can be understandably bewildered by the intensity of her partner's response to her physicality and justifiably afraid that touching him back will signify an intent to engage in sexual intercourse, and the young man cannot understand why she is not instantly aroused by his awkward attempts to caress: "He thinks of touching as a sexual starter—once he places his hand on a girl's body, he expects that her sexual motor will automatically shift to high gear" (Masters and Johnson, 1975, p. 250).

In such situations, if the two people do not communicate their feelings, they may come away from such encounters with misconceptions about each other's intentions and sexual identities. And even when sexual relationships are formed, the meaning of touch can remain imprisoned in its adolescent connotation—it is still regarded as a means to an end. This can be true even of partners who do not regard touching as a simple trigger for sexual intercourse. For such men and women, it becomes part of a repertoire of techniques, a science of stimulation, a skill and a service which can be transferred to a new location and a new partner—and, as such, touching simply becomes a prolonged and impersonal means to an end.

But, in fact, touching can be an end in itself. It is a way of relating without words and of bridging the gap which is a part of the reality of having separate bodies, thoughts, and feelings. Interviewed on the subject, one woman said: "Touching . . . is a kind of communication and if you're not getting something back, it's like sitting and talking when nobody is listening, or nobody is answering" (Masters and Johnson, 1975, p. 234). "Out of touch" is an apt phrase. It suggests loneliness, which is perhaps most painful when it is experienced in a relationship with a self-absorbed, uncaring, and unresponsive partner, one who distorts the multifaceted message of touching for the sake of his or her own temporary physical gratification. But touching has the potential for being a continual source of sensual pleasure both in and out of bed. If one frees it of its bondage as a prelude to a sexual encounter, touching becomes a way of suffusing one's daily experiences with sensuality, and, especially for steady partners in and out of marriage, it becomes a natural way of reaffirming loving ties.

Sex: A Topic for Scientists

Prior to the pioneering research of Alfred Kinsey in the 1940s, we had access to little scientifically gathered information about human sexual behavior. Much of our information was based on fallacy and folk notions. Early attempts by biologists and behavioral scientists to investigate sexual behavior were not well received by either professionals or the general public. In fact, sexual activity has, until recently, not even been considered a proper topic for the open scrutiny of scientific analysis. Furthermore, religious and community standards have condemned most studies of human sexuality, especially firsthand observations of human subjects under controlled laboratory conditions.

THE KINSEY REPORT

Sexual Behavior in the Human Male (Kinsey, Pomeroy, and Martin, 1948), better known as the "Kinsey report," was an instant best seller at the time it was published, despite its formidable scientific appearance. Alfred Kinsey and his associates interviewed over 12,000 American men and analyzed the results to describe patterns of prevalent sexual behavior. Kinsey's findings were attacked on methodological grounds, although it was his subject matter which was the chief cause of criticism. His work has stood up well for almost thirty years and has formed the basis for most subsequent studies of human sexuality.

Perhaps the most significant contribution of the Kinsey report was its revelation of the discrepancy between what was commonly thought to be the norm for male sexual behavior and what men reported they actually did, during both premarital and extramarital sexual encounters. The large percentage of males who had engaged in at least one homosexual encounter, as well as sex with animals, surprised the reading public.

In 1953 Kinsey and his associates published *Sexual Behavior in the Human Female*, which was based on interviews with 8000 females and provided much the same kinds of information about women's sexual behavior that the first Kinsey report did about men's. More than any other sex research, the Kinsey report was responsible for establishing the legitimacy of the scientific investigation of sexual behavior. The fact that the voluminous scientific report, full of statistical charts and graphs, was a commercial publishing success is evidence of the general public's willingness to sanction sex research, as well as the public's need for information about sexual behavior.

MASTERS AND JOHNSON: THE SEXUAL RESPONSE CYCLE

The first widespread research based on observations of changes in male and female physiology during masturbation and coitus was completed by

William Masters and Virginia Johnson in 1965. Using specially designed cameras and instruments for recording and measuring internal and external responses, Masters and Johnson were able to observe, for the first time, the physiological factors of sexual response. Masters and Johnson were not the first to study human subjects under laboratory conditions, but they were the first to study a wide range of volunteer subjects (700) over an extended time period (ten years). At first shunned by the medical profession, the study has been responsible for establishing the physiology of sexual response as a legitimate field of medical inquiry. The Masters and Johnson report has already spawned a number of laboratory studies designed to gather additional information and answer some of the questions it raised. In addition, the data collected by Masters and Johnson made an important contribution to the development of successful methods of treating problems of sexual dysfunction. Like the Kinsey report, the Masters and Johnson study dispelled some commonly held misconceptions about the way the body functions in sexual response. Perhaps the most significant finding is the discovery that men and women are more alike than different in bodily response to sexual stimulation. On the basis of observations of more than 10,000 orgasmic responses, Masters and Johnson concluded that all men and women, regardless of the source of stimulation, experience a specific sequence of bodily changes, which these researchers have termed the *sexual response cycle* (Masters and Johnson, 1966). Men are generally more predictable in their responses; women are capable of a greater variety of responses, especially late in the response cycle. For the purpose of describing bodily changes and placing them properly in the continuum of sequenced changes, Masters and Johnson arbitrarily divided the cycle into four phases, although they could just as well have divided it into three or eight parts for their descriptive purposes.

THE EXCITEMENT PHASE Changes that occur with the onset of sexual arousal are the result of a phenomenon called *vasocongestion*. Vasocongestion is the engorgement of body tissues with an increased supply of blood, usually resulting in changes in the size and color of the affected tissues. In men, vasocongestion is most obvious with the appearance of the engorged penis in a full erection. The penile erection is controlled by nerve endings in the lower end of the spine and not by the brain, thus placing it beyond the voluntary control of the brain, although sexual arousal may be induced not only by tactile stimulation but also by all manner of mental and emotional stimuli. In women, the onset of the excitement phase is signaled by lubrication, somewhat like perspiration, on the lining of the vaginal walls. Most women experience this first response as a moist sensation in the vagina.

The vaginal walls are extremely elastic, and when the woman is sufficiently aroused, they will accommodate a penis of any size. Attempts to penetrate the vagina before the female has become aroused can be painful and can result in a diminution of sexual desire rather than stimulation. While the vagina is flexible and elastic during coitus, the walls stretch only enough to accommodate the size of the penis inserted. The notion that some penises are too small to maintain contact with the walls of the vagina is a false one. In some women the clitoris may increase in both length and diameter. Normally positioned beneath the skins of the major and minor lips, the clitoris may, during the excitement phase, protrude from beneath the protective "hood."

In both men and women there are extragenital responses involving other parts of the body during the excitement phase. The nipples of both men and women may become erect and increase slightly in diameter. For women this may occur any time between late excitement and early plateau-phase levels. In men, when it occurs, it usually appears late in the plateau phase. The excitement phase is also marked in women by an increase in the size of the breasts.

While both men and women are capable of stimulation by a variety of sensory experiences (tactile, olfactory, and mental), men seem to be capable of arousal by a greater variety of cues, particularly visual ones. Women tend toward arousal by touching (Kaplan, 1974). When the source of stimulation remains at a constant level, both men and women pass fairly rapidly from the excitement phase into the second and more highly aroused state of sexual tension.

Distractions such as a loud noise, a change in lighting, or the sound of talking or music may cause a temporary loss of the penile erection and a slowing of the lengthening and expanding actions of the vagina. Most men and women attempt to prolong the excitement phase by consciously controlling the level of sexual tension. Men may often experience several partial losses of erection before reaching the plateau phase.

THE PLATEAU PHASE   The plateau phase is essentially a more highly aroused state of sexual tension. In the male the penile erection continues until it reaches its maximum fullness just before orgasm. The glans increases in diameter and deepens in color to a dark purple. The testes increase to about $1\frac{1}{2}$ times their original size and pull up tightly against the perineum. A few drops of a mucoid liquid may be secreted from the urethra during prolonged periods of plateau-phase excitement. This fluid, which is secreted from Cowper's gland, may contain a few drops of active sperm. Knowledge of this fact is important for persons who choose coitus interruptus as a method of birth control. Impregnation can occur when there is semen in the preorgasm discharge, even though the penis may be withdrawn from the vagina before ejaculation.

In the female there is further vasocongestive activity in the genital organs. The inner two-thirds of the vagina continues to lengthen and balloon into a saclike receptacle for the seminal fluid at the entrance to the uterus. The increased vasocongestion in the minor lips and the outer third of the vaginal barrel causes the vaginal outlet to protrude even more, and the diameter of the vaginal outlet is slightly reduced, which results in increased pressure on the penile shaft. When this "orgasmic platform," as Masters and Johnson have termed it, is formed, a woman almost never fails to achieve orgasm.

THE ORGASMIC PHASE The orgasmic response is nearly identical in both men and women. It is characterized by a series of muscle contractions in the pelvic region and surrounding the anal sphincter. In the male, contractions begin in the secondary sex organs located in the perineal cavity (the vas deferens, the seminal duct, the prostate, and the ejaculatory duct). This first set of contractions is experienced by the male as a feeling of "ejaculatory inevitability." It is followed almost instantaneously by more powerful contractions of the urethral muscles. Most of the ejaculate is discharged after the first three contractions, but it continues to be created in lesser amounts by contractions which may continue up to eight times.

The female experiences bodily reactions nearly identical to those of the male. Her contractions, however, may expand over a longer time sequence, lasting from ten to thirty seconds. For the female, contractions occur simultaneously in the muscles surrounding the orgasmic platform and in those surrounding the uterus, causing her to report a feeling of total pelvic contraction.

In both men and women there are are involuntary contractions of other muscle groupings. In most men and women there is a contraction of the facial muscles during orgasm, causing some people to seem to grimace. Both men and women, but women more often than men, may experience spasms of the abdomen and buttocks during orgasm. In both men and women there is a rapid increase of blood pressure and heartbeat which can reach peaks identical to those which athletes experience at the height of physical exertion.

The great majority of men in the study experienced what Masters and Johnson called a "refractory period" immediately after orgasm, lasting from two to five minutes into the resolution phase. During the refractory period, men seem to be incapable of restimulation. Women, on the other hand, have the ability to sustain the level of sexual tension at midplateau levels and to achieve an infinite variety of orgasms. Some women experience a series of seemingly connected orgasms, one right after another, until they reach a final orgasm, which is usually described as the most intense and exhausting. Other women may, like the majority of men in the study, be satisfied and exhausted after the first orgasmic contractions. In studies instituted after publication of the Masters and Johnson study, men have been reported to experience multiple orgasms in much the same way that women do, without losing any, or only a few, of the preorgasmic levels of tension. The men involved in these studies, however, reported that they do not generally ejaculate each time they experience orgasmic contractions (Tavris, 1976).

THE RESOLUTION PHASE During the resolution phase most of the parts of the body that experienced changes return fairly rapidly to their prestimulated state. The penis is reduced to half its erectile length and diameter in the first few seconds following orgasm. The return to its usual size occurs more slowly after the initial loss of erection. The disengorgement of the female genitals is slower than that of the male. It may take several minutes for the vaginal outlet and vaginal barrel to return to their prestimulated size and color. In some men and most women a fine film of perspiration may appear over the body in the first few minutes following orgasm. In men, however, postorgasmic sweating is usually confined to the palms of the hands and the soles of the feet.

VARIATIONS ON THE THEME

A straightforward description of the physiology of sex is apt to imply that a straightforward approach to lovemaking—intercourse between a man and a woman lying face-to-face, with the man on top (the "missionary" position)—is the normal way, or the best way, or the preferable way to achieve orgasm. In nearly every state, the missionary position is the only legal way to have sexual relations, even for those who are married. But cross-cultural studies, historical investigations, and surveys of our own present-day society illustrate that the human imagination has not given short shrift to the expression of sexuality and that most people continue to regard the way a couple make love as a question of mutual consent rather than legality.

Books ranging from the *Kamasutra* and *The Perfumed Garden* (Indian and Arabian treatises, respectively, on lovemaking) to contemporary manuals and popular guides to sex provide instruction in the various positions that partners can use when they engage in sexual intercourse. To these positions (some of which seem suited only to double-jointed acrobats) partners add their own varieties of time and place. But the "theme" of sexual activity is not limited to intercourse—the activities of foreplay are often used as ends in themselves, that is, as substitutes for intercourse. One example of this is the oral manipulation of the female genital area—technically termed *cunnilingus*. The female genitals are stimulated by means of kissing, sucking, and using the tongue to press and probe the labia minor, clitoris, and vestibule. Another example is *fellatio*, in which the male genitals are stimulated orally by means of stroking and sucking the area of the glans and manipulating the scrotum. Oral sex is colloquially termed "sixty-nine" when the partners are involved in simultaneous oral stimulation of each other's genital area.

The question of variation and norms is an important one to keep in mind when considering problems of sexual functioning. It is unfortunate, for example, that such a premium has been placed not only on orgasm per se, but also on simultaneous orgasm, as though all the pleasures of sexual activities are, at best, subordinate to climax and as though the "best" climax is something which is objectively definable.

One of the criticisms leveled against the Masters and Johnson description of sexual functioning concerns this very emphasis on orgasm and, specifically, on the woman's ability to experience orgasm during intercourse. Although the Masters and Johnson study concludes that the orgasm results from stimulation of the clitoral hood (rather than the vaginal walls), the stimulation itself is nonetheless linked to the stroking action of the penis. That is, orgasm during intercourse is treated as the norm, and the inability to experience orgasm under these conditions is termed "coital orgasmic inadequacy."

One of the people to challenge this interpretation is Shere Hite, who conducted a survey of 3,000 women, ranging in age from fourteen to seventy:

> Masters and Johnson's theory that the thrusting penis pulls the woman's labia, which in turn pull the clitoral hood, which thereby causes friction on the clitoral glans and thereby causes orgasm sounds more like a Rube Goldberg scheme than a reliable way to orgasm.
>
> It is not that the mechanism doesn't work. It does: if you pull any skin around the area it can stimulate the clitoris. But the question is, does thrusting do this effectively? The answer would seem to be that, for most women, without some special set of circumstances, it does not (1976, pp. 168–169).

In fact, only about 30 percent of women who were questioned for the Hite study claimed that they were able to achieve orgasm regularly from intercourse.

Problems in Sexual Functioning

Despite its limitations, the work of Masters and Johnson remains significant for many reasons. Not the least is that it demonstrates that all persons, when sufficiently aroused, go through a predictable sequence of bodily changes which culminate in orgasm and, for the man, in ejaculation of seminal fluid. Furthermore, Masters and Johnson have pointed out that when the source of stimulation remains constant, the changes proceed fairly rapidly and with regularity toward culmination.

Both men and women may experience reversal of the response cycle several times in the course of one cycle to orgasm. Most men, for example, experience partial and sometimes total loss of vasocongestion in the penis several times during one sexual response cycle. Since vasocongestion occurs primarily internally for women, reversal is less obvious. Women do experience reversal in the distending and opening actions of the vaginal barrel. Reversals are common in all people and have no bearing on one's ability to ultimately complete the cycle. Indeed, as we have seen, most people deliberately vary the level of sexual stimulus in order to prolong the pleasure of lovemaking.

But all people, some of the time, experience an inability to complete the sexual response cycle to orgasm or even to initiate it—that is, to become aroused. This happens especially when one is extremely tired or is suffering from illness. Furthermore, some people have repeated difficulty over long periods of time completing the cycle to orgasm and resolution.

The sexual response cycle is essentially a reflex action triggered by one or more nerve centers in the central nervous system. Experiments with paraplegics, for example, have demonstrated that the penile erection is a reflex triggered by a nerve center in the lower third of the spinal column. More recent research has suggested that other parts of the nervous system, including centers in the upper two-thirds of the spinal column and the brain itself, may be responsible for triggering bodily changes that result in sexual arousal. The particular nerve center involved

PROBLEMS IN sexual functioning are often aggravated by a fear of communication.

seems to depend on the source of the sexual stimulus—tactile, visual, or fantasy (Kaplan, 1974).

Just as a variety of stimuli may generate the reflexes that constitute the sexual response cycle, distractions may interrupt the cycle. We have noted that a loud noise, a change in lighting, or the sound of talking or music may inhibit the reflexive response and cause total or partial loss of vasocongestive reactions, but so may more internalized disturbances such as thought processes or expectations of how the body should react. For example, many men in treatment programs for the problem of premature ejaculation report early sexual encounters in the back seats of cars or with prostitutes where there were pressures to complete the act in as little time as possible. The learned behavior—that is, premature ejaculation—often continues even when there are no longer any time constraints.

IMPOTENCE

Impotence is the inability of a man to achieve or maintain an erection to the point of successful coitus. Masters and Johnson have found that the causes of male impotence generally involve feelings of fear and anxiety. The man who has experienced impotence several times in succession may become so anxious over his inability to attain and maintain an erection that he engages in what sex therapists have termed *spectatoring*. He becomes an observer of his own sexual response, waiting for an erection or watching to see whether an erection will return. This thought process tends to override or inhibit the original sexual stimulus which triggered his erective reflex, thereby contributing to his impotence.

Another cause of male impotence may be the fear of an inability to satisfy a real or imagined demand of the sex partner. Believing that penile size has a direct bearing on a woman's pleasure, some men with penises of less than average size, for example, may assume a priori that they are incapable of producing the fullest sexual satisfaction in their partners. A more detailed knowledge of female anatomy in general, and of his partners likes and dislikes in particular, should serve to dispel a man's anxieties on this score.

PREMATURE EJACULATION

The term *premature ejaculation* refers to a fairly prevalent disorder in which a man experiences orgasm either before or immediately after entry into the vagina. Actually, mutual requirements determine whether the male is ejaculating too soon. Masters and Johnson therefore regard a man to be a premature ejaculator if he cannot control his ejaculation long enough to enable his partner to achieve satisfaction a minimum of one-half the times they engage in intercourse (1970, p. 92). However,

Helen Singer Kaplan believes that the most important aspect of prematurity is not how quickly ejaculation occurs or whether it occurs before the partner achieves orgasm, but simply the absence of voluntary control over ejaculation once a certain level of arousal has been reached (1974, p. 290).

Several causes of premature ejaculation have been theorized. Freudian theory interprets the phenomenon as an indication of unconscious, but strong, sadistic impulses toward women. Another theory regards premature ejaculation as the result of an oversensitivity to erotic stimuli. Kaplan, however, suggests that the problem is one which develops in the learning process. Anxiety, guilt, and conflict may be factors. In terms of treatment, however, they are important not in themselves, but as they interfere with the perception of sensory feedback necessary for controlling the ejaculatory reflex:

> Premature ejaculators do not clearly perceive the sensations premonitory to orgasm, which, in turn, deprives them of the regulatory power of the higher nervous influences. As a result, reflex discharge, i.e. ejaculation, occurs automatically i.e. ejaculation, occurs automatically when the physiological threshold of excitation is reached (Kaplan, 1974, pp. 300–30l).

Kaplan's methods of treatment are therefore similar to the biofeedback techniques which have been used in achieving voluntary control of autonomic functions, such as the rate of heartbeat. For example, in the course of sexual activity, the male partner is taught to get "in touch" with the sensations which he experiences prior to orgasm. These conscious experiences of his excitement levels can eventually lead to control of the ejaculatory reflex.

GENERAL SEXUAL DYSFUNCTION IN WOMEN

The word *frigidity* has been used not only as a covering label for female sexual problems but also as a term connoting grave emotional failing in women thus "afflicted." Partly as a result of a better understanding of physiology and certainly in some measure because of the influence of feminists, sex researchers and therapists have been trying to replace the term with more specific, and less deprecatory, explanations and analyses of problems women experience in sexual relationships.

For most women sexual problems appear to derive from inadequate or inappropriate stimulation or from conditioned inhibitions against the open expression of sexuality. As with men, deep psychological conflicts may be factors in sexual dysfunction among women, but they do not have to be treated directly unless efforts to modify the present sexual behavior fail.

Kaplan uses the term *general sexual dysfunction*, rather than *frigidity*, and interprets it to mean both a general lack of erotic feelings and, on the physiological level, a lack of vasocongestion in response to sexual stimulation: "She does not lubricate, her vagina does not expand, and there is no formation of an orgasmic platform" (Kaplan, 1974, p. 342). Women with general sexual dysfunction are not necessarily incapable of achieving orgasm. They are usually found to be women who have never been erotically aroused with any partner or whose inability to be aroused seems to be related to the specific sexual situation.

Being inhibited in terms of sexual expression may be related to a reluctance to be open and to take any initiative in other matters. It is also true that women who experience general sexual dysfunction are often encouraged to accept their lack of response as normal. Successful treatment, therefore, is contingent on the willingness of both partners to view erotic arousal as a mutual right.

> It is the aim of sex therapy to facilitate the woman's abandonment to the sexual experience by changing the sexual system in which she functions . . . [and] the therapist attempts to implement this goal by creating a non-demanding, relaxed and sensuous ambience which permits the natural unfolding of the sexual response during lovemaking. The couple is encouraged to communicate openly about their sexual feelings and wishes, which helps to foster such ambience (Kaplan, 1974, p. 365).

The woman is encouraged to initiate coitus after she has been sufficiently aroused. Then, just as the premature ejaculator is taught to focus on his sensations prior to orgasm, the woman with a general sexual dysfunction learns to attend to physical sensations in her vagina. The couple are also given instructions in a variety of specific techniques for developing each other's sensuous and erotic capacity. This is especially helpful when the couple are confronting immediate obstacles to arousal in the course of lovemaking.

FEMALE ORGASMIC PROBLEMS

While treatment for general sexual dysfunction may enable a woman to become sexually aroused, it does not necessarily enable her to achieve orgasm. Some women are able to achieve orgasm only in certain situations. Others say they have never experienced orgasm, whether by means of intercourse or with more direct forms of clitoral stimulation. Women in this latter category may feel deprived, embarrassed, depressed, or defeated by their problem, or, as in the case of one of the women interviewed for the Hite study, they may feel angry that their status is considered abnormal:

> I resent the pressure placed on me and other women to have orgasms. Every time I read a survey that says Masters and Johnson or other researchers have found that X percent of women almost always have orgasms, I feel psychologically inadequate. But except when I read about the expectations for women's performances, I feel quite satisfied regarding my sex life (Hite, 1976, p. 117).

Unlike some therapists, Kaplan believes that orgasmic problems must be treated as a separate entity. Psychotherapy and behavior-modification techniques are coupled in the therapy program. The patient is helped by means of psychotherapy to work through fears, guilt, and hostility which consciously or unconsciously may inhibit her from releasing her sexual feelings and relinquishing control over her body, thus reaching orgasm. In the behavior-modification techniques using a step-by-step procedure with sexual experiences, the patient is taught how *not* to interfere with the orgasmic reflex.

VAGINISMUS

Sometimes observed in conjunction with the female sexual problems described above is *vaginismus*, an involuntary spasmic contraction of the muscular opening to the vagina. It is prompted by real, anticipated, or imagined attempts to penetrate the vagina and, in fact, precludes the possibility of intercourse. Kaplan treats vaginismus as a separate problem, since many women who experience it are otherwise sexually responsive and capable of having orgasms through noncoital means.

Vaginismus may result from repeated frustration with a partner who is impotent, or the woman's fear of vaginal penetration may be related to a physically and/or psychologically traumatic experience, such as rape. An inhibition toward intercourse may also develop from a repressive upbringing, marked by excessively strict religious and/or parental prohibitions (Masters and Johnson, 1970, p. 252). Feelings of anger or hostility toward the partner also can create a deep reluctance about, or fear of, engaging in intercourse and can manifest themselves as vaginismus.

Depending on the relationship of the partners involved, vaginismus may or may not be problematical. But it does often create feelings of inadequacy and guilt in the woman and anger and frustration in the man. Again, treatment, at least initially, is directed at the immediate obstacles to successful intercourse, rather than at deep-rooted disturbances. Kaplan and her coworkers often begin treatment by bringing the patient into a relaxed and nondemanding environment and then slowly and repeatedly attempting manual dilation of the vagina. The goal of this first phase of treatment is to diminish the patient's anxiety and phobic reaction to coitus. The partner may or may not be present, depending on what is most comfortable for the patient (Kaplan, 1974, p. 240).

DEALING WITH SEXUAL PROBLEMS

Methods for treating sexual disorders have only recently been accorded widespread attention and concern. In fact, acknowledging sexual dysfunction as a legitimate topic for discussion and investigation is itself a comparatively recent trend, especially as it concerns women. Cultural, religious, and social prohibitions against the open expression of sexuality have always been severe in relation to women. At the same time that men were expected to have urgent sexual needs that had to be either repressed or properly channeled, women were barricaded from any acceptance or understanding of their own sexuality.

> Women's sexual role? . . . She had none—other than that of a seminal receptacle. . . . Everyone knew—or at least all men knew and most women pretended—that "nice" women had no sexual feelings, that respected wives only submitted in the hope of conceiving and that "those women" who freely responded sexually simply weren't the kind you married (Masters and Johnson, 1975, pp. 3–4).

It is no wonder, then, that sexual dysfunctions in women were seldom understood or ever given serious consideration. Like most medical literature produced over the centuries, descriptions of female sexual functioning were written by men. Misconceptions and myths were generated and perpetuated, leaving both men and women in a profound state of ignorance concerning each other's sexuality. Part of the legacy of keeping women in the dark, sexually speaking and otherwise, is what Ruth Herschberger refers to as the *total responsibility theory*:

> According to this doctrine, if the wife is satisfied it is due to the outstanding virility of the husband; while if she is not satisfied, it is because his virility failed. . . . We thus find in marital relations a most unrealistic dogma: that the man is solely responsible for the presence or absence of sexual satisfaction in either party (1970, p. 96).

The notion of man as the sex expert, however, is slowly giving way to a concept of a more equitable distribution of sexual responsibility. Therapy is aimed at helping each partner deal with individual problems as well as at developing the kind of cooperation and communication which are vital to mutual satisfaction and a full expression of sexuality.

SUMMARY

Attitudes toward sex, for the most part, have been extreme. Until recently, and among most groups, there has been an attitude favoring the repression of sex except for purposes of procreation. Today there is an almost total acceptance of any and all expressions of sexuality in the media. The older attitudes still linger, and so each of us must still come to terms with his or her own sexuality. A first step is knowledge of the human sexual response within the context of a loving relationship.

Women's genitalia, being hidden, are more subject to misconceptions than those of the male. The clitoris, sometimes referred to as the "ecstasy organ," is the center of a woman's sexuality. Also sensitive to the touch are the labia minora (the minor lips) and the vestibule. The male sex organ, homologue to the clitoris, is the penis. The glans, or head, of the penis is the most sensitive area. The size of the penis bears no direct relationship to a man's sexuality or his ability to bring pleasure to his partner.

Sexual behavior is learned, and one way to explore one's own sexuality is by means of masturbation, the manipulation of one's own genitals to produce orgasm. Touching is a form of loving; touching gives pleasure and communicates affection. It is a mistake to view touching only as an invitation to love making and orgasm.

Scientists have only recently been able to gain public acceptance of studies of sexuality. Kinsey was a pioneer in the field and led the way for Masters and Johnson not only to talk to people about their sexual behavior but also to observe acts of intercourse in the laboratory. Masters and Johnson divided the sexual act, from arousal to orgasm and the final release of tension, into four stages, the sexual response cycle. They observed and minutely described the physiological changes that take place in each of the four stages: the excitement phase, the plateau phase, the orgasmic phase, and the resolution phase.

Coitus in the missionary position is the legal norm, and simultaneous orgasms have been considered the ideal. However, today most people seem to feel that sexual activity between two consenting adults may take any form that is pleasurable to those involved, as long as there is no risk of physical harm to either. There are a variety of positions in addition to the missionary position. Such sexual behavior as oral sex, both cunnilingus and fellatio, is often found pleasurable, either resulting in orgasm or as a preliminary to coitus.

An important aspect of the research of Masters and Johnson is their creation of effective therapies for sexual dysfunction in both men and women. Since sex is learned behavior, men who suffer from impotence and premature ejaculation are helped by learning to concentrate on the feelings in their bodies. Women who experience a general sexual dysfunction and are unable to become sexually aroused, women who do not regularly have orgasms, and women who suffer from vaginismus also can be helped by sex therapy.

CASE STUDY

Her View

After flunking out of college, Suzanne Ziegler moved back with her parents and got a job as a bank teller. She began to go out for lunch with Gerard Pierce, a twenty-nine-year-old fellow employee. Suzanne has dated since she was about twelve, and she says she engaged in petting when she was in high school and college. But her attraction to Gerard was to lead to even greater physical intimacy.

On their first evening date, they had drinks and a bottle of wine with their dinner. Suzanne was feeling high, and she agreed to stop at Gerard's apartment in order to sober up before going home. Gerard began to caress her, and Suzanne allowed him to take off her clothes. They engaged in sexual intercourse, but

Suzanne did not become as excited as she had expected. Since it was now quite late, Suzanne decided to remain overnight and did not call her parents until the following morning.

Suzanne's relationship with her parents is problematical. She wants to be close to them but feels that they are very authoritarian. Her father seems emotionally inexpressive, whereas her mother is easily upset—Suzanne remembers having water thrown in her face and having her hair pulled when she was a little girl. This year her mother kicked her and returned her Easter present of a potted plant because Suzanne did not finish the dinner dishes quickly enough. Her parents have always been disturbed by Suzanne's social activities. They worried about her when she lived in co-ed dorms, and they were dismayed when she went on a camping trip with a group of male and female college friends. When they received Suzanne's phone call about having stayed out with Gerard, they told her she would have to move out because she was setting a poor example for her three younger sisters.

On the Saturday of the very next weekend, Suzanne went apartment hunting, and that night she again stayed with Gerard. Gerard visited Suzanne the following weekend in order to help her move out, but Suzanne's parents would not let him into the house. Suzanne was now so upset with her parents that her work performance became impaired, and she was fired from her job. When Gerard did not call her for three weeks, she felt used, let down, and very angry.

Soon thereafter, Suzanne found a clerical job in a health-food store run by a fifty-year-old couple. During the third week, however, the husband began to make sexual advances, and Suzanne decided to quit. She registered at an employment agency and landed a position as a secretary to a pool of seven insurance agents.

After having a brief sexual encounter with someone she met at a discotheque and after turning down the sexual advances of another male acquaintance, Suzanne began dating one of the insurance salesmen, Tommy Turner. She delights in his expressed appreciation of her, and, when they are alone, she enjoys holding and stroking him. However, even though she has become more devoted to Tommy than to any previous boy friend, she wants to reserve sex for later. Tommy has asked her to share oral sex with him, but Suzanne feels that it is unpleasant and that a couple should first become comfortable with intercourse. Suzanne is afraid that Tommy might take advantage of her, even though she is pleased that he admires her appearance and has expressed a desire to see her naked. Frequently, after a date with Tommy, Suzanne masturbates while imagining that Tommy is touching her.

Suzanne moved back with her parents soon after getting the job with the insurance company. When she told her mother about how she enjoyed showing affection to Tommy, her mother made no comment. Later, however, her father claimed that Suzanne was obsessed with sex.

His View

Tommy Turner believes that women are fun to be with, but he would not want to marry any of the ones he has dated or slept with. Since his sophomore year in high school, Tommy has had intercourse with four or five different women each year. While he was completing his second year toward a business degree in a community college, he took a woman to a motel and became engaged to her three weeks later. They broke up four months later, when he joined the Army.

Tommy had been working in insurance sales for three years when he met Suzanne. He had been growing tired of living at home with his parents and bouncing from one girl friend to another. He finds Suzanne attractive, generous, warm, and sensitive, but he would prefer that she have only positive things to say about her family. (In general, he regards his own family as a close one.) Tommy thinks Suzanne's father is good-natured and jovial and likes talking with him about business and sports. He was surprised when Suzanne complained about his watching television with her father rather than taking her out for a walk. Tommy also finds it hard to accept that Suzanne is not close to her mother.

However, Tommy says that Suzanne's parents do make him feel uncomfortable about even holding hands with Suzanne. He was astounded by their rage over the fact that she was watching television with her head in his lap. He was further amazed when Suzanne told him that her mother locks her father out of the master bedroom and locks the bathroom door while she showers.

Tommy has realized that Suzanne herself is uneasy about sex, and he has decided not to pressure her. But he would like her to enjoy her physical self more, just as he enjoys and takes pride in his own body. He believes that his sexual experiences have taught him how to please a variety of women, and he tells Suzanne that he wants to teach her how to pleasure herself and him.

Interpretation and Questions

What influences and experiences have contributed to the way in which Tommy and Suzanne express themselves sexually? Was Suzanne interested only in sex in her encounters with Gerard Pierce? Do you think that Suzanne and Tommy have enough in common to share a meaningful sexual relationship? Are they sexually compatible? What effect do the attitudes of Suzanne's parents have on her sexual expressiveness? How common do you think Suzanne's and Tommy's experiences with sex are? Will their ways of interacting sexually lead to personal fulfillment and happiness?

STUDY GUIDE
Important Terms

vulva
clitoris
labia
mons veneris
penis
scrotum

resolution phase
orgasm
ejaculation
cunnilingus
fellatio
impotence

testes
vasocongestion
excitement phase
plateau phase
refractory period

premature ejaculation
general sexual dysfunction
orgasmic difficulties
vaginismus

Review Quiz

1 The _____ is the term for all the external female genitalia.
   a vulva
   b clitoris
   c labia
   d mons veneris

2 The counterpart to the female clitoris in the male is the:
   a scrotum
   b testes
   c penis
   d vas deferens

3 The Kinsey studies used the technique of _____ to study sexuality.
   a observation
   b the interview
   c the mail questionnaire
   d experimentation

4 During the excitement phase of sexual response:
   a penile erection occurs in the male
   b lubrication occurs in the vagina
   c the labia minora become engorged with blood and expand
   d all the above

5 The expansion of tissue as a result of an increased supply of blood during sexual excitement is called:
   a vasocongestion
   b orgasm
   c hyperventilation
   d none of the above

6 Men usually secrete a preejaculation fluid during the _____ phase of sexual response.
   a excitement
   b plateau
   c orgasmic
   d resolution

7 Compared with the male, the average female experiences orgasmic contractions which last:
   a a shorter time
   b a longer time
   c about the same amount of time
   d a length of time not yet determined by research

8 The period immediately after orgasm, lasting from two to five minutes, during which most men are incapable of sexual stimulation is called:
   a the plateau
   b the peak
   c the refractory period
   d afterplay

9 Comparing men and women, orgasmic potential seems to be:
   a about the same for both
   b greater for men than women
   c greater for women than men
   d still unknown

10 Cunnilingus and fellatio are:
   a medical terms for two positions of male-female sexual intercourse
   b two ancient Italian forms of birth control
   c two varieties of oral sex
   d names of sexual dysfunctions

11 Secondary impotence is:
   a inability ever to achieve or maintain an erection
   b inability to maintain an erec-

tion for coitus more than 25 percent of the time

c inability to engage in coitus a second time in one evening

d inability to maintain an erection with a second partner even though it is possible with a spouse

12 Male impotence is generally caused by:

a fear and anxiety

b "spectatoring"

c lack of confidence

d any or all of the above

13 Masters and Johnson classify a male as a premature ejaculator when:

a he ejaculates before his partner is satisfied more than 50 percent of the times they have sexual intercourse

b he has no voluntary control over ejaculation

c his sexual partner complains

d he ejaculates before the plateau phase is reached

14 Current thinking among researchers and sex therapists about the term *frigidity* is that it should be:

a used in relation to women who never reach orgasm

b used in relation to women who fail to reach orgasm more than half the time during intercourse

c used in relation to women who do not become sexually aroused

d replaced with more specific and less deprecatory terms

15 A disorder in women involving an involuntary spasmic contraction of the vagina is called:

a frigidity

b vaginismus

c colitis

d dyspareunia

Opinionnaire

Are your sexual attitudes liberal or conservative?

Agree	No opinion	Disagree		
———	———	———	1	There is never any justification for extra-marital sex.
———	———	———	2	Sex without love is immoral.
———	———	———	3	Homosexuality is just as normal as heterosexuality.
———	———	———	4	Sexuality should not be a legal concern.
———	———	———	5	The legal age for a female to consent to sexual intercourse should be lowered to fourteen.
———	———	———	6	Masturbation is as valid as any other method of sexual expression.
———	———	———	7	A female should feel as free to make sexual advances as a male.
———	———	———	8	Oral sex is unnatural.
———	———	———	9	All legal restrictions on the publication and sale of pornography should be removed.

——— ——— ———

10 A person who has had many sexual partners in the past is more likely to be
unfaithful in marriage than someone who
has had few.

Exercise

The three jokes* below depict situations which are sexual. Read the jokes and
then, on the basis of your first feeling reaction, rate each according to how
humorous you found it.

1   A little boy and a little girl were sitting in a bath together. The little girl looked
down at the little boy and asked, "Can I play with that?"
"Of course not," said the little boy. "You've broken yours."

Not funny at all   1   2   3   4   5   Very funny

2   A man was walking along a street in London, when he saw a pub called THE
TWO QUEERS. Intrigued, he went inside and walked over to the man behind
the bar. "Excuse me, sir, but can you tell me why this pub is called THE TWO
QUEERS?"
The bartender looked puzzled and replied, "I really don't know. Maybe
my wife can tell us. GEORGE!"

Not funny at all   1   2   3   4   5   Very funny

3   A woman was sitting at a bar, having a drink, when a man walked over and
took the seat beside her. "Would you be interested in having sexual intercourse with me?" he asked.
Outraged, the woman swung her purse and knocked the man to the floor.
Furiously, she jumped on him, pulling his hair and banging his head against
the floor. Standing up, she delivered several kicks to his ribs as he cringed in
pain. Finally, she turned and resumed her seat at the bar.
The man pulled himself up with the aid of the bar stool. Painfully he
remarked, "I guess there's no point in even asking you for a blow job."

Not funny at all   1   2   3   4   5   Very funny

Now consider your rankings and the details of the jokes. What do your ratings say
about your sexual values? Why did you find some jokes funnier than others? Did
you find anything offensive in them? If so, what? If this exercise has been useful in
helping you to understand your own sexual values, read Wesley J. Adams's "The
Use of Humor in Teaching Human Sexuality at the University Level," *The Family*

---

*Many jokes, especially those with sexual connotations, have been part of oral tradition so
long that acknowledgment to the originator becomes impossible. The author is grateful to
Maury Bennett and Judy Corwin for their input in this section.

Coordinator, October 1974, **23**, 365–368, for a further comment on jokes and sexuality.

Projects for Class or Home Study

1   Pornography is often inaccurate in depicting the physiology of sex. Read a graphic description of sex in a pornographic novel. How does the account correspond with what you learned in this chapter?

2   Some marriage manuals have also been criticized for presenting sex as "work." Training, fitness, practice, and expertise are recommended as "keys to sexual success." Read one or two manuals on sex. Do they present sex as work or play?

3   Many persons are unaware of their own preferences in sexual attractiveness. Imagine the person whom you find most sexually attractive. Now list those qualities which make the person attractive to you. Would the same qualities in someone else make that person as attractive sexually?

4   Write out a list of euphemisms or slang words which mean sexual intercourse. How many of them have aggressive connotations? Why is this so?

5   Sex, they say, sells. For one day try to remain aware of all the mass-media presentations which use sex and sex symbolism for audience appeal. Note the ads you see in your morning paper, the words of songs you hear on the radio, billboards you see on your way to work, store windows you pass when you go to lunch, and the television programs you watch in the evening. Is the assertion that this is a sex-oriented society justified?

Suggestions for Further Reading

Comfort, Alex (Ed.) *The joy of sex: A Cordon Bleu guide to lovemaking*. New York: Crown, 1972.
>   This explicit guide to lovemaking is illustrated with many drawings, both in black and white and in color. The emphasis is on the description of sexual techniques.

Ellis, Albert. *Sex without guilt*. New York: Grove Press, 1965.
>   The author is a practicing psychotherapist with a distinctive approach to behavioral problems called *rational emotive therapy*. Ellis has made sex his specialty, and he explains his viewpoint in this book.

Heiman, Julia R. The physiology of erotica: Women's sexual arousal. *Psychology Today*, April 1975, **9**, 90.
>   The author reports a study in which women were more aroused by films showing explicit sex than by those showing romantic sex, a finding contrary to what had earlier been believed.

Hite, Shere. *The Hite report*. New York: Macmillan, 1976.
>   A discussion of women's sexuality—their likes and dislikes and their complaints and recommendations—based on the self-reports of over 3000 women.

Katchadourian, Herant A., and Lunde, Donald T. *Fundamentals of human sexuality*. (2nd ed.) New York: Holt, 1975.

A thorough discussion of sexuality from both the biological and the cultural points of view. The book includes an interesting section on sex in art.

Masters, William H., and Johnson, Virginia E. *The pleasure bond*. Boston: Little, Brown, 1975.

Intended for the general reader, this book covers most of the issues surrounding sexuality. It contains an excellent discussion of commitment and sexuality.

Maykovich, Minako K. Attitudes versus behavior in extramarital sexual relations. *Journal of Marriage and the Family*, November 1976, **38**(3), 693–699.

This survey of the sexual attitudes and behavior of 200 women in Japan and the United States is typical of how research in sexuality is done by sociologists. The author concludes that important cross-cultural differences in extramarital sex exist.

Sex counseling over the telephone. *Sexual Behavior*, August 1972, **2**(8), 22–25.

This program, which has now expanded to other major cities under various names, is described as it operates in New York City.

Answers to Review Quiz

1-*a* 2-*c* 3-*b* 4-*d* 5-*a* 6-*a* 7-*b* 8-*c* 9-*c* 10-*c* 11-*b* 12-*d* 13-*a* 14-*d* 15-*b*

5

MARRIAGEABILITY

On a steaming July evening in 1962 in a small California town, a procession of gleaming hot rods carrying teenagers cruises slowly up and down the main street. Some of the cars have been beautifully modified. One candy-apple red 1958 Chevy Impala, for example, is magnificently decked-and-channeled and tucked-and-rolled. Raucous rock-and-roll music blares from many of the car radios, and some of the occupants bump and grind to the rhythms of the music.

Some of the hot rods are full of young men, others contain only young women, and still others are occupied by members of both sexes. Occasionally, the occupants of one car will whistle at, shout at, or talk to those in another car as the autos slowly pass one another or stop at a traffic signal. At times, the teenagers in one car will invite one of the youths from another vehicle to join them. Frequently, a car will pull off the main drag into the parking lot of the local drive-in restaurant to check out the people in the cars parked there or to "hang out," waiting for some action. This scene, typical of those in the film

American Graffiti, was part of the American courtship ritual in the late 1950s and early 1960s.

Dating

Not too long ago in Germany, young people from surrounding rural areas would pour into a village for church services on Sunday morning. In the evening, they would pair off and promenade up and down the main street, just as in the 1960s young Americans promenaded in their cars, perhaps singing long into the night. Later, the couples might disappear into the bushes to make love. The whole courtship process, however, had evolved under the auspices of the community, and the young people were supervised and encouraged by their elders. Although similar supervised systems prevail in parts of Europe to this day, more and more countries are adopting the freer American system (Shorter, 1975).

CHARACTERISTICS OF DATING

What is meant by the term *date* or *dating*? A date has been defined as a planned event involving an activity to be shared by two single persons of the opposite sex:

> It may be planned many months or just minutes in advance; it may involve only the one couple or another couple as well, or it may take place within a group. In any case, an event becomes a "date" only when one person (usually but not necessarily the male) asks the other to share in the activity. They then form a paired relation, publicly recognizable, for the duration of the event. The pairing may be loose, casual, and tentative; or it may be highly tenacious and exclusive (Saxton, 1972, p. 145).

Dating serves a number of functions. First, it is a form of recreation and entertainment, and it involves no commitment for either party beyond the sheer enjoyment that it offers (Winch, 1974). However, as sociologists Pepper Schwartz and Janet Lever (1976) found in a study of a college mixer, getting together with a member of the opposite sex can be a traumatic ordeal rather than a pleasant experience. The mixer is the traditional social device used by colleges and high schools to get members of both sexes together. At a mixer, males and females achieve maximum exposure with the least possible risk of being rejected or of ending up with an undesirable partner. Not surprisingly, then, none of the women interviewed by the investigators—and only one of the men—claimed to like mixers. Throughout the affair, all the participants are aware of being constantly evaluated and of being either desired or rejected. One young woman, for example, made the following observation about this popular form of social gathering:

I generally think mixers are grotesque. There you are, a piece of meat lined up along a wall in this herd of ugly females. You try to stand casually as guys walk back and forth and you know you're on display. You just want to crawl up the wall. Then you're asked to dance by these really gross creatures. I'm so revolted by the whole thing (Schwartz and Lever, 1976, p. 421).

The second function of dating, as Waller (1937) pointed out in his famous study entitled "The Dating and Rating Complex," is that of achieving status. The individual's rank in the status system depends on such things as his or her date's attractiveness and personality and on whether the date belongs to a prestigious fraternity, or sorority, or other organization. Thus, one Yale junior observes:

There have been times when I've seen a girl, and, you know, I imagined I might not get along too well with her just from talking with her, but she was so good looking that I just wanted to be seen walking into the dining hall with her or something like that, something prestigious (Schwartz and Lever, 1976, p. 419).

A third function of dating is socialization: It provides men and women with the opportunity to learn how to behave in each other's company and to become acquainted with the opposite sex. The fourth function is related to the third: Dating also enables young people to explore their own personalities as they interact with members of the opposite sex and to learn about the personalities of others. Thus, the dating experience is a kind of testing ground. Fifth, dating facilitates mate selection, enabling one to test a succession of relationships with individuals of the opposite sex. Finally, dating prepares the person for more extensive socialization into marital and other adult familial roles. "Dating provides an opportunity to explore the personality and values of another human being in a situation of erotically tinged, fun-oriented recreation" (Winch, 1974, pp. 398–399).

THE DATING SCENE TODAY

Dating among American youths now is quite different from what it was in the recent past. For one thing, more adolescents are dating. One study (Kopecky, 1976), for example, found that 93 percent of American teenagers go out at least on an occasional date, compared with 51 percent in 1960. Second, dating today is more informal. Says one sixteen-year-old girl: "I think it's [dating] kind of archaic. Years ago it meant going out with a boy who would call you up and ask you out. Today, so many kids go out in groups instead, the word itself is often useless" (Gilliam, 1973, p. 106).

In support of this attitude, Kelley (1974) states that today's youth engage in a form of courtship he calls "thinging," in which they do their own thing when out on a date. A couple may date on Saturday nights, for example, but each is free to date others on weekdays. Or two young people may begin dating fairly steadily and then, after a month or so, separate and begin randomly dating others. Thus, couples are free to do what they want to do when they want to do it. As one seventeen-year-old boy observes: "Dating makes me think of calling up a girl a few days in advance and asking her to go out to dinner or something. Most of the time, I just see a girl at school or on the street and ask her out." Another girl states: "People don't pair up that much anymore. Even dances are more or less a group thing" (Gilliam, 1973, p. 106).

Also changing are the reasons for dating. In a study in which she compared dating among Harvard students in 1964 with dating among them in 1970, Rebecca Vreeland (1972) found many differences between the 1964 students and the 1970 students. For one thing, the 1964 Harvard men saw recreation as the chief reason for dating. The 1970 students, by contrast, believed that finding a female friend was the most important reason. Students in the more recent sample were more interested in companionship than in sex or recreation. This finding was supported in James Wittman's (1971) analysis of the dating patterns of rural and urban Kentucky teenagers; he found that "being with someone you enjoy" was more important than prestige or the security of going together.

The Harvard men in both samples also rated being a good conversationalist as an important asset of one's date. Among the 1970s men, conversation and sex tied for the key attributes of a date. Other desirable characteristics included intellectual sophistication and an effervescent personality. But high school youths apparently have different criteria. In a

IT IS sometimes easier to meet a date in the company of same-sex friends.

study made by Dorothy Place (1975) of adolescent girls in 1952, and again in 1972, for example, it was found that the girls in the more recent sample valued a good personality, good looks, and a good physique in a date, whereas the 1952 girls considered a pleasant personality, a good sense of humor, and being a good sport to be desirable characteristics.

The importance of conversation also emerged in the part of the Harvard study that dealt with actual dating behavior. The 1964 students believed that "fun" events—going to movies and to parties—were the foremost dating activities. The 1970 students, however, leaned toward private activities, such as sitting and talking. For the Harvard men of the 1970s, Vreeland concludes, "learning about another individual's personality and securing one's own identity were the most important functions of dating" (1972, p. 68).

But George Dickinson (1971) found that the preferred dating activities of high school youths differed from those of college students. Dickinson found that neither black nor white high school youths ranked sitting around and talking high on their list of dating activities. Instead, the white youths preferred movies, bowling, and driving around, whereas the blacks liked to attend parties and dances. Parking was another prime activity, especially for white females: some 64 percent of the white girls stated that they courted or parked on dates, but only 21 percent of the black females said that they took part in such activities.

GOING STEADY

One of the principal stages of the pairing process is going steady. Kelley (1974), for example, found the stages of contemporary American courtship to be random dating, "thinging," going steady, and engagement. Going steady means regularly dating only one person for a period of time (Landis, 1969). The practice offers the youngster security because he or she always has a date. But it also has the limitation of preventing one from meeting a variety of other people and gaining valuable interpersonal experience. Going steady was the preferred dating status for youth in the 1950s. Today, however, the practice appears to be dying out. One seventeen-year-old girl, for example, observes: "I think it's [going steady] a dying form of relationship in my school. A couple of my friends still go steady, but I know it's not what I want. I don't want to be tied down" (Gilliam, 1973, p. 135).

And a nineteen-year-old Illinois boy feels the same way about this practice:

> I see the [going steady] System as a trap, a way of conditioning guys to marriage from the age of twelve. By the time they grow up, they are so used to being tied down that they don't know anything else; then they get married. There's only one way to fight it. Men of America, start going out with more than one girl. If one starts tying you down, let her go! If one gets that

class-ring gleam in her eye, drop her. Be tough! don't give any girl the upper hand (Byczek, 1973, p. 106).

CHANGING SEX ROLES

The social movements of the 1960s changed traditional ideas about sex roles. Before the 1960s, these roles were fairly rigid; the male was expected to be aggressive, and the female was expected to be passive. In the words of two female college freshmen:

> In the classic case the guy asks the girl out and makes all the necessary arrangements. This typical situation could include an activity such as a movie, football game, picnic, party, or just a drive. He arranges for transportation and sets the day and time. Once on the date, he lays out the bread, opens doors, offers the girl food, "leads" her because he knows where they are going. In short, he's the guide. This type of date is popularly associated with male aggression because etiquette dictates that the *girl* wait for the guy to call her up and ask her out (Dankman and Cooley, 1971, p. 94).

But all this is changing. A poll by a popular magazine found that most of its young women readers (93.4 percent) had at one time or another taken the initiative and asked a boy for a date. The women sometimes suggest dating activities, and some even pay their own share (Kopecky, 1976).

Two freshmen women at the University of California conducted an interesting study for a sociology course to see what would happen if they reversed the usual situation and asked men out on dates. The women decided to take the role that the male usually assumes: they would contact the date, make the decisions, make the arrangements, and lead the men about. The two women had more than twenty "reverse dates," but they found that their biggest problem was being too aggressive. Indeed, none of their subjects ever called back to ask for another date. The lesson the two learned was that the man must be allowed to make some of the decisions: "A girl can be aggressive to a point but . . . carrying it too far makes a guy uncomfortable and often surly. . . . We can ask them out. But . . . the success of the date depends on letting him make some of the decisions and do some of the managing" (Dankman and Cooley, 1971, p. 145). The women, incidentally, received an A on their paper.

SEX AND DATING

One of the most important aspects of dating is the sexual experience that one may or may not have during the date. Sexual intimacy is a delicate subject, and one study found that adolescents are still insecure about it (Kopecky, 1976). In the study, 93 percent of the adolescent girls reported that they had kissed a boy on their first date. When asked for their

SELF-REPORTS BY COLLEGE MEN OF SEXUAL AGGRESSION AGAINST A DATE

In a study of unmarried college males, 87 percent reported at least one case of sexual aggression toward a date since entering college. More extreme reactions occurred on "pick-ups" or first dates.

Reactions	"Pick-up" and first date		Occasional date		Regular date and "pinned"		Total %
	N	%	N	%	N	%	
Screaming and fighting	13	44.8	7	12.7	7	11.9	17.9
Crying	5	17.2	5	9.1	20	33.8	18.7
Pleading	9	31.1	16	29.1	19	32.2	26.5
Quarreling and turning cold	2	6.9	27	49.1	13	22.1	36.9
Total	29	100.0	55	100.0	59	100.0	100.0

Source: Kanin, 1969, Table 1.

opinion of what constitutes going too far in matters of sex, the girls gave a variety of answers. One girl, for example, thought that anything beyond kissing was too much. Another believed that limitations on sex were conditioned by "how long you've been going with a guy, how serious you are, where you are, who's around" (Kopecky, 1976, p. 35).

There is no doubt, however, that the sexual freedom begun in the 1960s is continuing today. Morton Hunt (1974), for example, compared sexual behavior in the 1970s with that studied by Kinsey in the late 1940s. Hunt found that half of the modern seventeen-year-old male college students had engaged in premarital coitus, a figure that was more than double that of the comparable group from Kinsey's example. There was an increase in the incidence of sexual intercourse off the campus too. Nearly 75 percent of the seventeen-year-old noncollege males had engaged in coitus, whereas slightly more than two-thirds of the comparable males in Kinsey's sample had done so. For females, the increase is even more remarkable. The proportion of modern women in their late teens and early twenties who had had premarital intercourse was about twice that of the women in the Kinsey sample.

What are some of the reasons behind these changes in sexual attitudes and behavior? They may have resulted, says Hunt, because parents allow their children to own cars at early ages or because they allow their sons and daughters to go unchaperoned on weekend jaunts. Indeed, a study by Graham Spanier (1976) found that dating frequency and premarital sexual intercourse among high school and college students are interrelated: The greater the dating frequency of an individual, the more premarital intercourse he or she is likely to engage in. Another factor could be the easing of rules by colleges which permit males and females to visit one another in their dormitory rooms.

Finally, says Hunt, the new sexual freedom does not reflect a growing promiscuity among modern youth. Rather, "They regard premarital

ONLY A couple in love would sit out in the rain watching an empty tennis court.

coitus, in general, as thoroughly justified when it grows out of and expresses a legitimate relationship, but much less so when it is a purely sensuous and casual indulgence'' (Hunt, 1974, p. 151).

Choosing a Partner

"You can marry anyone you want to. It's a free country, isn't it?" Many of us have heard statements like this, for, theoretically at least, a great many members of the opposite sex are potential marriage partners. In reality, however, there are a number of sociocultural, biological, and geographical factors that seem to filter out the final choice of a mate, and the partner that one finally chooses is, in most cases, remarkably like oneself.

PROPINQUITY AND PHYSICAL ATTRACTION

The first factor in the filtering out of potential partners is *propinquity*, or nearness. It is obvious that two people cannot meet, date, and mate if they never have the opportunity to do so. Thus, individuals who live in the same city or neighborhood are more likely to meet and to be attracted to each other than people who live worlds apart (Back et al., 1977). A study of married people by Alfred Clarke (1952) found that slightly more than one-half of the couples he studied lived within sixteen blocks of each other during the period in which they were dating. In another study, Joseph Marches and Gus Turbeville (1953) found that 43 percent of their subjects resided within a twenty-block radius and that 21 percent lived only five blocks apart.

However, as sociologist Robert Bell (1975) indicates, propinquity is a reflection of other factors. People who live in the same neighborhood, for example, are frequently members of the same race, the same social class, and perhaps the same ethnic group. If neighborhoods were more mixed, the effect of the propinquity factor in mate selection would probably be considerably reduced. Indeed, as Webber (1963) points out, this is becoming increasingly true for members of the middle and upper classes who use modern technology, including telephones, automobiles, and airplanes, to conduct business and to vacation in all parts of the world, where they are likely to meet many other people.

The second filtering factor in mate selection is *appearance*. Most people are initially drawn to others on the basis of physical attractiveness. As one adolescent girl observes: "Everybody says looks don't mean anything, but they do. I like dark hair because it seems more there. I like them taller than me—about six feet" (Place, 1975, p. 163).

A study by social psychologists Walster, Aronson, Abrahams, and Rottmann (1966) supports this emphasis on physical appearance. After arranging a dance at the University of Minnesota, these investigators matched male freshmen with female freshmen. Each male was told that he had been matched with a date whose personality was similar to his, but in reality the subjects had been randomly paired. Each man was asked to rate his date on the basis of attractiveness as well as personality. At the same time, the investigators also graded all the females for attractiveness. Results showed that the men liked their dates for the most part because of their physical attractiveness. However, a study by Eugene Mathes (1975) found that in subsequent dates with the same partner, personality assumes the dominant role in determining liking and may even weaken the effects of physical attraction.

ENDOGAMY

The other filtering factors in the mate-selection process are dependent upon *endogamy*, in which one marries someone who is a member of the same general group. Groupings important in endogamy include age, social class, race, religion, and ethnic group.

AGE People tend to marry those who are close to them in age. The age at first marriage is different for different sections of the population. Members of the lower socioeconomic strata, for example, tend to marry at a younger age than members of the upper classes. Men are likely to marry women who are about two years younger. In 1975, the median age at first marriage for American women was 21.1 years, compared with 23.5 for men (U.S. Bureau of the Census, 1976b).

SOCIAL CLASS Social class is undoubtedly the most all-inclusive factor in mate selection because it involves the variables of education, income, occupation, and, as we have seen, the neighborhood in which one lives. People of the same social class often have similar values and attitudes, and thus the class factor may be one of the most important elements in mate selection (R. Bell, 1975). If people marry out of their class, it is men who tend to marry women of lower social class; women are more likely to wed men of higher class.

In the past, sororities and fraternities on college campuses performed the function of assuring that members of the upper middle class selected mates from their own class by exposing members to potential mates only within the fraternity-sorority system, thus protecting them from socially undesirable partners (Scott, 1965). Some prestigious schools, for example, invited only students of comparable social class and educational attainment to mixers and other social affairs in which mate selection played an important role (Schwartz and Lever, 1976). However, such practices are not observed in the great majority of American universities today because such overt social-class distinctions are not considered in good taste, even though they are still observed by many of today's young people.

TO THE casual eye the chances for a lasting relationship seem good for this couple; they are of same age, same social class, and same race.

RACE Race has long been the most powerful of the endogamous factors of mate selection. Even today, despite the changes in race relations that began in the last decade or so in America, interracial marriages are rare. Hugh Carter and Paul Glick (1970), for example, examined the data of the 1960 census and estimated that black-white unions amounted to less than 1 percent of all marriages in this country. But another researcher, David Heer (1974), found that black-white marriages in the period 1953–1964 definitely increased in certain states. However, because of the reporting procedures of the states and because many states prohibited interracial unions at the time of Heer's report, it is difficult to arrive at an exact figure. Heer also points out that in most black-white unions a black man marries a white woman, both of whom are usually from the same class.

The attitudes of the young appear to be divided on the issue of interracial pairings. Asked about the importance of race and religion in dating at her school, one eighteen-year-old Massachusetts girl replied: "[Race and religion do not matter] . . . at my school. No one seems to care much about one or the other. We're all people, and everyone does his or her own thing" (Gilliam, 1973, p. 106). However, when the same question was put to a seventeen-year-old Chicago girl, she replied: "There isn't much mixed dating at my school. Many blacks, I know, feel a strong sense of nationalism and unity and they'd look down on their black peers going with a white person" (Gilliam, 1973, p. 106).

RELIGION Most religions do not encourage members to marry those of different faiths, and members appear to be adhering to the teachings of their churches in this matter. Carter and Glick (1970), for example, found that slightly more than 78 percent of American Catholics marry other Catholics, 91 percent of the Protestants marry other Protestants, and nearly 93 percent of the Jews marry others of their faith. Of course, as Robert Bell (1975) notes, the strength of one's faith will also influence the decision to marry outside one's religion.

As William Stephens (1970b) indicates, there are other factors in mate selection, some of which can be used to predict the success or failure of a marriage. Among these are the length of acquaintance before marriage, whether the woman becomes pregnant before marriage, whether either partner—or their parents—has ever been divorced, and where the couple live. All factors considered, Stephens concludes, the evidence appears to support the idea that conservative people and conservative marriages stand the best chance of success. For a lasting marriage, Stephens counsels a woman to marry:

> . . . a Rotarian who is active in his church, who gets on well with his parents, who has never been divorced, who is about your age, whom you have known for years. Don't get pregnant first. Don't marry without your parents' blessings. Don't marry until you are out of school. Marry your own kind, *vis-à-vis* religion and social-class position. And stay out of big cities (1970b, p. 195).

Living Together

In 1968, Linda LeClair, a Barnard College student, became the focus of national attention when it was revealed that she was living with a former Columbia University student. Her atypical living arrangement and her subsequent battle with university administrators who sought to eject her from school were judged so newsworthy that *The New York Times* chronicled her story on its front pages. *Time* magazine thought the event was important enough to merit a feature article entitled "Linda the Light Housekeeper." In short, the media and the university authorities were shocked at such flagrant disregard of sexual mores.

INCIDENCE OF LIVING TOGETHER

Today, Linda's living arrangements would not evoke such interest from university authorities or the media because living together is no longer news. On college campuses all across the nation, unmarried men and women live together without attracting any comment. Living together is a practice that, like dating, engagement, and marriage, is now recognized by most social scientists as a significant phase in the lives of young and not-so-young people.

In a review of studies on the subject, Eleanor Macklin (1974) found that the number of college students living together at the schools she studied ranged from 10 to 33 percent, depending on such factors as the location of the school, housing and parental regulations, the ratio of male to female students, the sampling methods of the investigators, and the investigators' definition of the term. In her own study, Macklin (1972, 1974) discovered that 31 percent of her sample had cohabited at some time. And the practice is not limited to college campuses; the 1970 census, for example, revealed that 143,000 couples reported living together, an increase of 800 percent over the 1960 figure. Even senior citizens are part of the phenomenon—the 1970 census found that some 18,000 couples over sixty-five were living together. (Most of these senior citizens have not married each other because by doing so they would forfeit some of their social security income.)

THE LIVING-TOGETHER EXPERIENCE

What is meant by the term *living together*? Some researchers refer to the phenomenon as *cohabitation*, some label it a *consensual union* (CU), some call it *living together unmarried* (LTU), and some describe it as *unmarried liaison* (UNMALIAS) (Lobsenz, 1974). Eleanor Macklin (1972, 1974) calls the practice *cohabitation*, which she defines as "having shared a bedroom and/or a bed with someone of the opposite sex (to whom one is not married) for four or more nights a week for three or more consecutive months" (Macklin, 1974, p. 55).

Couples living together do not perceive their relationship as a trial marriage or as an engagement. Instead, for the majority of the cohabitants:

> Living together seems to be a natural component of the strong, affectionate dating relationship—a living out of what used to be called going steady. The relationship may grow in time to become something more, but in the meantime it is to be enjoyed and experienced because it is pleasurable in and of itself (Macklin, 1974, p. 59).

In her study of Cornell students, Macklin found that students live together in a variety of arrangements. These include living with a roommate of the opposite sex in a co-op without sexual involvement and with both roommates romantically involved with others, sharing a room in a dormitory or fraternity house, and sharing a room with another couple who are also living together. But the most typical arrangement is for the girl to move into the man's room, or vice versa, in an apartment which is shared with others. Freshmen students tend to share dormitory rooms, whereas sophomores, juniors, seniors, and graduate students live in apartments or houses off campus. In most cases, the couple make no initial deliberate decision to live together. Instead, they gradually drift into the relationship. As one twenty-six-year-old secretary noted, "Jerry would stay overnight once or twice a week. Soon he was staying over four or five nights. After a while it seemed foolish for him to go back to his own place at all, or to pay rent on an apartment he hardly used" (Lobsenz, 1974, p. 184).

Macklin found that one-half of the couples in her sample slept together seven nights a week. In the other half of the sample, the woman spent five nights with the man, returning to her own room two nights a week to visit her friends. Surprisingly enough, Macklin also found that some couples had lived together for more than three months—some sharing the same bed—without having sexual intercourse.

In practical matters, Macklin found that few, if any, cohabitants pooled all their money, but the couple typically did share expenses for entertainment and food. Household chores, such as shopping and laundry, were usually done together, although the woman normally attended to cooking and housecleaning.

What are some of the reasons for living together? Among the most obvious are changing sexual mores that have lifted many of the constraints which had limited sexual relations. Then, too, many universities no longer consider themselves to be standing *in loco parentis*; they have liberalized dormitory visiting hours, permitted co-ed dorms, and allowed students to live off campus. A third reason for the increased incidence of living together is the availability of various effective means of contraception, as well as liberalized abortion laws. Fourth is the high probability of divorce, especially among young people, coupled with the desire for a

COUPLES WHO live together for any length of time do not really differ from their married counterparts.

more extensive premarital relationship before making a commitment to marry (Peterman, Ridley, and Anderson, 1974).

To these may be added a number of interpersonal reasons. Among these are feelings of loneliness experienced by students at large universities, the superficiality of dating, the desire for more meaningful relationships, and the emotional rewards gained from living with another person who really cares. Another reason given by some cohabitants is the desire for freedom and the chance to realize one's own identity. One formerly married graduate student, for example, observed: "What I like about our arrangement is the feeling I have about being my own person. With my wife, it seemed to me that I was always having to be something that she or her family wanted me to be. I had no real identity of my own" (Thorman, 1973, p. 252).

WHO LIVES TOGETHER?

Are individuals who live together different in any significant way from those who do not? The answer to this question is, "Yes and no." Henze and Hudson (1974), for example, examined the family and personal characteristics of cohabitants and noncohabitants. The researchers found that there were no important differences in family characteristics (urban versus nonurban home and disciplinary roles of parents, for example) between the two groups. But differences did emerge in individual personality factors. Students who lived together, for example, tended to be less religious, to be more liberal, and to use drugs.

In their study of Penn State students, Peterman, Ridley, and Anderson (1974) found that there was no relationship between cohabitation and grades. Interestingly enough, the male cohabitants were less likely to be majoring in physical sciences; the female counterparts tended to be studying behavioral sciences or the arts. As for religious beliefs and practices, Peterman and his colleagues found few differences between cohabiting and noncohabiting males. However, a large number of Catholic women reported cohabiting experiences, compared with a low number of Protestant women. A study of the psychological profiles of cohabiting college students by Catlin, Croake, and Keller (1976) found that cohabitants are apt to be more nonconformist and asocial than noncohabitants. And the male cohabitants tended to be more sensitive and idealistic than their noncohabiting counterparts.

Finally, cohabiting students felt that their relationships were of much higher quality than those experienced by noncohabitants. The same sentiment was expressed by 90 percent of the couples in Macklin's Cornell study; by and large, these students felt that their experience was successful and pleasurable and that it made them more mature, fostering personal growth.

As Lobsenz (1974) suggests, most couples who live together believe that they have a greater commitment to each other than married couples.

MORNING CONVERSATION with morning coffee is a part of the intimacy of couples who live together.

Cohabitants express their deeper commitment with such sentiments as, "I'm here every day because I want to be, not because I took a vow to be," or "We work very hard on our relationship because we want to, not because we're forced to for the sake of children, parents, or friends." Furthermore, some living-together couples believe that their arrangement makes it possible to be more honest when discussing differences than couples in typical marriages can be. As one man observes: "In marriage a serious fight can be terribly frightening, with its implications of a breakup. But Janet and I are separate to begin with, so we can fight without that fear" (Lobsenz, 1974, p. 186).

But there is a "Catch-22" of sorts for people living together. A relationship grows and matures only if the partners make increasingly greater commitments to it. The catch for cohabitants is, as Lobsenz observes, the greatest commitment of all—marriage, in which the couple emotionally and legally commit themselves to each other on the deepest level. If they really seek deep commitment, then, cohabitants must eventually consider marriage.

PROBLEMS OF LIVING TOGETHER

As the foregoing discussion suggests, living together is not always a bed of roses. There are numerous problems, both practical and interpersonal, which continuously threaten the permanency of the relationship. High on the list, especially for college students and other young people, is the attitude of the parents toward the living arrangement. So negative are some parents' views on the practice that an estimated 50 percent of the cohabitants have not told their parents (M. S. Miller, 1976). One father, for example, refused to allow his son to sleep with his lover in the same room when the couple visited for a weekend. "No whores in my house," the father shouted when told of the young couple's arrangement at school (M. S. Miller, 1976, p. 44). Another father refused to speak to his son for a whole year when he learned that the young man was living with a woman at school. But other parents are able to take their child's view of the situation. One mother, learning that her twenty-year-old daughter was cohabiting with a man, philosophically observed: "That's fine—it will save sheets." And a father said to his son, "Dammit, I was born twenty years too late" (M. S. Miller, 1976, p. 46). Finally, many parents come to terms with the situation by not knowing about it (or by pretending not to know) or by accepting it since they feel powerless to change it.

Interpersonal problems, too, plague those who choose to live together outside marriage. Some cohabitants believe that living together is just as personally stunting as going steady in that it locks them into a relationship that prevents them from dating others and sharpening their social skills. Others feel that living together will induce them to ignore commitment and to concentrate on themselves and their own happiness, rather than on that of the partner. Another problem involves individual freedom and sex. Theoretically, at least, the people in a living-together relationship are free to date and have sex with others because they are not married. Yet many cohabitants admit that they hesitate to do so because it would make their partners jealous or uneasy and could very well sabotage the feelings of emotional closeness that the two have for each other.

Then, too, cohabitants often find themselves slipping into tradition-al marital roles. In many cases, the woman gets stuck with the household tasks, even if she is employed. Finally, many cohabitants, especially those who live in small towns, must assume a masquerade of being married. Often, such couples must pretend to be man and wife to avoid problems with landlords, utility companies, employers, and even neigh-bors (Lobsenz, 1974).

However, this problem may vanish in the not-too-distant future. As one West Coast lawyer observed, "They're taking the sin out of living in sin" (Mancini, 1977, p. 25). The attorney's optimism stems from a recent court ruling in which Michelle Triola, who had lived with actor Lee Marvin for six years, may be awarded 1 million dollars because the actor decided to terminate their relationship. In handing down a preliminary decision, the jurists observed that an agreement to share assets and property obtained while living together is binding even if the couple are not married. According to the California jurists: "The mores of society have indeed changed so radically that we cannot impose a standard based on

alleged moral considerations that have apparently been so widely abandoned by so many" (Mancini, 1977, p. 25).

SUMMARY

At first glance the purpose of dating seems to be recreational—to have a good time. Other underlying functions are the achievement of status, socialization into the mysteries of manners and etiquette, the exploration of one's own maturing identity, mate selection, and the learning of marital and other adult roles. Today dating is more casual than in the past, but a purpose of dating expressed by the students in one study is to find companionship with a member of the opposite sex.

Sex roles are changing, and it is no longer true that the young man is exclusively the initiator; young women frequently pay their own way and participate in the management of the occasion. Two people who spend a great deal of time together and care for each other often see no reason not to extend their relationship to include sexual intercourse.

A person may go out with someone who is from another social class or is of a different religion or with someone who lives a great distance away; however, most people marry someone who is from a similar background and who lives or works nearby. Physical appearance is an important cause of attraction, but endogamous factors that are good predictors of mate selection are age (most people marry someone close to their own age), social class, race, and religion.

Living together, or cohabitation, is an arrangement that has become accepta- ble to a large degree on the campus and in the larger cities. Couples who live together do not usually pool their resources, as married couples do; they may share living expenses or participate with several others in cooperative housing. Sociological explanations for cohabitation as an institution point to changing sexual mores and the relative effectiveness and availability of contraception. Psychological explanations emphasize the emotional rewards of intimacy and the support of a caring person.

Parents may constitute a problem for young people living together. In a small town, such a couple may have to hide their status. In addition, cohabitation may constitute a burden in terms of commitment or a restriction on other friendships.

CASE STUDY

Eight months ago Margaret Hall met Barry O'Sullivan over coffee and doughnuts after Sunday-morning services at the Episcopalian Student Center on the campus of a small, private Eastern university. Barry telephoned Margaret two days later to invite her to an art movie. They quickly became steady dating partners. Eight months later Barry proposed marriage.

Her View

Margaret has always thought of herself as being rather independent. She paid her college tuition partly by working at a number of campus jobs, partly through a government education loan, and partly by maintaining a scholarship. In this way, she earned her B.A. and M.A. in French and German. She traveled with a girl friend to France one summer and toured Austria alone during another. After two years of teaching German in a city high school, Margaret enrolled in a doctoral program in comparative literature at an Eastern state university.

At the university Margaret worked diligently toward her degree and also developed an active social life. She especially enjoyed going out on Friday evenings for beer and pizza with a group of graduate students who met through the university's Episcopalian Student Center. Frequently, other events such as movie parties, picnics, or dates were initiated at the Friday-night gathering. By the time she had completed her four-year degree program, Margaret had both a Ph.D. in hand and a fairly good idea of what she wanted in a husband. She once wrote in her diary: "My husband should be a professional or university type who is self-assured, kind, friendly, and interested in other people and who has many interests and a genuine personal concern for me. I want him to be successful in his field. Of course, he should be someone I find personally attractive. He should be independent and interested in other cultures and international concerns."

When she was offered an instructor's position at a small, private university, Margaret moved into an apartment three blocks from the campus and began her new job and her search for a compatible person to share her life with. She attended various university and church functions and quickly met several people. She recalls the day she first met Barry. "His eyes had an appealingly direct look about them. He seemed to know where he was going. But he looked young. I was afraid he was mistaking me for an undergraduate. I was relieved when we started dating that he didn't mind that I am two years older. I'm glad Barry has completed an M.A. in sociology and wants a Ph.D."

Barry and Margaret have discussed their plans for their own future careers and their common desire both for children and for cross-cultural travel or work experiences. Margaret worries, however, that both she and Barry feel unsuccessful in their present work. "I keep telling myself I was hired because I was seen as the most capable candidate. And objectively I think I'm doing OK. But I feel like I need to grow up to my position, somehow." She worries that Barry may be saying that he wants a Ph.D. just to impress her or because she has one. Margaret believes that Barry will be an excellent professor. She has encouraged him to apply to the best sociology programs, even though this might mean they would be separated for awhile. She was upset when Barry was willing to enter a mediocre program in the same school where she was teaching just to remain near her. The two spend most of their waking and sleeping hours together, with the exception of the time spent at work. Margaret feels that Barry's gentle and affectionate concern for her is nurturing a new expressiveness in her. She treasures Barry's gentle lovemaking and feels that the loss of it would be the most difficult aspect of a separation. In spite of this, she has asked Barry for a one-year delay in their proposed marriage. She wants the opportunity to feel successful professionally and to see how Barry settles into his professional preparation without her help or influence.

His View

Barry has always considered himself an activist. When he was in high school, he worked in recreational centers with young people from poor families, and he joined a moratorium at his university in the Southwest to protest the Vietnam war. Immediately after graduating from the university where he earned a degree in sociology, he entered the Peace Corps. After two years in the Peace Corps, Barry decided to go East for his graduate education. Within a month of his arrival on the East Coast, he moved into a dingy basement apartment in a poor section of the city. Although he had no formal training in teaching, the superintendent of city schools awarded him a provisional certificate to teach the social sciences. He taught full time in an ancient school attended primarily by minority-group children.

In return, he was obliged to take a few credits in education each school year toward eventual full accreditation. Three nights a week he attended classes at the city college for his M.A. in sociology, and on Saturday afternoons he took the required credits in education. Although his schedule was full, Barry found time to make new acquaintances. He dated several women over the course of his two-year master's program.

When Barry and Margaret first met, it was not unusual for them to attend a movie, a concert, and a lecture at City College within the same week. They also enjoyed talking in a favorite restaurant and spending quiet evenings at his apartment or hers. At these times, they discussed their feelings for each other and explored their hopes for the future.

Although he has never formulated a formal list of criteria for a future wife, Barry says, "I always expected that my future wife would have *at least* an M.A. I want her to be a professional and someone who will challenge me to grow, both personally and professionally." He likes the fact that Margaret has international experience and friends; he introduced her to his family and friends as Dr. Margaret Hall, with a twinkle in his eye which seemed to convey both pride and a touch of humor.

Barry is supportive when Margaret describes her feelings of inadequacy at work. He reminds her that she is a sensitive and conscientious adviser to the undergraduates assigned to her. And he points to her careful preparation for teaching and her occasional satisfaction with a lecture as an indication that she is a good teacher. But he is increasingly unhappy with his own work; he feels that only a handful of his adolescent students are learning to apply the concepts he is teaching them to their own lives and experience. Many are mediocre students who admire and respect him, but a few are unruly and "unreachable, at least by me."

Barry is pleased that Margaret encourages him to prepare for teaching college students. He has applied to several graduate schools and has decided on one which is across the country from his present position. He was deeply disappointed when Margaret declined to follow him, but he agreed to a one-year separation *if* Margaret would promise to marry him the following summer. He understands that she wants a year to work on developing herself, but he is adamantly against any suggestion that she might need two years. With a frown and an expression borrowed from his Irish father, he said, "Opportunity has a forelock in front, but is bald behind. I'll wait a year for you, but not two. I love you with all my life and breath. But I need a firm decision from you. Now, are we engaged, or not?"

Interpretation and Questions

Given the criteria Margaret and Barry have for their future mates, do you feel they are compatible? Why or why not? Do you think they know each other well enough to make a wise decision about marriage? What do you think of their decision to be apart for a year? If you were Barry or Margaret, how would you expect yourself and your fiancé or fiancée to spend the year of separation?

STUDY GUIDE

Important Terms

dating
status system
mate selection
propinquity
endogamy
social class

cohabitation
consensual union
unmarried liaison
trial marriage
in loco parentis

Review Quiz

1 Dating serves a number of functions. Among them is:
   a to have a good time
   b to learn good manners
   c to rid oneself of sexual frustrations
   d none of the above
2 Most young people who date:
   a make formal arrangements
   b always go alone
   c date only one person at a time
   d are apt to meet as a group
3 The purposes people give for dating include:
   a prestige
   b security
   c being with someone you like
   d being seen with someone important
4 According to studies, desirable characteristics for a person one dates include:
   a good looks

   b attractive personality
   c good conversational ability
   d all the above
5 Going steady:
   a is no longer a common practice
   b is still an important part of adolescence
   c is discouraged by parents because it too often leads to sexual intimacy
   d is a good way to be sure of having a date every Saturday night
6 Which of the following statements is closest to the facts?
   a Most people would find it objectionable for a woman to ask a man for a date.
   b Attitudes toward sex roles are changing; researchers do not know to what extent it is considered acceptable for a

woman to initiate dating or make sexual advances.

c Most people would see no reason why a girl should not call up a male acquaintance and ask him for a date.

d Most girls are deterred from aggressive dating behavior by their parents' admonitions.

7 Which of the following statements is true?

a The noncollege males in Hunt's study (1974) had engaged in sexual intercourse by the age of eighteen to a greater extent than college males.

b Kinsey found in 1948 that noncollege males had more sexual experience than college males.

c Nearly twice as many women in Hunt's study who were in their late teens and early twenties had engaged in sexual intercourse as women in this age group in Kinsey's sample.

d All the above.

8 People are attracted to each other because:

a they are of different religions

b they are of the same race

c they live at a great distance from each other

d they are from a different social class

9 Which of the following statements is true?

a Opposites attract. People like those who are unlike themselves.

b Birds of a feather flock together. People are attracted to those who are like themselves.

c Beauty is only skin-deep. Looks are not an important factor in attraction.

d All the above.

10 A person has the best chance of

remaining married if he or she marries:

a someone whose politics are conservative

b someone who is about the same age

c after having finished school and reached the age of twenty-one

d all the above

11 Which of the following statements is true?

a Living together is no longer considered shocking to most people.

b Many parents condemn their own unmarried children for living with a member of the opposite sex.

c Living together is a commitment to another person which can be considered a stage in the process of mate selection eventually leading to marriage.

d All the above.

12 The percentage of students living together at schools where researchers have studied this phenomenon has ranged from:

a 0 to 10

b 5 to 15

c 10 to 33

d 25 to 50

13 Living together:

a does not necessarily mean that a couple share an apartment

b may mean that a couple sleep together several times a week

c may not necessarily mean that a couple have sexual relations

d all the above

14 The phenomenon of cohabitation has been explained by:

a the promiscuity of the younger generation

b the lack of commitment of people to each other these days

c the assumption of responsi-

bility on the part of universities for the moral conduct of
attending students

d improved methods of contraception and legalized abortion

Opinionnaire

Agree	No opinion	Disagree	
———	———	———	1 It is acceptable for an unmarried couple who are living together to have children.
———	———	———	2 Children should not be allowed to go out on a date before they reach adolescence.
———	———	———	3 Interracial dating is not a good idea.
———	———	———	4 A woman should feel free to invite a man out on a date.
———	———	———	5 An adolescent who does not date is missing a valuable growth experience.
———	———	———	6 In choosing a marriage partner, it is not important that a person have values similar to your own.
———	———	———	7 There should be laws governing who may marry whom.
———	———	———	8 All couples ought to live together before they marry.
———	———	———	9 Parents should not have any control over whom their teenage children date.
———	———	———	10 There is no reason why men should not date and marry women ten or more years older than themselves.

Exercise

Mate selection has sometimes been described as a funneling process in which eligibles are eliminated through a succession of filters based upon background characteristics. To see how this process works, answer the following questions honestly:

"Would you marry someone ————?"

POTENTIAL
MARRIAGE
PARTNERS

1   of a different social class
2   of a different race
3   of a different religion
4   much older, or younger
5   physically or mentally handicapped
6   with very different central values

If you answered "no" to any of the questions, you have in fact "filtered" certain persons out as potential marriage partners. Can you think of other filters? How do social expectations contribute to this process? For a more elaborate description of the filter theory, see Kerckhoff and Davis (1962).

Projects for Class or Home Study

1 Many computer dating companies will furnish copies of their questionnaires without obligation. Try to obtain some questionnaires. What information is requested? Do the questions touch on the characteristics that you consider important in a dating partner?

2 Social scientists are currently studying what happens when women take the initiative, ask men for dates, and make sexual advances. What do you think the typical male reaction to this would be?

3 Ask a number of persons, old and young, what they think about unmarried couples who live together. What arguments do those who are in favor of the practice use? What about those who are opposed?

4 Listed below are a number of qualities that some people value in a dating partner. Place a 1 before the quality you feel is most important, a 2 for the next most important quality, and so on.

_____ Physical attractiveness
_____ An affectionate nature
_____ Honesty
_____ Good conversational ability
_____ Wealth
_____ A good sense of humor
_____ Intelligence
_____ Considerateness
_____ Good taste in clothes

Suggestions for Further Reading

Austen, Jane. *Pride and prejudice.* (First published in 1813) New York: Dell, 1959.
Jane Austen's masterpiece describes mating conventions among the gentry at a time when the role of money and family background was discussed more openly.

Baldwin, James. *If Beale Street could talk.* New York: New American Library, 1974.
The experience of living together without marriage depends partially on how others react. In this beautifully told story, a young couple receive warmth and support from one family and hostility from another.

Blood, Robert O., Jr. *Love match and arranged marriage.* New York: Free Press, 1969.
There are different conventions governing the selection of marriage partners. This book contrasts those in Japan with those in the United States.

Cameron, Catherine, Oskamp, Stuart, and Sparks, William. Courtship American style: Newspaper ads. *Family Coordinator,* January 1977, **26**, 27–30.
The authors studied courtship through newspaper ads as a bargaining

process. The article reveals our marriage values by describing how people advertise themselves.

Macklin, Eleanor D. Cohabitation in college: Going very steady. *Psychology Today*, November 1974, **8**, 53–58.

Larger numbers of college students are forming partnerships and living together. The author believes that the practice fosters personal growth, maturity, and higher grades.

Roth, Philip. *Goodbye, Columbus.* New York: Bantam, 1959.

In this novella, Roth explores a passionate love affair between an upper-class Jewish girl and a working-class Jewish boy. The book shows how powerful background factors are in personal relationships.

Stafford, Rebecca, Backman, Elaine, and Dibona, Pamela. The division of labor among cohabiting and married couples. *Journal of Marriage and the Family*, February 1977, **39**, 43–57.

Women in both groups still do most of the household work, but cohabiting couples share more household jobs than married couples do.

Answers to Review Quiz

1-*a* 2-*d* 3-*c* 4-*d* 5-*a* 6-*b* 7-*d* 8-*b* 9-*b* 10-*d* 11-*d* 12-*c* 13-*d* 14-*d*

6

GETTING ALONG

The truth as I see it is that contemporary marriage is a wretched institution. It spells the end of voluntary affection, of love freely given and joyously received. Beautiful romances are transmuted into dull marriages, and eventually the relationship becomes constricting, corrosive, grinding, and destructive. The beautiful love affair becomes a bitter contract (Cadwallader, 1975, p. 27).

For eight years we had created a very exclusive marriage. . . . We had some disagreements—typical ones over money, sex, and children—but for the most part our relationship was peaceful, happy, satisfying. Our marriage was far better than we had ever imagined marriage could be (M. Paul, 1975, p. 85).

Two views of marriage, two extremes. The first is that of a much-married professional writer; the second, that of a marriage counselor. There is truth in each, but the great majority of American couples would probably describe their own marriage as lying somewhere in between.

What is the nature of this commitment? According to sociologist William Stephens, marriage can be formally defined as "a socially legitimate sexual union, begun with a public announcement and undertaken with some idea of permanence; it is assumed with a more or less explicit marriage contract, which spells out reciprocal rights and obligations between spouses, and between the spouses and their future children" (1970a, p. 205). As Stephens points out, there are a number of important elements in this definition. The first, "socially legitimate sexual union," means that sexual relations between husband and wife are sanctioned by society. The second phrase, "begun with a public announcement," indicates that the bride and groom make their new relationship public by announcing their marriage to society and its institutions—to relatives, friends, and neighbors, as well as to the state and, in most cases, the church. The third phrase, "with some idea of permanence," means that the couple do not consider their union to be temporary—it is neither a one-night stand nor a short-term relationship that will dissolve in a few months or years when either or both parties lose interest.

The final phrase in Stephens' definition—"assumed with a more or less explicit marriage contract"—is perhaps the most important, at least in the eyes of society and its institutions. The legal status of the marital contract satisfies two social requirements. Financial responsibility is fixed so that the state will not be left with the responsibility of supporting women and dependent children. The state also encourages marital unions in order to produce legitimate offspring and to limit sexual activity to the legal boundaries of marriage.

So, as Stephens points out, entering into a marriage means assuming a number of obligations. The groom, for example, is enjoined by the state to provide shelter, food, and clothing for his bride and any children that they may produce. The responsibilities of the bride, in return, are "to live in the home established by her husband; to perform the domestic chores (cleaning, cooking, washing, etc.) necessary to help maintain that home; to care for her husband and children" (Schulder, 1970, p. 147).

Marital Adjustment

[A marriage] is not so much a joining, with its implications of smoothly meshing two separate personalities into one unit, as a relationship with its implications of two diverse people trying to bridge the differences that naturally exist between them (Lasswell and Lobsenz, 1976, p. 4).

This statement, made by a team of marriage counselors, captures the essence of marital adjustment. In order to make their marriage a success, both spouses must constantly adjust so that the needs, wants, and expectations of each are met.

THE NATURE OF MARITAL ADJUSTMENT

What is the nature of marital adjustment? As Jessie Bernard (1964) points out, adjustment includes all those actions which tend to bring about functional changes in a relationship. Adjustment, then, is a process rather than a stable phenomenon; it means that there is continuous interaction between the spouses, "an interaction determined by the institutional

THIS COUPLE are among those rare and fortunate people who can look back on fifty-six years of shared experience.

specifications of the relationship, by the nature of the partners themselves, and by the quality of the relationship between them" (Bernard, 1964, p. 678).

The goals of adjustment are complex. In some cases, the goal may be immediate; for example, the wife may want to end a temporarily irritating situation by giving in to the husband. Or the goal may be some future reward, as when a couple scrimp so that the wife can finish her college education. Other goals include presenting a good front to the outside world and finding that elusive thing called "happiness."

The targets of adjustment in a marriage are the habits, attitudes, and values of the spouses. A husband may adjust his behavior to his wife's ideals if he gives up his habit of yawning and acting bored when she is trying to discuss an important matter with him. Similarly, a wife may adjust herself to her husband's recreational tastes by accompanying him to football games on Sunday afternoons rather than visiting her mother. Or both may change their intellectual values by reading more and watching fewer situation comedies on television.

PROBLEMS IN MARITAL ADJUSTMENT

Satisfaction in marriage depends upon the degree to which the spouses interact with each other so that the needs, wants, and expectations of each are recognized, respected, and satisfied. In the simplest terms, a need is a condition that exists when there is a deficiency of something. As psychologist Abraham Maslow (1954) notes, human beings have five kinds of needs which occur in a definite hierarchy. First are the fundamental needs for food, drink, sleep, shelter, and other physical necessities. Second is the need for protection against physical injury. Third come the emotional needs for love and affection. Fourth, each of us needs the recognition and respect of others. Finally, there are the needs for growth and self-actualization—needs which can be attained only after the other needs in the hierarchy have been met.

The self-actualizing individual is one who has learned to satisfy his or her own basic needs, rather than depending upon others to do this. He or she is supportive of others by being honest and constructive when interacting with them. Thus, the self-actualizing person can appreciate others for their sake rather than for what they provide in the way of meeting his or her own needs (Maslow, 1968).

Another approach to the importance of needs has been proposed by marriage counselors Marcia Lasswell and Norman Lobsenz (1976). Each partner counts upon the other to meet one or another need, and so the partners are mutually dependent. The more one partner depends upon the other for need satisfaction, the greater the dependency. Thus, according to this analysis, marital satisfaction depends, in large part, on how well the partners satisfy each other's needs. Satisfaction also depends upon the opportunities that one partner presents to the other to satisfy his or her own needs. It is important that each partner be made aware of the other's needs: "Self-analysis—finding out what your needs are, how well your partner meets them or how much you are frustrated by him or her in meeting your own—can yield a significant assessment of your marriage" (Lasswell and Lobsenz, 1976).

Many people tend to confuse their needs with their wants. Often they think of needs as being vital and genuine, and of wants as being quixotic and unreasonable. At times, it is easier for a husband to say what he does not want than what he does want. In many cases, a spouse will want something but will be unable to verbalize exactly what it is. For example, a husband may be "unhappy with the present situation," or a wife may observe that "the magic has gone out of my marriage." One couple, for example, came to Lasswell and Lobsenz because the wife thought her marriage was boring—"a grave without end"—but she was unable to pinpoint the exact problem. The following is an excerpt from one of her counseling sessions:

> WIFE: I can't live this kind of humdrum existence. Every day is just like the one before. Get the kids off to school, go to a job that's routine, come home, eat, watch TV and go to bed. The big excitement of the week may be a movie, if I'm lucky.
> HUSBAND (to counselor): Well, why do you think Sue has it so bad?
> WIFE: Well, what comes to mind is some variety—some surprises. I wish Dave would not be so predictable. . . .
> M. LASSWELL: What is "less predictable," Sue? Describe for me how you would like Dave to act.
> WIFE: Just not—so predictable. *You* know!
> ML: No, I don't know. Do you, Dave? . . .
> ML: And until we know what you want we won't know if the problem can be solved. It may turn out that Dave will see your point and that you both will agree that your position is valid. But until you let us know more concretely how Dave can meet your wishes, we aren't going to know if he can or will do it (Lasswell and Lobsenz, 1976, p. 9).

In addition to mutual need dependency and the identification and articulation of needs, marital satisfaction consists in fulfilling the expectations that each spouse has of himself or herself, of the partner, and of the marriage. The sources of such expectations include one's past experiences, one's goals in life, and one's values. Expectations can be simple ("I expect my wife to think about me often") or grandiose ("Our marriage will always be happy because my husband will always be a fantastic lover"). Not surprisingly, such unrealistic expectations can spell trouble for a relationship. In the early years of marriage, for example, problems emerge because the partners expect that their marriage will bring them continuous and lasting happiness.

SOURCES OF ADJUSTMENT PROBLEMS

Conflicting expectations of marriage constitute a problem in adjustment. In this respect, Jessie Bernard (1964) has raised the question, "Who adjusts to whom?" Ideally, one spouse voluntarily changes his or her behavior rather than being changed by the partner. But in real life, one partner often attempts to manipulate the other, to force change in the other's behavior. "Marriage may become an arena in which each spouse is attempting to make the other do the changing or adjusting rather than having to do the changing himself or herself" (Bernard, 1964, p. 681).

A study by George Levinger (1966), which shows that husbands and wives differ significantly in terms of the bases of their marital dissatisfaction, bears out Bernard's observation. Levinger found that such differences exist across socioeconomic lines. Levinger studied 600 couples who had applied for divorce. He examined marriage counselors' records and found that the spouses' complaints about each other could be placed into twelve definite categories. Among these were complaints about financial problems, physical abuse, drinking, neglect of home or children, lack of love, mental cruelty, and sexual infidelity.

The results showed that twice as many complaints were submitted by the wives as by the husbands. Not surprisingly, the nature of the complaints also varied. The wives complained ten times more than the husbands about physical abuse. Moreover, the wives lodged four times as many grievances as the husbands about excessive drinking and financial problems. In addition, the wives reported more complaints about neglect of home and children, lack of love, and mental cruelty. The husbands, by contrast, were more sensitive about only two matters: in-law problems and sexual incompatibility.

The nature of the grievances also differed according to social class. Lower-class wives, for example, complained about financial problems, drinking, and physical abuse much more than their middle-class counterparts. On the other hand, the middle-class women reported more charges about lack of love, infidelity, and excessive demands. "In general," concludes Levinger, "the evidence indicates that spouses in the middle-class marriages were more concerned with psychological and emotional interaction, while the lower-class partners saw as most salient in their lives financial problems and the unsubtle physical actions of their partners."

Another study (Cutler and Dyer, 1971) of sixty married couples who were attending college also found sexual differences in marital adjustment. Wives whose husbands violate an expectation react by talking about the problem, whereas the husbands take no action at all, adopting a wait-and-see attitude. As reported in the Levinger study, there are also husband-and-wife differences about different problems. Husbands, for example, tend to discuss openly questions about finances and money management, but not those concerning sexual intimacy. Surprisingly enough, the study also found that a negative reaction by one spouse can result in a positive adjustive response by the other. For example, if a wife complained to her spouse that he was not spending enough time at home, he would be more likely to respond by changing his habits than by arguing, complaining, or grumbling.

CORRELATES OF MARITAL DISSATISFACTION Are certain individuals or groups of individuals more susceptible to unsuccessful marital adjustment than others? Apparently they are. Karen Renne (1974), for example, studied marital adjustment in 5,000 spouses.

Renne came up with a number of findings, none of which should be too surprising. First, blacks with low income or little education tended to be more dissatisfied with their marriages than whites or people with adequate income or education. Second, couples who were raising children tended to be less happy with their marriages than those who had never had offspring or whose offspring had left home. Third, individuals who were chronically ill or disabled reported less satisfaction than healthy people. Related to this was the finding that those who reported being generally happy with life were also more likely to say they were happily married. By contrast, marital dissatisfaction was reported by those who drank heavily, felt isolated or chronically depressed, or had few or no close friends.

THE TWO MARRIAGES An interesting point is that of Jessie Bernard (1972), who views every marital union as actually consisting of two marriages— his and hers. Each of the two partnerships includes a separate set of needs, wants, and expectations. And the marriages of husbands are far superior—psychologically and socially—to those of wives.

In the first place, the mental health of married men is far better than that of their never-married counterparts. As Leo Srole and his colleagues (1962) found, the mental health of married men in all age categories is less impaired than that of single men. Moreover, Gurin, Veroff, and Feld (1960) found that nearly three times more married men than unmarried ones report that they are happy. There are fewer criminals among married males, and married men earn more and make greater career advancements than single men. Indeed, married men even live longer than unmarried ones.

For wives, being married is only half as good as it is for husbands, not only in terms of survival but for other reasons as well. As Bernard observes in her review of the research:

> Gurin, Veroff, and Feld, for example, found that more married women than married men have felt they were about to have a nervous breakdown; more experience psychological and physical anxiety; more have feelings of inadequacy in their marriages and blame themselves for their own lack of general adjustment. Other studies report that more married women than married

men show phobic reactions, depression, and passivity; greater than expected frequency of symptoms of psychological distress; and mental-health impairment (1972, p. 30).

Models of Adjustment

Most couples find ways to adjust to their problems so that their marriages are relatively happy, or at least not unhappy. Sociologists John Cuber and Peggy Harroff (1965), for example, identified five kinds of marital relationships, each of which can be associated with the presence of some prominent psychological characteristic.

FIVE TYPES OF MARRIAGE

Cuber and Harroff studied the marriages of 211 upper-middle-class individuals who had been married for ten or more years and who had never considered divorce. The researchers found in these partnerships five kinds of marriage. The first, the *conflict-habituated marriage*, thrives on tension and conflict, much of which is controlled.

A fifty-year-old male physician, married for twenty-five years, characterizes this type of marriage as follows:

> You know, it's funny; we have fought from the time we were in high school together. As I look back at it, I can't remember specific quarrels; it's more like a running guerrilla fight with intermediate periods, sometimes quite long, of pretty good fun and some damn good sex. . . . It's hard to know what it is we fight about most of the time. You name it and we'll fight about it. . . . (Cuber and Harroff, 1965).

In the *devitalized marriage*, all the mystery and spark of the relationship are gone. A marriage becomes devitalized usually some time during the couple's middle years. The partners spend little time together, have relatively few social encounters, and do not share interests and activities. They look upon the time they do spend together as "duty time," during which they entertain friends, share activities with their children, and fulfill community obligations. Some attention is paid by the wife to the career of the husband, and by the husband to the rearing of the children, but there is little real interest in common in these matters.

The *passive-congenial marriage* is quite similar to the devitalized marriage, the chief difference being that the partners have been apathetic toward each other from the beginning of the marriage. Again, as in the devitalized marriage, there is little conflict or tension in the passive-congenial marriage. On the surface, the husband and wife believe that they have much in common, but in reality they have little interest in their relationship. Usually, professional people who maintain this type of relationship are more interested in their careers than in their marriage.

The *vital marriage* is the exact opposite of the three types discussed above. The partners are closely linked psychologically—sharing and togetherness are the be-all and end-all of their existence. They must participate in all activities together for them to have any meaning. "The things we do together aren't fun intrinsically—the ecstasy comes from being *together in the doing*. Take her out of the picture and I wouldn't give a damn for the boat, the lake, or any of the fun that goes on out there." (Cuber and Harroff, 1965).

Finally, there is the *total marriage*, a type of partnership which resembles the vital marriage, except that the shared aspects are more numerous. There is no "pretense or show of unity to the outside world, and few areas of tension. Differences do arise, but these are managed in such a way that the relationship maintains its essential unity and vitality" (Cuber and Harroff, 1965).

The discussion by Cuber and Harroff emphasizes one important point: There is no such thing as perfect adjustment. There are adjustments in wondrous variety, each capable of producing stability, need gratification, and, more or less, happiness.

THE MARITAL BARGAINING TABLE

William Lederer and Don Jackson (1970) propose that marriage is a social system based on bargaining. These investigators have referred to the reciprocity or bargaining process as a system of quid pro quo, a Latin expression which means "something for something." In marriage, it means essentially the same thing as Scanzoni's idea of reciprocal exchange: If the husband does so-and-so, the wife will automatically respond in such-and-such a manner.

Quid pro quo behavior is a regularly recurring phenomenon among married couples. Typically, it is nonverbal and not formally recognized for what it is. Lederer and Jackson offer the following illustration of the way it works.

Suppose that a husband wishes to convert a spare bedroom into a study but is hesitant to do so because his wife thinks the project is too expensive. At the same time, the wife wishes to hire someone to do the housework, but the husband has refused because he feels that they cannot afford it. One day, the husband decides to go ahead with his plans for the study. A few days later, the wife hires a maid. "When the husband gets a bill for the maid at the end of the month, he goes into his now-comfortable study, writes a check for the maid (even though he previously thought he could not afford one), lights a good cigar, and congratulates his wife on how clean the house is. Something-for-something behavior has occurred—a *quid pro quo*—without spoken acknowledgement by either spouse" (Lederer and Jackson, 1970, p. 267).

Such an exchange is rarely a one-time event. It is part of a recurring behavioral pattern shared by the couple which serves to balance the partnership. The quid pro quo pattern is an attempt to assure that the parties remain equals, that one does not receive rewards to the other's detriment. The technique helps the couple maintain their dignity because both partners perceive this reciprocal behavior as just and satisfying. Once established and accepted by both, the quid pro quo pattern enables the partners to get through their days with a sense of security because both know what is expected of them and what to expect from each other. "Each has tacitly agreed to a behavior complex which he believes protects his own dignity, self-respect, and self-esteem in relation to the other party. Whether the actions are cruel or loving is irrelevant; both partners accept them, once the pattern is established" (Lederer and Jackson, 1970, p. 268).

Another feature of the quid pro quo pattern is that it is unconscious. As one wife observes:

> It must have happened very early in our relationship—we're not sure when—a subtle, unspoken agreement on how we would act with each other. Neither of us was consciously aware that we had developed a system, a set way of responding to each other, based around our fears of the consequences of being free and independent (Paul and Paul, 1975, p. 83).

Finally, a smoothly running quid pro quo system can be obstructed or unbalanced if one partner breaks the accepted ground rules. Such an obstruction may occur in the form of some outside influence or a change in the expectations or behavior of one spouse. The wife, for example, may make new friends whose ideas and lifestyles stimulate her. When she attempts to interject some of the new influences into her interactions with her husband, her behavior may upset their exchange system. "The predictable pattern is no longer predictable. Confusion and discord unbalance the relationship" (Lederer and Jackson, 1970, p. 269).

Actualized Marriage

As many contemporary researchers have noted, marriage is currently undergoing a shift from the traditional "institutional" type of relationship to one that emphasizes companionship. The *institutional marriage* involves a rigid, hierarchical structure that centers around the marital roles of the partners. The male partner plays the dominant role of husband-father-provider, whereas the female acts as wife-mother-housekeeper-child caretaker. *Companionate marriage*, by contrast, is based on equality, intimacy, and interpersonal interaction (Mace and Mace, 1975).

The fundamental problem with the institutional role-oriented marriage lies in the fact that the participants are concerned chiefly with performing their roles. The man, for example, may play his husband-provider role comfortably for years without ever really coming to know the other family members, who are also acting out their roles. In effect, a husband and wife who have such a relationship never get to know each other as persons because they are concerned only with each other's external, objective actions. They relate to each other on an I-It level, rather than an I-Thou level. Indeed, many marriage counselors have observed that it is not uncommon for couples to be married for fifteen or twenty years without ever really knowing each other (Regula, 1975).

The companionate marriage, on the other hand, stresses the value of interpersonal relationships. Couples involved in this kind of marriage are strongly interested in the inner dimensions of each other's lives—in the partner's ideas, feelings, values, and attitudes—rather than in external behavior alone. The couple are encouraged to develop interpersonal competence, which involves using their natural human abilities to control open-ended situations so that they grow in the direction of intimacy (Mace and Mace, 1975).

MARRIAGE AS PARTNERSHIP

Foremost among the contemporary thinkers who see the dissolution of traditional marital roles as signaling a new kind of marriage is psychologist Carl Rogers (1972). In Rogers's view, the abandonment of roles—roles dictated by one's parents, religion, or culture—is one of the threads that runs through all successful marriages. By throwing off these role expectations, a partner learns to live by "natural rhythms," to be himself or herself, and to grow as the relationship grows.

The role expectations of parents or social institutions box an individual in, and the relationship with the spouse either becomes stale or starts sliding downhill. For example, a young woman who had difficulty with her marriage says:

> You fall into a role even if you don't want to, which is so *awful*, of a husband is supposed to be this way and a wife is supposed to be this way, which is part of the reason, I guess, that I felt my life was over. . . . Dick is not likely to be a typical breadwinner husband and I'm not likely to want to stay home and clean house. So it put me in a big conflict because I'm thinking, "Well, I've *got* to be like this, I'm married, and I'm supposed to do this . . . " (Rogers, 1972, p. 43).

As Rogers observes, marriage is a cradle in which two individuals grow to an understanding of themselves, each other, and their marriage. The next element of a successful marriage is commitment. Both partners learn that they cannot reap any of the enriching rewards of marriage unless they are committed to each other and to their marriage. Commitment, then, is the second thread running through the successful marriage.

A husband and wife are not committed simply because they can tell each other "I love you" or say "We pledge ourselves to one another until death parts us." The committed partners see marriage as a process—a "flowing stream"—rather than a static contract which binds them and dictates the ways in which they can behave toward each other. Rogers defines commitment in the following statement: "We each commit ourselves to working together on the changing process of our present relationship, because that relationship is currently enriching our love and our life and we wish it to grow" (1972, p. 201).

Thus, each partner makes a separate commitment, but the work that is performed to make the marriage succeed is done by both of them. Together, the two must build a relationship of loving and living which focuses not on past or present difficulties but only on the immediate relationship. As one of Rogers's subjects observes:

> I haven't reached a goal or an end of anything, but I'm in the process of reaching it. And for me, it's just *being*, and it's not easy to do. A lot of times it would be a lot easier for me not to share some of the things that are going on with me. I think, "Oh, God, that's going to trigger this, which is going to trigger that, and as soon as I do that, you know, I'm in trouble, and our relationship is in trouble." I've always got to remember to share what I am *right now*, which is just being, and it's the *process*. And that works, and it's the only thing I've found that does (Rogers, 1972, p. 96).

The third element of a successful marriage, according to Rogers, is effective communication between the spouses. Commitment to the process of marriage is, of course, a fundamental prerequisite for effective communication. But there are others. One of these is risk taking, in which a partner decides to speak his or her mind about some troubling issue and in doing so "lays the relationship on the line." For example, the wife may say to the husband, "You know, honey, I'm not really satisfied with our sex life." When she does this, the wife is risking the relationship in order to change it for the better. Moreover, she is revealing to her husband a secret part of herself which he may reject or misunderstand, or he may perceive what she says as an accusation. Such a communication makes the person who has spoken vulnerable and often encourages the other to express his or her own sentiments about the matter.

The final element of a successful marriage is the realization that a satisfying relationship can enable one to become a separate self. What does this mean? First, it means that the individual who engages in self-discovery is continually attempting to understand his or her true inner feelings. Often, the person learns that complex and diverse feelings frequently conflict with what society says about the nature of such feelings.

Next, the individual accepts the fact that these complex feelings are a natural part of the self. By learning to accept the ugly and the beautiful, the normal and the bizarre aspects of selfhood, one becomes more of a person.

The third aspect of self-discovery follows logically from the first two: As the partners realize who they really are, they begin to drop the masks—the facades—that serve as their defenses. The wife "is not a frightened immature child, hiding behind the mask of a sophisticated glamour girl." The husband "may seem to be a living example of *machismo*, of supermasculinity, of strength, but he can drop that facade. Inside, he is often childish, dependent, in need of mothering, just as at times she needs the fatherly care which can mean so much to a frightened little girl" (Rogers, 1972, p. 207).

Next, each partner learns to decide the meaning of his or her own experiences rather than to accept the meanings that the spouse or society places on them. For example, traditional marriage requires that each of the parties not have any close opposite-sex friends (O'Neill and O'Neill, 1972). A wife should not cultivate a deep friendship with a man, nor should a husband maintain a close relationship with a woman. Yet one or both spouses may feel that such a restriction eliminates many people who are stimulating, supportive, and loyal.

An internal center of evaluation frees a partner from such constraints, making it possible to disregard the "shoulds" and "oughts" that society readily substitutes for internal values. As Emma Lewis notes: "A relationship between two people who try to live according to a philosophy or set of rules that goes against their nature will probably hurt him or her as well as others. That kind of relationship is certainly not 'free' or 'open.' I would describe it as 'masochistic.' " (1976, p. 133).

Finally, as one partner in a marriage grows into personhood, he or she will naturally encourage the other partner to do the same. Indeed, if inner growth is experienced by only one of the partners, the distance between the two can become insurmountable, and the marriage will probably be destroyed. But attaining one's individuality can be challenging, especially if the couple are raising young children. A young lawyer, for example, observes: "I think every young married couple knows that it's a struggle to maintain the quality of your intimate relationship when you have very small kids. It's even harder to find time for yourself, because then you feel guilty about shortchanging either the children or your spouse" (Jacoby, 1975, p. 126). As of 1975, about 180,000 couples had attended marriage enrichment programs.

Marriage Enrichment

As they have recognized the changing nature of marriage, many investigators have begun to abandon the traditional therapeutic approach to marital problems, which seeks to remedy the problems after they have developed. A new approach has evolved in which problems are prevented from arising by the encouraging of the growth of the husband and wife, both as individuals and as a couple. Such an approach is known by a variety of names, the most common of which is *marriage enrichment*.

THE NATURE OF MARRIAGE ENRICHMENT

Marriage enrichment has been defined as "the improvement of a relationship by the development of its unappropriated inner resources" (Mace and Mace, 1975, p. 132). In other words, a marriage-enrichment program offers a couple the opportunity to meet and encounter each other by increasing their awareness of themselves, of each other, and of their relationship. It uses the techniques of communication theory to teach partners about loving and learning to love. In this respect, then, it is an outgrowth of humanistic psychology, as developed by Maslow, Rogers, Fromm, and others.

The mechanics of marriage enrichment are quite straightforward. A group of husbands and wives—usually no more than six or seven couples—meet with a group leader for a specified period of time and participate in a variety of exercises and activities. The leader can be an individual trained in marriage problems, an unrelated male-female pair, or a married couple. The leader may play an authority role or may participate as a member of the group. The encounter can take place over the course of an intensive weekend in a motel, or the couples can come together at a certain number of weekly meetings. In one program developed by Robert Travis and Patricia Travis (1975), each couple collectively and individually discuss different aspects of their relationship, view films, and participate in various exercises in intimacy. At various stages of the program, each married couple engage in the mutual caressing of bodies and genitals, bathing, hair washing, and foot massage.

KEY IDEAS OF MARRIAGE ENRICHMENT

Some of the important concepts of marriage enrichment have been explained by Sherod Miller and his associates (S. Miller, Corrales, and Wackman, 1975). First is *awareness*, which basically means focusing on one's internal experiences—on feelings, thoughts, and attitudes. Each participant at an enrichment session is encouraged first to focus on self-awareness—on internal sensory, intellectual, and emotional processes and on how these are revealed in his or her actions. By becoming aware of themselves, the partners can learn who they are and how they feel. Each spouse is also directed to become aware of his or her partner's internal experiences, both by engaging in verbal communication and by taking the partner's role. A final form of awareness is the awareness of the relationship, which moves the emphasis away from the behavior of a single person to the interpersonal interaction of the two. The thrust of relationship awareness is to find the relationship's patterns—the ways in which husband and wife usually interact with each other in certain situations. For example, the couple are directed to discover whether both consistently state their feelings during interviews or whether one partner typically holds back his or her emotions.

A second important idea of marriage enrichment is *self-disclosure*, in which the partners openly and honestly communicate the feelings that they have become aware of having. Self-disclosure has been defined as taking the risk of revealing one's feelings and thoughts to another person who is important in one's life (Regula, 1975). Self-disclosure depends upon two conditions. First, the individuals must feel that an atmosphere of trust, acceptance, and compassion exists between them. Second, the disclosing person must be secure and have a high degree of self-esteem in order to overcome the fear of rejection that might result from self-disclosure.

Self-disclosure enables the partners to perceive each other's ideas, feelings, and responses to the environment. Mutual self-disclosure enables the spouses to discover each other's needs and how these needs can be met or frustrated. Most important, mutual self-disclosure helps individuals grow into self-actualizing people; by disclosing themselves to their partners they are enabled to get a better idea of their own identity as well as to become more intimate with their partners (Regula, 1975).

An important aspect of disclosure is that disclosure by one partner often encourages disclosure by the other. Thus, if one spouse reveals some deeply personal feeling, the other will most likely reveal something equally personal. The reverse, of course, is also true; if one spouse refuses to express his or her intimate feelings, the other spouse tends to behave in the same manner.

Finally, those who advocate marriage-enrichment programs believe that there are certain skills or behaviors that can be taught to help couples communicate more effectively. Individuals are encouraged to speak for themselves and to take responsibility for their own statements. Travis and Travis (1975) refer to this technique as using "I-language," which means employing the first-person pronoun to express feelings. In this way, the speaker assumes the responsibility for the ideas and feelings expressed. For example, Edward Stein (1975) asks his clients to express themselves in such terms as "I worry about . . . ," "I'd like to change the way I . . . ," and "I don't like the way you. . . . "

Another communication skill is that of using specific and concrete examples to illustrate why one feels as one does. And a final tool consists in using statements which verbally express what the individual is feeling at the moment. The effects that marriage enrichment has had on marriage have been summarized by Travis and Travis as follows: "In all the data to date, there has been a definite trend toward greater self and partner understanding, personal growth, interpersonal intimacy, warmth, appreciation, and development of the characteristics of the 'actualized' marriage" (1975, p. 165).

MARRIAGE ENRICHMENT IN ACTION

How does marriage enrichment actually work? Part of a twelve-hour course on the subject developed by Sherod Miller and his associates

(1975) has been described by Jane Brody (1976). In this course, a couple discuss specific marital problems in the presence of six or seven other participating couples and a leader. The program is designed to improve communication skills so that the couple can talk out problems in a constructive manner. During their conversation, the couple are encouraged to explore their feelings and perceptions and to attempt to see each other's viewpoints.

In one session, for example, a couple who had been married for eighteen years explored the problems caused by the husband's devoting excessive time to his business and neglecting his wife and home. The wife remarked to her husband:

> I would like to talk about the business and how much time it seems to be taking. I have the feeling that it's been pushing us apart just at the time in our lives when we should be able to do more things together. I feel a wedge in our relationship, and I'm a little frightened by it.

To which the husband replied:

> I'm glad you brought that up. I have also been feeling a certain distance between us, but I don't know why. I know that with the business making so many demands on my time and energy, I can't even think about doing the things we've talked about doing when the children were grown (Brody, 1976, p. 36).

During the course of their conversation, the counselor periodically interrupts to ask the other couples to criticize the way the couple were communicating. The counselor might ask the group whether the couple were actually expressing their true feelings and intentions or whether they were properly feeding back information to each other. The counselor might also ask whether the couple were avoiding statements that tended to blame, accuse, manipulate, or downgrade. Everyone is encouraged to contribute to the discussion. After the first couple finish their discussion, a second couple can volunteer to discuss a specific marital problem, and the rest of the group comments on the second couple's use or misuse of communication techniques.

The program offers a number of benefits to couples with marital problems. First, it gives them the communication tools that enable them to talk about their problems in a forthright manner. Second, it is a good leveler—it puts each partner on the same footing, avoiding the usual situation in which one is manipulative or aggressive and the other is passive or defensive. Finally, the program encourages couples to understand each other's position, and it deemphasizes the practice of trying to exert influence upon the other person to adopt one's own point of view.

SUMMARY

Marriage is a relatively permanent contract which spells out the reciprocal rights and duties between the spouses and between the spouses and any children they may produce. When a man and woman enter marriage, they must make a number of major adjustments.

The way the couple adjust to their new situation is determined by the marriage institution itself, by the personality of the spouses, and by the quality of their relationship. Thus, the marital satisfaction of both partners depends upon the degree to which their needs, wants, and expectations are mutually recognized and met. The happiness of the couple greatly depends upon the degree to which they satisfy each other's needs. Many couples, however, tend to hinder their adjustment by confusing their needs with their wants. Indeed, in many cases the spouses do not know what they want from each other or from the relationship.

Moreover, marital happiness depends upon the expectations each spouse has of himself or herself, of the partner, and of the marriage. Not surprisingly, husbands and wives have different expectations of marriage. One study, for example, showed that every marital union actually consists of two marriages—his and hers—and that his marriage is superior, psychologically and socially, to hers.

Most couples tend to adjust to marital problems in such a way that their unions remain relatively stable. Some marriages, for example, thrive on conflict, some on apathy, and some on sharing and togetherness. Other marriages appear to be based on reciprocity and bargaining, in which one spouse responds to the behavior of the other in kind.

An increasing number of Americans are abandoning traditional marital roles, seeking new ways to grow, and learning to respond to their own needs as well as those of their partners. Many of these individuals have forged successful partnerships which have a number of basic threads running through them. Among these are commitment, two-way communication, and the mutual opportunity for each partner to chart his or her own path to self-actualization.

Recognition of the shifting nature of marriage has prompted many investigators to change their ideas about marital therapies. Among the most widely used of the new approaches is marriage enrichment, which utilizes the techniques of communication theory. This approach offers the partners the opportunity to encounter each other by increasing their awareness of themselves, of each other, and of their relationship.

CASE STUDY

His View

Robert Sanderson met Carmen Blake in an Italian class during summer school at an Oklahoma college. Her effervescent conversations and folk singing provided him with a diversion from long and tedious hours in the biochemical laboratories.

For Robert, the attractive young woman was a source of companionship, support, and affection.

During July and August, Robert made love to Carmen in a small, rustic cottage at a nearby lake. He found her sensitive personality appealing and was delighted that she responded to his sexual advances. At the end of August, Robert sailed for England to study at Cambridge on a scholarship. He wrote to Carmen three times a week, and his fondness for her increased.

At Christmastime Robert scraped together the money for a trip to share the holiday season with Carmen and her family. He found Carmen somewhat despondent on his arrival, but after several days she brightened up in his company, especially after they became engaged and she accepted an emerald ring, her birthstone, as an engagement present. They planned to be married eighteen months after he earned his Cambridge degree.

In January, Robert returned to the gray, foggy, rainy cold of an English winter. Since mail does not provide the immediacy of a person's presence, he experienced an increasing sense of distance between himself and Carmen. During a tour of France and Germany the following summer, he concluded that he was not close enough to Carmen to marry her, and so he sent her a letter to break the engagement.

Shortly after Robert came home, he stopped by to see Carmen. He still found her attractive and wanted to date her, but he did not want to commit himself to marriage. Back in England, Robert discovered that he missed Carmen more and more, and in November he invited her to come to visit.

As a foreign visitor Carmen could not work, and Robert was pleased to have her all to himself. When they made love, he felt he could not ask her to use a contraceptive, and so he wore a condom during what they gauged to be her fertile period. They renewed their plans to marry in April during the Easter vacation. In early March they discovered that Carmen was pregnant. Although they agreed to marry, Robert felt cornered and robbed of his free choice.

During the first five years of their marriage, Robert secured three increasingly prestigious promotions as an industrial biochemist; each change of position involved a move of several hundred miles. Meanwhile, Robert encouraged Carmen to pursue her professional interest in folk singing. In their sixth year of marriage, Carmen wanted to move close to Nashville, the recording capital of country and folk music, in order to advance her career. For three weeks, Robert deliberated about all the economic, personal, and professional ramifications of such a move, but finally he agreed to relocate.

Robert is pleased with Carmen's success, but at times he wishes her career did not involve road tours. However, when she is away, he likes the relief from their petty disagreements and the chance it gives him to visit his own friends. Nevertheless, he does not consider her taking a month-long road trip twice a year an ideal situation. He does enjoy listening to her perform, even though he dislikes traveling from the suburbs to the downtown area in order to do so.

Robert tries to accept Carmen's absences, but he gets upset because he feels that she demands excessive emotional closeness just before she departs on a road tour and during their telephone conversations while she is on the road.

As a scientist, he prefers to keep his emotional expressions in balance. When asked whether he misses Carmen while she is away, he says "somewhat" or "to a certain extent." He knows that others consider him a success professionally and regard his marriage as happy. But he does not want to just "settle into" his relationship with Carmen. He sometimes thinks that perhaps the chemistry between them is wrong. He does not want their marriage to be dull, and he hates the continual squabbling; he wonders whether he should find someone more compatible while he is still young and attractive.

Her View

Carmen recalls seeing Robert in the summer school Italian class in his khaki shorts and thinking that he had "the neatest legs." But she was also impressed by his academic accomplishments. She says, "I was intrigued by intellectual people. I was thrilled to be asked on a date by someone who I read in the school paper had received a lot of academic awards. I think of Robert as the smartest person I know; you can throw Albert Einstein to the dogs. And my sorority sisters were enthusiastic about him, too." Carmen said she felt the need to see just one person because dating a lot of fellows distracted her from studying.

After having so much fun during the summer with Robert—the first man with whom she had shared herself sexually—Carmen missed him immensely. She was overjoyed with their engagement, and when Robert broke it the following summer, she was shocked. She was eager to pursue their relationship, and so she did not mind at all leaving her somewhat dull job as a travel agent to join Robert at Cambridge. She, too, felt her freedom of choice about marriage vanish with her pregnancy.

Carmen likes to have her feelings quickly understood by Robert. She plays practical jokes at work, but she desires direct, supportive communication at home. She says that what is important is not what is said but how it is said. She wants to be passionately in love with her husband, and she wants neither of them to do anything to turn the other off. She wants them to miss each other when she is away on tour. She needs to feel very close emotionally just before a tour; this sustains her while she is away, and she feels let down when Robert begins to withdraw before a tour or to talk only business during their long-distance telephone conversations. Before her last trip she proposed that they call each other at least every other night and discuss only personal matters. She also promised to return home for four days in the middle of every month to revitalize their relationship. They both have enjoyed this arrangement.

Carmen does not want Robert to feel obligated to see her perform, but she needs his support. She was greatly upset last week when he listened to only half an hour of her two-hour radio broadcast and then tape-recorded the rest, forgetting to turn the tape over while he watched a baseball game. She wants to please Robert. Last Thursday, when they planned to see a movie together, she rushed home from seven hours of rehearsal, changed clothes, and ate a little cottage cheese and tuna fish, thinking that Robert would be impatient. Instead, she found him leisurely sipping a whiskey sour on the sofa.

Carmen is satisfied with their sex life, but would like to be touched and gently hugged more even when they are not in bed together. Above all, she wants to be religious and to have a very personal relationship to God. She desires to be purified by a religious spirit and regards Robert's philosophical approach to religious topics as too impersonal. Sometimes Carmen feels estranged from their son, David, since Robert involves himself so much with parenting while she's at rehearsal or performing on a tour. Though she would like Robert to respond to her more on a feeling level, she values peace at any cost even more highly.

Interpretation and Questions

What effect might Carmen's pregnancy have had on the decision of the Sandersons to marry and on their subsequent adjustment? How did their being abroad alone together away from their families affect their relationship? What influence may the Sandersons' moving four times in six years have had on their marriage? Are Robert, the scientist, and Carmen, the folk singer, compatible? Do you think Robert knows what he wants from Carmen? What differences do you perceive this couple as having, and how would you suggest they resolve them? What is your reaction to Carmen's making long singing tours several times each year?

STUDY GUIDE

Important Terms

role
marital adjustment
family life cycle
conflict-habituated marriage
devitalized marriage

passive-congenial marriage
vital marriage
total marriage
marital bargaining
reciprocity

Review Quiz

1 Statistics for the past few years indicate that the marriage rate is:
   a increasing slightly
   b declining slightly
   c staying about the same
   d impossible to determine
2 In the United States, the institution of marriage includes:
   a a legitimation for sex
   b the idea of permanence
   c a public announcement
   d all the above
3 Initial adjustment in marriage usually centers around:
   a child rearing
   b self-actualization

   c role performance
   d marriage enrichment
4 Which of the following statements is true?
   a The partner who adjusts most in marriage is the husband.
   b The wife must make the greater adjustment.
   c Both partners make an equal adjustment.
   d Research has not yet determined which partner makes the greater adjustment.
5 The main sources of information for couples who are learning marital roles are:

a the couple's parents and knowledge of their parents' partnerships
b the couple's friends
c marriage manuals
d high school or college courses in marriage and the family

6 According to Abraham Maslow, the first, most basic needs in the need hierarchy are those for:
a self-actualization
b recognition and respect
c love and affection
d the means of physical survival

7 The lower their income, the more likely it is that a married couple will be concerned with:
a self-actualization
b recognition and respect
c love and affection
d physical survival

8 Comparison of husbands' and wives' complaints to marriage counselors shows that husbands are more dissatisfied than wives with:
a the couple's sex life
b the amount of affection shown by the spouse
c the drinking habits of the spouse
d the financial aspects of the marriage

9 Over the life cycle of a family, satisfaction of both spouses _____ after the child-rearing phase and before retirement.
a increases
b decreases
c shows little or no systematic change
d fluctuates unpredictably

10 Comparing married and unmarried women and men, we find that those who are generally happier and in better mental health are:
a unmarried women
b married women

c unmarried men
d married men

11 In the passive-congenial form of marital adjustment, the partners:
a have lost the vitality which was once there
b have been apathetic toward each other from the beginning of the marriage
c thrive on tension and conflict
d are closely linked in a pattern of sharing and togetherness

12 Marital adjustment is characterized by:
a reciprocity
b bargaining
c quid pro quo
d all the above

13 Effective communication in marriage is seriously hindered by the lack of:
a mutual commitment
b willingness to take risks
c agreement to abandon traditional roles which are no longer functional
d all the above

14 A common misconception concerning marital adjustment is that "two become one." A separate identity can be maintained if the spouse:
a continually tries to understand his or her own inner feelings
b learns to accept the desirable aspects of his or her own character and to reject the undesirable ones
c interacts with the marriage partner on the basis of roles
d does all the above

15 Marriage-enrichment programs had enrolled about _____ couples as of 1975.
a 5000
b 180,000
c 5 million
d 100 million

Opinionnaire

Who adjusts to whom in marriage?

Agree	No opinion	Disagree	
———	———	———	**1** If a couple disagree on the frequency of sex in a relationship, the disagreement should be decided in favor of the person who desires sex more often.
———	———	———	**2** Couples should decide who will do which chores by common agreement.
———	———	———	**3** Ideally, the jobs around the house should be the responsibility of the spouse who is best able to do them.
———	———	———	**4** All recreational activities should be shared by both spouses.
———	———	———	**5** The wife's career is as important as the husband's.
———	———	———	**6** Couples cannot live together if one member is religious and the other is an atheist.
———	———	———	**7** For major purchases such as furniture, a car, or a house, couples should take turns in having the final decision.
———	———	———	**8** Both husbands and wives should continue the same relationships with their friends after marriage as before.
———	———	———	**9** There must be a head of the family in every marriage.
———	———	———	**10** Certain aspects of the husband-wife relationship should never be divulged to outsiders by either spouse.

Exercise

HOW MUCH ADJUSTMENT IS NECESSARY?

The following game can be played by any two people, whether they are intimately involved or not. Try the game with several partners to get an idea of how much adjustment would be necessary to live with a particular individual.

Instructions: Read each statement to see whether you would agree or disagree with its intent. Avoid qualifying a statement by rationalizing that you would agree under some circumstances and disagree under others. Be honest!

Have your partner record answers on a separate sheet of paper. Calculate your agreement score by dividing the sum of the "Agree" column by 20. Agreement scores on each of the subscales may be calculated by dividing number of agreements by 5.

	Yourself		Partner	
	Agree	Disagree	Agree	Disagree

A Value congruence

1 Pornographic literature will be on the shelves in my home. _____ _____ _____ _____

2 If I (If my partner) become(s) pregnant before we planned, I will want to have (encourage my partner to have) an abortion. _____ _____ _____ _____

3 I will always refuse financial help from my parents or in-laws. _____ _____ _____ _____

4 My children will never be punished by spanking. _____ _____ _____ _____

5 Religious holidays will always be observed. _____ _____ _____ _____

B Sexual congruence

6 I would not be upset if my mate went to dinner alone with a member of the opposite sex. _____ _____ _____ _____

7 I may occasionally have sexual intercourse with someone other than my spouse or steady partner. _____ _____ _____ _____

8 I am willing to experiment with any sexual behavior which will not physically harm me or the other person. _____ _____ _____ _____

9 I will not discuss past sex life with my present partner. _____ _____ _____ _____

10 I feel that sexual activity can be initiated by either me or my partner. _____ _____ _____ _____

C Behavioral agreement

11 If guests stay one-half hour later than I think they should because I have to get up in the morning, I will ask them to leave. _____ _____ _____ _____

12 I will quit an unsatisfactory job even if neither I nor my partner will be working for a time. _____ _____ _____ _____

13 I will remember my partner's birthday with a present each year. _____ _____ _____ _____

14 My partner will have to do an equal amount of the cooking as long as we live together. _____ _____ _____ _____

15 I will try to go out for a social evening twice a week or more with my partner. _____ _____ _____ _____

D Money management

16 I will have some money separate from my partner's which I never have to account for. _____ _____ _____ _____

17 Saving for a house is of higher priority for me than buying a new car. _____ _____ _____ _____

18 I will always use cash, rather than credit, for household expenses and clothing. _____ _____ _____ _____

19 I will have the major say concerning how any money I earn is spent. _____ _____ _____ _____

20 Adding to a savings account will take priority over spending money for entertainment. _____ _____ _____ _____

$$\text{Adjustment score} = \frac{\text{no. of agreements}}{20}$$

Projects for Class or Home Study

1 Using Cuber and Harroff's classification of five types of marriage, try to classify the marriages of couples you know intimately. Are they (1) conflict-habituated, (2) passive-congenial, (3) devitalized, (4) vital, or (5) total? Do some couples seem not to fit any of the classifications?

2 Write down the marital roles for a man and a woman who married in the 1950s. Now draw lines through all those roles which are out of place in the 1970s.

3 Interview a man and woman (preferably not close friends) and ask about their main complaints and their main satisfactions in marriage. Did the woman express more dissatisfaction? Was the man less willing to discuss complaints?

4 Call a few institutions which sponsor marriage-enrichment programs. How do they compare in terms of cost, time, etc.? Would you consider attending such a program to enrich your present or future marriage?

5 Adjustment literally means alteration in order to correspond or fit. Many persons have aspects of self which they feel are unalterable by marriage or any other relationship. What attitudes or behavior do you consider not up for "bargaining" in marriage?

Suggestions for Further Reading

Anderson, Sherwood. *Winesburg, Ohio*. New York: Viking Press, 1919.
    Anderson's short stories about small-town America concern people who cannot express themselves. One story, "Surrender," is about a woman who never adjusts to marriage because she cannot communicate her needs to her husband.

Horn, Patrice. How to enhance healthy sexuality. *Psychology Today*, November 1975, **9**, 94–95.

The author describes a program which attempts to aid couples in achieving an exciting sex life. The program is not for couples with serious dysfunctions but can be viewed as an aid to sexual adjustment.

Medley, Morris L. Marital adjustment in the post-retirement years. *Family Coordinator*, January 1977, **26**, 5–11.

Marital adjustment is a never-ending process. This clearly written article suggests that adjustment centers around four dimensions: self-esteem, interpersonal commitment, availability of resources, and goal consensus.

O'Neill, Nena, and O'Neill, George. *Open marriage: A new life style for couples.* New York: M. Evans, 1972.

The authors contend that monogamy can be free of mate ownership, self-denial, and much else that goes with traditional "closed" marriage. Readers can confront issues concerning the question of identity in marriage.

Stack, Carol B. *All our kin: Strategies for survival in a black community.* New York: Harper & Row, 1974.

Marriage adjustment must always take place within the confines of economic necessity and cultural community. This study concerns marriage and family life among lower-income black families.

Answers to Review Quiz

1-*b* 2-*d* 3-*c* 4-*b* 5-*a* 6-*d* 7-*d* 8-*a* 9-*a* 10-*d* 11-*b* 12-*d* 13-*d*
14-*a* 15-*b*

7

MAKING MONEY

> Expectations about work in American society reflect a strong Calvinist ideology; we have inherited a view that it is good to work hard and if you do not work hard, somehow you are an inadequate individual (Veroff and Feld, 1970, p. 208).

This attitude is reflected in newspaper articles about top-level executives, which usually stress their long, hard workday; they never leave the office before 10 P.M. and are back shortly after dawn. The reader is impressed by the feverish energy of these individuals and is convinced that they deserve to be in positions where fortunes are made and where their decisions affect large numbers of people. It is inferred that straining to put in an eighteen-hour workday is virtuous in itself and that anyone so driven must be a genius at his or her work. In countless subtle ways, people learn to admire complete commitment to work, even if this requires self-sacrifice.

Work

Almost everyone works in one way or another, even those who do not have a paid job. To study the concept of work and how it affects family interaction, sociologists define *work* as an activity from which the worker derives certain benefits (Clayton, 1975). Among those benefits are:

1 Salary or income; an occupation that is regularly scheduled, around which other activities are arranged
2 A personal identity; the way in which a person's status or position in the community is recognized
3 A way of making friends or acquaintances outside the family network
4 A means of feeling productive, significant in society, creative

JOB STATUS AND INCOME

Ours is a mobile society that allows for changes in status. It is quite conceivable that an assembly-line worker who studied for a degree at night or conceived of a new way to speed up production could be promoted to an executive position. Such a promotion would involve a change in status since status is based on both the type of work an individual does and the income derived from it.

Berger (1960) divides the status derived from work into three categories. The highest category includes work with which the individual can identify and which is satisfying. The lowest is work understood as a "direct threat to self-identification, an indignity, an oppression." In between is work "in which one neither rejoices nor suffers, but with which one puts up with more or less grace for the sake of other things that are supposed to be important—these other things being typically connected with one's private life" (Berger, 1960, pp. 218–219). Industrialization has shrunk the first and third categories and expanded the second, where money is the major reward.

High-status jobs require skill and knowledge. In addition to a handsome paycheck, they offer opportunities to make independent decisions without constant supervision and such fringe benefits as the option of owning stock in the company, good retirement plans, and a chance to travel. These increments are offered mainly to people in management positions. But union backing also adds prestige to other, less glamorous jobs. Garbage men, for instance, have more status than others who do maintenance work because garbage men in many areas have a strong union organization.

The more education the main provider has, the more likely the family is to be affluent. Income data still show the effects of discrimination in American society. Black families have lower median incomes than their white counterparts in each educational category.

MONEY INCOME, 1974

Race and years of school completed by head of family 25 years old and over	Median income
White families:	**$13,816**
Elementary school: less than 8 years	7,501
8 years	10,011
High school: 1–3 years	12,080
4 years	14,226
College: 1–3 years	16,139
4 years or more	20,267
Black families:	**8,255**
Elementary school: less than 8 years	5,736
8 years	7,184
High school: 1–3 years	7,238
4 years	10,283
College: 1–3 years	13,220
4 years or more	16,434

Source: Adapted from U.S. Bureau of the Census, 1975, p. 396.

Workers in any category who perceive their jobs negatively may continue to fulfill the basic requirements of their jobs but may avoid taking a real interest in the work. They will maintain a psychological distance between their sense of self and the work they are doing. They will see their real lives as lying outside their jobs (Berger, 1960). Other people, however, may dignify jobs that some would see negatively and endow them with meaning; for example, a janitor might have an image of himself as "guardian of the house."

Work and Marriage

"I told Jerry I don't want him home for lunch," Betty Ford said upon retiring as First Lady (Hunter, 1977). Widely respected during her husband's Presidency for her honest and realistic comments, Mrs. Ford's remark reflects the way some Americans live in the second half of the 1970s. Her statement suggests certain conventional assumptions about the relationship between occupation and home: A vigorous man is not seen in his house between breakfast and dinner. To those with such a perspective, home and job are separate spheres, each dominated by a marriage partner; the wife reigns in the emotional sanctuary of the home and family, and the husband performs an economic function. A man does not perform his major activity at home, just as he does not bring his children to the office.

While many Americans remember growing up in a family structured along these lines, such a segmented approach to life is being replaced in many homes by a marriage in which the division of labor between husband and wife is less sharp. Nevertheless, the traditional approach is worth understanding for the light it sheds on contemporary American thought.

FAMILY VERSUS WORK

There was a time when father, mother, brothers, and sisters worked at home to provide the family with food and other necessities—a time when work was a part of the rhythm of the family. Today, home and occupation not only are located in different places, but also are structured differently. The more clearly defined organization of work is essentially bureaucratic, with specialized jobs, many different levels of supervision, and hiring and promotion determined by explicit impersonal rules and standards. Relationships at work tend to be impersonal and relatively impermanent, depending on job tenure. A jobholder is usually expected to perform one role or function. Interaction is determined by specific, formal rules.

Relationships in the family, on the other hand, are more general, invading many realms of experience. Membership is determined not by rules but by biology. Family interaction is personal, emotional, and intense. The family is relatively long-lasting, each family evolving over a period of time its own rules and rituals (Aldous, 1969).

Work and family life make different demands upon the individual, and frequently these demands are in conflict, causing tension (Holmstrom, 1972). Since salaries pay the rent and food bills, the demands of the job are generally considered more compelling than the demands of the family. Sometimes the employee is required to move to another neighborhood or city to retain the job or receive a promotion.

There is a tension that exists between the demands of work and those of family. Traditionally, the family takes second place to the job, since it is the job that provides financial support. The occupational system often requires an employee to move, favoring the person whose family is agreeable to the change. Work and family conflict in the emotional involvement of jobholders who are committed to their jobs and whose jobs, in turn, demand the most commitment from them. This is particularly true at the managerial or professional level and generally is less important at the lower ranks of the occupational hierarchy.

In the case of some jobs, there is an underlying assumption that the duties will be performed by two people. The husband holds the designated position. Frequently, the wife of a management executive must take on certain responsibilities, such as entertaining other executives and their wives. She is not listed as an employee of the company, but she is expected, nevertheless, to do her part graciously for the firm and her husband. Often the husband's opportunity to move up in the company depends on his wife's willingness to expend her time and efforts in this way (Aldous, 1969).

DIVISION OF LABOR

Although it may not represent the statistical average, the division of labor within the white middle-class family of the past fifty years has, until recently, set the pattern for the nation. The traditional middle-class family can be conceptualized as an economic unit. Not only does the family spend its money as an economic entity, but, more important, in the assignment of tasks to sustain the group it operates as a unit. In the traditional family there is a division of labor according to sex and age. The father works outside the home and is the breadwinner. His paycheck supports the family's economic needs. The mother works within the household. She performs all household tasks and takes care of the children. As the children get older, they too have chores to perform around the house.

Traditionally, certain household tasks are left to the husband and father. In most conventional families the father is in charge of the yard work and has responsibility for maintenance of the house. The wife usually takes the initiative in maintaining ties with the extended family and in establishing and sustaining ongoing friendships and social activities.

According to the traditional pattern of the separation of home from work, each partner also has the responsibility for specific areas and types of communication. The wife holds the family together and expresses the emotional affiliation of the group. The husband's specialty is impersonal communication. Veroff and Feld (1970) point out that in the traditional division of labor in the family, the husband is seen as largely responsible for adapting the family members to changing conditions in the outside world that could affect them. The wife's responsibility is maintaining relationships between members of the family. Popular humor characterizes the family division of labor: The mother says, "I am responsible for the little things, like bringing up the children and organizing the budget to fit our income. Father is responsible for the big things, like when man will live on the moon and who will be the next President."

Today, the traditional division of labor exists in fewer and fewer families, and it is no longer considered to be the model after which to pattern one's own family. For example, 43 percent of married women now are at work outside their homes. With both adults working, arrangements have to be made to compensate for the absence of the wife from the home. As we shall see, there are different ways of accommodating to this new pattern, and there are consequent advantages and drawbacks for the various family members.

Men and Work

To date, the work life of most men has not been changed to any great degree by the increase in the proportion of women who work. It is true that some men may experience competition from women on the job or in the job market. But to a large extent, their attitudes toward work have remained the same.

For most men, work traditionally has been a major area in which to prove themselves and define their social value. Today, with assembly lines and automation and the rise in the proportion of people who work for big business, fewer workers can associate their own work with a finished product, and thus many men derive less satisfaction from their work itself than from their paychecks (Veroff and Feld, 1970). But the sense of dignity and identity is still, in effect, dependent on having a job. The money becomes not only a means in itself but also a symbol of a man's worth and status in society and in his own family.

Studying contemporary American life values, Yankelovich observes:

> The breadwinner—the man who provides for his family is the real man. . . . For almost 80 percent of the adult population, to be a man in our society has meant being a good provider for the family . . . which . . . also conveys overtones of adulthood, responsibility, intensity of loving care for others (1974, p. 22).

THE CORPORATION MAN

When President Carter first took office, he let it be known that he was not impressed by men who worked late at night and on weekends. He felt it was more important for a man to be home with his wife and family. Can a corporation man live up to President Carter's high expectations? Might a high-level executive survive competition without taking work home? And would he be happy spending leisure hours with his family if that were possible?

Evidence suggests that managers have difficulty leaving work in the office. Sometimes evening meetings keep them at conference tables until midnight. And on late-evening trains to the suburbs of large cities, hundreds of men carry slim briefcases packed with company reports and other office papers. Even before the trains chug out of the stations, executives are making notations on memorandums, just as if they were at their office desks.

A psychoanalyst studied the lives of 250 corporate managers through a series of interviews and psychological tests. In some cases wives and children were also studied. He tried to find out what motivates corporation executives to want managerial jobs, what kinds of behavior are encouraged and rewarded within corporations, and what kinds of personal lives these executives lead (M. Maccoby, 1976).

Qualities that were most obviously prized were "ability to take the initiative," "pride in performance," "self-confidence," "open-mindedness," and "flexibility." Other intellectual traits were also approved. More emotionally tinged qualities, such as honesty, sense of humor, and loyalty to fellow workers, fell much lower on the scale of importance. Compassion, generosity, and idealism were considered to be the least useful traits among corporation executives in this study.

In another study, sponsored by the American Management Association, it was found that competitiveness is associated with lack of consideration for others, need for recognition and approval, and greed for power. These three factors were named by managerial respondents. Top management was criticized for sometimes "breeding insecurity among subordinates by being closed-mouthed and manipulative, and for withholding information needed by lower managers for proper decisions" (Fowler, 1977, p. D1).

Therefore, while "head over heart" may be useful to the corporation, this type of development obviously can create problems in family life, where compassion and empathy are so important. It is difficult for a man to be a detached and manipulative executive at the office and a warm, loving husband and father at home. Unless wives and children are also strongly attached to the idea of success, at the price of emotional malnutrition, the employee, in becoming an absentee husband and father, may create unhappiness for himself and his family.

THE BLUE-COLLAR WORKER

E. E. LeMasters, who studied skilled construction workers—carpenters, plumbers, bricklayers, and roofers, for example—found that for "blue-collar aristocrats," as he called them, work is still the central theme of life. The men he observed enjoyed their work. It paid well and was interesting because there were problems to be solved. It offered variety and a chance to be outdoors. Some, like this worker, derived great satisfaction from the results of their efforts:

> I tell you, Lee, I get a hell of a kick when I drive around town and see a building I helped you put up. You know the Edgewater Hotel down by the lake? I did the paneling in the dining room. . . . Sometimes I drive down there just to see the damn thing. . . . (LeMasters, 1975, p. 23).

These men were also found to derive pleasure from the interaction that takes place at work with their fellow male workers. The men ride to work together in car pools, they eat lunch together, and after work they may stop at a favorite bar for a few beers before going home. Many blue-collar workers find more companionship with their "buddies" than with their wives. They do not expect to have their wives as friends (Veroff and Feld, 1970).

Blue-collar aristocrats believe that the primary responsibility of a "good" woman is to take care of her children and her household. Conflict often arises, however, when blue-collar wives work, as they frequently do, at white-collar jobs—such as bookkeeper, telephone operator, or clerk. The women develop skills in interpersonal relationships rather than in manipulating "things," as their husbands do. Many of

UNFORTUNATELY, few jobs today offer the pleasure of outdoor work, demand the performance of meaningful skills, and give the satisfaction of tangible achievement.

them would prefer a more companionate than traditional marriage. One wife complains:

> If you ask me, it's a hell of a raw deal. The wife has to raise the kids, take care of the home, jump into bed whenever the husband feels like it—and lots of times she has to hold down a job besides. They say that marriage is a 50-50 proposition—that is a pipe dream if I ever heard one. Seventy-thirty in favor of the man would be more like it (LeMasters, 1975, p. 43).

MALE UNEMPLOYMENT

A man must work to participate in the family. Without some kind of job he has no status or authority. Research done in the 1930s showed that a man loses power and influence over the actions of his wife and children when he is succeeded by one of them, or by an outside agency, as the family's means of support (Aldous, 1969).

The world falls apart for corporation executives when they lose their jobs or are unemployed for more than a short period of time. It is akin to being thrown out of the family. A retired corporation president, now a consultant, said as much to Studs Terkel:

> When a top executive is let go, the king is dead, long live the king. Suddenly he's a persona non grata. When it happens, the shock is tremendous. Overnight. He doesn't know what hit him. Suddenly everybody in the organization walks away and shuns him because they don't want to be associated with him. In a corporation, if you back the wrong guy, you're in his corner, and if he's fired, you're guilty by association (Terkel, 1972, p. 409).

Blue-collar workers enjoy taking time off for such things as hunting deer or fishing, but when there is no employment, they feel a loss of control. They frequently become alcoholic; they and their wives fight because the husbands are underfoot at home, interfering with established domestic routines. Obviously, both husband and wife are also disturbed by the loss of income (LeMasters, 1975).

Studying the chronically unemployed gives some insights into the destructiveness of unemployment and its probably negative effect on the family relationships. According to Tiffany, Cowan, and Tiffany (1970, p. 92), "The profile of the unemployed group reflects their low level of

WHAT WILL happen to these workers when the unemployment checks run out?

self-esteem; they see themselves as undesirable, doubt their own worth, often feel anxious, depressed, and unhappy, and have little faith or confidence in themselves." How can such people have a relaxed family life?

Women and Work

"There is a simple way to define a woman's job," Caroline Bird wrote in 1972. "Whatever the duties are—and they vary from place to place and from time to time—a woman's job is anything that pays less than a man will accept for doing comparable work" (p. 82).

Despite job discrimination, nearly 50 percent of all women in the United States hold jobs. A large proportion of these women are mothers. In 1950, 14 percent of mothers of children under six had outside jobs. By 1977, 37 percent of such mothers were part of the labor force (More Children Have Mothers Who Work, 1977).

Women, like men, frequently cite the need for income as the main reason for entering the labor market. It is increasingly difficult for families to live on one paycheck. Inflation keeps shrinking the value of the dollar, and, in general, salaries have not risen commensurately with current living costs. As early as 1972, working women were already contributing 38 percent of family income in the United States (C. Epstein, 1976). There is no evidence that this contribution has decreased in the ensuing years. The increasingly high rate of divorce and separation has also forced many women to fend for themselves and their children, increasing their participation in the labor market. And a large percentage of women work because they enjoy it.

JOB DISCRIMINATION

> Women are largely confined to sedentary, monotonous work under the supervision of men and are treated unequally with regard to pay, promotion, and responsibility. With the exception of teaching, nursing, social service, and library work in which they do not hold a number of supervisory positions and are often occupationally segregated from men, they make a poor showing in the professions (Hacker, 1951, pp. 62–63).

This was the way Hacker described the female role in American economic life in 1951. Since then the number of women in the work force has multiplied, but their occupational roles and job status have changed relatively little, despite acceptance of the principle of equal pay for equal work. Employers have found many ways of circumventing compliance with this ideal. Salaries are given on the basis of job titles, such as secretary, administrative assistant, or supervisor. If two people do similar

THESE UNION officials seem to run an exclusively male club, but women are slowly breaking into the ranks of union leadership.

work but the titles of their jobs are different, they will probably receive different salaries. Usually the salary of the woman is lower than that of the man. "Too often, women end up in clerical dead-end jobs, keep getting assigned more and more authority and responsibility as their experience and competence increase, but with no corresponding title or salary increase" (Suelzle, 1973, p. 331).

Laws against discrimination have not stimulated any great movement of women up the corporate ladder. In spite of increased tokenism at upper levels, affirmative-action programs, and lawsuits, women seldom appear at the top-management level (Bird, 1972). In 1975, only 2.3 of all people earning over $25,000 a year were women. And among workers in general, the discrepancy between the wages of women and those of men doing the same or similar work is widening. The Bureau of the Census reported that in 1957 the median income of males was about $4700 and the median income of females was about $3000; in 1969 males' incomes were about $7777, and females' were about $4500. *Current Population Reports* (U.S. Department of Commerce, 1974) shows the 1974 figures to be about $8379 and $3079, respectively.

The Two-Job Family

With 62 percent of those women who work married, the two-job family has become the standard rather than the exception. Probably the most important consequence of the fact that both husband and wife work is that the adjustments to the situation are often experienced as burdens. This is so because society provides no easy solutions for such families (Holmstrom, 1972). All our institutions—occupational, religious, educational—are structured on the assumption that most women will devote their time and energies to the care and support of their husbands and children. The families whose lives are patterned in this new way find that they are "swimming against the tide." There are very few facilities set up to provide good child care in convenient locations at reasonable cost. The rigid occupational structure makes it difficult for either partner to modify his or her work schedule, such as by working irregular hours or working fewer hours. And in our mobile society, in which the nuclear family is the norm, regular help from a relative cannot be counted on. Thus the two-job family is left to make its own ad hoc arrangements. Satisfactory solutions for the whole family require much effort and persistence.

HOUSEHOLD TASKS

Among less well educated couples, there is a greater likelihood that both will accept the traditional segregation of male and female tasks. For the most part, working-class wives do not expect assistance with household tasks except in emergencies even if they are working. This attitude tends to change with increasing amounts of education. Even if we compare those with a high school education and those with less than a high school education, we find a pronounced difference (Tepperman, 1970).

There is some evidence that husbands whose wives are in professions perform significantly more household tasks than husbands whose wives hold less prestigious jobs (Hoffman and Nye, 1974). But in any case, it is generally recognized that "no matter how much help the woman received, the domestic realm was defined ultimately as her responsibility; it was not defined as a responsibility to be shared equally by both spouses" (Holmstrom, 1972, p. 155).

Some couples, however, are working hard to achieve a new kind of unstereotyped marriage. For writer Anne Roiphe and her doctor husband, housework is human work, not women's work, and both share the daily tasks. She describes their relationship:

> While the word "helpmeet," old-fashioned as it may be, sounds like something to be added to a tuna casserole, it is in fact exactly the right way to describe partners in a marriage. There is only one way that two working people, with assorted children, a large dog, two cats and two guinea pigs can

make a home more than a hovel and less than a prison, and that's by a division of labor according to each's inclination and fancy (1976, p. 54).

The author says her husband markets and cooks because he enjoys these tasks and can arrange to do them during and after his workday. He also takes the children to the zoo when he is able. In addition to writing articles, helping clean up the house, and taking care of the guinea pigs, she meets the children at the school bus every day, bathes them at night, and enjoys spending time playing Monopoly with them and taking them to museums.

The solutions arrived at by the Roiphe family may not be suitable for others. The particular arrangements made will depend upon the personal preferences and general situation of the family. For example, hiring help to do housework or to care for children is feasible only when the family income is high enough to allow for such expense. Arrangements for child care outside the home will depend upon the availability of services and upon beliefs about what is best for the child. The greatest problem, of course, is the care of children under six, below school age. About 50 percent of these young children in two-job families are cared for in their own homes. Care in someone else's home by nonrelatives—family day care—has become increasingly common. Such care, for the most part, has consisted of unlicensed and private arrangements with friends or neighbors in the community. The other alternative has been a licensed day-care center or nursery.

DAY CARE

In the 1960s, federal Head Start programs were provided for preschool children from low-income families. The goal was not only to provide a baby-sitting service for working mothers but also to enrich the educational and emotional experience of the children. Day care was also intended to release welfare mothers for training and employment. The popularity of Head Start programs stimulated an interest in the educational benefits of day care for any child, and a broad day-care movement began to grow. Other forces which encouraged the growth of the movement included the steadily increasing employment of mothers and the growth of the women's movement, which views day care as a right and a means of offering women equal opportunity for education and employment. The result was that legislation was written to support the development of quality day care.

In 1971, Congress passed the Comprehensive Child Development Act, but it was vetoed by President Nixon. This bill was aimed at providing day care that would foster child development, not merely provide custodial supervision. Health care, nutritious meals, educational experiences, and social services would be offered, and parent participation would be encouraged. Such services would be made available to all families, not only to the poor and disadvantaged, and would be subsi-

GOOD DAY-CARE centers not only are a safe and friendly depository for children but also offer an opportunity for the early learning of social and intellectual skills.

dized and supported by a federal commitment (L. W. Hoffman and Nye, 1974). When Congress failed to override the Presidential veto, educational specialists began to raise questions about how desirable it is to rear children in day-care centers. They were particularly concerned about what they perceived to be the high cost of running such centers. Others continued to believe in the movement and hoped to see day care established in the future as a right. Meanwhile, although praised by many families who have used them, day-care centers have not been made available to most two-job families (L. W. Hoffman and Nye, 1974).

THE HUSBAND

If the two-job family is to function successfully, the husband must do more than merely tolerate the situation. His attitude depends on the way he was brought up, his expectations for family life, his self-assurance, and his feelings of competence in his work. How adequate he feels as a provider and how seriously he views his wife's work also affect his attitudes. The husband who objects to his wife's working may feel that she should be available exclusively to meet his own physical or emotional needs. Men who hold high-level jobs may fear that their careers will suffer if their wives are unable to entertain frequently.

But many husbands can no longer afford the luxury of traditional attitudes, insisting that their wives remain at home. There are many advantages for a man whose wife works outside the home. A working wife shares the responsibility for providing the family with a living, thus lightening the husband's economic burden. A husband may take risks which he would not have dared to take otherwise, such as accepting a low-paying job with good prospects for the future. He has the option of doing his work as he sees fit without fear of the consequences of dismissal. Many men can work at jobs which will never pay well but which they find satisfying. Finally, of course, a man with a wife who works may spend much more of his own money on himself and may enjoy hobbies and possessions he would never otherwise have been able to afford.

In addition, there are psychic benefits. Husbands find that working wives are generally better companions, better informed, more understanding about their work problems (Holmstrom, 1972), and more likely to have "something interesting to talk about" than nonworking wives. This seems to hold across social-class lines and under different work conditions—part-time, temporary, or long-term commitment. In some cases the partners influence and benefit from each other's work or may even engage in a joint enterprise. But in any case, the husband seems to benefit when the wife brings outside interests and experiences into their relationship.

There is a possible future benefit for all if the attitudes and practices relating to the two-job family continue to become more positive and result in bringing about larger changes in other institutions. It is felt that the quality of life for men, as well as for women, can be improved. If efforts to change the occupational structure as it is presently set up are successful, men will be able to lead more balanced lives. Holding a job will require less compulsive, competitive behavior and less single-minded devotion. Individual human needs for creativity and fellowship will have a greater chance of being met when work is oriented toward service rather than toward status. "Men cannot be liberated until American institutions permit part-time or flexible work schedules and inexpensive child-care facilities. But men will not liberate themselves until they reevaluate the culturally entrenched meaning of achievement and success" (Filene, 1976, p. 217).

THE WIFE

What about the women who do make it to the top and achieve success? Women with careers—not just jobs—who want both marriage and a family have few role models to follow in carving out a new lifestyle. It is not easy to be a pioneer, and such women are under a strain to perform well in both roles. The most common complaint of women executives is that they need a "wife"—someone to take their clothes to the cleaner, run their errands, and entertain their business associates at dinner—in short, someone to do the things that the wives of most successful men do.

The two-career-family arrangement is hardest on women who want or already have children. Even though men do participate to a greater extent than previously in bringing up children, the responsibility still lies mainly with the woman. Many women cave in under the pressure and decide to shelve their careers "temporarily" until the children are grown. The result is that women earn lower incomes, work at levels below their ability, and withdraw from the labor market at the peak of their careers. "As long as there is no decent day-care system, no simple way of finding competent and trustworthy household help, and no backup from employers, women who want it all—marriage, career, and children—will have to face the facts: they've got to be superwomen" (Kron, 1976).

Along with the difficulty of making practical arrangements for carrying out household responsibilities, there often are also barriers in the form of criticism from relatives or friends who hold the traditional view that the wife who works is neglecting her husband and children. Some women also are beginning to realize that as a kind of backlash of having liberated themselves from the drudgery of housework, they have had to sacrifice certain pleasures associated with family life. And, in fact, not all women want careers—some would prefer not to have to take any job outside the home and feel that their role as homemaker is an important one.

In a letter to *The New York Times* on March 2, 1977, a woman reader defends her right to stay home and cook: "What makes cooking more tedious than accounting, washing dishes more gruelsome than automotive repair, and food shopping more provincial than keeping shop?"

It is not incumbent on women to work outside the home. But as one researcher sees it, people are becoming more and more agreeable to the idea that it is all right for men to participate in household chores and for women to work for self-fulfillment even when it is not economically necessary. "Under the impact of the women's liberation movement a far greater flexibility has marked the relationship between the sexes" (Yankelovich, 1974, p. 29).

Furthermore, studies show that the physical, mental, and emotional health of employed mothers appears to be better than that of their nonworking counterparts. There is some guilt and anxiety about combining the roles of mother, wife, and worker, but these are not severe. Employed mothers are more likely to enjoy their activities and relationships with their children than nonworking mothers are. (This is true only of families with three or fewer children, however.) Working mothers are less likely to have excessive expectations for their children or for themselves as mothers. Working women have a sense of usefulness, importance, and competence. This, in turn, means that they often have a better self-concept and more self-esteem than nonworking mothers (L. W. Hoffman and Nye, 1974). The working woman is less limited in experience. Ideally, she leads a more fulfilling life, balancing her time and her energies between family and work.

MARITAL SATISFACTION

How satisfactory are marriages in which both partners have jobs? Is there any difference in marital happiness between two-job and one-job families? In the 1950s and early 1960s, mothers working full time reported slightly more conflict and tension and less marital happiness than others without jobs. By the late 1960s and the early 1970s, this effect seems to have disappeared, at least in the middle-income family. Recent studies of lower-income families, however, reveal less marital satisfaction when the wife is employed. Marital satisfaction in the two-job family was found to be greater if there were few children at home, if the wife enjoyed her job, if the husband's attitude was positive, and if the husband and wife had advanced education (L. W. Hoffman and Nye, 1974).

These findings corroborate Komarovsky's study of blue-collar marriage (1962). She found that family acceptance of working wives depended on various factors. There was greater acceptance if the children were of school age, if the job was part time, or if the wife was working so that the family could afford extras. The men in this study took great pride in their roles as providers. However, their attitudes were changing. They were sometimes jealous of their wives' relationships on the job and concerned about their own possible loss of power in the marriage; they were disappointed that their wives did not live up to ideal images of homemakers. Nevertheless, they recognized that their wives needed the satisfaction of a job. The men were also pleased with the additional earnings of their wives (Komarovsky, 1962).

Among families where wives work, the husband's job takes precedence. This is true whether wives are professionals or working only part time. Family locale is usually determined by the husband's job. It is usually the wife who, like it or not, adjusts. Although Holmstrom (1972) found that many husbands' job-related decisions are affected by the job interests of their wives, in the final analysis, the man's job has priority.

THE CHILDREN

It has long been believed that if a woman works, there will be dire consequences for her children. They will run the streets, fall into bad company, become juvenile delinquents, or worse. But research does not necessarily bear this out. It depends on the circumstances. Working mothers who obtain personal satisfaction from employment, who have adequate household arrangements, and who do not feel excessively guilty are as good mothers as those who stay home to care for their children, if not better. Generally, working mothers encourage independence in their children. Working mothers will try to compensate for leaving the house every day by setting aside certain hours to be with their children and by planning activities that they can enjoy together. Increased participation of the father in child care has positive effects on children, too. In short, the picture of children as victims of maternal deprivation caused by the fact that their mothers work is not supported if the mother likes her work and child care is adequate (L. W. Hoffman and Nye, 1974).

The daughters of working mothers derive special benefits. They are much more likely to rate high on independence, achievement, and positive self-concept than daughters of nonworking mothers (L. W. Hoffman and Nye, 1974). Successful women in various fields are more likely to be the daughters of employed women. This fact is attributed to the presence of a successful mother as a role model, to the encouragement of independence, and to a good relationship with a father who

THE CHILD of the working mother can be quite fortunate. This woman is an additional loving person in whom a little girl can place her trust.

encouraged achievement for women and at the same time accepted femininity (L. W. Hoffman, 1974).

Sons, too, are often better off when their mothers are working (Holmstrom, 1972). In the traditional one-job family, all the wife's energies must go into homemaking, and particularly child rearing. The traditional American mother is seen as overinvolved, possessive, and overly ambitious for her sons. As a result, the sons can develop narcissistic personalities and feel driven to seek self-aggrandizement through their careers. The woman who has a life and a job of her own to manage is less likely to seek her own fulfillment in the careers of her sons.

SUMMARY

People derive status as well as income from the work they do. Today the job is structured apart from personal life. Work is bureaucratically organized and impersonal. Often there is a conflict between work and home. In the traditional family the father works outside the home and supports the family; the mother keeps house and brings up the children. Today, in contradiction to the stereotype, 43 percent of married women work.

For men, work has been a major way of proving as well as defining themselves. Corporation men tend to devote themselves to their work to the exclusion of their families. Blue-collar workers prefer the male society of their buddies over the company of their wives. For a man at any level, unemployment means a loss of status, of self-esteem, and of position in the family.

The proportion of women employed outside the home is higher now than it has ever been before. However, women's role in economic life has not changed. Despite lip service to the principle of equal pay for equal work, discrimination keeps women in the poorer-paying jobs, and the gap between the median incomes of men and women is widening.

The two-job family is now the standard rather than the exception. Members of such families must decide on their own arrangements for housekeeping and child care, for there are no ready-made solutions. Each family makes its own compromises with household tasks. With the shortage of day-care centers, about 50 percent of small children are cared for in their own homes, mostly by relatives.

The husband has much to gain when his wife works. He no longer has the entire responsibility for family support, and in many cases he is free to spend some of his own money on things he enjoys, such as hobbies or sports equipment. He also gains a more interesting wife. Most wives must juggle their energies between home and work. If the wife likes to work, her family will benefit from her outside activities.

The two-job marriage seems to be happier if there are few children at home, if the wife likes her job, if the couple are well educated, and if the husband is pleased with the arrangement. However, the husband's work requirements take precedence over those of the wife. Children are seen as beneficiaries in the two-job family if the wife likes her work, the husband is cooperative, and there is adequate child care.

His View

Mark Sadecki has been working since he was ten. He had a paper route for four years and then got an office job supervising the distribution of the papers. Before he was sixteen, he also worked in a small grocery store, a fast-food restaurant, and a jewelry store. From the age of sixteen until he joined the United States Public Health Service three years later, he was a clerk in a large grocery store.

Mark's father did not finish high school and works on a factory assembly line. Four years ago he was laid off for a full year. Mark's mother completed high school, but illness has prevented her from working. Mark recalls that many times his parents worried about paying the rent and feeding the family. He often stops at the grocery store after finishing his various jobs and purchases food, never asking his parents to repay him. Mark's oldest brother went to graduate school and became a computer analyst, but he has never contributed much to the family. Another brother presently manages a large hardware store and lives at home, but he gives his parents no money. Mark's sister, four years younger than himself, is also at home.

Starting with his sophomore year in high school, Mark excelled in his courses, and in his senior year he decided he would like to be a lawyer. He was accepted at an Ivy League school but was offered no financial aid. Mark elected not to go to college for a year anyway since he did not know how he could pay back a huge loan. In April he decided to join the U.S. Public Health Service as a technical aide for four years.

Around the same time, Mark was becoming serious about Eileen Dolan, a girl he had been dating since the previous summer. But in August, when he was preparing to leave for his training in Texas, he and Eileen agreed that they would see other people while he was away. Seven weeks later Mark telephoned and asked Eileen if she would agree not to date anybody else, and he was delighted when she consented. He returned home four days before Christmas and surprised her with an engagement ring.

Mark and Eileen set the wedding date for a year from June. A few days after Christmas they opened a joint savings account. They also discussed various overseas public health assignments and decided on South Korea because they believed it would be inexpensive. They were disappointed, however, when Mark arrived there in February and discovered that prices were relatively high.

The following July, Mark began taking undergraduate courses in South Korea through an extension service of the University of Oklahoma. His supervisors allowed him just $1\frac{1}{2}$ hours for a class at midday. Since the bus ride from where he works to the school takes fifty minutes each way, he found it necessary to purchase a car. He discussed this with Eileen, and they decided on an inexpensive used model. Since he does not like to be in debt, Mark had his paychecks sent to the bank, and he arranged for direct monthly payments.

In their letters back and forth Mark has worked out a budget with Eileen. They know exactly how much he will make, and they have allocated various amounts for housing, fuel, food, clothing, and other necessities. Mark is very pleased that he and Eileen easily discuss and agree on money matters. When a financial question arises, they lay their cards on the table, consider their choices, decide on priorities, and arrive at what they consider the best solution.

Her View

Eileen Dolan grew up in a relatively wealthy family. Her father works as an engineer and her mother has two master's degrees and has done labor organizing as a nurse. Her parents helped one son through medical school and a second through law school, and both brothers have since married professional women. Eileen is presently a sophomore in college and is working toward a combined doctorate in psychology and sociology.

Because of her parents' financial position, Eileen did not have to work during school. But since she wanted some independence, she began baby-sitting at the age of ten. At fourteen she started a volunteer program for hyperactive, retarded, and handicapped children at a large hospital, for which she eventually received the Youth Achievement Award as Outstanding Woman of the Year in her county. Following this, she worked at a variety of jobs—tutor, cook, waitress, and record-keeper for a summer lunch program—up through the summer following her high school graduation.

In January she was hired as a counselor-driver for the YMCA, a job she still holds while attending college. The children she works with are economically deprived, many are emotionally disturbed or hyperactive, and some are considered predelinquents by the courts. Eileen finds satisfaction in knowing that when the youngsters are really down, they turn to her. Occasionally, on Saturdays, she takes some of them to a movie and treats them to a hamburger. Some of her charges still call her even though they have left the program.

Eileen met Mark Sadecki at a party and began dating him seven months later. She was impressed by his attitudes and sense of values. Once when she asked him what might happen if they had a child and she wanted to return to her profession, Mark said they would talk it over and, if it would work out better, he would stay home with the child. Eileen was thrilled with his reply and with the fact that they were communicating so well early in their relationship. Eileen is also happy that Mark believes in being honest and direct about his feelings and plans because she feels that "holding back" eventually results in major conflicts. Because of her background, however, Eileen has difficulty understanding how Mark could grow up in such poor circumstances. Her mother once criticized her for dating someone who was not going to college, but Eileen defended Mark by saying that he was very bright and just needed time to get his head together.

Now that Mark is overseas, Eileen works and studies hard to keep from missing him too much. They write to each other daily and manage to call once a month. Last Christmas, Eileen's parents surprised her with a round-trip airplane ticket to Korea so that she could visit Mark.

From her jobs, Eileen has saved $2000. She has to pay for her own air fare to Korea after the wedding, and she will need to buy several items, such as a toaster and a mixer, that are very expensive in Korea. Two weeks before the wedding she had to send Mark air fare for the flight home because school tuition and rent had consumed his recent paychecks. Eileen was worried about their financial situation until last Sunday, when she was given a bridal shower. Her friends and relatives were most generous. Eileen now hopes that she and Mark will be able to live somewhat comfortably as students. She is counting on working part time in a nursery school to supplement their income.

Eileen envisions herself and Mark someday opening a home for wayward and neglected children. She would help the youths with any psychological and social problems, and Mark would handle the legal aspects. She wants to have three children after she and Mark have gotten themselves settled professionally. Right now she is very excited about her wedding and thinks she has made a good choice. Eileen and Mark are writing the wedding ceremony themselves.

Interpretation and Questions

Might the differences in Mark's and Eileen's socioeconomic backgrounds affect their married life? What differences are there between Mark's and Eileen's work experiences and attitudes toward work? Do these experiences and attitudes fit in with traditional views on marriage, the family, and working wives? What do you think of the way Eileen and Mark handle money? How will their way of communicating affect their financial future? Is this a good time for them to marry? What should their financial priorities be?

STUDY GUIDE

Important Terms

work

division of labor

corporation man

blue-collar worker

job discrimination

day-care programs

two-career family

Review Quiz

1 The sociological definition of work includes:
  a a salary or wage
  b social status
  c a personal identity
  d all the above
2 In industrialized societies, most work is characterized as:
  a that with which the individual can identify and which is personally satisfying
  b that which is an indignity and oppressive for the individual
  c that which is neither abhor-
  rent nor self-satisfying, but necessary in order to obtain a living
  d that in which craftsmanship is important
3 In industrialized societies, the relationship between work and the family includes:
  a separation of home and job into distinct spheres
  b the belief that men and women should have equal responsibility for both home and job

    c the expression of more intense personal feelings on the job

    d all the above

4 The percentage of married women who are presently part of the United States labor force is about:

    a 12 percent

    b 26 percent

    c 43 percent

    d 78 percent

5 A study of corporate managers showed that among personal qualities most prized by executives were:

    a compassion

    b generosity

    c idealism

    d the ability to take the initiative

6 A study of skilled construction workers, or blue-collar "aristocrats," shows a high degree of work satisfaction in those occupations because:

    a they pay well

    b the men can see the results of their labors

    c they can interact with their fellow male workers

    d all the above

7 In their marital lives the blue-collar aristocrats:

    a find more companionship with their wives than with their buddies

    b may be unhappy with their wives but have no complaints about marriage in general

    c believe that a woman's responsibilities are to her home and her children

    d have become domesticated and have lost their independence

8 Studies covering the decade between the early 1960s and the early 1970s show that:

    a increasing numbers of women are working because they enjoy work

    b few women are working because they need money

    c fewer married women now enter the labor force than formerly

    d the percentage of women in the labor force has decreased over the past decade.

9 Women, in contrast to men, have:

    a a higher rate of absenteeism on the job

    b less serious career commitments

    c less psychological ability for jobs requiring logic and planning

    d none of the above

10 Federally supported day-care programs begun during the 1960s have:

    a expanded in the 1970s

    b gradually become a right for all working mothers

    c lost federal support and come under attack by some public officials

    d been criticized by almost all families who use them

11 If the education level of a **couple** is high:

    a there is a greater likelihood that both husband and wife will accept the traditional segregation of male and female household tasks

    b the husband does more of the household work

    c the wife expects less assistance with household tasks

    d all the above

12 The two-job family can expect to face problems after a child is born because of:

    a inadequate day-care systems

    b difficulty in finding competent household help

    c lack of support from employers for time off

    d all the above

13 Studies of the relationship be-

tween marital satisfaction and two-job families have shown that:

a middle-income two-job families have lower satisfaction than one-job families

b in lower-income families there is less satisfaction if the wife is employed

c there is greater satisfaction in the two-job family if there are more children at home

d if the husband and wife have less education, there is greater satisfaction in the two-job family

14 Some of the benefits men may receive from having their wives work include:

a greater income

b having wives with more interests and growth experiences outside the home

c the possibility of working together

d all the above

15 Children who are raised in families where the mother works outside the home:

a have more negative self-concepts if they are daughters

b are more independent than children raised in families where the mother does not work

c have problems because their mothers have excessive expectations for them

d have feelings of inferiority if they are sons

Opinionnaire

Agree	No opinion	Disagree		
_____	_____	_____	1	Few women today find satisfaction in the responsibility and care of a home.
_____	_____	_____	2	Children are shortchanged if both parents work.
_____	_____	_____	3	A woman who works outside the home will be a more interesting partner than one who does not.
_____	_____	_____	4	A husband should be as prepared to move the household to further his wife's career as she would be to do the same for him.
_____	_____	_____	5	Two-job families will necessarily experience more conflict than those in which only the husband works.
_____	_____	_____	6	If a wife's income is greater than her husband's, trouble is sure to occur.
_____	_____	_____	7	Women who choose to work outside the home voluntarily should also expect to have primary responsibility for the housework.
_____	_____	_____	8	Unemployment is serious for a man but not for a woman.
_____	_____	_____	9	On the average, women will have to be absent from their jobs more than men.
_____	_____	_____	10	Husbands who become fathers should receive "paternity" leave so that they can help care for their infants.

Exercise

Many gains have been made in the past decade concerning women's rights. How much job discrimination still exists?

Ask a number of persons to read the following résumé and then fill in the rating scales below, using separate sheets of paper. Half your respondents should see a résumé with a female first name, and half should see one with a male first name (e.g., Laurence Smith and Laura Smith). You also may want to modify the résumé by changing marital status from married to single; see whether this causes a change in ratings. The applicant is applying for a high school teaching position.

Be sure to discuss with your respondents what their reasons for the ratings were. Do home and family responsibilities or the possibility of pregnancy influence women's ratings?

Résumé

Name: _____ Smith   Age: 26

Marital status: Married,
                one child

Address: 6400 Westland Road   Telephone: 666-6666
         Uptown, N.Y. 10101

Education:

    Fremont High School   Diploma, 1968
    Fremont, Rhode Island

    St. John's College   B.A., 1972
    Annapolis, Maryland   Major: Secondary education

    University of Maryland   M.A., 1974
    College Park, Maryland

Academic awards:

    Dean's List, 1971, 1972

    Phi Beta Kappa, 1972

Work experience:

    Graduate teaching assist-
    antship   1973, 1974

    Substitute teacher:

        Onataka County public
        schools, New York   1975

Interests and hobbies:

    Writing poetry, playing tennis

Career goals:

    Teaching and administration in secondary school

Assume that you are a high school principal and receive the above résumé. Rate the applicant on the following categories:

Poorly qualified	1	2	3	4	5	6	7	8	9	10	Well qualified
Low teaching potential	1	2	3	4	5	6	7	8	9	10	High teaching potential
Poor prospect	1	2	3	4	5	6	7	8	9	10	Excellent prospect
Low priority for hiring	1	2	3	4	5	6	7	8	9	10	High priority for hiring

Projects for Class or Home Study

1 Legislation has helped to decrease discrimination against women, older persons, and others. Look through your newspaper's classified ads. Does the wording contain any subtle biases against married women?

2 Make an appointment to go through a day-care center. The personnel in most centers are eager to answer questions about their programs and their philosophy of child care. Does the center have educational goals? Are the people working there safety-conscious? Are they interested in providing role models?

3 Many times working women find themselves excluded from neighborhood activities organized by nonworking women, whether deliberately or not. Conversations concerning children and the PTA often leave the working woman with little to contribute. See whether you can observe this phenomenon. What effect do you think it has on the working woman?

4 Assume that you are one member of a partnership in which both partners work a full eight-hour day. Make a list of household chores for each of you which you think represents an equitable division of the work to be done.

5 A large part of most men's identity derives from their work. Do you believe the same will be true for women in the future? Are there any work roles now which provide such an identity for women?

Suggestions for Further Reading

Burke, Ronald J., and Weir, Tamara. Relationship of wives' employment status to husband, wife and pair satisfaction and performance. *Journal of Marriage and the Family*, May 1976, **38**, 279–287.

This research report shows that working wives are better satisfied and perform more satisfactorily than nonworking wives. However, husbands of working wives are less satisfied and perform less well than those of nonworking wives.

Holmstrom, Lynda L. *The two-career family*. Cambridge, Mass.: Schenkman, 1972.

A sociological study of the division of labor and of competitiveness in—and of the occasional breakdown of—families in which both the husband and the wife work.

LeMasters, E. E. *Blue-collar aristocrats: Lifestyles at a working-class tavern.* Madison: University of Wisconsin Press, 1975.

A study by a longtime observer of family life of the cream of the blue-collar world. LeMasters observed these skilled workmen during their leisure hours, talked to their wives as well, and wrote of them with affection and respect.

Liebow, Elliott. *Tally's corner.* Boston: Little, Brown, 1967.

A study of black street-corner men in Washington, D.C. This book shows how working at marginal jobs has a negative impact on marriage and family life.

McGrady, Mike. *The kitchen sink papers: My life as a house husband.* Garden City, N.Y.: Doubleday, 1975.

A satirical account of one husband's role reversal. The book contains humor and insight.

Steinbeck, John. *The grapes of wrath.* New York: Viking Press, 1939.

What happens to a family when there is no work? According to Nobel Prize winner Steinbeck in this tale of the Okies in the thirties, they endure.

Theodore, Athena (Ed.). *The professional woman.* Cambridge, Mass.: Schenkman, 1971.

A collection of fifty-three articles on career patterns and discrimination in work. Some articles discuss the impact of work on marriage.

Answers to Review Quiz

1-*d* 2-*c* 3-*a* 4-*c* 5-*d* 6-*d* 7-*c* 8-*a* 9-*d* 10-*c* 11-*b* 12-*d* 13-*b* 14-*d* 15-*b*

8

SPENDING MONEY

Money is a tangible item; it can be earned, saved, counted, and spent for numerous goods and services. It is impossible to imagine a world without money—the era of self-sufficiency, when the majority of people lived off the land and clothed and fed themselves by their own labor, has long since disappeared. Even young children today know that money is buying power for toys, movies, and other luxuries. A child with money sees how easy it is to buy friendship and popularity; the child has experienced the subtle control money offers to those who have it. Money is the ultimate symbol of power because it buys what we value most—security, luxuries, escape from boredom, and the means to direct and control others.

Considering all that money may mean to an individual, it is not surprising that handling finances is often a major source of conflict for married couples. Rarely do husband and wife agree on how much money they need, how their money should be spent, and who should control the purse strings. A study by marriage counselors reveals that

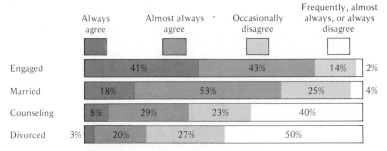

	Always agree	Almost always agree	Occasionally disagree	Frequently, almost always, or always disagree
Engaged	41%	43%	14%	2%
Married	18%	53%	25%	4%
Counseling	8%	29%	23%	40%
Divorced	3%	20%	27%	50%

DEGREE OF AGREEMENT ON FAMILY FINANCES
The degree of agreement on family finances is high among engaged couples. It decreases sharply thereafter, mirroring the difficulties encountered in handling money. *After Landis and Landis, 1973, p. 323. Copyright © 1973. Reprinted by permission of Prentice-Hall, Inc., Englewood Cliffs, N.J.*

only 18 percent of the married couples in their sample "always agree" on finances. Of the couples with problems serious enough to bring them to counseling, 40 percent said they "frequently or almost always disagree" on family finances (Landis and Landis, 1973). Thus, money can become an emotional issue between husband and wife, one that may trigger bitter arguments and even threaten marital stability. Handling finances is the ultimate challenge to a couple's ingenuity, emotional maturity, and respect for each other.

Feelings about Money

Long before marriage, attitudes about money have been formed by family patterns and childhood experiences. A child reared in an economically deprived family and one from an upper-middle-class environment may harbor very different attitudes about the importance of money. A boy reared in an atmosphere of economic austerity may rebel by demanding every luxury money can buy, or he may become exceedingly stingy, saving most of his income and denying himself and his family necessities as well as pleasures. A girl from a wealthy family may expect the material circumstances of her marriage to match those of her childhood, or she may willingly accept the challenge of living on a smaller income. Whatever the financial background, each man and woman will bring his or her own concept of money to marriage.

MONEY: A SOURCE OF CONFLICT

The change from courtship to marriage presents the first set of problems for newlyweds in regard to money. Not only do couples rarely discuss finances during their dating years, but they also usually spend freely at this time. Movies, restaurants, and excursions are all part of romance, and two young people who need to support only themselves feel free to spend money on their own pleasure. Once a couple marry, they no longer can spend in any way they choose. They are accountable to each other. With the first child, the financial picture takes a drastic turn. Their income must be stretched to cover the costs of child care as well as the basic necessities like rent, food, and clothing. Both husband and wife may feel the pinch keenly, and they may even resent their family status for robbing them of their former freewheeling life.

Agreement on how to handle money requires an essential agreement on norms, values, and goals. Let us take the case of Sharon and Jim, for example, who shared a common middle-class background but who had very different ideas about how money should be spent in a marriage. Sharon's childhood had been extremely home-oriented. Her mother had been a model homemaker who had made her home a pleasant retreat from the outside world and the focus of all family activity. When Sharon married, she wanted to create just such a homelife for herself and Jim. She cooked gourmet meals and decorated her house with great care. Her home and family were her first consideration, and she had every expectation of spending the greatest portion of the family income on them.

Jim, on the other hand, came from a sports-minded, fun-loving family who belonged to social and athletic clubs and did a great deal of entertaining. Jim had always loved these costly activities, and he expected to continue this way of life after his marriage to Sharon. He spent a large portion of his income on club memberships, sports equipment, and entertainment. Sharon resented these expenditures because she did not share Jim's enthusiasm for such activities. Jim, in turn, resented Sharon's nagging about money and her emphasis on their home, which to him was just a place to rest between activities.

Jim and Sharon quarreled often about money because money meant different things to each of them. Jim's income, although adequate, could not support two different lifestyles. Unless they could reach some agreement on how they wanted to live their life, Jim and Sharon seemed doomed to personal and financial problems (Dowd, 1971).

Sharon and Jim are typical of the many couples who find money a source of conflict in their marriage. According to marriage counselors at the Family Service Association of America, "handling finances is one of the major emotional battlegrounds of marriage" (Lobsenz and Blackburn, 1969). Counselors cite two principal reasons for problems among young couples: the use of money as a weapon to control or punish a spouse and immature or unrealistic attitudes toward earning, saving, and spending money.

Disagreement about financial goals is another area of potential conflict. However, this may be the easiest financial area to discuss because the goals are so concrete. A couple are quite likely to talk at great length about spending their money on raising children and having a family. Do they want to save their money for a down payment on a home of their own? Is one spouse willing to work while the other is being trained for a better-paying job? Or do they both want to work and spend their money on travel, hobbies, or political causes? What about support for an aged parent or a brother or sister who wants professional training? A husband and wife must find some areas of compromise on financial goals—both immediate and future—if they hope to keep their marriage running smoothly.

YOUNG MARRIEDS

When a young couple marry, their immediate financial picture is determined by several factors: the financial background of the man and woman, their age, and their education. For example, a young man or woman from an affluent family may bring a generous financial gift to the marriage. A couple in college or graduate school may even be supported by one set of parents until all education is completed. Such a situation will postpone the moment of financial truth, however, when the two young people are left on their own to support themselves.

One of the universal problems of newlyweds is a modest income combined with the heavy financial burden of furnishing a home and setting up housekeeping. Often there are college loans to be repaid. A study by the U.S. Bureau of the Census (1975, p. 398) shows that income is lowest when the head of the family is twenty-five or younger (income levels slowly increase until ages forty-five to fifty-four, when income potential is at its peak). In addition to age, education will affect a couple's immediate earning potential. College graduates generally earn more than high school graduates, although income will vary among occupations. A trained auto mechanic whose skills are in demand is likely to earn more than a college graduate with a B.A. in history and no specific job prospects.

But even when income is sufficient, young couples often suffer from inexperience in handling money and the desire to live above their means. Bob and Sandra, for example, had excellent financial prospects when they married. Both were college graduates with teaching degrees and the good luck to find jobs in their field. They earned identical starting salaries of $9000. In addition, Sandra's father, a well-to-do physician, presented her with a new car when she graduated, and he gave the couple a $5000 cash wedding present. With a joint income of $18,000 plus a good financial head start, this couple anticipated few financial problems. But neither Bob nor Sandra had ever budgeted money before; they really had no idea how far their income would stretch. Yet both expected to be able to live well on $18,000 a year. They moved into an expensive luxury apartment at a cost of $500 per month (plus $30 to garage Sandra's car). They opened charge accounts in every major department store, and they furnished their entire apartment. Since shopping was a favorite pastime, they enjoyed buying new working wardrobes, which Sandra supplemented with glamorous at-home outfits. Entertaining their new friends, evenings out at restaurants and theaters, and a vacation in the Bahamas all added up to a substantial amount at the end of a year. In addition, Bob and Sandra were surprised to find that everyday expenses took a greater bite out of their paychecks than they had expected. Besides food and rent, there were the costs of heat and electricity, car maintenance, telephone service, and health and life insurance. It was a real shock when the bills began to pile up, and the newlyweds discovered that not even two salaries were sufficient to meet their expenses. The problem was quite simple: Bob and Sandra were living a $50,000-a-year dream while earning an $18,000-a-year reality.

Managing Money

The example of Bob and Sandra illustrates that even two-income families can experience financial problems without proper money management. But generally, two-income families have a good financial edge over couples with only one wage earner. In most cases, a family's total net income (the amount of money earned after taxes) will be higher with two incomes than with one. Two teachers will earn twice as much as one, and an insurance salesman and a secretary will probably do better than one engineer. Of course, there are exceptions to this rule, but all two-income couples have one great advantage: The family is not dependent on a single income.

The value of two sources of income is perhaps most apparent to those couples who have children. If a husband and wife ever calculated the cost of rearing just one child from birth to marriage, including expenses for medical care, clothing, food, education, and extras, they would probably find the sum total to be staggering. In purely monetary terms, children are the ultimate financial burden to a marriage. To begin with, the cost of giving birth, including the doctor's fee and hospitalization for mother and infant, is now about $1200, according to the Health Institute of America (The Costs of Having a Baby Today, 1976).

But birth is only the beginning of a new set of expenses that continue to grow with the child. The costs of medical care, clothing, and equipment are obvious ones; in addition, a couple may find they need a bigger apartment or a new home to accommodate their growing family. The economical compact car may have to be replaced with a station wagon. And just when two incomes are needed most, the woman of the family will probably stop working to devote several years to child rearing. Even if a woman does continue to work, the family income will be drastically reduced by child-care expenses and the costs of household help, convenience foods, and other goods and services that help save time and energy.

It should be obvious by now that two people—much less a family with children—cannot live as cheaply as one or as harmoniously. As we have seen, money may become a source of marital conflict because it is an inevitable part of life. We must all pay bills, meet expenses, and then stretch whatever money is left to buy consumer goods and services which we feel will enhance the quality of our lives. Problems occur most frequently when husband and wife function separately, without regard to the joint financial needs of their marriage, or when inexperience and poor money management create financial problems which lead to personal hostilities. With children, there is an even greater need for coordinated spending by means of a realistic budget.

BUDGETING

A budget is simply a plan or guideline for managing money. It shows where and how money is being spent, and it helps a couple distribute their money to suit their individual needs. Each household budget will be as unique as the couple who plan it. One couple will allot a large sum for clothing and entertainment because their jobs require that they dress well and entertain lavishly. Another family with a child on the way may try to save as many dollars as possible each month in order to buy a crib, clothing, and other necessities for the baby.

A well-planned budget helps make the most of any income. Couples who do not work with a budget are often amazed to find their money simply leaking away. Perhaps they know that rent and car payments total a certain amount each month but beyond that they do not have the vaguest idea of what happens to their money—how much they spend for food, clothing, medical care, and entertainment, for example. A couple operating without a budget of any kind find it difficult to save or to reach the financial goals they have agreed upon.

A budget provides a realistic view of income and outgo, and it answers the most basic question: "Where is our money going?" Most couples are aware of basic, fixed expenses, such as rent and utilities, but until they use a budget, they can rarely achieve balanced spending on food, clothing, entertainment, or even phone bills and department-store charges—all the variable expenses that drain off income. A budget is likely to keep a couple out of debt by showing what they can and cannot afford.

The personal benefits of budgeting are equally important in easing money tensions between husband and wife. A couple cannot plan a budget without a discussion of financial needs and wants. In some cases, this may be the first occasion for a husband and wife to air their feelings about money and how it has affected their marriage. A man who thinks his wife is overly cautious about luxuries may see for the first time that his income simply does not stretch far enough to include a late-model car. And in a household in which shopping duties are handled by only one partner, a budget can provide the clearest evidence of rising costs of such things as food, dry cleaning, and clothing for the children—and thus settle any questions about "what happened to all the money."

IN PLANNING a budget, couples must determine whether certain items are luxuries or necessities. Available finances may require "compromise" buying, such as the purchase of a used car rather than a new one.

Budgeting opens a dialogue between husband and wife that may ease a lot of unspoken grievances. Planning together gives a couple the chance to reach an agreement on financial goals and to work together to achieve those goals.

PLANNING A BUDGET

Before starting a budget, financial experts suggest keeping a cash-flow record of all expenses (Gross, 1976). This is simply a record of how and where money is being spent, and it is usually an eye-opener. For a month or two, both husband and wife record every penny they spend and the reason for the expenditure. After a few months, spending patterns become apparent, and a couple can ask themselves whether they are using their money to their best advantage: Do they really want to spend so much money on restaurant meals, cosmetics, or clothing? In this way, the cash-flow record becomes a budget guide, showing where expenses can be cut.

Another useful diagnostic tool is a balance sheet of assets and liabilities. Assets are what you have, and liabilities are what you owe. Under assets go such items as cash in savings and checking accounts, stocks and bonds, the market value of your house, and even the approximate value of furniture, a car, or jewelry. Liabilities include any debts, outstanding bills, loans, car payments, and the balance due on a mortgage (How Much Are You Worth? 1976). With a list of assets and liabilities, a couple are ready to assess their net worth. If assets exceed liabilities, they are in good financial shape. If, however, their liabilities are greater than their assets, the family is in debt, and a budget can help. In this situation, all flexible expenses should be drastically reduced so that any extra money may be used to help pay off existing debts.

For convenience and simplicity, most budgets are planned on a monthly basis, since so many fixed expenditures are paid that way. One begins by dividing the net income (the money brought home after taxes) by 12; this is the exact amount available for budgeting each month. Out of this money, all bills and loans must be paid, and the rest will be juggled to provide whatever extras a couple want. Let us say the joint net income for a family of three is $15,000. Divided by 12, this provides $1250 a month for budgeting. Here is how a sample budget might look:

Fixed expenditures		Variable expenditures	
Rent or mortgage and taxes	$350	Food	$200
Insurance:		Clothing	75
Health	20	Medical care	40
Life	10	Entertainment	60
Car	20	Baby-sitting	40
Utilities:		Charity	25
Gas	25	Miscellaneous	50
Electricity	40	Savings	100
Phone	30	Total	$590
Car payment	125		
Car maintenance	40		
Total	$660		

The variable expenses provide the greatest challenge to any budget, for this is the only area in which money can be juggled around. If our hypothetical couple are expecting another child and want to increase their savings by $20 a month, they will have to cut back on clothing or entertainment. If the rent is raised, the extra money will have to come from the variable expenses. To work properly, a budget should be flexible, changing with a couple's needs, growing with a growing family, and adjusting to salary increases, salary cutbacks, or the demands of inflation. Without a budget, a couple are likely to spend money impulsively and run short when a large quarterly payment or credit-card bill is due. With a realistic, flexible budget, they have a chance to meet their expenses, stay out of debt, and perhaps find the money to buy whatever luxuries are most meaningful to them.

HEALTH INSURANCE

One of the variable expenses that can actually impoverish a family, whether or not they have a budget, is illness. In the 1970s, medical-care

MEDICAL-CARE PRICES, AVERAGE ANNUAL CONSUMER COSTS

	March 1975	Dec 1975	March 1976
Physicians' fees	165	178	184
Semiprivate hospital rooms (daily)	228	249	262
Drugs and prescriptions	117	122	124
Dentists' fees	159	166	169

Source: U.S. Bureau of the Census, 1976c, p. 24.

costs have risen faster than the prices of all consumer goods and services combined. The cost of a semiprivate hospital room averaged $262 per day in March 1976, and this has been the fastest-rising item in medical services since 1971. Prescription costs, too, have risen tremendously, reaching an annual rate of increase of 7.4 percent in 1975 (U.S. Bureau of the Census, 1976c, p. 24). The result is that the cost of medical care has become so prohibitive that few families can afford to pay for a major illness, an operation, or even a hospital stay without help from health insurance.

Medical-care prices have been among the most rapidly rising consumer-goods prices in recent years, as is shown in the accompanying table.

Health insurance plans such as those of the nonprofit organizations Blue Cross and Blue Shield help to defray hospital bills and doctors' fees during a hospital stay. These organizations offer several different plans that provide varying amounts of coverage. A variety of health insurance plans are available from private insurance companies. Many of these plans will pay the beneficiary a sum of money for each day of illness under specified conditions.

The nonprofit health insurance organizations are the most widely used, since the profit-making health insurance plans usually cost more or have fewer benefits. Thousands of physicians and hospitals across the country participate in the nonprofit organizations. This minimizes red tape and the need for financial references and helps facilitate hospital admittance for the patient. Also, many companies and employers partici-pate in group Blue Cross/Blue Shield plans and pay part or all of the cost of coverage for their employees. The private health plans also offer group rates and are bought by many companies for their employees. Any group accident and sickness insurance plan is always the least expensive insurance available (Lasser and Porter, 1961). If a company, employer, or other organization offers a group health insurance plan including cover-age for children, a family would be wise to take advantage of this opportunity. Individual plans are almost always more expensive than group plans, or coverage is less complete, and the buyer must be wary of deceptive advertising or vague and misleading claims (Nuccio, 1967).

One popular form of personal insurance is *major medical*, known in the business as "tragedy" insurance. Major medical often takes over when other policies end, providing coverage for serious accidents and long illnesses. There is usually a deductible clause, ranging from $50 to $1000; beyond that amount, the insurance company may provide benefits as high as $4000 to $20,000 (Nuccio, 1967).

The Credit Game: An American Dilemma

Jim and Barbara were one couple who never argued about money. Both had grown up in blue-collar, middle-class homes, where there were few luxuries but always plenty of food to eat and decent clothes to wear. They met in college, where both worked hard at part-time jobs to help finance their education. When they fell in love and decided to marry, they agreed to wait until Barbara graduated so that they could count on two incomes and start off on a financially sound basis. But their practicality ended there. Once married, their hunger for all the luxuries they had never known during childhood and adolescence overwhelmed their better judgment. Barbara had an excellent job as a medical secretary, earning nearly $10,000 a year. Jim made slightly less as a management trainee at a large department store. With a combined annual income of $19,000, this couple felt rich; they saw no reason to delay buying all the wonderful things they wanted so badly.

It was thrilling for Barbara, who had always bought her clothes at discount stores, to open charge accounts in all the finest department stores, and Jim encouraged her to make expensive wardrobe purchases. Next the couple purchased a sports car with a number of options. They could not pay cash because they had no savings, but the salesman was glad to sell them an expensive model on time, with "leisurely payments they could easily afford." Jim took out bank credit cards and charged all the sports equipment he longed to have. He treated Barbara to fancy dinners at high-priced restaurants and to a two-week trip to Spain—the couple's first real vacation together.

With credit cards in hand, Jim and Barbara went on a year-long spending spree. Each month they paid the "minimum balance due" on each credit card, and the finance charges began to build. Without a budget, they had no idea they were living significantly beyond their means. Two years later, Barbara gave birth to a son, and now their problems really became serious. Barbara stopped working, which meant a drastic cut in the family's income just at the time when extra money was needed most. Jim and Barbara were so heavily in debt by now that they had to take out a loan just to cover doctor and hospital costs for the birth of their son. Medical insurance pays only a small portion of the cost of pregnancy, on the theory that it is voluntary and therefore budgetable (The Costs of Having a Baby Today, 1976).

At this point, Barbara and Jim owed more money than they could possibly pay off in any one month. They let car and furniture payments slide for a few months so that they could catch up on department-store bills, but soon they had to borrow more money to pay their most pressing creditors. They owed hundreds of dollars in interest payments alone and had absolutely no savings to fall back on. What had begun as an honest desire to live well and enjoy all that money could buy soon ended in a nightmare of bills, debts, and angry creditors.

THE CREDIT TRAP

Buying on credit has become an American way of life. Over 190 billion dollars' worth of consumer credit was extended in 1975 (Don't Let the Credit Pushers Trap You, 1976). About one-third of all households in the United States use one or both of the two major bank credit cards. Seven out of ten holders of bank credit cards use the "minimum payment" feature which leads to finance charges (Don't Let the Credit Pushers Trap You, 1976). This is just one of many credit traps. A credit-card owner must distinguish between "previous balance," "new balance," and "minimum payment due" or "amount now due" on each monthly bill. This last item is always the smallest. If, for example, the "new balance" on a department-store bill is $150, the "minimum amount due" may be as low as $30. Paying the $30 fulfills the bill requirements. The only catch is that now a finance charge (usually between 1 and 1.5 percent per month) is added on the unpaid balance of $120. If this payment pattern is kept up for a number of months, the finance charges can become almost as burdensome as the price of the original merchandise purchased.

There are numerous psychological traps operating behind credit buying. A credit-card holder enjoys immediate gratification through immediate purchasing power. No more gazing in store windows, longing for the day when enough money has been saved for the new living-room furniture. Buy it now, enjoy it now, and worry about paying for it tomorrow—these are the powerful incentives operating behind credit buying. Using credit is also easy, fast, and convenient. Department stores cater to credit customers, mailing them glossy brochures, signaling them before every major sale, and even offering special treatment at the store itself.

Since credit is such an essential aspect of the American economy, it would be unrealistic to expect that a family would never take advantage of it. Credit is best used for major purchases for which the buyer simply could not pay cash. Buying a home or condominium is the most obvious example and is a very good use of credit, particularly in an inflationary period. For many couples, a home or apartment represents their single most valuable asset, and one that is likely to increase steadily in value over the years as property values rise with inflation (How Much Are You Worth? 1976). If a car is necessary for commuting to work or for getting from place to place in the suburbs, it may be just as wise to finance the purchase of the car and enjoy it when it is needed most. And department-store credit cards can help a homemaker buy clothing and furniture on sale.

But for many couples, the lure of the credit card is just too hard to resist. Some people are truly "spendaholics"—they are happy only if they can buy something, and it is very difficult for them to walk through a store without making a purchase. A credit card in the hands of a spendaholic is a dangerous weapon that can easily lead to debt.

A cash-only policy is a sensible budget idea for a family with too many debts and bills. Paying cash may not always be feasible, but it is one great way to simplify income and outgo—with cash, you can spend only what you have.

Loans

Even a well-budgeted family may find that available cash, savings, and income often are not enough to cover unusual financial needs. When a major purchase or expense arises—for example, a home, a car, or a college education—the family will probably look to an outside source for financial help in the form of a loan. All loans through formal institutions are expensive because the borrower is charged interest on the money used, with rates ranging from 5 to 30 percent and more. Because rates vary greatly among lending institutions and according to the type of loan offered, it pays to shop around and consider all options before borrowing (Quinn, 1976).

Credit unions, which are membership groups established by certain unions, employers, or organizations, are a good source of loans for members. Interest rates are usually low, and loans may be paid back slowly, without penalty, or through payroll deductions.

Savings banks and *savings and loan associations* have limited lending power, perhaps offering personal loans or passbook loans. Interest rates at these institutions are generally slightly lower than those at commercial banks. Any savings bank depositor can get a passbook loan at a low rate of interest. This means that a depositor will borrow his or her own money and still earn interest on whatever remains in the account. Since the bank will lend only up to the amount already in the savings account, it is generally wiser to withdraw and use the money than to borrow against it. However, if the rate of interest paid by the bank is relatively high and the savings account is for educational or retirement purposes, it might be better to borrow against savings.

Commercial banks are the largest source of loans, offering any kind of loan an individual may qualify for. Interest rates will vary greatly according to the type of loan and the qualifications of the individual who is borrowing the money. The criteria for assessing the borrower's qualifications may include his or her income and credit rating and the security or collateral offered.

Home mortgages are probably the most common loan sought by married couples. When a couple buy a house or condominium for $45,000 with a cash down payment of $5000, they then have to borrow the

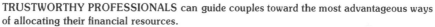

TRUSTWORTHY PROFESSIONALS can guide couples toward the most advantageous ways of allocating their financial resources.

remaining $40,000. A commercial bank will lend the couple the $40,000 using the house as security; if they cannot meet the payments, the bank can legally assume ownership of the house.

Interest rates on mortgage loans depend on several factors. Mortgage rates vary from year to year according to real estate values, the area of the country, and the prime rate—a fluctuating rate, controlled by law, which is the lowest rate a bank can charge any borrower. The amount of money used as a down payment will also affect the interest rate. A bank is likely to charge a lower rate to an individual who can put up more money. The ability to make a large down payment assures the bank of the individual's financial worth and means that the bank is risking less of its own money on the loan. Similarly, a person's occupation can sway a banker's judgment—physicians or business executives, for example, who show large earning potential are considered better risks than individuals with low income or a poor record of earnings.

Instant loans are available to holders of commercial bank cards. Bank-card loans, usually up to $1000, are easy to get but expensive; interest rates may start as high as 18 percent. Checking accounts at commercial banks often offer overdraft checking, with an automatic line of credit up to a specified amount. When a person overdraws a checking account, the bank instantly lends money to the account and then charges interest ranging from 12 to 18 percent.

Finance companies are the most expensive commercial lenders, with interest rates running as high as 18 to 36 percent. Although consumers are now protected by the Truth-in-Lending Act, which requires any lender to state the true annual percentage rate of a loan, finance companies should still be regarded as a very expensive source of money. Any family that qualifies for a loan from a savings institution, commercial bank, or credit union should avoid finance companies.

Family, friends, and employers should not be overlooked as a source of loans either. Many couples borrow cash from their parents to increase the down payment on a home, and a trusted employee may feel comfortable enough to ask for a loan or advance from the boss. The advantages of such loans are obvious: High interest rates and stringent payment terms can be avoided. If the loan is not repaid promptly, however, strained relationships may result. In addition, "strings" are frequently attached to loans from relatives and employers, and such loans may involve a personal commitment which the borrower is unwilling to make.

Recent legislation—the Federal Equal Credit Opportunity Act—is intended to end credit discrimination based on sex or marital status. As part of their compliance with the regulations of this law, lenders may not inquire whether the applicant is divorced or widowed, nor may they automatically require, as part of their own policy, that a husband cosign for credit even if the woman applicant has already shown that she is credit-worthy. However, it is possible that these and other regulations may be only as airtight as state equal-credit laws help to make them. Furthermore, creditors are given a considerable amount of time in which to comply with the new legislation (Kramer, 1976). In summary, then, women have, and for some time probably will continue to have, more difficulty than men in their credit transactions.

Protecting Family Income

Every family has to face the possibility of losing the chief breadwinner through death. *Life insurance* is a means of maintaining financial solvency even if this should occur. Most families do not build up sufficient financial reserves during the child-rearing years to meet the contingency of a provider's death without serious hardship if there is no life insurance.

There are two kinds of life insurance. *Term insurance* provides for payment of a "face" amount designated on the front of the policy if death occurs within a specific period of time, or a term. After the term expires, the person may renew the policy, but at a higher rate because of increasing age and a higher probability that death will occur. After age sixty-five, the policy usually cannot be renewed. Some term insurance policies also contain provisions for conversion to the second type of insurance, in which cash values accrue with the policy upon renewal.

Cash-value insurance policies have various names and involve various arrangements—ordinary life, whole life, twenty-payment life (in which premiums are paid up at the end of twenty years), endowment policies (in which the individual is "endowed" with income from the policy after a specific period), and so on. These policies contract to pay a face amount, usually in some multiple of $1000, if the beneficiary dies. Premiums are substantially higher than those for term insurance, but they do not increase—payments remain constant after being established according to actuarial figures at the insured's age when the policy is begun. The policy need not be renewed at intervals; it remains in effect as long as premiums are paid. As payments continue, a cash value accrues. Eventually the insured may elect to receive the cash value in a lump-sum payment, accept paid-up insurance for life or for some lesser period, or receive monthly cash payments. Cash values can also be used as collateral for loans, or loans may be made from the insurance company, in which case the face value of the policy is reduced until the loan is paid.

Policies which accrue cash values may appear to be superior to term insurance in every way, but there are other considerations. First, whole life policies may put a strain on the budget of newlyweds because of their higher monthly cost. Second, whole life is never a prudent investment or savings plan. Returns on money paid in are far less than those on money that is deposited in a savings institution, with interest compounded. Saxton (1972) provides a comparison showing that term insurance is actually a better buy if the difference in cost between term and whole life is invested at 5 percent interest. The catch, of course, is that many persons are not disciplined enough to invest the difference and leave it for years to accumulate interest.

Investment

Savings are generally designated as money set aside for relatively short-term goals, whether for a specific item or for general need. Institutions which may be used to save while the money earns interest include banks, credit unions, and savings and loan associations. However, large sums of money which do not need to be designated for emergency needs or specific items can more profitably be *invested*.

Investment is necessary to prevent the erosion of money's purchasing power. Inflation has exceeded 6 percent per year recently, and so money in a savings account earning 6 percent interest annually is actually losing ground in purchasing power.

The number of investment possibilities is almost unlimited, depending upon whether one is more interested in yield (annual return) or growth (appreciation in value). One possibility is the purchase of government bonds from a commercial bank. Many families invest in common or preferred stocks. There are over 1600 stocks listed on the New York Stock Exchange, and they run the gamut from highly speculative to extremely conservative and from high yield, no growth potential to no yield, high growth potential. Most financial experts recommend that before making any investments, however, a family should have a home mortgage, enough savings to cover emergency situations, and health and life insurance.

SUMMARY

The meaning of money and priorities for spending money vary to an extraordinary degree—even for people brought up in the same financial circumstances. Disagreements over money thus constitute a potential source of conflict for many couples. This may be particularly true of newly married young couples who find themselves in a poor financial position because of the expenses of setting up a home and keeping house.

Because of the myriad of expenditures they make, many people are not sure what happens to their income. A budget allocating exact amounts for each category of expense is often a good solution. A careful accounting for several months of each item of expense is a first step. Expenditures should be classified as either fixed or variable. Budget changes can be made only in regard to the variable expenditures.

An important budget item is medical care. Health insurance provides the best means of paying the bills which accrue from a serious illness. The most desirable form of health insurance is a nonprofit group plan.

Buying on credit is a widely used way of enjoying a house or other major purchase while paying for it. However, buying on credit may be a trap for people who purchase more than they can realistically pay for. Loans are another form of credit. It is best to shop for a loan since terms may vary from one lending institution to another. Credit unions, savings banks, savings and loan associations, and commercial banks lend money and charge interest for it. Finance companies should be avoided because of their high interest rates.

Life insurance is one means of providing an income for the family in case of the death of the major wage earner. A form of investment in addition to savings deposited in a savings bank is the purchase of stocks or bonds through a stockbroker. Government bonds may be purchased at a commercial bank.

CASE STUDY

Her View

Seven months ago Corine Peters, a charming and vivacious thirty-two-year-old, moved away from her husband of thirteen years because of differences over spending money. Corine likes to spend freely. She says money makes life enjoyable in the present. Corine's father abandoned her and her mother when she was three, and so she does not remember him. But her mother had a merchant-marine boy friend who brought Corine ornate and expensive gifts when he returned from the sea. She still treasures the English china tea set and several luxurious-looking handwoven and painted shawls from Singapore that he gave her. Because of her desire for expensive possessions, when she was a junior in high school she went to work part time at a McDonald's hamburger outlet, and on Saturday mornings she worked as a dentist's receptionist.

When Corine married Phillip, they took advantage of low-rent public housing until they could save enough from their meager earnings to afford more spacious quarters. Corine worked as a counter girl at a McDonald's for a year before becoming a clerk for the public gas and electric company. Three years later, Corine was convinced that they should move to an apartment she felt was more suitable, especially since she wanted more space for their new son, and they moved out of the project. Since by then she had become a receptionist in a bank, she was confident that she and Phillip could soon buy a house of their own, and she considered the move temporary until they could save for a down payment.

About a year ago Corine became convinced that Phillip might never consent to the purchase of a house. She wanted one in a middle-class community with three bedrooms and a spacious yard. She arranged for her brother to lend her the

$6000 she needed as a down payment on a $53,000 house, and he cosigned with her for the bank loan needed to purchase the property. Then she moved out of the apartment with her two sons, aged eleven and nine. Corine's house lies 67 miles across the state line from the bank where she works. She is willing to ride a bus that distance twice each day in order to own her dream house.

After the separation, Corine requested and received $75 a month in support payments for each child. When she purchased $750 worth of new living-room furniture, she asked Phillip for a $500 loan and promised to repay it in ten months, but she defaulted on the first two smaller payments. She frequently charges smaller items that she cannot pay off for two or three months, and so the interest charges and future purchases keep her in debt. Two years ago, in an effort to control her credit buying, she destroyed all her credit cards. But since then she has gradually reacquired her cards and is currently in debt for four months.

His View

Phillip has great difficulty spending more than small amounts of money at a time. He is a steady worker and is generally easygoing and even-tempered. Phillip's parents were divorced when he was seven. His mother remarried two years later, and he established a fairly close relationship with his stepfather, who provided for him as best he could with his earnings as a janitor. Phillip remembers his gift of a bicycle when he was twelve and a little transistor radio when he was fifteen. Phillip still regards himself as his mother's dutiful son. He remembers, for example, that when he was fourteen his mother insisted that he be in the house by eight in the evening. Then she would regularly send him out an hour or so later to search for his younger brother, who was generally playing basketball with his buddies. Phillip's mother lived around the corner from the apartment where he and Corine originally lived for eight years. He visits his mother at least weekly, never with Corine, and he was reluctant to move from that area. He protested that a new apartment would double their rent.

For the first eight years of his marriage Phillip drove a laundry truck. He would have liked to join the Marines, but his low academic scores prevented him from doing so. He took a U.S. Department of Labor manpower training course geared toward enabling the enrollees to pass civil service tests. Phillip passed the ambulance-driver test, but there was a possibility that a job in the fire department would soon open up, and Corine encouraged him to wait for this more prestigious, better-paying position. He took her advice, and five months later he began his training as a fireman.

After Corine moved to her own house with the two boys, she intimated to Phillip that if he would locate an attractive apartment in a community where they might purchase a house within a year, she would return to him. This placed Phillip in a bind. He loves Corine and wants to be a father to his sons, and yet as a municipal employee he must live within the state where he works. Furthermore, he felt that any house Corine would find acceptable would entail a 40- to 50-mile train ride to and from work. On top of the stress of his job, Phillip would find such a ride unbearable.

Nevertheless, Phillip used his days off to locate an apartment that would be suitable for Corine. He made an appointment for her to see it, arranged to have the walls painted her favorite colors, signed the lease, and put down $650 for a security deposit and one month's rent. Two days later Corine called and informed him that she just could not bring herself to sell her house. She said she could not give up her dream of owning her own home and all it symbolized to her, and she refused to return to him.

However, Phillip has not brought his relationship with Corine to an end. His station-house buddies prod him to find a girl friend who will not put him through so many trials, but he intends to keep seeing Corine and the boys. He makes the child-support contributions faithfully, and he willingly lent her $500 for her new furniture. The family usually spend at least one day of each weekend together. Phillip and Corine frequently stay overnight at each other's homes and enjoy sex together. Phillip even consulted Corine when he decided that he needed a car if he was going to be visiting his family regularly.

Interpretation and Questions

Corine and Phillip Peters clash not only over how much money to spend but also over what to spend it on. What he considers satisfactory living conditions she regards as impoverished disgrace. If you were Corine, would you continue to encourage Phillip to loosen up his spending habits or allow your aggravation at his reluctance to spend drive you away? If you were Phillip, how would you handle Corine's spending sprees? If you were Phillip, would it disturb you that Corine looked to her brother for financial help? Do Corine's middle-class aspirations and spending habits really enable her to achieve middle-class financial security? What is the meaning of money to Corine? What does money mean to Phillip? Do you think better communication about money would solve any problems in this marriage?

STUDY GUIDE

Important Terms

net income
budget
cash-flow record
assets
liabilities
fixed expenses

variable expenses
prime interest rate
term insurance
ordinary (or whole) life insurance
common stocks

Review Quiz

1 The two most common causes of conflicts over money among young couples are:

a unrealistic attitudes toward money and the use of money to control one's spouse *b* too much money and too many choices for spending it

    c poverty and being forced to spend money only for survival needs

    d interference from in-laws and bad advice from friends

2 Income potential is at its peak when wage earners are:

    a under twenty-five

    b between thirty and forty-five

    c between forty-five and fifty-four

    d between fifty-five and sixty-five

3 In 1976 the average cost of giving birth to a child was about:

    a $300

    b $600

    c $900

    d $1200

4 Two types of expenses included in all budgets are:

    a personal and business items

    b fixed and variable expenses

    c assets and liabilities

    d weekly and monthly expenses

5 Net income is defined as:

    a all money earned

    b the money left after taxes

    c the money left after bills have been paid

    d none of the above

6 The Federal Equal Credit Opportunity Act makes it illegal for:

    a creditors to inquire whether an applicant is divorced or widowed

    b a creditor to require that a husband cosign for credit for his wife

    c a creditor to discriminate because of sex or marital status

    d all the above

7 If a credit-card holder wishes to pay a bill in full, the _____ must be paid.

    a previous balance

    b new balance

    c minimum payment due

    d amount now due

8 Interest rates on small loans are usually lowest when obtained through:

    a credit unions

    b banks

    c commercial savings and loan associations

    d finance companies

9 Mortgage rates for the purchase of a new home may vary depending upon:

    a real estate values

    b the prime interest rate

    c the area of the country

    d all the above

10 Term insurance:

    a never increases in cost

    b usually cannot be renewed after age sixty-five

    c cannot be converted to whole life

    d all the above

11 Cash-value insurance policies are of several types, including:

    a term

    b medical

    c ordinary life

    d none of the above

12 One advantage of insurance policies that accrue cash values is that:

    a they cost less per month than term policies

    b they furnish a prudent savings plan

    c premiums do not increase

    d all the above

13 If the purchasing power of money is to be retained over a long period, the money must:

    a be kept at home

    b be invested in government bonds

    c be kept in a bank checking account

    d be invested at a return higher than the rate of inflation

14 Experts recommend that before investing in stock, a family should:

    a have a home mortgage

    b have savings for emergencies
    c have life insurance
    d all the above

Opinionnaire

Agree	No opinion	Disagree	
_____	_____	_____	1 Couples should decide how they will spend the major part of their income before they marry.
_____	_____	_____	2 When a couple live together, one is usually liberal about spending, while the other is cautious.
_____	_____	_____	3 How much money a couple have has nothing to do with whether they will be happy in marriage.
_____	_____	_____	4 The average newly married couple will be unable to meet normal household expenses unless both husband and wife work.
_____	_____	_____	5 A written budget is unnecessary for any couple who use common sense in money management.
_____	_____	_____	6 Buying clothing and furniture on credit will get a marriage off to a bad start.
_____	_____	_____	7 Life insurance for the primary breadwinner should be purchased during the first year of marriage.
_____	_____	_____	8 Wives should be able to assume loans just as their husbands can even if they are not employed outside the home.
_____	_____	_____	9 Credit cards are certain to get most newlyweds further into debt than is wise.
_____	_____	_____	10 The only reason a couple should ever consider a loan is for a home mortgage.

Exercise

The following table is designed to help individuals clarify their values concerning money and expenditures. Couples or groups may wish to compare responses to gauge the degree of consensus. For purposes of comparison, groups may be divided into younger and old persons, men and women, or married and unmarried people.

FINANCIAL PRIORITIES INVENTORY

First, imagine that you and your spouse will be living on a very low income when you are first married.

Second, examine the list of budget items below. Choose the budget item you think is the most important. Write the number of this item in box A below. Now choose the budget item you think is next most important. Write the number of this item in box B. Then write the numbers of the eight next most important budget items, in order of importance, in the remaining boxes.

1	Appliance repairs	
2	Bank and finance charges	
3	Books, magazines and papers	
4	Car insurance	
5	Car payments	
6	Car upkeep	
7	Church contributions	
8	Clothes—his	
9	Clothes—hers	
10	Community chest	
11	Disability insurance	
12	Donations to other organizations	
13	Dry cleaning and laundry	
14	Educational expenses—books, tuition	
15	Entertainment—movies, alcohol	
16	Food and household supplies	
17	Furniture	
18	Gasoline	

1 Appliance repairs
2 Bank and finance charges
3 Books, magazines and papers
4 Car insurance
5 Car payments
6 Car upkeep
7 Church contributions
8 Clothes—his
9 Clothes—hers
10 Community chest
11 Disability insurance
12 Donations to other organizations
13 Dry cleaning and laundry
14 Educational expenses—books, tuition
15 Entertainment—movies, alcohol
16 Food and household supplies
17 Furniture
18 Gasoline

19 Gifts—Christmas, birthdays, etc.
20 Haircuts and beauty salon
21 House repairs
22 Life insurance
23 Insurance on personal property and house
24 Mail
25 Medical insurance and doctor bills
26 Miscellaneous
27 Phone
28 Professional or union dues
29 Rent or mortgage payments
30 Savings
31 Spending or incidentals money—his
32 Spending or incidentals money—hers
33 Supplies, etc., for anticipated baby
34 Taxes on property and house
35 Utilities—electricity, water, etc.
36 Vacation

A	B	C	D	E	F	G	H	J	K

When you have a number in each box, A through K, check to see that the number of the most important budget item is in box A. Boxes B through K should contain the numbers of the budget items second through tenth in importance. Do not leave any boxes without a number.

Source: Adapted from Rolfe, 1974, Table 1. Copyright © 1972, David J. Rolfe.

Projects for Class or Home Study

1 The text indicates that the starting salary of a college graduate may not always be higher than that of a non-college graduate. Select about ten positions at random from the "help wanted" section of the daily newspaper which require a college degree. Compute the average entry-level salary. Now do the same for ten positions which do not require a degree. Which salary is higher?
2 Keep a cash-flow record for one month, including all expenditures. Were you aware of how you spent your money?
3 On the basis of your cash-flow results, set up a budget with fixed and variable expenses.

4 Loan institutions are required to give loan costs in total monetary figures rather than confusing percentages. Contact a credit union, a bank, a savings and loan association, and a finance company. Ask each for total costs on a new-car loan of $4000 to be repaid in thirty-six months. How do they compare?

5 Much consumer education is available for the asking. To plan an investment program for the future or evaluate one you already have, call a stockbroker and ask for free literature that will help you compare stocks, bonds, and ways to shelter income from taxes.

Suggestions for Further Reading

Coles, Robert. The cold, tough world of the affluent family. *Psychology Today*, November 1975, **9**, 67–77.
  The author points out that money has meaning beyond what it will buy and that affluence may breed families without the resourcefulness needed in emergencies.
Cox, Frank D. *Youth, marriage and the seductive society*. Dubuque, Iowa: Wm. C. Brown, 1967.
  Chapter 7, entitled "Economic Entrapment: The Modern Slavery System," is a thoughtful comment on how married couples are seduced into money problems. Alternatives are offered.
Cutright, Phillips. Income and family events: Family income, family size and consumption. *Journal of Marriage and the Family*, February 1971, **33**, 161–173.
  This article is an example of how sociologists study some of the meanings of money in the family and of how patterns of expenditure can be interpreted in terms of behavioral principles.
Mace, David R. *Getting ready for marriage*. Nashville, Tenn.: Abingdon Press, 1972.
  A well-known marriage counselor explores aspects of financial planning before marriage.
Smith, Carlton, and Pratt, Richard P. *The Time-Life book of family finance*. New York: Time-Life, 1969.
  Every family should possess one basic monetary guide. This one is thorough, well written, and easy to understand.
Weinstein, Grace W. *Children and money*. New York: Charterhouse, 1975.
  This book explores the neglected areas of how children, from the preschool years through adolescence, learn about money, "from piggy bank to checking account."

Answers to Review Quiz

1-*a* 2-*c* 3-*d* 4-*b* 5-*b* 6-*d* 7-*b* 8-*a* 9-*d* 10-*b* 11-*c* 12-*c* 13-*d* 14-*d*

9

MANAGING CONFLICT

Conflict appears to be a natural ingredient of social interaction. A world war, a blood feud among factions or related groups, a rumble between gangs of urban youths, a brawl among spectators at a sporting event, and a squabble between husband and wife are all examples of conflict. Behavioral scientists have often disagreed about the meaning of conflict in social life. Some, such as psychologist B. F. Skinner, imply that conflict is a negative force which disrupts and destroys. Humanistic psychologists like the late A. S. Neill see the positive side of conflict, relating it to the possibilities of change in relationships and to individual freedom. Both viewpoints have merit.

Marital conflict, like the marriage relationship itself, has the potential of bringing either grief and unhappiness or growth and increased understanding. Conflict is inevitable in an intimate environment like marriage because the persons involved have different perceptions of the world. When they enter marriage, most newlyweds are in many ways strangers. They have lived different lives for twenty or thirty years, and they have different values, attitudes, customs, and expectations.

> Many of these factors will be similar, to be sure, or these particular individuals would not have been drawn together in the first place, and their relation would certainly not have survived dating and engagement. However, inevitable dissimilarities will be present in the relation, and they will invariably be a source of some conflict (Saxton, 1972, p. 230).

In fact, even the same person tends to view the same situation differently on different occasions, and so the probability that two people will agree on everything is very small indeed. If we cannot escape conflict, the alternative is to make it function positively.

The Nature of Conflict

Two steps are involved in managing marital conflict. First, some understanding of its nature and course is necessary. As we shall see, conflict can occur whenever two or more persons behave in ways that bring out underlying feelings of hostility and antagonism. Second, specific skills and orientations must be learned by the married couple. The nature of marital conflict is illustrated in the following account provided by George Bach and Peter Wyden:

> MARCO (confidentially): I don't think you can really appreciate how sensitive I am about my Italian background.
> SYLVIA (sympathetically): Sure I do! I've felt it ever since I met you.
> MARCO (seemingly relieved): OK, then, you make sure you never call me a "wop," not even as a joke!
> SYLVIA : OK, I understand.
>   More than a year later the Pollettis were at a party, and Marco thought that Sylvia was dancing entirely too much with a friend of his. When they got home, he was terribly angry. Both had had too much to drink. A *Virginia Woolf* free-for-all ensued during which Marco, quite unjustly, called Sylvia a "whore." Sylvia, understandably provoked . . . called him a "stupid wop." . . .
>   He broke up their *Virginia Woolf* stalemate with a loud guffaw and said: "Hey, I guess that's sort of funny. I know I told you never to call me a 'wop' but I was only testing you. I don't really mind. I guess it's about time I told you what I'm really sensitive about. What bugs me more than anything is here I am 34 years old and I ought to be getting ahead much faster at the office. I don't think I'll ever make it there and it worries the hell out of me."
>   Sylvia, greatly relieved, said, "Oh, I don't care! I love you anyway. If things get tough, I can always go back to work" (1968, pp. 81–82).

What is really happening in this squabble? First, the basis for the fight was laid far in advance when the husband apparently revealed something about himself to his wife. In the marital relationship, each partner knows all the intimate details about the other's personality and behavior patterns. When one spouse reveals something personal to the other, he or she is really saying, "I trust you to know this about me." Then, when that spouse uses the revelation in marital combat, the trust is felt to be betrayed.

Second, the event which triggered the conflict described above was soon forgotten. Such events are usually unimportant except as the immediate precipitators of fights, and couples who continue to focus on them are wasting time and growth opportunities.

Third, there was an underlying problem which contributed to the conflict. In this instance, Marco was distressed about his job, but the reason for the outburst could have been any of a hundred small issues. Indeed, many conflicts arise from the thoughtless behavior of one party and nothing more. The husband, for example, might leave his clothes scattered all over the bathroom floor, the wife might use his razor to shave her legs, he might nag her about leaving the cap off the toothpaste, and so on.

However, chronic conflict, in which small incidents always become major disruptive problems for the couple, must be understood by considering not just the immediate event but also the prior predisposing causes. The figure below depicts chronic conflict as a function of certain underlying problems, or causes, which incline the couple to enter into conflict. These causes are grouped into three categories: value differences, situational stresses, and deprivation of personal needs. These categories are interrelated and thus may influence one another.

A MODEL OF CHRONIC CONFLICT
Certain conditions predispose a couple to marital conflict, but conflicts usually begin with some specific event. The predisposing causes may be compounded, as the arrows indicate.

Predisposing causes

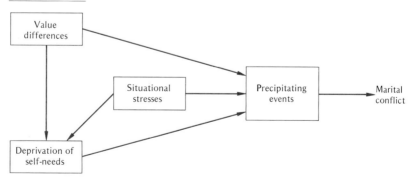

VALUE DIFFERENCES

Values are the standards and ideals that guide one's behavior. Social psychologists have identified six major groups of values which an individual may hold in varying degrees of importance (Allport, Vernon, and Lindzey, 1951):

Theoretical values are characterized by a dominant interest in the discovery of truth and by an empirical, intellectual approach to life.

Economic values emphasize useful and practical ideals.

Aesthetic values place importance on form and harmony. Such ideals enable one to judge and enjoy each unique experience from the standpoint of its grace, symmetry, or fitness.

Social values are characterized by altruism and philanthropy.

Political values emphasize personal power, influence, and renown; they are not necessarily limited to politics.

Religious values are concerned with the unity of experience and the comprehension of the cosmos as a whole.

Possession of different interests and values does not necessarily lead to chronic conflict in marriage. As we saw in Chapter 5, the theory of mate selection is based on the attraction of opposites. Thus, a woman whose values are primarily economic may be happily married to a man who has an aesthetic approach to life, and the relationship may profit from the complementarity. The couple's varying interests and values may encourage new experiences and growth for each.

On the other hand, a union between people with totally different values may engender conflict because each spouse assigns different priorities to different needs and wants. For example, a husband may propose the purchase of an admired work of art, only to find that his wife is opposed because she thinks that the installation of carpeting in the living room is more important. An argument ensues. The effect of this argument—and of all future ones—on the marriage will depend to some extent on whether the couple understand that value differences exist between them and that these differences affect their day-to-day living.

A second common type of value conflict is seen in couples who begin marriage with similar values but change their values as the relationship matures. For example, if one spouse continues his or her educational development while the other works, their attitudes and values will almost certainly begin to diverge. Similarly, religion may come to play an increasingly important part in the life of one spouse, but not of the other.

Value conflict may also be stimulated and reinforced by changes in society. For example, suppose that one couple, married for twenty years, were raised in traditional sex-role molds. Now they find that a growing number of people are challenging these sex roles and, in effect, challenging the choices upon which they have based their lives. This conflict in values may be "brought home" if, for example, the wife's own attitudes begin to change. Perhaps she is talking about returning to school or entering the job market, or she may have joined a "rap" group in which she and other women explore their feelings about their marital and social status. During this time, the husband and wife may experience considerable uncertainty and confusion about values which they once accepted unquestioningly. If the husband's viewpoint does not alter along with his wife's, the difference in values could well emerge in the form of marital conflict.

The speed with which societal values change may also affect the quality of marriage—and the potential for marital conflict in industrialized nations. Thus, in his book *Future Shock*, Alvin Toffler (1970) predicts that rapid value changes will lead to more "serial" marriages in our society. Specifically, he predicts that marriage customs will have four "trajectories," or phases. The first phase, trial marriage, will be for the young couple not planning to have children. A second stage will be a relationship formed solely for the purpose of bearing and rearing children. The third marriage will be formed by persons with grown children who will share similar values. A fourth marriage may be necessitated if one or both partners retire from work.

Although some couples may progress through the four stages with the same partner, Toffler believes that the trend will be toward changing partners at each phase to minimize conflict.

SITUATIONAL STRESSES

Recent studies have asked husbands and wives to rank the things that they disagree about most. Letha Scanzoni and John Scanzoni (1976), for example, have summarized the results of three studies of major conflict areas in marriage. Four of these conflict areas—money, child-related matters, friend-related matters, and kinship-related matters—center around situational stresses. Of the five remaining areas, three are related to underlying value differences. These areas are the ways the couple spend their leisure time; certain activities such as excessive drinking or gambling, adultery, and the like; and the marital roles of the partners, including the division of labor in the household. A final area in the Scanzoni study, commonly referred to as "tremendous trifles," can involve either situational or value stresses; such trifles are the common, everyday events that can trigger a conflict.

As is the case with value differences, couples often fail to realize that specific issues or events are not as important in marital squabbles as situational stresses. If in-law problems are producing stress for a couple, their dialogue should focus on ways to reduce the stress rather than on the specific derogatory remarks that triggered a fight.

One interesting study on situational stresses found that the stresses which set off conflict are not isolated. Instead, the problems seem to cluster in general patterns. Jerzy Krupinski, Elizabeth Marshall, and Valerie Yule (1970) analyzed the problems in 641 marriages presented to a marriage counselor by either or both spouses over a one-year period. An average of 5.9 problems were presented for each marriage in the sample. The investigators were able to correlate some 143 problems into six general clusters. For example, the first cluster of problems centered around interpersonal hostility which was manifested by violent quarreling. This cluster contained such problems as money management and child rearing, as well as the husband's antisocial behavior (jealousy and intolerance) and lack of control (quarreling, loss of temper, and violence). The wife responded to the husband by nagging him or by walking away from the argument.

Another cluster of problems revolved around the wife's assuming a domineering role characterized by constant nagging and distrust. She tended to accuse the husband of being unfaithful or of being an inadequate provider. The husband would retaliate by criticizing her money management and her scolding attitudes and, in some cases, by deserting her. Among the other clusters of marital problems found by Krupinski and his colleagues were interpersonal alienation, shown by lack of communication and quarreling, and complete avoidance, characterized by either partner's walking away from the relationship.

DEPRIVATION OF PERSONAL NEEDS

All of us possess images of self which require recognition (identity verification), expansion (growth), and relatedness through contact with others. Individuals enter marriage partially as a means of self-fulfillment. When one spouse's personal needs are not met, the other may be seen (often wrongly) as responsible, and conflict may result. How is deprivation of personal needs manifested in actual behavior? This question is perhaps best answered by the following account, given by a family therapist:

> Thirty-four-year-old Tom and thirty-year-old Wendy, married for six years and parents of a four-year-old son, came to me because of sexual difficulties. In reality their problem was communication.
> Wendy's version: "For several nights in a row, Tom ate his dinner very quickly and said he had to go back to work. Even during dinner he acted uninterested in my conversation and completely ignored my objections to his working late every night. I grew increasingly resentful. One night Tom returned home after midnight, woke me, and with no exchange of words, began to make love. I felt extremely hostile. When we finished, he had a temper outburst at me."
> Tom's version: "I had been involved in a very important project which might mean life or death for my firm. The deadline was approaching and I had to work very hard. I felt under great pressure. I needed comfort. On the night

in question I came home exhausted and dispirited. My sexual advances this time weren't for sexual reasons—I wanted a tender contact. Instead, Wendy was more distant than ever, just when I needed her most. It made me furious and I lost my temper" (Fensterheim and Baer, 1975, pp. 169–170).

By learning where the real problems were—in needs for recognition, security, and belonging—and how to communicate the needs, the couple managed the chronic conflict.

Communication

During all the waking hours that they spend together, a married couple are constantly communicating. A kind or harsh word, a kiss, crying, a long silence, a slap, a glance, a gift—all are used to transmit messages from one person to the other. Indeed, as one student of interpersonal communication writes, "One cannot *not* communicate" (Watzlawick, 1964).

What is meant by communication? Psychologist Sven Wahlroos defines communication as "any behavior that carries a message which is perceived by someone else" (1974, p. 4). The behavior can be verbal or nonverbal, and the message carried by the behavior can be intended or unintended. Moreover, the party receiving the message may perceive it either consciously or unconsciously, and the message may come through distorted or undistorted.

Communication breakdowns are at the heart of virtually all marital conflicts. This is particularly true of the tacit or unspoken variety because the behavior for both parties is open to interpretation—or misinterpretation. Tacit communication, as sociologist Jessie Bernard (1964) points out, is not precise and is quite hard to decipher. After a bedtime argument, for example, one spouse may turn over and move to the far side of the bed, hoping that this will elicit an apology or just any sort of response. The other partner, however, is likely to read this "body language" as rejection and a desire *not* to discuss the situation. Without further clues, intentions remain obscured, and more reasons for conflict are created.

In one of the most extensive studies to date on working-class marriages, Mirra Komarovsky (1962) examined some of the reasons why her subjects were dissatisfied with their marital communication. Komarovsky found that there were four major themes of dissatisfaction: boredom, overall meagerness of communication, mutual misunderstandings, and the mate's indiscretions. It was found that wives express far more discontent about marital communication than husbands; some 90 percent of the wives were dissatisfied with their marital communication. Typical of the wives' comments was the following:

I used to talk to him a lot when we were first married, but now I can't talk to him at all. He kinda draws away from me. Sometimes I think that all he wants

FACE-TO-FACE communication can be emotionally difficult, but it is an essential step toward resolving conflicts.

me around for is to cook for him and the kids and then to leave him alone. I don't know too much about him because he's so close-mouthed (Komarovsky, 1962, p. 138).

Komarovsky offers several explanations for this phenomenon, one of which is that the American ideal of masculinity prevents men from expressing certain grievances. The wife may be accused of being a "griper" by her husband. In fact, this is often just his way of precluding communication and thus avoiding a confrontation not only with her emotions but with his own as well.

OBSTACLES TO COMMUNICATION

Why should individuals experience such difficulty communicating with each other? One outstanding reason is that communication is a highly personal process. As Michael Burgoon points out:

If we probe more deeply into the perceptions, attitudes, and psychological make-up of the people involved in the process, and the way they use language to express themselves, we may wonder if communication can succeed on anything but the most elementary level. For even when people share a language and a common cultural background, they are ultimately isolated from each other's "reality" by differences in their personal histories and by the feelings and expectations they associate with words, the symbols of this reality (1974, p. 151).

Indeed, it is the very personal nature of the communication process that is responsible for the obstacles to effective communication. According to Burgoon, these obstacles include selectivity, frozen evaluation, polarization, and bypassing. *Selectivity* is the tendency to choose from among the communications we receive the one containing ideas and attitudes that mirror or support our own. A husband who does not like his mother-in-law, for example, will tune himself out if his wife begins recounting her mother's virtues to him.

Certain physiological conditions—hunger, fatigue, illness, and so on—can interfere with one's interpersonal communication so that only certain environmental stimuli are attended to. During her menstrual period, for example, a woman may continuously focus on the physical changes and discomfort that she is experiencing, which will interfere with her ability to communicate with her husband. One woman observes: "The week before my menstrual period has always been a hard time for me. I'm restless, irritable, and nervous. I'm less tolerant of mistakes in myself and others. Things that I normally don't notice irritate me and make me angry. I cry easily" (Paul and Paul, 1975, p. 115).

The second roadblock to effective interpersonal communication is *frozen evaluation*, which occurs when a person clings to an idea or assumption that no longer reflects reality. Many husbands, for example, may think of their wives as weak-minded, fragile, passive, and docile because men have been socialized to think of women in these terms and also because such an evaluation reinforces the notion of male superiority. Even after the women's movement exposed the false assumptions behind such labels, the evaluations remain so ingrained—or frozen—that a number of people still hold onto the old stereotypes.

The third hindrance to communication, *polarization*, involves oversimplifying reality by resorting to "either-or" judgments. One aspect of polarization is that it suggests a limitation of choices. A wife who thinks in terms of polarities may believe that her method of rearing children is the one and only way. If her spouse makes a suggestion which does not conform to her methods, his suggestion is ignored. In her simple either-or world, his advice cannot be correct.

The fourth obstacle is the problem of *bypassing*, which results when the sender and the receiver of a message find themselves at different levels of understanding. They may be saying the same thing but using different words to express themselves, in which case they perceive a conflict where none exists. Or they may think that they are in agreement when, in fact, they are using the same words to mean different things. In either case there is a failure to communicate—the intended meanings of the sender are bypassing those of the receiver (Burgoon, 1974, p. 169).

PSYCHOLOGICAL BLOCKS

In addition to the general barriers, there are a number of psychological impediments that prevent spouses from communicating with each other. As Herman Lantz and Elaine Snyder (1969) point out, the first of these is an attitude of hopelessness. Some partners see marital problems as part of the order of things. Such people must accept marital strife because they cannot deal with it. For example, one husband on a drinking spree knocked out his wife's upper front teeth. At her friends' suggestions, the woman went to a marriage counselor, but she became hostile at his questions and even defended her husband: "He only knocked out my uppers, he did leave the lowers" (Lantz and Snyder, 1969, p. 361). Apparently, this woman had given up on the possibility that her relationship with her husband could ever change and so had resigned herself to suffering his physical abuse.

Other individuals may hesitate to talk to their spouses about marital problems because they fear that their complaints will anger their partners. Some of these people lack the courage to confront their partners with marital grievances. Still others are afraid to air their grievances to their spouses because they fear that doing so will result in the termination of the marriage.

IMPROVING MARITAL COMMUNICATION

John Strong (1975) has proposed a program designed to facilitate communication and so help resolve marital conflict. According to Strong, one must develop the skills necessary to understand oneself and one's partner in a conflict situation. Two of these basic skills—listening and speaking effectively—sound simple, but people appear to have a great deal of difficulty in mastering them. One must learn to listen to the messages one's partner is transmitting and to adopt positive attitudes and responses such as acceptance, empathy, feedback, and, when appropriate, silence. A good listener also avoids adopting negative attitudes and taking negative actions. These include defending one's position, offering advice, trying to enter the conversation before being invited, not having time to listen, and taking a rigid position on the issue at hand.

Speaking, which also must be learned, involves transmitting thoughts, feelings, and needs to one's partner. One is speaking positively when one prefaces threatening remarks, assumes responsibility for statements, invites the participation of the listener, and grants the listener the right to be understood. One should avoid the negative aspects of speaking, including adopting an attitude of superiority, speaking too slowly or rapidly or loudly or softly, and talking to fill a silence. "If one or both of the individuals in a relationship do not learn the skills of listening and/or speaking, communication becomes a matter of one-way or two-way monologue—messages sent without understanding" (Strong, 1975, p. 273).

THE IMPORTANCE OF FEEDBACK An essential ingredient of two-way communication—briefly mentioned by Strong—is the principle of *feedback*. The use of feedback involves checking oneself to be sure that one understands his or her spouse's statement and feelings. Repeating a partner's statement slowly and carefully aloud often helps avoid complications and the introduction of irrelevant issues during an argument. For example, saying, "Now let me get this straight. As I understand you, you mean that . . . " often prevents misunderstanding and escalation of conflict.

Researchers George Bach and Herb Goldberg (1974) have perfected this technique to such a degree that they teach it as part of their program for fighting fairly. According to these investigators, feedback "is a form of active listening that restates what was heard, to the total satisfaction of the person whose statement is being fed back." The person engaging in the feedback is not to reinterpret or to read into his or her partner's statement anything that is not there. According to Bach and Goldberg, both parties must engage in feedback immediately after one of them makes a statement. Neither may make a statement or respond to another's statement before repeating what the other has just said. The following example of the technique is offered by the two investigators:

> JERRY: The thing I like most about you is your generosity. You always offer to help me financially when I need something. That gives me a sense of security and safety.
>
> JERRY'S FATHER (feeding back): What I hear you saying, Jerry, is you like me for my money and that it makes you feel good knowing that I'll always give it to you when you need it.
>
> JERRY: No, you didn't hear me right at all. When you said I like you mainly for your money, you distorted what I said (Bach and Goldberg, 1974, p. 6).

Feedback, say Bach and Goldberg, performs a number of valuable functions during a conflict. For example, it forces the parties to listen carefully, preventing the tendency of one partner to prepare a reply while the other one is speaking. Bach and his colleague note that in their training sessions differences begin to disappear as the partners begin to listen to each other and to keep the issue that they are arguing about in the foreground.

Violence: The Far Side of Marital Conflict

For many couples, marital conflict does not end with verbal exchanges but spills over into physical violence. Thomas J. Cottle, in his book *A Family Album*, reports the following conversation conducted with a twelve-year-old boy:

> "They fighting?" I asked quietly.
>   "Just about every night. . . .

"Mother too. Both of them. Screaming, hitting. Wrestling each other all over the place. Breaking furniture. The whole thing. Then they're all right for two or three nights, then they're back at it. . . .

"I don't know. It was just one night, I heard them yelling. They used to do that so I was kind of used to it. But like, this one night, I think maybe it was New Year's Eve I was in bed and they were fighting, and Mom kept telling Dad they were going to wake us up, but he kept yelling at her. Then he pushed her or hit her, and she fell. I waited for a while and then went in there," Mordecai pointed behind him in the direction of the living room, "and she was lying on the floor. She had this big cut over her eye. I had to push Dad away, which isn't easy with Dad" (1975, p. 34).

How often such scenes occur is difficult to say, but they probably happen more frequently than most people would guess. Steinmetz and Straus (1974), two sociologists who have studied violence in the family, discuss the results of the few meager studies on husband-wife violence and note their conflicting results. The best estimate, they feel, is that 56 percent of all couples will use physical force on each other at some time during their marriage.

Among the most notable of the early studies of violence in the family is that conducted by Marvin Wolfgang (1956). This investigator analyzed homicides that occurred in Philadelphia between 1948 and 1952. He found that 41 percent of all the women homicides were wives who had been murdered by their husbands and that 11 percent of the male homicides were husbands who had been killed by their wives.

Another more intensive study by Richard Gelles (1974) found that violence is a significant phenomenon in family life. Indeed, the cases of violence that are reported and recorded may be only the "tip of the iceberg," beneath which may be a much more widespread amount of daily violent family behavior. Gelles studied eighty families representing both middle and lower socioeconomic classes. The results showed that more than half of the eighty families reported incidents in which one partner pushed, kicked, slapped, choked, threw an object at, or knifed the other. In a quarter of these families, husband-and-wife assaults occurred on a regular basis from six times a year to once a day. The husband was usually the more violent of the partners. About 47 percent of the husbands struck their wives at least once, whereas 25 percent of the men struck their wives from six times a year to once a day.

Several kinds of marital violence were detected. Normal violence, for example, comprises those incidents which are routine and sometimes even regarded by family members as a necessary outlet for their emotions. In most cases of normal violence, however, the husband assaults the wife. Secondary violence is a fight that results when the participants are attempting to resolve another conflict. This type of behavior usually occurs when one partner comes to the aid of a child who is being punished by the other.

One type of violence that is not usually recorded is the threat of violence. Gelles found many incidences of threatening behavior by husbands—punching holes in walls, kicking down doors, firing guns, smashing dishes. These acts were committed as a way of warning the wife that she would receive the same kind of treatment if she continued her behavior. One divorced wife, for example, observed:

> He had a violent temper, in fact I've got bullet holes at the old house in the walls to prove it. He also put his fist through the walls a couple of times. One night he went into the bedroom and the next thing I knew the gun went off and there was a bullet hole in the wall, and he slammed the gun down and out of the house he went (Gelles, 1974, pp. 73–74).

Gelles also attempted to learn how violent families differ from nonviolent families in terms of age, education, occupational status, and income. For the age variable, he found that there is violence among family members of all ages but that conjugal violence is most widespread among the middle-aged. Gelles also found that less well educated husbands tend to resort to physical violence more frequently than their better-educated counterparts. This finding supports that of Mirra Komarovsky (1962), who studied blue-collar marriages. Komarovsky found that 27 percent of the husbands in her sample who had less than twelve years of education quarreled violently with their wives, compared with 17 percent of the husbands who had a high school education. Similarly, 37 percent of the wives with less than twelve years of schooling engaged in violent quarrels, whereas only 4 percent of the wives with a high school education exhibited this form of behavior.

As for occupational status, Gelles found that husbands with low occupational status—truck drivers, laborers, and so forth—were involved in more incidents of family violence than other husbands in the sample. Similarly, reports of violence were more numerous among low-income husbands than among those with high incomes. It should be noted here that it is difficult to be certain of the correlation between violence and the educational background or economic and professional status of the husband. Recent statements by battered wives suggest that violence may be more prevalent in white-collar families than studies have thus far shown. As housing and child-care facilities as well as emotional support become available to battered wives—thus encouraging them to disclose their condition—it should become possible to develop a more accurate profile of this form of family violence.

Handling Conflict Creatively

As we have seen, conflict is not intrinsically pathological or destructive. It has a number of positive functions, some of which have been pointed out by social psychologist Morton Deutsch (1969). For example, conflict prevents relationships from stagnating by stimulating interest. Venting differences and learning how to manage the conflict which may ensue allow for the development of emotional intimacy. Conflict clears the air; it brings problems to light and presents the possibility of solutions. Finally, conflict enables people to test their abilities and to grow emotionally and intellectually.

Since conflict can be beneficial, one might wonder whether there is a way to harness it. In other words, can a husband and wife employ conflict creatively to better themselves and their marriage? A number of behavioral scientists believe that this is possible. Among them are George Bach and Peter Wyden (1968).

Bach and Wyden have proposed an interesting approach to the problem of managing marital conflict which consists of learning how to fight fairly and constructively. This theory holds that there are certain ways to start, wage, and end a fight. There are even certain times and places to do battle. If the partners fight according to this method, most conflicts can probably be resolved with a minimum of psychological scars. Bach and Wyden's five rules for fighting creatively are discussed below.

GIRDING FOR BATTLE Creative fighting really begins with the internal dialogue. Before starting a fight, the partner who feels aggrieved should talk it over with himself or herself. During the internal conversation, a husband might ask himself: "Do I really have a complaint to lodge against my wife? Or do I just want to get the best of her?" "How important is this complaint? Am I being realistic about it, or am I blowing it all out of proportion?" In many cases, such dialogues take the place of actual conflict and prevent fighting altogether.

LEVELING Next comes the process of leveling. The partners should communicate to each other, as clearly and as simply as possible, their positions and their intentions. For example, the best way to discuss how one's spouse feels about something—to get a fair fight started—is to ask him or her point blank: "C'mon, honey, tell me what's the matter. I'm sure we can work it out." Then the couple can bring the problem into the open and decide whether it is important enough to fight over. If it is, they can then set a time and place for fighting.

FIGHTING CREATIVELY In creative fighting, the husband and wife should always avoid situations in which one spouse wins all and the other loses all. The goal of fighting should not be a knockout, a total victory for one party. Rather, the spouses should fight to improve the overall relationship. Attempting to KO a partner—to win at any cost—can turn one into a guerrilla fighter whose chief weapons are dirty tricks. Both partners should win something, and so they must solve the problem by bargaining and compromise.

When a conflict arises, it is important for a spouse to identify the issue and say that he or she wants to discuss (fight about) it at a particular time and in a particular place. This gives both partners a chance to cool down and organize their thoughts so that they can present their case logically and clearly, sticking to the issue. Both parties also can think up proposal and counterproposal during the postponement period. Many conflicts explode and ramify because this rule is not observed. In some instances, for example, one partner will start the fight when the other is not ready for it. He or she may be on the way out the door, for example, or trying to buckle down to some task that demands concentration. Moreover, different people fight best at different times. Some, for example, fight best in the morning, whereas others are good night fighters. The best places for fighting also differ among individuals. In some cases, it is a matter of territoriality; the husband may fight best in the den, whereas the wife may prefer the kitchen.

WATCHING THE BELT LINE Another important principle in constructive fighting is to make sure that one's psychological "belt line" is properly adjusted so that it is neither too high nor too low. The belt line is the point above which verbal blows can be absorbed by an individual and hence are fair and endurable. Blows below this point, by contrast, are considered unfair and intolerable.

Some individuals are supersensitive about virtually all matters, and their belt lines are up around their necks. Any verbal blow leveled at them by their spouse, then, is bound to be painful. These people cry "Unfair" every time their spouse criticizes them or approaches them with a complaint. It is extremely important that such a person openly display his or her belt line so that the partner is aware of its location.

ENDING A FIGHT Many married couples try to avoid fighting because they simply do not know how to terminate fights. Others do not like to fight because they are afraid that in the end they will lose more than they will gain. Still others fear the possibility that a fight will end in violence, separation, or divorce. Under ideal conditions, a fight ends when both parties have had their say and have gotten all the venom out of their systems. The best way to discover whether this point has been reached is simply to ask. If the parties have difficulty resolving the conflict—if the same accusations are being repeated back and forth, for example—they should pause, declare a truce, and make a date to resume the fighting at another time. A fight can be considered ended when the partners have made up. If they have decided that they cannot resolve the conflict on their own and require outside assistance, this is in itself a more constructive development than if they had not confronted their problems.

Marriage Counseling

In most cities and towns, the troubled partners can choose from quite a variety of professionals who will try to help with marital problems. Some of these therapists call their work *marriage counseling*, some call it *marriage and divorce counseling*, and some call it *marital therapy* or *family therapy*. Some are trained as members of the clergy, some as social workers, some as psychiatrists or psychologists, some as physicians, and some as sociologists or educators.

The American Association of Marriage Counselors (AAMC) recommends that all counselors have an advanced degree from a university or other approved institution of higher learning and at least three years of professional experience (Kephart, 1966).

Furthermore, as Hilda Goodwin and Emily Mudd (1969) point out, a capable marriage counselor has, during the course of his or her training and practice, acquired certain basic information, attitudes, and skills. This knowledge includes a grasp of human biological and psychological development, an understanding of psychodynamic theory, a knowledge of social and cultural factors that may influence clients, a familiarity with the principles of role interaction, and an understanding of counseling skills. Moreover, a good counselor is thoroughly familiar with all aspects of marriage—emotional, sexual, economic, and religious. The goal of the marriage counselor is "not to effect any drastic change in the personality of either partner, but to help each to perceive his own reality, the reality of the partner, and that of the marriage more clearly" (Goodwin and Mudd, 1969, p. 97).

Marriage counselors can be found by inquiring at a church or synagogue or by contacting the American Association of Marriage Counselors, Alcoholics Anonymous, Legal Aid and Defender, or the Salvation Army. Counselors use a variety of different techniques. They may provide their services free, they may charge as much as $100 a session, or they may base their fee on the client's ability to pay. Generally, a therapist meets with the client couple, with the client family, or even with a group of client couples or families.

How effective are the various forms of marriage counseling? J. Richard Cookerly (1973) conducted a preliminary study of the major types of marriage counseling available today and found that, by and large, each produces a different outcome. According to Cookerly, there are six major types of counseling, which can be broken down into three pairs: individual interview and individual group counseling, concurrent interview and concurrent group counseling, and conjoint interview and conjoint group counseling. In the first pair, a counselor works with one spouse in interview or group sessions; in the second pair, the therapist sees both spouses in separate interviews or group sessions; and in the third pair, the counselor sees both spouses together in interviews or group sessions.

Cookerly examined the files of a private counseling center and obtained the records of 773 former marriage-counseling clients—360 white males and 413 white females. The clients represented all socioeconomic classes. Next he determined which of the six forms of marriage counseling each of the clients had participated in. Then he consulted the center's follow-up data to determine whether the counseling had helped the marriages.

The results showed that the interview of both spouses together was most successful, followed by the conjoint group method. Surprisingly, Cookerly found that separate interview counseling of both spouses—the form most widely practiced today—was ranked either least or next-to-least effective.

SUMMARY

Conflict may occur in any social interaction, and it is inevitable in the intimate environment of marriage. In chronic conflict, small incidents continually evolve into major problems. Differences in values and interests may cause chronic conflict if they are extreme and occur in a number of areas. Value conflict may develop in the course of a marriage and may stem from changes in society as a whole. Chronic disputes can also be caused by situational stresses and by lack of satisfaction of a need for something which either partner perceives as necessary for self-fulfillment.

Failures in communication are at the root of nearly all marital conflicts. People may selectively perceive what they wish to hear rather than what is being said, or they may be distracted by physiological conditions. Another obstacle, frozen evaluation, occurs when people hold onto beliefs and attitudes that are no longer consistent with reality. Polarization is "either-or" thinking, which can prevent two people from finding compromises for their differing opinions. Bypassing occurs when intended meanings are misperceived. Some couples also fail to communicate because they have given up hope of working out their problems or because they fear the consequences of expressing themselves openly.

Marital conflict may result in physical violence, including homicide, or may involve the threat of such violence. In fact, an intensive study has found that violence is a significant phenomenon in family life that seems most widespread among the middle-aged. The level of daily family violence may be higher than reported and recorded cases indicate.

Conflict can serve positive functions, such as allowing for greater emotional intimacy in relationships and presenting the possibility of finding solutions to marital problems. Conflict can be handled creatively by carrying on an internal dialogue before a fight starts, by leveling with one's partner, by avoiding total win-or-lose situations, and by recognizing the psychological "belt line" of one's partner.

Fighting constructively may resolve conflicts or suggest the need for outside help. While they may have different training backgrounds, marriage counselors, at their best, are thoroughly familiar with all aspects of marriage and are skilled at maximizing interpersonal communication. Of the six major types of counseling, the interview of both spouses together seems most successful. Least effective is separate interview counseling of both spouses.

Her View

Ten years ago, at age twenty, Lorraine married Harvey to escape her parents. Lorraine identifies closely with her father, who is a successful general contractor. He is an impatient man and a perfectionist. Lorraine remembers that when she was a child, she and her father regularly walked to the corner store after dinner for the evening paper. She generally got a penny bubble-gum ball and always wanted a black one. One night her father said he was tired of purchasing several pieces of gum to obtain a black one. She promised that she would accept any color, but she was so choked up with disappointment when she got an orange one that she could not put it in her mouth all the way home. Her father expects his wife to wait on him, likes to smoke and gamble, and will eat only steak when he dines out.

Lorraine's mother and aunts have devoted their lives to domestic excellence. Lorraine resents housework, and yet she feels guilty when her house is not in perfect order. She fears that her mother will discover some dust behind a dresser when she visits. Lorraine considers her mother very controlling. Lorraine remembers being greatly disappointed at age five because when she squirmed a little while her mother was pinning up her Easter dress, her mother refused to finish fixing the dress. Last year while Lorraine was visiting her parents and had a cold, her mother took her to see the family doctor under the pretense that the appointment was for herself.

Though she was brilliant in math and a winner of scholarships, her parents insisted that Lorraine live at home and not in the college dormitories, imposed an 11 P.M. curfew, and gave her an allowance of only $2 per week. She has a master's degree in psychiatric social work and worked in a public school for the first two years of her marriage before she became pregnant. She found the decision to return to work four months ago an agonizing one. Her mother accused her continually of neglecting her two preschool children, and she herself felt guilty that she was not fulfilling her motherly duties. She also questions her husband's sincerity in supporting her desire to work as a professional outside the home. She believes Harvey is "only humoring her to keep her in his service" by taking more responsibility for child care and household chores.

Among her girl friends, Lorraine is the best organizer of luncheons and receptions for their get-togethers, since she makes decisions quickly and executes them in a burst of energy. She gets upset by Harvey's deliberating for months about redecorating the house and by his trying to do several garden and household tasks at once. When she wants some repairs done in the house, she likes to have her father come over immediately without consulting Harvey. Harvey's habit of giving the children their baths ten or fifteen minutes after the time she sets infuriates her.

Lorraine says that she married Harvey because she believed she could control him. She even says she wishes she were a man because then she could be more assertive and have more social opportunities. Although at work she enjoys following her supervisor's directives, she does not respect Harvey. She reminds him that she still resents his having let the dishes pile up in the kitchen sink nine years ago when she had pneumonia.

Lorraine avoids sharing herself much with her husband and fears that she could never be personally intimate with a man. She complains that Harvey comes home and talks and talks when she has her hands full with the two children and is cooking dinner. Now that she is considering a separation, Lorraine refrains from communicating with Harvey because she is afraid he would take this to mean that she is committed to him.

During their six months of courtship Harvey displayed no more affection than a good-night kiss, and Lorraine considered him a relief from other guys, who were "all hands." But he disappointed her by not being a more demonstrative lover after marriage. She regards sex as "a reward for him when he has been a good boy by helping me during the day." Now Lorraine says she is "working for her freedom money." She is demanding release from their relationship and says she wants a separation after she has saved up enough to live on her own.

His View

For his part, Harvey sincerely supports Lorraine's desire for a professional career, and he willingly drives the children to the baby-sitter's before work. He wonders why she constantly criticizes him. He remembers that when they first got married, they talked of sharing fifty-fifty, and he feels frustrated that they have to resort so frequently to fighting. Harvey is aware that Lorraine prefers not to sit down and talk the moment he comes home, but he complains that when the children are in bed, she avoids him by taking hour-long baths upstairs. He would like to be able to be more open with her and reveal his insecurities about work, but he feels she would not really listen.

Harvey dislikes the fact that they sometimes go for weeks without sexual intercourse, but he does not feel right about making love when they are at odds with each other. He complains that Lorraine often does not join in sexual foreplay and submits passively to him. Furthermore, he feels hurt and discouraged that he has adjusted his schedule to accommodate her working and has made changes in his personal habits, such as showering daily, to please her (as a bachelor he bathed once a week whether he thought he needed it or not). Despite all, Harvey professes his love for Lorraine and does not want to be separated from his children. But he is getting tired of putting up with her abuse, even though he loves her.

Interpretation and Questions

Describe the conflict between Harvey and Lorraine. How does Lorraine see herself as a woman, and how does this influence her relationship with Harvey? How does Lorraine see Harvey? What are the needs of each in the relationship? How can they learn to communicate their needs?

Important Terms

chronic conflict
value differences
situational stresses
communication
selectivity
frozen evaluation

polarization
"normal" violence
secondary violence
leveling
psychological "belt line"
marriage counseling

Review Quiz

1 Conflict has the potential of bringing to the intimate relationship:
  a grief and unhappiness
  b personal growth
  c increased understanding of the spouse
  d any or all of the above

2 Unemployment, as a predisposing cause of some marital conflict, is best considered:
  a a situational stress
  b a value conflict
  c a lack of satisfaction of personal needs
  d an immediate precipitating event

3 Social psychologists have identified _____ major groups of values which orient individuals toward life.
  a two
  b six
  c ten
  d 100

4 According to Toffler, marital conflict can be decreased by:
  a increasing the number of single people
  b encouraging couples to remain together longer
  c structuring marriage around four trajectories

d postponing marriage until middle age

5 Research shows that the most frequent cause of marital conflict is:
  a money
  b disagreement over children
  c friends
  d in-laws

6 A husband who constantly asks his mother for child-rearing advice without consulting his wife may be unaware that _____ can cause conflict.
  a value conflict
  b situational stress
  c lack of satisfaction of personal needs
  d precipitating events

7 Communication can be:
  a verbal
  b nonverbal
  c unintended
  d all the above

8 In a study of working-class marriages, Komarovsky found that:
  a husbands and wives were about equally satisfied with the quality of marital communication
  b husbands were more satisfied with marital communication than wives

229

**MANAGING
CONFLICT**

c wives were more satisfied with marital communication than husbands

d almost no one expressed dissatisfaction with marital communication

9 People who psychologically "tune out" any communication which is negative about themselves are being:

a selective

b polarized

c frozen in evaluation

d all the above

10 Polarization, as a hindrance to communication, is illustrated by:

a a wife who insists that twice a week is the only normal frequency for sex

b a husband who is willing to spend only one-eighth of the weekly income for food

c a parent who insists that unless a teenager wears his hair a certain length, staying-out privileges will be revoked

d any of the above

11 Telling one's partner, "You seem to be saying . . . " is an example of the communication technique called:

a empathy

b feedback

c listening

d escalating

12 The best estimate we have of the frequency of marital violence is that about _____ percent of couples will use physical force on each other at some time during their marriage.

a 10

b 20

c 50

d 100

13 In constructive fighting the goal should be to:

a avoid having one partner win and the other lose

b pick a time and a place for the fight which are acceptable to both partners

c stay above the psychological "belt line"

d accomplish all the above

14 A recent study indicates that the most successful form of marriage counseling takes place with:

a both spouses together

b a separate interview for each partner

c the conjoint group method

d both spouses in separate group sessions

Opinionnaire

Agree	No opinion	Disagree		
_____	_____	_____	1	It is natural to attack someone verbally if that person hurts your feelings.
_____	_____	_____	2	The fewer fights a couple have, the better adjusted they are.
_____	_____	_____	3	Couples should agree not to bring up certain subjects during a fight.
_____	_____	_____	4	Anyone guilty of child abuse or wife abuse must be mentally ill.
_____	_____	_____	5	One should express all feelings when fighting with an intimate.
_____	_____	_____	6	It is possible for a couple to have a good relationship in which there is never any fighting.

—— —— ——

—— —— ——

—— —— ——

—— —— ——

7 Some fights may have effects that a couple can never overcome.

8 Regardless of how a couple try, there will always be a winner and a loser after every fight.

9 The reason almost all fights occur is that a person cannot see things from someone else's point of view.

10 There is never a reason for one spouse to hit the other during a fight.

Exercise

Below is the chart which Bach and Wyden developed for scoring a fight between intimates. While you probably will not want to score every fight you have, the chart can help you to understand the principles of fighting constructively. Think back to the last fight you remember clearly and fill in the graph (or save it until your next one). Consult the text descriptions of fighting constructively.

THE FIGHT ELEMENTS PROFILE

1	2	3	4	5	6	7	8	9
Reality	Injury	Involvement	Responsibility	Humor	Expression	Communication	Directness	Specificity
Authentic, realistic	Fair, above belt	Active, reciprocal	Owning up	Laugh with relief	Open, leveling	High, clear, reciprocal feedback	Direct focus	Specific
+								
0								
−								
Imaginary	Dirty, below the belt	Passive, or one-way	Anonymous or group	Ridicule clowning or laugh-at	Hidden or camou-flaged	Static, one-way, no feedback	Displaced focus	General "analysis"

The "plus" (+) positions on the profile represent good (or "bonding") styles of aggression.
The "minus" (−) positions represent poor (or "alienating") styles of aggression.
The middle (0) positions indicate styles rated as neutral, irrelevant, or unobservable.
The profile is complete when one line is drawn to connect all nine dimensions, intersecting each dimension at the appropriate level (+ or − or 0). When the line stays predominantly above the "0" level, the fight was fought in a predominantly bonding style. When the line stays predominantly below the "0" level, the fight was fought in predominantly alienating style.
Source: Bach and Wyden, 1968.

Projects for Class or Home Study

1 Consider a recent fight you have had with an intimate. What was the immediate precipitating event? Can you trace the real problem to value differences, situational stress, or lack of satisfaction of personal needs?

2   Watch a family situation comedy on television. Is conflict handled realistically? Do couples use the techniques described in the text for fighting constructively?

3   One positive value of feedback is that it shows your interest in the other person, since it represents an effort to understand that person correctly. Try feeding back a person's communication in your next conversation. Do you sense a positive or a negative reaction? How would feedback affect a verbal fight with that person?

4   Read several newspaper accounts of child abuse or wife abuse. Do the aggressors or their victims seem to have any similar characteristics?

5   Where is your psychological "belt line"? List some verbal comments which you could not absorb. Would all persons' belt lines be at the same level yours is?

Suggestions for Further Reading

Bach, George R., and Goldberg, Herb. *Creative aggression: The art of assertive living*. New York: Avon, 1974.
    The authors feel that being "nice" and nonaggressive leads to problems.
Berkowitz, Leonard. The case for bottling up rage. *Psychology Today*, July 1973, **7**, 24–31.
    The author differs from many behavioral scientists in believing that expression of hostile feelings leads to further hostility.
Brickman, Philip. *Social conflict*. Lexington, Mass.: Heath, 1974.
    This is the most comprehensive collection of readings on conflict available. Many are directly related to family conflict, and others have implications for intimate relationships.
Brownmiller, Susan. *Against our will*. New York: Simon and Schuster, 1975.
    An account of rape as a form of violent male domination. This form of attack is treated as a political act of humiliation.
Johnson, David W. *Reaching out: Interpersonal effectiveness and self-actualization*. Englewood Cliffs, N.J.: Prentice-Hall, 1972.
    Two chapters provide further thoughts on conflict and practical exercises for helping make conflict more constructive. Chapter 7 is on listening skills, and Chapter 9 is entitled "Constructive Confrontation."
Updike, John. *Of the farm*. New York: Knopf, 1965.
    Novels are based upon conflict, either internal or external. In this book a man, his new wife, and his stepson visit a farm owned by the man's mother. Subtle, often unspoken conflict changes and solidifies relationships.
Winter, Gibson. *Love and conflict*. Garden City, N.Y.: Doubleday, 1961.
    The author explores how modern society is related to conflict. He feels that high levels of anxiety prevent us from talking out our conflicts creatively.

Answers to Review Quiz

1-*d*   2-*a*   3-*b*   4-*c*   5-*a*   6-*c*   7-*d*   8-*b*   9-*a*   10-*d*   11-*b*   12-*c*   13-*d*   14-*a*

10

DECIDING TO HAVE CHILDREN

Many people assume that family planning is far advanced in both concept and practice in the United States today. For one thing, our scientific understanding and technological skills appear equal to the task of providing us with safe and effective methods of birth control that are also easily and widely accessible. But such expectations do not coincide fully with the reality of the situation. There are, for example, more sophisticated methods of birth control available than ever before, but periodic reports in journals and newspapers indicate that many of these methods are far from being both unequivocally safe and completely effective. Furthermore, almost one-half of the 4 million teenage girls estimated at risk of unwanted pregnancy have no access to the most effective birth control methods and no reliable sex and birth control education, either in school or elsewhere (Planned Parenthood Federation of America, 1976).

There are, however, other aspects of the situation which suggest that the matter of having children is not being left wholly to chance.

The fact is that fewer babies are being born to women of childbearing age, and the average size of families is decreasing. In 1975, according to the Center for Health Statistics, the birthrate was at a record low of 14.8 births for 1,000 persons. This continues a downward trend in birthrates which began in 1972 and which, if it continues, may culminate in zero population growth by the next century (Illegitimate Rate of Births 14.2%, 1977).

Making a Choice

Birthrate statistics make it clear that many couples are deciding to limit their families. But far less evident is whether, in deciding to have children at all, couples are guided by an in-depth consideration of pertinent questions. No matter how much a child is wanted or how carefully it is planned for, its arrival will cause an irrevocable change in the lives of its parents. Inevitably, a large amount of their personal privacy will vanish. Their ability to schedule their time and activities will be greatly affected. Furthermore, the couple accustomed to two incomes may find it very hard to get by with only one, even if the wife intends to return to work when the child is older. These pressures, separately or in combination, can easily cause a deterioration in the husband-wife relationship.

As shown in the accompanying table, close to half the births that occurred from 1966 to 1970 were unplanned. Women with college degrees were somewhat more successful at family planning than their less well educated sisters.

UNPLANNED FERTILITY, 1970

Race and education	Most likely number of births per woman	Percent of births that were unplanned, 1966–1970
White:	**2.9**	**42**
College:		
4 years or more	2.5	32
1–3 years	2.8	39
High school:		
4 years	2.8	42
1–3 years	3.2	44
Less	3.5	53
Black:	**3.7**	**61**
College:		
4 years or more	2.3	21
1–3 years	2.6	46
High school:		
4 years	3.3	62
1–3 years	4.2	66
Less	5.2	68

Source: Adapted from U.S. Bureau of the Census, 1975, p. 57.

FINANCIAL ASPECTS OF THE DECISION

At first glance it may seem mercenary to think about a baby in terms of dollars and cents. But two people cannot live as cheaply as one, and the addition of a third is an even more expensive proposition. It begins, of course, with obstetrical care for the expectant mother, hospital and delivery costs, clothing and medical care for the baby, and a crib for it to sleep in and toys for it to play with; but it does not end there. Over the eighteen years to come, during which the parents are responsible for supporting the child, the list of expenses snowballs: housing that provides enough room, medical care, dental care, clothing, food, nursery school, baby-sitters, incidental school expenses or even the expense of private schooling, unexpected expenses for illness or accidents, summer camps. . . . The list goes on and on.

A conservative estimate suggests that the cost of rearing one child is about 2½ times the family's annual income; thus for a family with an income of $20,000, the cost of raising one child would be $50,000. This expense is likely to come early, when the husband is just beginning his career and the wife has had to abandon hers temporarily. Research indicates that married couples who have not achieved the standard of living they desire are more likely to use contraceptive techniques and defer child rearing (Bahr, Chadwick, and Strauss, 1975).

EMOTIONAL ASPECTS OF THE DECISION

Sociologist Alice Rossi (1968) has suggested that the major point of transition in a couple's life is not marriage but the first pregnancy. She points out that the role of parent is highly demanding (and, in fact, is a commitment that cannot be revoked), that couples have little or no training for it, and that it happens abruptly, with a very brief transition period of only a few days in the hospital. A number of studies confirm the fact that the first child brings extensive to severe crisis to young parents (Dyer, 1963; LeMasters, 1957).

It is important for couples to question their motives for having children. Do they plan to have children because "everyone has kids" or because two sets of in-laws have made it clear that they are looking forward to being grandparents? Do they feel, deep down, that being a parent somehow makes a man more masculine? Is the woman influenced by pronatalism, the set of beliefs which teaches that motherhood is woman's fulfillment? Are they hoping that the arrival of a baby will help to bridge the growing gap in a husband-wife relationship that seems to be falling apart at the seams?

For many couples, children can be one of the most rewarding aspects of their marriage. But children are *not* a constant source of joy and pride, they are *not* always pleasant people to have around, and, despite our best efforts, they are never just what we hoped they would be. A child is not a computer, to be programmed with the unfulfilled wishes and dreams of

THE ARRIVAL of a baby is especially joyful if parents have planned for it.

parents. Psychologists now understand that such programming can often result in badly damaged individuals, perpetually torn between the desire to please their parents and the desire to please themselves.

One of the greatest pleasures of parenthood is that of guiding the development of a new little person, watching the child as it grows from helpless infancy into competent adulthood. Providing the kind of steady guidance necessary is never an easy job, and there are sure to be some very rocky intervals along the way. Nonetheless, this aspect of parenthood can be immeasurably rewarding.

Another reason for choosing to become parents is the desire of the husband and wife to share their love by extending it to their children. If the marital relationship is sound to begin with, there is always enough love to go around. If the relationship is shaky, one partner or the other may feel that because of the child, he or she is not getting enough love and may react with resentment against the child. The parent who announces, "My child is the most important thing in the world to me" is often using the child as a way to punish the spouse. The effects on the child who is manipulated in this way can be devastating. Parental love should be a natural, logical outgrowth of marital love rather than a substitute for it.

"Are we ready to have children?" This is perhaps the most important question of all. It involves financial, personal, and career considerations. "Can we support a child now?" "Does it appear that we will be able to support one in the future?" "Do we have enough room to provide privacy for ourselves and the child as well?" There is some evidence that college students consider the overpopulation question in deciding how many children to have (Corman and Schaefer, 1973). In response to this problem, some may consider the alternative of adopting all their children or of adopting one or two and placing a corresponding limit on the number of natural-born children they have. But it is not clear whether the matter of overpopulation influences actual practice.

The questions keep coming: "Is our chosen lifestyle flexible enough to include children, or would the presence of a child be a complete disruption?" "Are we ready to make the transition from the closed intimacy between husband and wife to the open intimacy among family members?" "Are we ready to share our love, rather than reserving it only for each other?" "Do we really like children, or do we only like the idea of having children?"

Some considerations are perhaps more applicable to the wife, since the mother usually provides the greater amount of child care during infancy and early childhood. "Am I set on having a career other than homemaking?" "Am I willing to drop that career at least for a few years?" "Is my career the kind that I can easily take up again after a long period away from it?" "If I do resume my career, will the double responsibility be too great a burden for me?"

Finally, there are considerations dictated by our increasing understanding of genetics and the transmission of certain heritable diseases. In the case of some diseases, such as sickle-cell anemia, Tay-Sachs disease, and hemophilia, prospective parents can be tested to see whether they are likely to transmit the disease. In the case of others, there is as yet no way to predict whether the disease will appear in children. Diseases such as diabetes and certain types of cancer seem to run in families. If such a disease has appeared in both their families, a couple should realize that the odds are greatly increased that it will appear in their children.

Family Planning

Once a couple make the decision to have children, a new question arises: "When shall we have them?" Modern methods of family planning allow a couple not only to decide whether to have children but also to determine when they will be born.

At this point in our discussion, we should distinguish between birth control and contraception. *Birth control* involves any method of preventing or spacing the birth of children. *Contraception* refers specifically to any means of preventing conception from taking place. And *family planning* is a catchall term that includes both birth control and contraception.

Today a wide variety of family planning methods are available. Some are more effective than others. Used singly or in combination, however, they all can help couples to carry out any decision they may make regarding parenthood or nonparenthood.

The assumption can be made that illegitimate births, in most cases, are unplanned. According to the accompanying table, the rate of illegiti-

RATE OF BIRTHS TO UNMARRIED WOMEN
(NEVER MARRIED, WIDOWED, AND DIVORCED)
AGED FIFTEEN TO FORTY-FOUR,
PER 1000 BIRTHS, BY AGE OF MOTHER

	1950	1973
Total	141.6	407.3
Percent of all births	3.9	13.0
Rate	14.1	24.5
Age of mother:		
Under 15 years	3.2	10.9
15–19 years	56.0	204.9
20–24 years	43.1	119.1
25–29 years	20.9	43.1
30–34 years	10.8	18.5
35–39 years	6.0	8.2
40 years and over	1.7	2.6

Source: Adapted from U.S. Bureau of the Census, 1975, p. 57.

mate births almost quadrupled between 1950 and 1973, despite the considerable drop in the birthrate during that period (24.1 per 1000 in 1950 and 14.9 per 1000 in 1973).

THE REPRODUCTIVE SYSTEM

Presumably it is no surprise that humans reproduce through the act of sexual intercourse. However, a number of men and women have a mistaken or limited understanding of their own reproductive systems and of the way a child is actually conceived. Perhaps this accounts for confused notions about birth control and about how contraceptives work or what happens when they fail to work.

A new life form begins when a single male reproductive cell—called a *spermatozoon* or *sperm*—penetrates and fertilizes a single female reproductive cell—the *ovum* or *egg*. If its development is unhindered, the fertilized egg, containing genetic characteristics from each parent, eventually develops into the specialized cells and tissues that constitute a human being.

Female reproductive cells and sex hormones are produced in a pair of organs known as the *ovaries*. On about the fourteenth day of a

A HUMAN FETUS at an early stage of development in the uterus. The placenta is a protective layer of tissue through which nutrients pass to the fetus.

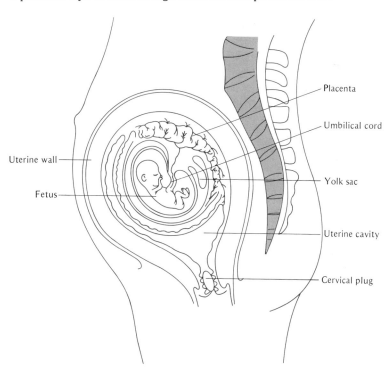

menstrual cycle that lasts approximately twenty-eight days, an egg is released from one of the ovaries and usually passes into one of the two *fallopian tubes.* Each tube forms a passageway between an ovary and the *uterus,* the part of the female reproductive structure in which a fertilized egg would normally begin its nine-month development into a human fetus. If the egg is not fertilized, it completes its journey through the tubes and is released from the body along with a mucous membrane and blood supply that line the uterus during the menstrual cycle. If conception occurs—that is, if an egg and sperm cell unite—the uterine lining helps to provide protection and nourishment for the fertilized egg.

Male reproductive cells and sex hormones are produced in the reproductive organs known as the *testes.* Connected to each testis is a coiled tube some 20 feet in length and of nearly microscopic thinness—the *epididymis*—in which the sperm collects. Each of these tubes joins with one of two ducts, the *vas deferens,* which, in turn, lead to glands called the *seminal vesicles.* The vas deferens continue from the vesicles to the *prostate gland.* Here they merge with the urinary tract from the bladder to form the *urethra,* the single duct which runs the length of the penis. At ejaculation, sperm and fluids from the seminal vesicles and prostate gland mix to form the milky substance called *semen.*

When the male experiences orgasm during intercourse, he ejaculates approximately 20 million sperm cells into the vagina of the female. Out of this number only a few dozen are able to survive and pass through the *cervix,* the narrow and mucus-filled passageway to the uterus. Once in the uterus, the sperm cells may continue to propel themselves toward the fallopian tubes. In order for there to be a possibility of conception, a mature egg must be present in one of the fallopian tubes, and the sperm cells must enter the correct one. Of those sperm which succeed in reaching the outer layer of the ovum, only one will achieve penetration.

If the egg is indeed fertilized, it immediately begins to divide into a multicelled structure. As it forms, this structure is normally moved through the remaining length of the fallopian tube and into the uterus, where it implants and continues to develop. One of the first steps in this intrauterine development is the production of rudimentary sperm or egg cells. Thus, early on, the new life form begins to develop its own ability to participate in reproduction and perpetuation of the human species.

METHODS OF FAMILY PLANNING

Given a general background in how reproduction occurs, we can now better appreciate how conception and birth can be prevented. Methods of family planning can be divided into four categories: behavioral, mechanical, chemical, and surgical. We shall discuss the merits and drawbacks of each method in turn and perhaps touch upon a few of the myths and fallacies that have grown up around this most important subject.

A SURVEY OF FAMILY PLANNING TECHNIQUES
USED IN THE VICTORIAN AGE (1882 TO 1920)

Family planning technique	Percentage of women using (N = 45)
Douching	36%
Rhythm	32%
Withdrawal	22%
Condom	9%
Diaphragms	12%

Source: Based on Gaylin, 1976.

Family planning is not new or modern. Birth control was practiced not only by the Chinese in ancient times but by many so-called primitive people throughout the world. A recently discovered survey of forty-five urban women taken around the turn of the century, as shown in the accompanying table, found that 82 percent used some form of family planning. Percentages equal more than 100 because some women reported using more than one technique.

ABSTINENCE Abstinence is a totally effective means of family planning. It requires no equipment and no drugs—only a heroic amount of self-control. Simply stated, it involves total avoidance of sexual intercourse except at times when children are actively desired. Effective as it may be, it is wholly unacceptable to most couples, for very obvious reasons.

WITHDRAWAL (COITUS INTERRUPTUS) This behavioral method of family planning has been known for thousands of years and has been utilized by every human society which recognized the father's part in the process of conception. References to withdrawal are found in the earliest books of the Old Testament and in the Jewish Talmud. As its name implies, withdrawal involves removing the penis from the vagina before ejaculation occurs.

In theory, withdrawal should be a very effective method of birth control. In practice, however, it has a number of drawbacks. Physiologists now understand that the actual ejaculation of semen is often preceded by an uncontrollable glandular secretion of fluid from Cowper's gland which may contain sperm. Thus, by the time withdrawal has occurred, enough sperm-bearing fluid may already have entered the vagina to enable conception to take place.

From the psychological standpoint, withdrawal may be particularly unrewarding to both husband and wife. Although the husband will probably reach orgasm after withdrawing, he is forced to pull away just at the time when he desires to be closest to his wife. The wife may find herself deprived of stimulation just at the moment when she is about to experience her own orgasm. In such a situation, the two partners inevitably feel separated at the time when they should be closest.

THE RHYTHM METHOD A balance between abstinence and careful timing, the rhythm method is still the only means of family planning condoned by the Roman Catholic Church and certain other religious groups. The practice of the rhythm method requires an understanding of when the woman's ovulation (releasing of an egg from one of the ovaries) is most likely to occur. If a reliable means of predicting the exact date of ovulation were available, this method might have more than the 70 percent effectiveness which it now does.

The simplest method of rhythm planning involves charting the woman's menstrual cycles over a period of one year. Taking into consideration both the longest and the shortest possible cycles and assuming that ovulation will occur on approximately the fourteenth day before menstruation begins, it is theoretically possible to plot the "safe days" and the "baby days" within the cycle.

Once again, theory is easier than practice. Stress, either physical or emotional, may delay or induce ovulation. Physical illness may have the same effect. Perhaps the final testimony to the unreliability of the rhythm method as a practical means of family planning is the suspicion among researchers that ovulation in women, as in several other species of animals, including cats and rabbits, may actually be induced by the act of sexual intercourse, possibly stimulated by the muscle contractions that accompany orgasm.

Several attempts are being made to make the rhythm method more reliable. For a number of years it has been possible for a woman to take her "basal body temperature" every day upon awakening, using a specially calibrated thermometer. The basal body temperature drops sharply just before ovulation and rises even more sharply after ovulation occurs. However, there is still some uncertainty as to how long both egg and sperm may survive in the woman's genital tract, and so the basal body temperature measurement is not yet a completely reliable guide to the duration of the fertile period.

More recently, an experimental test has been developed which can detect chemical changes in the mucus secretions of the cervix prior to ovulation. If a simple test can be devised which allows a woman to check her own cervical secretions at home—perhaps using a chemically treated paper which changes color on contact with cervical mucus—it is probable that family planning using the rhythm method will become much more reliable than it now is.

DOUCHING There is some question as to whether douching, or injecting liquid to wash out the vagina after intercourse, should be considered a chemical or a mechanical method of birth control. Essentially, the douche is an attempt to wash sperm out of the vagina before they can travel upward toward the waiting egg.

Douching is almost as old a practice as withdrawal. It is also the basis for many old wives' tales. Many young people in the rural regions of this country, for example, firmly believe that a douche of warm Coke or 7-Up will kill the sperm. It will not. Others believe that a douche of certain herbs in infusion will do the job. It will not. Any value that douching may have is due to the liquid itself rather than the contents of the liquid, and this "flushing out" of the vagina is by no means a reliable method of family planning. Sperm move quickly, helped along by the uterine contractions that occur during intercourse. They move considerably faster than the woman can, in her frantic run to the bathroom after intercourse has taken place. The douche may reinforce her peace of mind, but it has only a minimal likelihood of preventing conception.

Many of the chemical preparations that are advertised specifically for contraceptive douching may have a damaging effect on the tender tissues of the female genital tract. All in all, douching is by itself an extremely unreliable means of contraception. However, it may have a place in backing up other methods, as we shall discuss a little later.

CONDOMS   Most methods of birth control must be implemented by the female partner. The condom, however, is a method which has long been used by men, although its original purpose was the prevention of venereal disease rather than prevention of pregnancy. The condom is familiarly known as a "rubber," "sheath," "skin," or "prophylactic." It

CONDOMS.

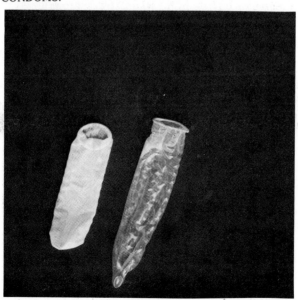

consists of a thin "glove" for the erect penis, made of latex or, in certain more expensive versions, of the intestinal gut of newborn or unborn lamb.

Typically, the condom appears as a rolled-up sheath, which is unrolled to fit over the erect penis just before intercourse takes place. Usually the condom has an extension or "nipple" at the end, which provides a receptacle for the semen and prevents it from splitting under the pressure of ejaculation. Condoms are readily available; they are sold over the counter in drugstores and, in some states, in vending machines in men's rest rooms. Since the latex may have deteriorated in any condom that is purchased from a vending machine, a man is well advised to procure his supply from a drugstore.

The condom is a highly effective method of contraception. Used in conjunction with a diaphragm (see below), it may be almost 100 percent effective. For an individual who routinely has many sexual partners, the condom is an important device for protecting against the transmission of venereal disease.

If the condom is so effective, why is it not the preferred method of contraception? For one thing, its use involves interruption of sexual foreplay so that the man may put the device on. For another, some men report that the condom lessens sensation during intercourse. On the other hand, in some countries, such as Japan, the brightly colored and decorated condoms are used as an aesthetic enhancement of the sexual act.

THE DIAPHRAGM Mechanical means of contraception which involve blocking the entrance to the cervix with a foreign body have been known to Europeans for at least 300 years and to aboriginal peoples for much longer. The writings of Casanova, that legendary lover, speak of women who capped the cervix with the shell of a squeezed lemon in order to prevent conception. American Indian women frequently used a ball of buffalo tallow or even buffalo dung to achieve the same results. But it was not until the 1880s that the diaphragm, a modern method for blocking the cervix to the penetration of sperm, was evolved.

The diaphragm is a thin circular rubber membrane supported by a flexible wire rim. Secured in place, it covers the cervix completely and is firmly wedged under the pubic bone. To back up its contraceptive effect, the diaphragm should be smeared with a spermicidal jelly before insertion and should remain in position for at least six hours after intercourse.

Properly used, the diaphragm is about 95 percent effective as a contraceptive measure. However, there are certain problems which may work against its effective use.

First of all, the diaphragm must be carefully fitted by a physician to the individual woman and must be refitted periodically—always after childbirth and ideally once a year. The woman must remember to install it

DIAPHRAGM.

before intercourse, and once installed, it must remain in position for many hours. Douching before removal of the diaphragm is often advised. Some women find the process of installing the diaphragm distasteful. Others find that these careful preparations detract from the spontaneity of lovemaking. And in certain women, the muscular contractions that occur during orgasm may dislodge the diaphragm from its position. But in most instances, the failure of the diaphragm can be attributed to its position on the shelf of the medicine cabinet rather than over the cervix, where it should have been.

THE IUD The IUD, or intrauterine device, is probably the most effective of the mechanical means of birth control. It consists of a small plastic or metal object which must be inserted into the uterus by a physician or a medical paraprofessional. Insertion is usually performed toward the end of the woman's menstrual cycle, at which time the cervical opening is relaxed and slightly expanded. IUDs come in a number of sizes and shapes, and current research will probably add to this variety. Most IUDs have small threads or strings that protrude from the cervix, allowing the woman to check and be sure that the device is still in place. All the IUDs have about a 92 to 98 percent rate of effectiveness.

Just how the IUD prevents pregnancy is only now beginning to be

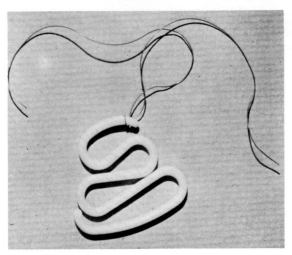

IUD.

understood in detail. Researchers believe that rather than preventing conception, the IUD serves as an irritant which prevents the embryo from becoming implanted in the lining of the uterus. Because of its contra-implantation nature—that is, because it does not prevent conception—it is classified as a birth control device rather than as a contraceptive.

At first glance, the IUD would seem to be the ideal method of birth control. Once it is installed in the uterus, the woman needs to take no further precautions against pregnancy. However, many doctors advise that an IUD be removed every few years for inspection. If the woman decides to have a baby, fertility returns as soon as the IUD is removed. Like all methods, however, the IUD has its drawbacks. Many women experience severe cramping and a very heavy menstrual flow for the first few months after insertion. In some women, particularly those who have never had a child, the IUD may be spontaneously expelled by uterine contractions. Women with fibroid tumors of the uterus or those who are prone to pelvic inflammations are advised not to use the IUD. Cases of

DISPOSITION OF APPROXIMATELY 1 MILLION PREGNANCIES AMONG TEENAGE GIRLS, 1975

Postmaritally conceived marital births	261,500
Premaritally conceived marital births	95,200
Out-of-wedlock births	225,500
Miscarriages	120,000
Abortions	340,000

Source: Adapted from Planned Parenthood Federation of America, 1976.

pelvic infections and perforation of the uterine wall have been reported in connection with the IUD. Questions concerning the effects of long-term use have yet to be answered.

SPERMICIDES Chemical methods of contraception have long been known, or at least postulated, by primitive peoples. Women of certain South American tribes drink a "tea" made from the leaves and roots of a plant which is supposed to cause temporary sterility. For a long time scientists discounted such claims. Now, however, it appears that they may be perfectly valid, and research is directed toward isolating the chemicals which might be responsible.

Spermicides—foams, jellies, or liquids containing an active sperm-killing ingredient—are an important chemical means of contraception. However, most of these methods should be used in conjunction with a mechanical method. Totally ineffective are those spermicides—usually in the form of vaginal suppositories—that are advertised under the euphemistic name of "feminine hygiene supplies." No such suppository ever prevented a pregnancy from taking place, unless that pregnancy was doomed to failure from the beginning.

The foams and jellies, however, are quite another matter. It is always recommended that a spermicidal jelly be used with the diaphragm, and such a jelly can also add to the effectiveness of the condom. The spermicidal foams, on the other hand, are meant to be used alone. Most of them are efficient spermkillers, but they do have certain drawbacks. The foam must be injected into the vagina just before intercourse and again if intercourse is to be repeated, which causes an interruption in sexual foreplay. While it may assist with lubrication, some couples complain about the extreme slipperiness caused by the foam. Foams also tend to be rather messy and to leak out of the vagina onto bedclothes and underwear. Finally, some couples report that the foams have an irritating effect on the sensitive genital tissues.

THE PILL Oral contraceptives are perhaps the best-known chemical method of family planning. When using the pill, a woman continues to excrete her uterine lining through menstruation, but she is prevented from ovulating. In other words, no fertile period occurs. Taken exactly according to directions, the pill has an effectiveness of nearly 100 percent.

The contraceptive pill is an extremely potent drug which changes the hormonal balance of the female reproductive system and may affect a variety of other body functions. The most widely used pill is the "combination" type, containing synthetic versions of two female hormones, estrogen and progesterone. It is usually taken for twenty-one days of each menstrual cycle, starting on the fifth day after menstruation

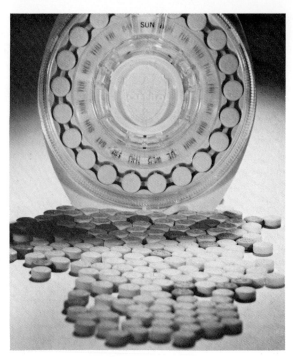

BIRTH CONTROL PILLS.

begins. Ovulation, and the risk of pregnancy, may occur if even one pill in the sequence is skipped.

Most obvious of the pill's advantages is its almost perfect effectiveness when taken as prescribed. It has no more mental association with the sexual act than the taking of a vitamin tablet. One of the pill's desirable side effects is that it frequently makes menstrual cycles regular and the menstrual period shorter in those who have previously had difficulty with menstrual irregularity or excessively long and heavy periods. In fact, quite apart from its contraceptive effects, it is often prescribed for such conditions. The known disadvantages of the pill, however, are growing, and its safety has been debated for a number of years.

Every package of contraceptive pills carries a warning required by the Food and Drug Administration listing the undesirable side effects that the pill has been known to cause. These include nausea, headache, dizzy spells, depression, high blood pressure, high blood sugar, breast tenderness, and darkening of the skin. It is worth noting that all these are also side effects of pregnancy and that the pill works, in effect, by simulating pregnancy where none actually exists.

A more serious side effect of the contraceptive pill is abnormal blood clotting, accompanied by the potential for fatal or crippling blockage of a blood vessel in the brain, heart, or lungs. There is an unusually high incidence of such clotting among women who take the pill, and it is estimated that 3 out of every 100,000 users of oral contraceptives will die annually because of blood clots which obstruct the flow of blood through the body (Goldsby, 1976). Advocates of the pill point out that the percentage of fatalities among women taking oral contraceptives is actually lower than the percentage of fatalities resulting directly from complications of childbirth. Nonetheless, the FDA has now issued a further recommendation that women over forty years of age avoid the pill, since the incidence of abnormal blood clotting is appreciably higher in that age group. It is further advised that women of any age take the pill for no more than ten consecutive years and that it be alternated with some other form of contraception.

Certain women should not take the contraceptive pill at all. Contra-indications are a medical history of abnormal bleeding between menstrual periods, disease of the liver, cancer of any reproductive organ, and abnormal blood clotting. Certain other women, including those with a history of mental depression, uterine fibroids, epilepsy, diabetes, migraine headaches, asthma, high blood pressure, heart disease, or kidney disease, should take the pill only under conditions of very close observation by a physician. And all women who take the pill should have a yearly gynecological examination.

A recent study of 17,032 women also found an impairment of fertility among women after use was discontinued. While the impairment diminishes with time, there is still a difference in pregnancy rates thirty months after use of oral and nonoral contraceptive techniques is discontinued (Vessey, Doll, Peto, Johnson, and Wiggins, 1976). As shown in the accompanying table, women who have been on the pill are likely to wait longer to deliver a live-born or stillborn child than those who have been using a diaphragm.

It should be clear that not all the returns on the pill are in yet and that much remains to be learned about it. A woman's decision to use the

PERCENTAGE OF WOMEN WHO HAVE NOT YET COMPLETED A PREGNANCY AFTER STOPPING CONTRACEPTION IN ORDER TO CONCEIVE

Months after cessation	Percentage who have not yet completed a pregnancy	
	Diaphragm	Pill
12	44.9	69.3
18	24.4	31.7
24	17.0	20.7
30	11.8	16.4

Source: Adapted from Vessey, Doll, Peto, Johnson, and Wiggins, 1976.

contraceptive pill, therefore, should be made in consultation with her physician, after weighing the advantages and disadvantages of this method.

THE "MORNING-AFTER" PILL This pill is designed to be used only as an emergency measure after intercourse has taken place. It consists of a high-dosage estrogen compound which causes the uterus to contract and expel its contents. To be effective, it must be taken within five days after intercourse has occurred. The morning-after pill should not be considered a method of family planning. It invariably produces a number of uncomfortable side effects, including nausea, vomiting, and painful abdominal cramps. However, it has a definite value as an emergency measure and is frequently administered as part of the routine treatment of rape victims.

STERILIZATION Sterilization is a contraceptive technique which is usually permanent and irreversible. Available to both men and women, it should be chosen only by those who have given it careful consideration and made a final decision to have no more children.

The sterilization procedure for men is called *vasectomy*. It is a minor operation that can be performed in a doctor's office and requires no hospitalization. After a local anesthetic is administered, a small incision is made in the scrotum. Through this incision the vas deferens on each side is either cut or tied off. Sperm cells can no longer reach the urethra and instead are reabsorbed by the body.

Some minor postoperative pain and swelling usually occur after vasectomy, but most men are ready to resume sexual activity within a week. For several weeks after vasectomy the couple are advised to use a backup method of contraception, since some sperm may remain in the genital tract until after the first few ejaculations. By the end of the second month after vasectomy, microscopic examination of the semen will usually confirm that sperm are no longer present. The man is now sterile, and no further contraceptive measures are necessary.

Until only recently, sterilization for women involved major surgery. The procedure, called *tubal ligation*, is performed under general anesthesia and requires a hospital stay of several days. A large abdominal incision is made, and both fallopian tubes are severed or cauterized so that eggs released by the ovaries can no longer reach the lower tubes and the uterus. Menstrual cycles continue, and the ovaries release their eggs as usual. But with the tubes cut or tied, there is no way in which an egg and sperm can meet.

A newer technique shows promise for making sterilization a much safer and simpler procedure for women. Officially known as *laparoscopic sterilization*, it has acquired the nickname "belly-button" or "Band-Aid" operation. The procedure takes only a few minutes to complete, can often be done under local anesthesia, and is usually performed on an outpatient basis with no overnight hospitalization necessary.

A ¹/₂-inch incision is made just below the navel, and the laparoscope—a hollow, lighted tube—is inserted. Carbon dioxide gas is forced into the abdominal cavity to distend it so that the abdominal organs can be clearly seen through the laparoscope. Through the same incision, or through a second tiny incision slightly lower down on the abdomen, another instrument is inserted, and the fallopian tubes are cauterized or permanently closed with a clip made of inert plastic. The carbon dioxide is now allowed to leave the abdominal cavity, the instruments are withdrawn, and each tiny incision is closed with a single stitch and can be covered with a Band-Aid.

The only usual aftereffects of the laparoscopic procedure are a tendency toward cramping for a few days and a slight bloating caused by retention of some of the carbon dioxide, which is soon absorbed. The woman can usually resume all her activities immediately, including sexual relations. The tiny scars which remain become nearly invisible within a very short time.

ABORTION Abortion is the surgical termination of pregnancy before the fetus has developed enough to survive on its own. It cannot really be considered a method of family planning, but it is, in fact, a way of preventing unwanted births.

Until recently, most state laws allowed abortion only when the physical or emotional health of the mother might be damaged by the birth of a child, when there was medical reason to believe that the fetus might be abnormal, or when the pregnancy resulted from rape. In 1973, however, a Supreme Court ruling struck down most state laws forbidding or limiting abortion. Abortion during the first two trimesters of pregnancy is now legal, although the state retains the power to regulate second-trimester abortions in the interests of maternal health. The decision concerning whether an abortion is to be performed during the first trimester of pregnancy is now arrived at solely by the woman and her physician.

Many advocates of abortion consider the Supreme Court ruling most important because it officially recognizes the right of a woman to control her own body. However, the medical aspects of the ruling are probably even more important. Thousands of women have died from illegal abortions that were often performed by persons with no medical training, under appallingly unsterile and unsanitary conditions and without even the benefit of anesthesia. Equally tragic are the deaths of those women who, in desperation, tried to abort themselves. Since the 1973 ruling, such cases have become infrequent. Abortion, performed by a qualified physician under the same sterile conditions that obtain during any other type of surgery, is a safe procedure.

During the first trimester of pregnancy, abortion can be performed in two ways. The old method, which is still used occasionally, was the "D and C"—dilation and curettage—in which the cervical canal is artificially enlarged to admit a spoon-shaped curette, with which the lining of the uterus is scraped away. A newer technique is *aspiration* or *vacuuming* of the uterus. This new procedure is much safer than a D and C, and the incidence of postoperative complications is much lower than in the case of the older method.

Abortion during the second trimester of pregnancy is a much more difficult procedure and more dangerous to the woman. In the *salting-out* technique, a strong saline solution is injected into the uterus to kill the fetus. Within a few hours uterine contractions much like those which occur during labor begin, and the body of the dead fetus is expelled. The fetus may also be removed by *hysterotomy*, a surgical procedure resembling cesarean section.

Since 1973, the number of abortions has probably increased greatly, although accurate data on earlier periods are hard to obtain. The District of Columbia has had over a 3 to 1 ratio of abortions to live births since 1973. Other highly urbanized areas have reported high abortion rates as well, but in more rural states abortion is still rare. Mississippi had only two legal abortions per 1,000 live births in 1973 (U.S. Bureau of the Census, 1975, p. 58). About 80 percent of the legal abortions have been performed prior to the twelfth week of gestation, and approximately two-thirds of them have been performed on unmarried women.

SUMMARY

With a declining birthrate and a decrease in the average size of families, it appears that many couples are deciding to limit the number of children they will have. But it is important that couples also consider when to have children and whether they should have them at all. One factor that enters into the decision is the financial one—that is, the medical, clothing, school, and other expenses for which parents are responsible until their offspring are eighteen years old. Another major factor is the emotional impact of having children. Included among a range of issues that parents are advised to consider are their motives for having children, their desire to share with the child the time and love once reserved for their own relationship, their ability to cope with the child's own problems in growing up, and the willingness of the wife to withdraw temporarily from a job or career. Parents are also advised to consider the possibility of heritable diseases.

Family planning includes two concepts: birth control, which involves any method of preventing children from being born or of spacing the birth of children, and contraception, which refers to any means of preventing conception from taking place. Conception occurs when the male reproductive cell (sperm) penetrates and fertilizes the female reproductive cell (ovum). In the normal process, the fertilized egg then becomes implanted in the uterus and begins its development into a human fetus.

There are behavioral, mechanical, chemical, and surgical methods for preventing conception or controlling birth. Among strictly behavioral methods (all safe), abstinence is unrealistic for most couples, withdrawal is psychologically unrewarding and not completely effective, and present rhythm methods are about 70 percent effective. Among mechanical methods, the condom is safe, is quite effective when used with a spermicide, and is a good preventive against the transmission of venereal disease. The diaphragm is also safe and, used properly, is about 95 percent effective. The IUD can be almost 98 percent effective, but it entails considerable risks which vary with the user. Among chemical methods, douching is of negligible effectiveness, but spermicides have general value as supplementary contraceptives. The oral contraceptive is the most effective single method of birth control, but its usefulness is marred by a number of risk factors. The potential effectiveness of the morning-after pill is very limited, and its use can produce severe physical discomfort. Sterilization involves surgical procedures which permanently prevent conception. Abortion is the surgical termination of pregnancy before the fetus becomes independently viable.

CASE STUDY

His View

Ralph Richard Brodner became acquainted with Maria Elena Ruiz nine years ago at a musical rehearsal for the celebration of the twenty-fifth anniversary of the appointment of the local Catholic bishop. Ralph was then studying for the priesthood, and Maria belonged to a community of nuns. Friendship between Ralph and Maria blossomed, and in time Ralph was sure he was in love with her. The fourth of seven boys, he had entered the seminary after grammar school. He had never dated in his twenty-three years. Now, however, he had become disillusioned with the loneliness and sacrifice that he foresaw would be required of him as a priest.

At the end of the summer Ralph decided that the priesthood was not for him. Maria chose to remain in the convent, but she promised to remain "friends" and to correspond regularly. Ralph returned to his hometown and found a job as a caseworker at a home for delinquent boys. As the year progressed, his letter writing increased, and Maria reciprocated. Ralph visited Maria at Thanksgiving and Easter. In May, Ralph was overjoyed to hear that Maria was agreeable to marriage, and they planned an August wedding. A simple but personalized ceremony was held in the town where the two had met, and both families gathered for the occasion. Ralph sang a love lyric that he had composed, and they exchanged wedding promises that they had written themselves.

Ralph willingly moved to a neighboring state so that Maria could complete her last two years of college. He agreed with her that they should not start a family while she was still in school. He imagined they might someday have children, but he was in no rush. He wanted to be settled into a place he liked and the kind of work he preferred before making that decision. For now he wanted mainly to bask in the pleasure of Maria's company.

Two years later Ralph yearned to return to the lovely and serene town where they had met. He took a low-paying, part-time position teaching math and counseling at a boarding school for girls. At year's end, he concluded that teaching was not for him, since he did not want the hassle of disciplining youngsters and was unwilling to put out the effort to obtain a regular teaching certificate. He was proud of his guitar playing, but he regarded a musical career as demanding too much grueling travel. For two years he pieced together an income from several jobs—clerking at a sporting-goods store, teaching guitar to young-sters, and selling insurance door-to-door. Three years ago he decided that he wanted a steady, good-paying, non-service-oriented job. He responded to an ad placed by a computer firm. Though he had no background in the field, he was chosen from among seventeen applicants for a position as junior manager. Eight months ago he volunteered to manage the evening shift, though it would mean being with Maria only in the late evenings and on weekends. Ralph is confident that he has found the work he likes and that promotions will be forthcoming. Four months ago he and Maria purchased an attractive and spacious house with lots of yard room.

Ralph listens with some hesitation to Maria's comments about wanting children. His best buddy, Edward Smith, became a father ten months ago. Edward told Ralph that sexual intercourse was cumbersome during the last several months of pregnancy and that his wife was too sore from delivery for six weeks after the birth to have sex. Ralph enjoys sex and does not like to think of forgoing it. Another friend, Steve Tanzi, told Ralph that he had been present at the delivery of his daughter. Ralph wants to share meaningful experiences with Maria, but he is not sure he could withstand the bloody aspects of the birth process. Edward also recounted that he had difficulty adjusting to finding his wife occupied with the baby when he came home, to not having the baby asleep when he was interested in having sex, and to being awakened by the baby several times during the night.

Her View

Maria entered the convent after graduating from high school. She had dated, but never seriously. Maria liked Ralph a lot, but she was ambivalent about choosing him over the religious community that she had wholeheartedly joined two years before. She had grown up with three brothers and four sisters and had engaged in numerous coeducational activities in high school. She was eager to pursue a lifestyle that would contribute to the fulfillment of others, possibly in education.

In September Maria returned to her classes at the sisters' college. She became close to one of her lay professors, Mrs. Diane Ramirez, who taught child psychology and was the mother of three. Maria visited her professor's home several times a month and sometimes baby-sat for the children. Between classes and at meditation time, Maria reflected on her future. Most of all she wanted to be a loving, giving person. She saw how Mrs. Ramirez and her husband tried to help each other grow by communicating their personal selves and supporting each other in discovering their individual talents, and she was impressed by the sensitive way in which they reared each child as a unique person. As the months passed, Maria's feelings for Ralph grew warmer, and she assented to marriage.

Maria's sister had secured a job as a key-punch operator in a town 20 miles from Ralph's home, and the sisters shared an apartment during the summer. Maria designed all the floral arrangements and bouquets for the wedding and had made the colorful invitations by hand. She wanted to major in theater and dance and was very pleased when Ralph was willing to move to a neighboring state so that she could attend the college she had selected as the most appropriate. She wanted to be free of child-care responsibilities at least while completing her degree, and she also wished for abundant time to enjoy Ralph's companionship.

After finishing college, Maria also longed for the natural beauty and tranquillity of the town where they had fallen in love. For the first year she taught dance and directed a theater group at the girls' boarding school. She renewed her acquaintance with Mrs. Ramirez and wondered how long it would be before she had a baby. Jobs were hard to find for a couple of years and Maria worked as a short-order cook, clerked in a dry-cleaning establishment, taught dance in adult education classes, and sang at weddings. Despite their low income and the fact that they moved to a slightly more spacious and somewhat more attractively decorated apartment each year, Ralph and Maria were able to save about $800 a year toward a house. Though she did not regard her work as very fulfilling, Maria liked playing tennis with Ralph on weekends, found dancing or singing to his guitar playing exhilarating, and enjoyed his gentle and pleasuring lovemaking.

Maria experienced a surge of confidence and strength three years ago when Ralph decided to work for the computer firm. Eighteen months ago an old friend recruited her to help direct a series of courses on nutrition in the local high school. She has since taken several college courses in the subject and finds her return to teaching invigorating. Maria misses Ralph while he supervises the evening shift. About a year ago she told Ralph she would like to think about starting a family. She is nearing thirty and considers herself neither too young nor too old to bear and raise children. Maria talks a lot with her girl friends about motherhood. She thinks it would be beautiful to share a birth experience with Ralph since she believes that parenthood is really a joint project. Her friend Rita is a year older and is also considering what motherhood would mean to her. They lunch together at school, and a couple of times a week their conversation centers on becoming mothers. Maria has witnessed many joyful moments shared by her friends and their children, but she questions whether the daily routine of child care will consume all the time she feels she needs to grow as a person and to cultivate her professional talents. She worries that three of her close friends, including Mrs. Ramirez, have been divorced in the last year. Maria is not sure how her life will be affected, but she quietly and hopefully anticipates that she will become pregnant in the coming year.

Interpretation and Questions

How do you think the backgrounds of this couple are affecting their present situation? What do you think about Maria's motives for wanting children? Do you feel that Ralph's reservations about having a family are serious, or are they just minor concerns which will work themselves out once a decision is made? Will the recent purchase of a home influence the couple's decision? What would be the impact of a baby on Maria's personal and professional development? How might a child affect Ralph's and Maria's marital relationship? Do you feel they are ready for the responsibility of children?

STUDY GUIDE

Important Terms

pronatalism
family planning
birth control
contraception
abstinence
coitus interruptus
rhythm method
douching
condom
diaphragm

intrauterine device (IUD)
spermicides
birth control pill
morning-after pill
sterilization
vasectomy
tubal ligation
laparoscopy
abortion

Review Quiz

1 It is estimated that _____ of the 4 million teenage girls at risk of having an unwanted pregnancy have no access to reliable birth control methods and devices.
   a one-tenth
   b one-quarter
   c one-half
   d three-quarters

2 The belief that children are desirable evidence of a woman's fulfillment is called:
   a pronatalism
   b family planning
   c birth control
   d zero population growth

3 Most methods of birth control:
   a are perfectly safe
   b are very dangerous
   c are completely effective
   d have the drawback of being ineffective, hazardous in one way or another, or both

4 The term which refers specifically to means of preventing conception from taking place is:
   a birth control
   b contraception
   c family planning
   d abortion

5 Withdrawal is an unsatisfactory method of birth control because:
   a sperm may be contained in the preejaculation fluid from Cowper's gland
   b the two partners must pull away from each other at the moment they want to be closest
   c it is less reliable than other methods
   d all the above

6 The only means of family planning condoned by the Roman Catholic Church is:
   a withdrawal

b the rhythm method
c douching
d abortion

7 The contraceptive device that is also effective in preventing the transmission of venereal disease is:
a the condom
b the diaphragm
c the IUD
d the pill

8 The intrauterine device (IUD):
a is a birth control device rather than a contraceptive
b is about 70 percent effective
c must be reinserted after every menstrual period
d can never be inadvertently expelled by a woman

9 The contraceptive pill prevents birth by:
a aborting the fetus after conception has occurred
b obstructing the sperm from entering the vagina
c stopping ovulation
d permanently sterilizing a woman

10 _____ prevent(s) the fertile period of the woman's monthly cycle from occurring.
a Withdrawal
b The IUD
c Spermicides
d The pill

11 At present, the "morning-after" pill:
a works by dissolving the contents in the uterus
b has no undesirable side effects
c must be taken within five days to be effective
d all the above

12 The form of sterilization called *vasectomy* involves:
a cutting or tying off the vas deferens tube
b a generally irreversible operation
c minor pain and some swelling for a few days
d all the above

13 Abortion is a relatively safe procedure if performed:
a in the first trimester of pregnancy
b after the fifth month, when the woman can "feel life"
c on a married woman
d all the above

14 In choosing a method of birth control:
a it is a good idea to consult a doctor
b people must decide for themselves what seems best
c one must consider one's own health and sexual pleasure
d all the above

Opinionnaire

Agree	No opinion	Disagree		
_____	_____	_____	1	No couple should have more than two children.
_____	_____	_____	2	A woman is not truly fulfilled until she has given birth.
_____	_____	_____	3	Children will be cared for and loved whether they are planned or not.
_____	_____	_____	4	Use of contraceptives takes all the spontaneity out of sex.
_____	_____	_____	5	Couples who are poor have as much right to have children as well-to-do couples.
_____	_____	_____	6	No couple should have children during the first year of marriage.

_____ _____ _____ 7 Couples should agree on exactly how many children they will have before they get married.

_____ _____ _____ 8 Birth control is the responsibility of the female in a relationship.

_____ _____ _____ 9 Most people would find the rhythm method unacceptable as a form of birth control.

_____ _____ _____ 10 Any mechanical means of birth control will decrease enjoyment of the sexual act.

Projects for Class or Home Study

1 Ask childless people of your acquaintance to estimate how much it costs to raise a child. Are the estimates realistic, using the $2^{1}/_{2}$-times-family-income formula?

2 Planned Parenthood has local chapters in most cities. Call and ask for free literature on family planning.

3 In the near future, technology may permit bringing a fetus to term in an artificial womb. What are the advantages of such a procedure? What are your feelings about it?

4 Ask several friends and acquaintances to find out whether they were planned or not. Is there a tendency for younger persons to be planned?

5 The Lamaze Method of Child Birth Education and the La Leché League can provide information on natural childbirth and breast feeding, respectively. How do you feel about these practices?

Suggestions for Further Reading

Boston Women's Health Book Collective. *Our bodies, ourselves: A book by and for women.* New York: Simon and Schuster, 1971.
   Written by a group of women concerned about their own health, this book contains an excellent chapter each on reproduction, venereal disease, and birth control. The emphasis is on choosing and using a birth control method that is good for the individual.

Cochrane, Susan H., and Bean, Frank D. Husband-wife differences in the demand for children. *Journal of Marriage and the Family*, May 1976, **38**, 297–307.
   The authors suggest that economic factors are often taken into account in deciding how many children to have but that the economic future of a family may have a different meaning for husbands and wives.

Dixon, Ruth B. Hallelujah the pill. *Trans-action*, November–December 1970, **7**, 44–49.
   The author discusses the impact of oral contraceptives on women's position in society. She concludes that the birth control pill has not made women free.

Golantry, Eric. *Human reproduction.* New York: Holt, 1975.
   This brief, up-to-date paperback contains excellent graphics and a clear, concise treatment of reproduction.

Greely, Andrew M. Catholics prosper while the church crumbles. *Psychology Today*, June 1976, **10**, 44–51.

 The impact of religious attitudes on birth control can be very strong. In this article, the Catholic position is criticized by a priest.

Rainwater, Lee. *And the poor get children*. Chicago: Quadrangle, 1960.

 This study has become a classic and still contains some of the best insight in print into sex, contraception, and family planning in the working class. The text is supported liberally with interview excerpts.

Thompson, Jean. *The house of tomorrow*. New York: Harper & Row, 1967.

 An autobiographical account of a twenty-year-old college girl who goes to live in a home for unwed mothers.

Answers to Review Quiz

1-*c* 2-*a* 3-*d* 4-*b* 5-*d* 6-*b* 7-*a* 8-*a* 9-*c* 10-*d* 11-*c* 12-*d* 13-*a* 14-*d*

11

WATCHING CHILDREN DEVELOP

Becoming a parent is not confined to the matter of bearing children. After a child is born, many parents find themselves unprepared for the work and responsibilities involved, and too often they are unprepared for their own feelings toward the child's behavior. Undoubtedly, one of the most complex tasks anyone can undertake is that of rearing a child. But training for parenthood has not been systematically provided in our society, and widely divergent views are promulgated as to the "proper" way to rear children. Parents today suffer as a result of contradictory evidence from the "experts," changing attitudes toward sex roles, and, in particular, an honest dilemma regarding values—strictness versus permissiveness. E. E. LeMasters overheard the following remark in a tavern: "They're always talking at school about whether we understand our kids. By God, I think it's more important that kids understand their parents" (LeMasters, 1975, p. 116). The speaker finds it difficult to understand why children, whose basic needs are taken care of and who are free of adult responsibilities and hardships, should be given any special consideration.

Other people, however, emphasize the fact that children are not to be trained like so many smart little animals. This school of thought considers children to be people, like the rest of us. They have feelings; they can be hurt; they respond to love and praise; they have ideas of their own; and, most important, they are incredible learners, sopping up information about the ways of the world. At Summerhill, a private school in England founded by A. S. Neill and based upon the concept of allowing children complete freedom to learn for themselves, a writer-photographer recorded his first impressions:

> The children were immediately friendly and straightforward. If someone objected to being photographed at a particular moment, or objected for one reason or another to your presence in their room, they just said so, and that was that, for no one in Summerhill is more important than anyone else (Walmsley, 1969, p. 1).

Science cannot furnish guidelines for deciding which of the two viewpoints expressed above concerning the treatment of children is correct. Science does not deal in prescriptions. The values of parents—and, to a great extent, the society in which they live—determine rules, often contradictory, for rearing children. But research has provided us with an abundance of information concerning the way children grow, what their needs are as they develop and mature, and their different responses to their environment as they grow older. In fact, some of the best researchers and theorists of the twentieth century have devoted themselves to the question of the family's influence on child development. Equipped with this information, parents may be able to address themselves to child-rearing issues with greater understanding and confidence.

Early Development

The early physical development of children is an area in which systematic observation has provided a more or less standard profile. If a child's growth does not conform, it does not necessarily mean that there is something wrong; individual differences are expected to emerge. But within any given age group, children do seem to share certain abilities and to behave in many similar ways. Extreme differences between one's own child and other children of the same age may suggest problems in development. Standards of growth, therefore, provide parents with a way of knowing when to seek professional help and advice (Mussen, Conger, and Kagan, 1969).

Though new parents may be reluctant to admit it, all newborns have the same general features, with variations in size and weight. Newborns are usually reddish and wrinkled, with puffy eyelids and smoky bluish

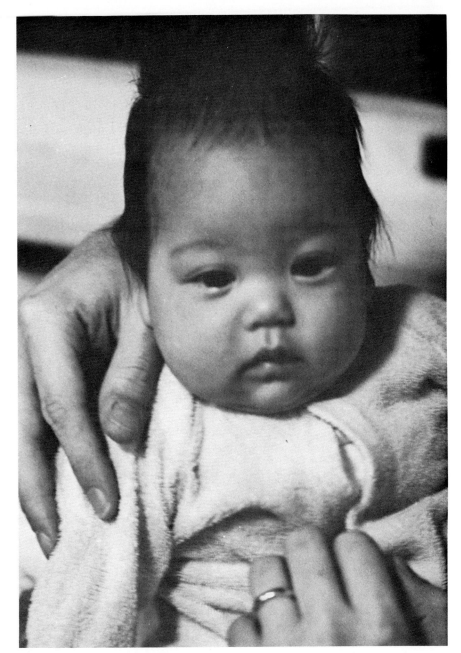

THOUGH SHE now needs a parent's support just to sit up, this four-month-old infant may be soloing in three months' time.

eyes. Their heads are large in comparison with their trunks, and their legs, as one new father remarked, look like those of a 67-cent-a-pound bowlegged chicken.

As in prenatal development, growth proceeds from the head down. During the first year or so, the head makes up one-fourth of the child's total height; by about age seven, the head makes up only one-eighth of the total height. Development also tends to occur from the spinal cord outward to the extremities. In no other period, except before birth and during adolescence, are there such remarkable changes and growth as in the first twelve months of life. Within the first four weeks of life, the lungs begin to function regularly, and breathing is no longer erratic. The heartbeat steadies, body temperature becomes stable, and the muscles become less flaccid.

The development of motor skills in the first year of life—for example, sitting and standing—is largely a factor of maturation. Parents may try to get their child to perform these skills ahead of schedule, but it is usually an exercise in frustration for all parties involved. Until a particular child's muscle tone, coordination, and nervous system have developed, he or she is simply incapable of doing certain things. The schedule varies, but a child is generally able to sit up without support by seven months, creep at the age of ten months, stand alone at fourteen months, and walk alone at fifteen months. (It is interesting to note that some babies may start to walk as early as nine months.)

In accordance with the principle that growth works outward, control is gained first over movement of the arms and legs. After that, the infant begins to acquire manual dexterity. Initially, the movements of the hands and fingers are random and clumsy. The infant tries to pick up any large object in the immediate vicinity and vainly tries to put it into his mouth. But at about the age of five or six months, the hands and fingers are able to grasp smaller objects and to coordinate with the infant's intentions. When he sees something he wants, he is able to move toward it, reach for it deliberately, grasp it in his hand, and—he is successful this time—put it into his mouth (Piaget, 1936).

During the first year, one also notices dramatic differences in the infant's ability to perceive the environment. The newborn seems unable to distinguish between the various people in the environment, though it is difficult to be certain of this. But such ability is quite evident by the age of five to six months. For example, at this time, infants may become anxious about strangers, suggesting that they are able to make perceptual distinctions between those people and objects which are usually in the "scheme" of the everyday world—and hence familiar—and those things which are alien (Spitz, 1946). Also, before the age of four months children apparently have no concept of permanence. When the mother leaves the room, she ceases to exist for the infant—which explains why departure may be accompanied by crying. A five-month-old knows that the mother and father are separate beings but cannot conceive of their independent existence. It is not until the age of twelve to eighteen months that the child is able to understand that there are permanent objects in the world. They may be hidden for the moment—like a toy under a blanket or a father playing peekaboo. But once having seen these objects, the child knows they are still there, somewhere.

Theories of Child Development

In the course of child rearing, nearly all parents believe they have stumbled upon certain "truths" about child development. Quite possibly their discoveries could be supported by any of a number of studies or experimental investigations conducted by professionals in the field. But to formulate a theory of child development requires much more than random or isolated observations of one's own child.

At present, there is no single theory which provides a comprehensive and complete explanation of all the mechanisms of growth and features of psychological development. Partly because of the enormous amount of information that has been gathered on the subject, each theory of child development focuses on only certain aspects of the process. The theories also vary in their interpretations and explanations of different kinds of behavior. However, all current theories agree that children enter the world with certain capabilities and that development is the result of some degree of interaction between heredity and environment. The differences between theories are partly a matter of emphasis.

The psychoanalytic theories of Sigmund Freud and Erik Erikson are concerned more with personality and emotional development than with physical development. They propose that a child is born with certain innate biological structures which strongly influence the response of the child to the environment. Both Erikson and Freud conceive of the

THE SOCIAL PROCESSES OF CHILD DEVELOPMENT
A human infant is an unsocialized bundle of drives, all "id" in Freud's term. Without others to interact with, the infant would not survive. Language gives the child the capacity for feeling, knowing, and seeing the self. These qualities eventually lead to a functioning adult who can exercise inner control and direct his or her way through life's alternatives.

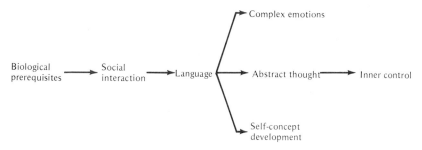

development of an infant from childhood to a healthy maturity as a struggle to conquer different innate needs and urges at successive stages in the process. Erikson, however, is more sensitive to the effects of the social environment on the individual than was Freud.

Learning theorists regard biological factors as only minimally important. Children's behavior is seen as an almost direct result of learning from experiences in the environment. Children learn to behave in ways that seem to bring rewards and avoid punishment. They also observe and imitate the behavior of important people in their environment, such as parents and teachers.

A third approach to child development focuses on the cognitive processes—reasoning, thinking, and problem solving. The most important researcher in the field of cognitive development is Jean Piaget. Like the psychoanalytic theorists, he proposes that the child's development is, in part, an unfolding or maturation of inborn tendencies and that these tendencies interact with the child's physical and social experiences in the environment. In the process of adapting, the child tries to understand, to order, and to shape the world at the same time that he or she is being shaped by it. The changes in behavior which result from this continuous process of interaction characterize the process of child development, according to Piaget (1952).

Stages in Development

The concept of stages is commonly used in explaining intellectual and emotional development. Piaget, concerned with the process by which the child acquires the skills needed for thinking and for manipulating the environment, suggested that intellectual development occurs in a series of fixed stages. The abilities a child gains in one stage are brought into the next, where they are integrated with new cognitive abilities and dimensions in experience. Cross-cultural studies seem to support Piaget's notion that the sequence of stages is the same for all children. However, the rate at which one child passes through these developmental stages appears to be strongly influenced by the environment (Cole, Gay, Glick, and Sharp, 1971).

BABIES

Piaget describes the cognitive development of infants from birth to twenty-four months as the period of *sensorimotor* intelligence. The information a child gains about the world through the development of sensory and motor skills forms the basis for a more complex probing and understanding of the environment. It is during this period, for example, that a child's eyes and fingers develop and coordinate, making it possible to reach out and intentionally grasp objects. The sensorimotor period is divided into six substages, which Piaget sees as gradual and continuous, but inflexible in respect to sequence (Piaget, 1952). The child progresses from reflexive activity—such as crying and sucking—to a basic understanding of the relationship between his or her own body and the objects in the environment.

Foundations for symbolic activity, such as the use of language, are formed during the sensorimotor stage. George Herbert Mead, a social psychologist, has described a possible sequence of events leading to such activity. He divided development of symbolic understanding into three stages: the preparatory stage, up to eighteen months; the play stage, from about eighteen months to seven years; and the game stage. A child begins to babble, usually before the sixth month. At that time, a trained linguist can pick out all existing basic sound units of the language. By one year to fifteen months, children may have acquired a few words. But at this stage much language use is simply expressive, and the child often repeats words without intending to designate objects. For example, a child, upon seeing a ball, may accurately name the object but then toddle through the house repeating the world *ball* without intending to communicate anything. This is, however, preparation for later symbolic use of language (G. H. Mead, 1934).

During the first twelve months, the baby is also changing emotionally in some important ways. Erik Erikson describes people's lives in terms of the resolution of eight crises, from each of which a positive or negative self-image is gained. These progressive crises build on the foundation of preceding ones, but each crisis may often be re-resolved in the light of additional maturity.

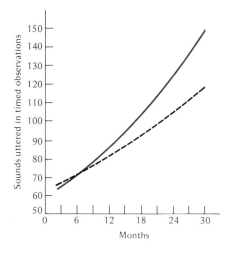

DEVELOPMENT OF SPEECH IN CHILDREN OF PROFESSIONAL AND LABORERS' FAMILIES
Children begin with the same capacity for speech development, but the progress of those in professional families (solid line) is faster than the progress of those in laborers' families, as this early study showed. *Adapted from Orvis C. Irwin, Infant speech,* Scientific American, *September 1949,* **181***(3), 24. Copyright © 1949 by Scientific American, Inc. All rights reserved.*

Erikson describes the first year of life as a stage given to the resolution of the basic trust-versus-mistrust crisis. Basic trust is "the essential trustworthiness of others as well as a fundamental sense of one's own trustworthiness" (Erikson, 1963). Basic mistrust, a view of the world as an unsafe and unpredictable place, is the opposite personality set. Basic mistrust leads to such self-defeating actions in older children as whining or picking fights, to a poor sense of self-esteem, and to a reduced ability to deal with others in a positive way.

This first stage in Erikson's model coincides with and expands Freud's first psychosexual stage of the human ego—the oral stage. During this time of life, according to Freud, all sensation and satisfaction center in the mouth. Feeding, sucking, and, during teething, hard rubbing and chewing are the baby's primary concerns. This innate need for sucking is all-important and must be satisfied before the subsequent stages can be achieved (S. Freud, 1949).

According to Erikson, the development in normal babies of a sense of basic self-trust or self-confidence depends in large part upon whether their needs are met (especially in the first three months) in a loving and consistent manner. Babies who are picked up for cuddling and feeding or changing every time they cry learn to trust that other people will respond to them. Their confidence will increase because someone else cares about them. For Erikson, this is not the time to teach independence—the newly formed self-concept is really too fragile to bear adversity. Children who are left to "cry it out" or who scream themselves into the next feeding time only become more frantic and frightened.

INFANTS' REACTIONS TO ADULTS' DEPARTURE
Children's awareness of the difference between family and nonfamily members increases with age, as shown by the amount of crying in the first minute after departure of a stranger (black line), mother (gray line), and father (color line). *Adapted from Jerome Kagan, Do infants think?* Scientific American, *March 1972,* **226***(3), 79. Copyright © 1972 by Scientific American, Inc. All rights reserved.*

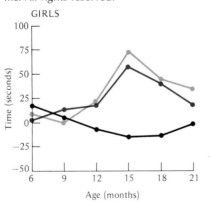

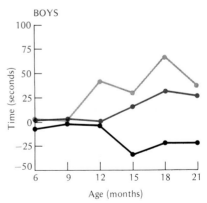

Erikson points out the importance of the maternal figure at this early stage; human trust is built on the bonds between the infant and a nurturing parent. Husband and wife usually want to share this vital role. Thus if the mother is nursing, the father might take over the other aspects of the baby's care—bringing the baby to bed to be nursed or changing diapers.

Current studies suggest that it is the response to the infant's cries and the amount of interaction and contact with the mother at such times that affect the strength of the maternal attachment (Schaffer and Emerson, 1964). The importance of continual close physical contact with either parent is dramatically illustrated in a study made by René Spitz (1945) of forty-five babies in a foundling home. Most of the time the infants were isolated in small cubicles and had no human contact although the nursing care was excellent and the babies were visited by a doctor daily. A follow-up study made eighteen months later revealed that one-third of the infants had died; the remaining children showed retarded physical and mental development. Spitz attributed the dramatic number of deaths to the lack of human contact as well as the lack of any kind of visual or emotional stimulation.

TODDLERS: TWELVE TO TWENTY-FOUR MONTHS

At the toddler stage, curiosity about the environment is insatiable, and energy is unflagging. Toddlers gain greater control over their muscles, including control of bowel and bladder, and they begin to exercise their will and the right to autonomy. Intellectually, they are becoming able to create and manipulate mental representations of things by using symbols.

Freud described the second and third years of life as the anal stage, when pleasure becomes centered on the sensations of holding back and releasing the sphincter and urethral muscles. Following Freud, Erikson sees the crisis of the second year as autonomy versus shame and doubt. Toilet training is used as a symbol for this crisis, since it involves the necessity for children to gain a measure of self-control over their bodies, something in which they take pride and pleasure.

Autonomy implies an ability to control oneself, with a resultant sense of pride and self-confidence. Its opposite, for Erikson, is shame and doubt about one's worth and ability to control one's actions. Shame can occur either as a response to an overly stern and restrictive parent who allows the child no leeway or in response to the anarchy of the child's own conflicting impulses—"I want to please Mommy by doing this, but maybe it would be more fun to do that." Either way—obeying the parent or following the "naughty" impulse—leads to discontent with oneself, or shame. Parents can help guide the child toward autonomy by striving for a "middle ground"—not being overly strict, but at the same time providing guidance so that a two-year-old, for example, is not left to decide alone when it is time to come in from the rain! Avoiding excessive strictness is especially important in the area of toilet training. Several studies (e.g., Bostock and Shackleton, 1951; Sears, Maccoby, and Levin, 1957) indicate that punishing bed wetters does not improve the situation; in fact, it seems to have the opposite effect. Guidance and support appear to bring the best results.

PRESCHOOLERS: TWO TO FIVE

Personality develops during these years partly as a result of the way in which problems of gender, identity, and expressions of anger are dealt with. The problem of identity in the preschool years, particularly the year from two to three, presents a striking similarity to the problem of identity in adolescence. In fact, this preschool year has been called the "first adolescence" (Dodson, 1970). It is a time of storm and stress, of negativism and rebellion. All these are reactions to the struggle to define oneself, in opposition to one's parents.

But parents may notice a change in their child when he or she is past the third birthday. Things are not so tense all around. Suggestions are no longer greeted by automatic rejection. Language is getting clearer all the time, and the child seems generally more self-assured. This period has been described as an "age of equilibrium" (Ilg and Ames, 1955).

Erikson described the stage from ages three to five or six as one of conflict between initiative and guilt. Children now have lots of energy, and, it is hoped, they have developed an abiding sense of trust and confidence in their own ability to control themselves and to perform successfully at their own level. Autonomy now becomes more focused and directed as the child begins to attempt more and harder physical and mental feats. A sense of initiative will be the outcome of the conflict if the child succeeds in most of the activities attempted. Guilt is the product of frustration and the inability to deal with failure or disappointment. On the one hand, the child has become aware of all the things he or she can do. On the other hand, a rudimentary conscience is at work, limiting the possibilities. This time is comparable to later adolescence, when fiery idealism is tempered with realism.

Guilt at age four or so also arises from the high level of sexuality during what Freud characterized as the "first genital stage." From about age three to age four, pleasure is phallic, resulting from the stimulation of the genital area. The second stage, from age four to age five, is also phallic, but it centers on a strong attraction to the parent of the opposite sex. This is the period of the Oedipus and Electra complexes in the male and female, respectively. According to Freud, the resolution of the oedipal conflict finds the child turning from the futile attempt to win the opposite-sex parent and emulating the same-sex parent. Freud originally

THE OLDER SIBLING, male or female, is often regarded as a protector and "provider" for younger members of the family. This young girl listens raptly while her brother negotiates business with the ice-cream vendor.

believed that the oedipal period was rooted in physical maturation. However, early anthropological research showed that there are societies in which no oedipal conflict develops. Examples of such cultures include those in the Trobriand Islands (Malinowski, 1927) and the island of Samoa (M. Mead, 1928).

Intellectually, great advances are made in this stage of tremendous curiosity and energy. Children's attention spans lengthen, and their improved coordination enables them to carry out more preplanned and precisely executed activities. Unlike developments during the preceding period of sensorimotor intelligence, in which an infant can connect actions and perceptions only one at a time, without a cohesive overview, representational thought—coming at around age two in the preoperational period—enables the preschooler to grasp many events at once. Past, present, and future can be considered in one effort. Representational thought enables children to decide what they would like to play with and where they will play with it at a particular time. It also expands their world to include contemplation as well as concrete action. Children during this period begin to deal intellectually with numbers and quantities, such as size. Finally, representational thought becomes codified and socialized—that is, children can share their thoughts with a friend (Piaget, 1952).

Piaget observed certain limits to this new mode of thinking. One of his central themes is the egocentric nature of preschool children's thought. They find no need to examine their own logic, and consequently they are unable to think about their own thought processes. The process of playing with other children forces them to realize that their thinking must interact with that of others.

The power of reasoning at this stage is limited in other ways. It is static. Children may perceive and focus on the beginning and end of a process—for example, the ingredients that go into a chocolate cake and the finished product—but it is extremely difficult for them to conceptualize the stages required to mix and bake the cake.

At this stage, errors in judgment result from what Piaget terms *centration*. This is a tendency to focus on one aspect of an object or situation and to fail to balance various other features involved. Reasoning may be based on memory: "Every time Mommy puts on David's coat, they go out. She is putting his coat on; therefore, they must be going out." The logic of a preschooler is also greatly influenced by wishful thinking. Matthew wants dinner. His mother says it is not ready yet, and so he climbs into his high chair because he associates it with eating and believes that sitting there will make food materialize, independent of his mother's estimate of the waiting time. Finally, the preschooler's reasoning is flawed by transduction—the child connects two unrelated events because they occur simultaneously. If Ellen goes to bed at dusk every night, she may assume that staying up will prolong the hours of daylight.

As the child matures, contacts with peers become more frequent and more influential. Such social interaction is often characterized by play activity. Parten (1932) has categorized children's play behavior and has noted changes in the size of play groups as children become older. At first, children play independently. By the age of two, they engage in parallel play, playing independently of, but in proximity to, another child or several other children. By the age of four, children are playing together at the same activity—in fact, they spend a quarter of their playtime in a group. Mead observed that children enter a postlanguage play stage which lasts until age seven. Older preschoolers often play at roles, such as mother and father, an important activity which improves their interaction skills (G. H. Mead, 1934).

MIDDLE CHILDHOOD: SIX TO ELEVEN

During the years from about six to eleven, the personality, already formed, solidifies, becoming more distinct and more predictable. This is a period of more intellectual than physical development, although there

AS CHILDREN MATURE, they begin to enjoy playing with others in addition to engaging in solitary amusements.

may be a small growth spurt between six and eight years. Most children's bodies change in shape, however, conforming more to adult proportions of head-trunk-limb relationships. Genetics, health, and diet influence growth. Growth, in turn, has an influence on personality. Large, well-coordinated children are often looked up to by their peers. They may excel in athletics. This approbation develops feelings of self-confidence, causing such children to assume leadership in other areas as well.

The age of six seems to be almost universally regarded as a milestone in child development. The family circle opens, and children enter school to acquire a working knowledge of the skills and facts necessary to function in society. They also come into greater contact with other children, and peers begin to exert a counterinfluence to that of the parents. Members of another race or class may be encountered for the first time, and children become aware of differences between themselves and other children.

The individuals who are most importantly involved in the formation of self-concepts are termed *significant others*. Between the child's second and fourth years, these people are primarily family members. But during middle childhood, as the self-concept begins to stabilize, the range of significant others widens. Same-sex peer groups begin to exert considerable pressure on children after they begin school. Teachers initiate the systematic comparison of children in the grading system, which also has an important impact on how the self-image develops (E. J. Green, 1973).

The focus of children's attention shifts at around age seven from the emotional involvements within the family to the challenge of learning to deal with the outer world as a worker. This, then, is the period of industry versus inferiority (Erikson, 1968). During this time, jobs are done and enjoyed for the sake of their execution. In the past, many projects were begun and abandoned, but during the period of initiation, goals are set more realistically and are achieved more often.

Children at this age are practicing continually. They practice games until they are mastered. They often begin music or dance instruction or participate in athletic activities. The child's feeling of accomplishment is the reward for the hours spent studying, reading, practicing, or playing the same thing again and again. Inferiority, the opposite resolution of this developmental stage, comes only when the goals set by the child, the parents, or society are beyond the child's ability to achieve. A sense of industry may be gained when a child successfully joins a peer group and functions well with other children intellectually. The other danger during this period, Erikson points out, is that the child may become so immersed in "work" that work is perceived as the only important aspect of the world.

Piaget terms years from ages seven to eleven the *concrete operational period*. To him, an operation is a process which changes the child's environment (Piaget, 1960). The preoperational child can change things through the process of thought, while the sensorimotor child can do so only with actions. The child who has arrived at the concrete operational stage can go one step further and think about real, concrete things in systematic ways. However, seven-year-olds cannot easily think about abstractions. They classify reality by concrete objects, rather than by abstractions. Attention can now be focused on more than one aspect of something simultaneously. Conservation of volume can be grasped; John at two may think a tall, thin beaker holds more than a short, wide one, but by the time he is eight, he knows this is not necessarily true. Teaching boys and girls cooking helps to reinforce such concepts. Sequential order becomes understood. The making of a cake is now known to proceed from the assembling of the ingredients to mixing, molding, baking, and finally decorating.

Thinking also becomes more socialized and less egocentric. The opinions of other children are taken into account. In G. H. Mead's terms, the child is able to take the role of another, that is, to place himself or herself in another's position (1934). The rules of a game become of

TELEVISION CAN have a strong impact on children, who are in the process of learning roles and piecing together an understanding of their world.

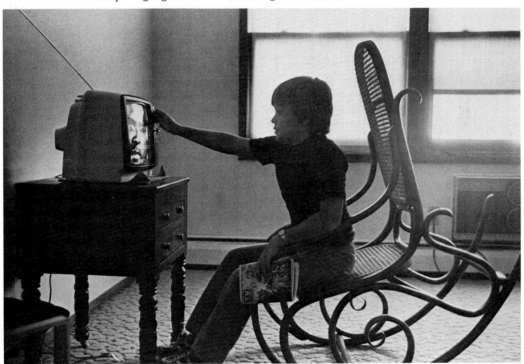

paramount importance. Children may make them up, but while they are in effect, status attaches to their successful observation.

Thinking in the middle years of childhood is typically more flexible than earlier, but also there is more awareness of the distinction between fact and fantasy. A four-year-old talks about the trip she and a friend will take out west, but a scornful older sister knows that two kids on a wagon, fortified with a banana and four cookies, will not get more than a few blocks from home.

ADOLESCENCE: TWELVE TO EIGHTEEN

Adolescence is the bridge between childhood and adulthood, a time of great stress and of tremendous physical, intellectual, and emotional change. It is a time of testing boundaries, both those imposed by the self and those imposed by others. In the process of testing, changing, and questioning, a deepened sense of self is formed.

One aspect of adolescence is the two- to four-year period called *puberty*, during which sexual maturity is reached. Puberty involves both physical and psychological change. The sexual organs become capable of adult functioning, and hormonal changes cause secondary sexual characteristics to appear. Girls begin to menstruate and to develop hips and breasts. Boys begin to develop pubic and facial hair, and their voices become lower. However, secondary sexual characteristics do not make their full appearance until after puberty. Breasts grow larger, and beards heavier, in later teen years.

The development of sexual maturity is preceded in both boys and girls by a tremendous growth spurt. Except for the first six months of life, in fact, adolescence is the period of most rapid growth. Unfortunately, for some adolescents, growth is uneven, with the hands and feet growing more rapidly than the arms and legs. The resulting gawky and ungainly appearance can be one of the trials of this stage of life. Eventually, however, such discrepancies even out. Gains are made in height and weight. The amount and distribution of fat change, and the proportion of bone and muscle tissue increases. The growth spurt for girls usually begins between the ages of eight and eleven and peaks at the middle of the twelfth year. From then on, growth tends to slow down, and it ceases in most cases between the ages of fifteen and eighteen. During the period of maximum growth, girls grow about $3^{1}/_{2}$ inches in one year and gain about 11 pounds. Boys begin to grow between the ages of eleven and fifteen and reach a peak at fifteen; between the ages of fourteen and fifteen they may grow 4 to 5 inches and gain 12 to 14 pounds. Boys continue to grow until age nineteen or twenty. This differential pattern of growth accounts for much of the agony of adolescence, during which time girls tend to be larger and more sexually developed than boys, to the consternation of both sexes.

Intellectually, adolescence is a time of great advances. Piaget classi-

DIFFERENT CHARACTERISTICS OF ADOLESCENTS WITH HIGH AND LOW SELF-ESTEEM

High self-esteem	Low self-esteem
Close relationship with father	Distant from fathers
Jewish faith	Catholic or Protestant
Only children	Later-born children
Fewer psychosomatic symptoms	More psychosomatic symptoms
Not sensitive to criticism	Sensitive to criticism
Not isolated; many friends	Detached; few friends

Source: Adapted from Rosenberg, 1965.

fies the years from age eleven to age fifteen as the *period of formal operations*. Formal operations represent the highest level of cognition. During late adolescence and early adulthood, the ability to acquire and utilize knowledge reaches a peak. Between the ages of eleven and fifteen, children become able to think in abstract terms. They can generalize before this time, but it is now easier to think in terms of abstract universals such as "freedom" or "blueness." According to Piaget, children at this age can think in terms outside the realm of their experience and deal with propositions contrary to fact. An interest in theoretical problems and hypothetical solutions develops, as does the ability to deal with abstract symbols, as required, for example, in logic or algebra. Indeed, it is the adolescent's increased ability to form hypotheses that causes some of the teenager's typical problems of decision-making. Like toddlers who say "no" to everything because they have just discovered that option, adolescents are able to envision many alternatives, which can cause them to doubt their own judgment.

Adolescent interest in theoretical ideas also can lead to a high degree of idealism and to lengthy discussions with peers about solving social problems. Another example of adolescent idealism is the teenage "crush," which is of brief duration but great intensity. Such crushes are also a way for the adolescent to try out different images, since the object of the crush may mirror or complement aspects of the young person who has it.

In addition to abstract and logical thought, thinking becomes more mobile and flexible and less egocentric. Finally, adolescents begin to think about the process of thought itself and to be extremely aware of the thoughts of others.

The crisis of adolescence, according to Erikson, is the resolution of identity versus identity diffusion. This stage encompasses the Freudian genital stage, during which time sexual feelings are in resurgence after the latency period between ages seven and eleven. According to Freud, such sexual feelings initially focus on members of the same sex, but eventually the average individual becomes sexually oriented toward members of the opposite sex. In addition to this sexual confusion, the adolescent must rework his or her solutions to crises resolved earlier in childhood.

The main concern of individuals during this period, according to Erikson, is their identity. Having mastered certain formal skills in the previous stage, adolescents are concerned with whether the way the world perceives them coincides with the way they view themselves, and they must deal with the important question of how to connect the roles and skills they have acquired with the real occupations of the world. Roles and identities are tried on for size in an effort to integrate these factors, and, as Erikson points out, others must be appointed to play devil's advocate for the testing of ideas. The assumption of enemies is the other side of the coin of adolescent crushes, platonic and otherwise.

Role diffusion is a danger at this stage. Adolescents who have a poorly conceived identity or who have doubts about their worth are especially likely to have difficulty settling on an occupation. To compensate for this confusion, adolescents "overidentify" (Erikson, 1963) with heroes of cliques and crowds, to the point of "falling in love" with a hero of the hour.

Adolescents are even more attracted by the peer group, and more influenced by their friends, than young people in the middle years of childhood. For example, in one study (Brittain, 1963), 338 high school girls were presented with hypothetical situations requiring decisions and were asked whether parents or peers would be more influential in helping them arrive at their decisions. In general, peers were thought to

THE INFLUENCE OF PARENTS AND PEERS

Item	More influential	
	Parent	Peer
Which course to take in school		X
Which boy to go steady with	About the same	
How to be selected for a school honor	X	
Whether to report boy who damaged school property	X	
Whether to enter beauty contest or be a cheerleader	X	
How to dress for football game and party		X
Whether to be beauty contestant or appear on TV program	X	
Which dress to buy		X
Which one of two boys to date	X	
Which part-time job to take	X	
Whether to report adult who damaged public property	X	
How to let boy know she is willing to date him	X	

Source: Adapted from Brittain, 1963, p. 389.

OFTEN IT IS young people who most eloquently reflect the capacity for living in the moment and enjoying the indefinable pleasure of simply being alive.

be more influential in such areas as how to dress, but parents were still considered role models in areas with long-term consequences.

In the middle years of childhood, children band together in same-sex groups. After puberty, as interest in the opposite sex increases, a same-sex group usually bands together with a clique of the opposite sex. There is a fairly rigid hierarchy of status in such cliques. Membership furnishes a setting for the formation of a few intimate friendships, which supplant the close ties between parents and child at this age. Popularity is often influenced by membership in the right clique, since adolescents are often extremely clannish and intolerant of any out-groupers or less well accepted members of the peer group. One is either "in" or "out," and those who are "in" help reinforce one another's shaky identities by stereotyping themselves and the enemy. This willingness to conform to win acceptance, plus the adolescent intellectual bent for idealism, may explain the attraction of spiritual cults for many youths.

Adolescence is a time, then, of many conflicts between parent and child. Sexual tension is created on both sides by the maturation of one's offspring into a sexually attractive man or woman. The mother feels a little threatened by the beauty who now lives with her and her husband, and the father is aghast as young men come to court the child who used to love *him* best. Conversely, both parents are threatened by the manhood of their boy, who only a few short years ago could not be persuaded to talk with members of the opposite sex.

Emotionally, adolescents are struggling for independence and for a definition of their self-image. This cannot be achieved if they still perceive themselves as attached to their parents. The right to make their own decisions, on the basis of their own values and judgment, is what is really at stake in arguments over what time to be home or what mode of dress is appropriate.

Self-esteem depends upon a number of factors, but parental interest in the adolescent still seems to be primary. In a survey of over 5,000 adolescents in high school, most of the factors which correlated with self-esteem were also correlated with parental interest (Rosenberg, 1965).

SUMMARY

An understanding of how children develop physically and intellectually is a valuable aid for parents, who, for the most part, have little direct knowledge of children until their own are born. Children grow according to specific patterns: from the head down and from the trunk to the extremities. Growth is sequential, and learning proceeds according to physical maturation. Children cannot walk or talk until their bodies have developed the physical capacities to do so.

The most influential theories of child development are the psychoanalytic theories of Freud and Erikson, learning theory, and cognitive theory as developed by Piaget. All these theories are developmental; that is, they are explanations of sequential stages of development. During the first year of life, according to Erikson, healthy babies learn to trust the adults who care for them. Freud describes this as the oral stage, during which sucking and eating are of primary concern. The foundation for the acquisition of language is laid, and most important, babies in their first year take control over their bodies, turning over, sitting, pulling themselves up to their feet, and perhaps taking their first steps and mouthing their first words.

Toddlers are busy people—curious, into everything, and eager to learn. This is Freud's anal stage, given over to the control of the sphincter and urethral muscles. Toddlers become autonomous, in control of their own bodies. Between the ages of two and five, children seek to define themselves as separate from their parents. This is a stormy period, sometimes called the "first adolescence." At this time children develop initiative, and they succeed in projects they undertake. Intellectually, they develop the ability to think symbolically, to grasp many events at once, and to deal with numbers and quantities. Their logic is still faulty, however, in that they make casual connections between two simultaneous but unrelated events.

Middle childhood sees children interacting on their own outside the home. The school begins to exert influence in the socialization process. Grading begins, and problems raised by status and place in the hierarchies of peer and school groups must be confronted. Children become more sensitive to social situations and learn to put themselves in the position of others.

Adolescence sees the final preparation for adult life. Physically, adolescents grow to their full size and develop their full sexual potential. Adolescents learn to think in abstract terms. Roles are tried and rejected. Peer groups become important influences, causing conflict with parents. In Erikson's terms, adolescence is the time of identity formation.

CASE STUDY

1 Toddler

Kim Schwartz is an active sixteen-month-old toddler. The first child of a professional couple, Kim has received a lot of attention. An eight-week veteran at walking, Kim still walks with a widespread stance and topples at the slightest provocation. She moves quickly, however, and with a lot of self-assurance.

Kim knows a few words—"Ma-ma," "Da-da," "hi," "bye-bye," "nose," "ear," "bah" (for "bottle"), and "no"—but she leans more toward activity and exploration than toward mastering the finer intricacies of language. She can often be found peeking impishly out from under the table at dinnertime or busily emptying out the contents of a closet, cabinet, or brown paper bag at other times. She sings a kind of happy tune to herself while she does this. She likes to eat, and she enjoys a variety of meats, fruits, vegetables, cereals, and breads. She strongly prefers helping herself to small morsels of these with her own two hands, though she has begun to explore the use of a fork and spoon.

Kim is distractible. Time for eating is not clearly distinct from time for playing for her, and so she often decides to empty her milk glass onto the tray of her high chair or to carefully drop each morsel of her meat, bread, and vegetables into Ma-ma's water glass while she is not looking. She has a tremendous desire to please Ma-ma and Da-da. Thus in response to their upset voices and faces when she makes a mess on her food tray, she may, in a burst of inspiration, swipe the whole mess onto the floor with a smile that clearly means, "See, I cleaned it up!" When the Schwartzes find Kim playing with something dangerous or something valuable, they attempt to substitute another object for it. They allow Kim, for example, to pour water from one container to another at the table, but not milk.

Although Kim used to go to bed earlier than her parents, now she insists on staying up. It may take Mrs. Schwartz two hours to get her to go to sleep. She has not found a solution for Kim's wakefulness and is hoping it is just a phase that will pass. She is also concerned that Kim has begun to say "no!" whenever she is offered any of a variety of foods at dinnertime, although Kim actually goes ahead and eats about as well as always.

Interpretation and Questions

Should Kim be allowed to play in every cabinet and closet, or should some specific area be designated as "hers"? Do you think that Kim is misbehaving when she puts her food into her mother's milk glass? How would you handle this incident? Why do you think Kim is wakeful at night? How should Mrs. Schwartz handle Kim's bedtime. Do you think Kim is a pampered child?

2 Preschooler

Charlene Brown is a self-possessed five-year-old with a sunny disposition. Until recently she could usually be found in her mother's company, busily plying her needle to a scrap of cloth if her mother was sewing or happily stirring up an imaginary stew in her little pans on her stove if her mother was preparing dinner.

Six months ago, Charlene's new cousin, "baby Ann," and her parents came from another state to visit. Mrs. Brown had prepared Charlene for the visit by telling her about baby Ann. Charlene was excited about the visit, and she giggled with delight as she sat beside Ann and her mother on the ride home from the airport. Ann, who was barely five months old, responded with giggles and smiles of her own. Throughout the visit, Charlene was delighted to play beside baby Ann, who sat in her plastic carrier, basking in her older cousin's attention and attempting to mimic Charlene's every motion. Charlene would dance and sing for Ann, and Ann would shriek delightedly and wave her hands and feet. Charlene asked to hold the baby and exhibited a look of total pleasure and pride when she was allowed to do so.

Recently Charlene started kindergarten, and Ann, who was now able to stand alone but was not yet walking, and her parents came for a second visit. Charlene showed only a token interest in Ann this time, and she spent much more time showing her aunt and uncle her school bag and its contents, displaying some pictures she had drawn at kindergarten, and telling them about what she did at school. Her mother notes, ruefully, that "Charlene talks back to me now, just like Willy and Jackson [her brothers, who are two and three years older than Charlene], and she's always off playing with them now, whenever they'll let her. And she's always hanging onto her Daddy these days. I'm really feeling left out."

Interpretation and Questions

Why do you think Charlene was interested in babies six months ago but is not now? Should her mother try to make Charlene play with Ann now? Can you account for Charlene's recent change of loyalties from her mother to her father? Do you think Charlene will ever become interested in her mother or babies again? If so, when? Why? What is a "tomboy"? Do you think Charlene is or will be a tomboy? If you were Charlene's mother, would you want her to be more interested in domestic concerns than in things that happen in the world outside the family as she grows up? Why?

3 Middle Childhood

Carlos Ramos is a quiet and rather shy seven-year-old. He admires his father, who
has a great interest in, and facility with, mechanical devices. Carlos's mother
recalls the crestfallen look on her son's face on Christmas morning when he
turned the plastic ignition key in a pedal-propelled racing car and discovered that
its motor did not really work. She reports that Carlos, unlike his older sister Anita,
who spends hours pretending with her dolls, has always preferred real things.

Carlos is fiercely proud of the small go-cart his father bought him for his
birthday. Although his father thought the go-cart was too expensive for such a
young child, he relented and bought it when Carlos asked to be allowed to collect
pop bottles in order to earn enough money to purchase the cart. Although he
collected bottles diligently for three months, the money he earned was a small
fraction of the cost of the cart. When his father noticed Carlos's deep disappointment with his meager earnings, he told Carlos that he had decided to buy the cart
for him. Carlos was ecstatic and has taken excellent care of his cart. He does not
allow his friends to operate it unless he is there to supervise, and his sister is not
permitted to touch it.

Recently Carlos's aunt and uncle, whom he had not seen for two years, came
for a visit. After showing his uncle his go-cart, Carlos sat quietly while his family
and relatives joined in animated conversation around the dinner table. He
seemed especially to observe every gesture and motion of his rather heavyset,
bearded uncle. After dinner his mother noticed that Carlos had slipped away to
his room, where she found him in front of a mirror scotch-taping a paper beard
and a cellophane moustache onto his face. She laughed merrily and asked Carlos
to come out and show everyone his "new face."

Interpretation and Questions

If you were Mr. Ramos, would you have bought Carlos a go-cart? Is Carlos a
pampered child? Is he responsible? Why do you think Carlos put on a beard and
moustache after observing his uncle? Was Mrs. Ramos right to share her
amusement at Carlos's "new face" with the others? How would you have reacted
to this situation? Do you think Carlos needs to learn to use his imagination?

4 Adolescence

Mary Ellen O'Riley is sixteen years old. She is the fifth child in a family of six
children. Michael, who was two years older than Mary Ellen, was killed in a
hunting accident last year. Her oldest sister is married. Mary Ellen thought of
herself as being a happy-go-lucky person until recently. She says, "I always got
along with everybody," and she adds, "and I guess I took a lot of things for
granted. Like I always thought my family was great and that everybody just got
along with everybody." Mary Ellen finds herself feeling upset with her parents a
lot of the time. She is not sure why she is so irritable. "It seems," she says, "like
they are always on my back. It's like they make a big deal out of everything."

Mary Ellen started dating six months ago. She became very fond of a young man two years older than herself. "Sonny was different," she says. "He wasn't like all the other guys; he didn't just want to do what everybody else was doing. He thought a lot about things. I guess I'm like that, too." Mary Ellen was depressed when Sonny decided to start dating someone else. "I'm not sure I want to get involved with someone else. It hurts too much."

Mary Ellen is particularly distressed that her relationship with her father changed sometime during the past year. She says, "I remember when he used to hold me on his lap on the porch swing when I was a little girl. He used to say if anybody ever wanted to take his little girl away from him, he'd knock him to the moon!" She does not think she has ever felt really close to her mother. She is aware that her mother and father sometimes argue over money matters or about how to discipline the children. "I just wish I didn't know all that," she says. "If this is what growing up is like, I'm not sure I want to grow up."

Interpretation and Questions

Why do you think Mary Ellen is less happy-go-lucky than she used to be? What do you think happened to the close relationship between her and her father? Does Mary Ellen's irritation with her parents mean that something has gone very wrong in their relationship? How would you try to relate to Mary Ellen if you were her parent?

STUDY GUIDE

Important Terms

Jean Piaget
sensorimotor intelligence
representational thought
egocentric thought
preoperational thought
centration
transduction
concrete operations
formal operations

Sigmund Freud
oral stage
anal stage
Oedipus complex
Electra complex
genital period
maturation
puberty

Erik Erikson

trust versus mistrust
autonomy versus shame
initiative versus guilt
industry versus inferiority
identity versus role diffusion

G. H. Mead

symbolic interaction
significant others
play stage
game stage

Review Quiz

1 Most children are able to walk alone at about:
   a six months
   b nine months
   c one year
   d fifteen months

2 The theorist whose ideas place the greatest emphasis upon innate biological factors in childhood development is:
   a Sigmund Freud
   b Erik Erikson
   c Jean Piaget
   d George Herbert Mead

3 According to Jean Piaget, children learn mainly through _____ activity before twenty-four months of age.
   a symbolic
   b sensorimotor
   c centration
   d formal

4 The use of symbolic language, in which a child begins to put together two-word sentences, is associated with the theories of:
   a Freud
   b Erikson
   c Piaget
   d Mead

5 According to Erikson, an infant develops trust when his or her mother:
   a makes constant and nurturing responses when the child cries
   b feeds the child on schedule
   c emphasizes oral activity

   d fosters independence by leaving the child unattended

6 In a study by René Spitz of infants in a foundling home, it was shown that lack of physical contact eventually resulted in the death of _____ of the children.
   a 10 percent
   b one-fourth
   c one-third
   d one-half

7 Punishing children for wetting the bed:
   a has no effect
   b usually improves the situation
   c usually has an undesirable effect
   d has not been studied

8 Freud's Oedipal and Electra complexes:
   a occur in the male and female, respectively
   b do not occur in some societies
   c are characterized by a high level of sexuality
   d all the above

9 A preschool boy's error in judgment may result in his being pricked by a thorn because he was paying attention only to the beauty of a rose and was ignoring the thorns. This is called:
   a egocentrism
   b centration
   c wishful thinking
   d transduction

10 Parallel play, in which children play alongside other children but independently of them, is characteristic of ages:
   a six to ten months
   b two to three years
   c four to five years
   d six years and above

11 According to Erik Erikson, the period of industry versus inferiority occurs:
   a during the first year of life
   b at age three
   c between the ages of seven and eleven as the child begins to deal with the outer world as a worker
   d during adolescence

12 Most children are able to take the role of another person, or see things from that person's point of view, by age:
   a one
   b three
   c five
   d seven

13 During the developmental period known as *puberty*:
   a girls begin to menstruate
   b growth in height is completed
   c sexual behavior occurs for the first time
   d all the above

14 During adolescence, peers are more important than parents in setting standards concerning:
   a jobs
   b how to dress
   c whom to date
   d whether to report someone who damaged property

15 Adolescents with high self-esteem are more likely to be
   a distant from their fathers
   b Catholic or Protestant rather than Jewish
   c only children
   d sensitive to criticism

Opinionnaire

Below are listed ten childhood behaviors. In the blanks, write the earliest age at which you believe the average child can perform each behavior. Do respondents in your class who are parents give answers that are different from those of respondents who do not have children?

Average age

_____ 1 Thinking in terms of abstract universals such as "blueness"

_____ 2 Standing alone

_____ 3 Understanding sequential order in thinking

_____ 4 Riding a bicycle

_____ 5 Focusing eyes

_____ 6 Tying shoelaces unassisted

_____ 7 Sitting up without support

_____ 8 Understanding that there are permanent objects in the world

_____ 9 Distinguishing family members from strangers

_____ 10 Understanding that the relationship between grandparent and parent is the same as that between child and parent

Exercise

FAMILY CONSTELLATION AND CHILD DEVELOPMENT

Personality development is affected by whether one has siblings and by one's birth order. Below are listed six clusters of personality traits. Decide which cluster best describes you; then check to see whether that cluster is supposed to be characteristic of your family constellation. The first three clusters apply to men, and the second three to women. Try it on your friends.

1   *a* Loves to lead and to assume responsibility
    b Is sensitive and shy around women
    c Is interested in property and possessions
2   *a* Is a ladies' man
    b Has a cavalier attitude toward material possessions
    c Is not very interested in making male friends
3   *a* Prefers the company of older persons
    b Prefers "motherly" women
    c Is above becoming involved in the internal rivalries of groups

4   *a* Likes to give orders
    b Tends to overexert herself
    c Discourages men from flirting with her
5   *a* Finds herself often in competition with other women
    b Needs guidance from others
    c Can attract men more easily than other women
6   *a* Depends upon the care and attention of older persons
    b Feels that material wealth is unimportant
    c Would be willing to give up a job in order to marry

SIBLING PATTERNS

1   Brother with brothers
2   Brother with sisters
3   Male only child

4   Sister with sisters
5   Sister with brothers
6   Female only child

The sibling patterns are based upon descriptions given by Walter Toman (1976). For more information and precise descriptions of different patterns, see Toman's theory of family constellation.

Projects for Class or Home Study

1   Read a few cartoon strips featuring the Peanuts crowd. Pay special attention to the quality of their interactions and their use of language. Are the vocabulary and level of thinking characteristic of one of Piaget's classifications?
2   Some psychologists believe that children have different activity levels throughout childhood. Obtain a number of family snapshots of yourself and your brothers and sisters and rate the amount of activity shown by each child on a scale of 1 to 5. Average your ratings. Do your averages correspond with your parents' perceptions?

3 A simple experiment can show the existence of egocentrism in thought. Ask a four-year-old boy with one brother, "How many brothers do you have?" He will probably answer correctly. However, if you ask him, "How many brothers does your brother have?" he will probably become confused. What is the difference between the two questions?

4 To illustrate the quality of interaction where there is no role taking, tape a few minutes of a conversation between four- or five-year-olds. Does the interaction seem disconnected? Why do the children often fail to respond to one another's comments?

5 Ask a number of your friends whether they had "imaginary playmates" in childhood. What functions did they serve?

Suggestions for Further Reading

Back, Kurt, et al. *Social psychology.* New York: Wiley, 1977.
   Chapter 2, "Socialization," is an analysis of the interdependence of innate genetic inheritance and learned behavior within the context of evolution. Behavior is seen as dependent for its emergence on the interaction between heredity and environment.

Bettelheim, Bruno. Joey: A "mechanical boy." *Scientific American*, March 1959, **200**, 116–127.
   Child development can go awry for a number of reasons. This article describes a schizophrenic child who converted himself into an electrical machine because he did not dare to be human.

Elkind, David. *Children and adolescents: Interpretive essays on Jean Piaget.* New York: Oxford University Press, 1974.
   The famous psychologist's writings are scattered among a number of books and scholarly papers. In this volume, his most important ideas are organized in a clear, cohesive fashion.

Green, Ernest J. et al. Marriage and family. New York: McGraw-Hill, 1977.
   Chapter 7, "The child in the family," is useful for the discussion concerning child development and parent-child interactions. There is also a section on alternatives to traditional child-rearing methods.

Hemingway, Ernest. *The Nick Adams stories.* New York: Scribner, 1972.
   Many novelists have written of their childhood, but few have revealed as much of their personalities as Hemingway. These stories are arranged chronologically, following Nick Adams as he grows to maturity and acquires the moral standards which identify the author.

Keller, Helen. *The story of my life.* New York: Airmont, 1965.
   Blind and deaf, Helen Keller struggled to achieve the social standards of others. This book is one of the most perceptive accounts ever written about childhood socialization.

Lewis, Michael. The busy, purposeful world of a baby. *Psychology Today*, February 1977, **11**, 53–56.
   The author describes techniques infants use to control their environment. He also claims that infants possess a self-concept *before* they have the language to demonstrate it to others.

McClintock, Jack. The Edith Project. *Harper's Magazine*, March 1977, 21–24.
A controversial man claimed he could develop his infant daughter into a genius—and then did it. This article tells how the twenty-five-year experiment has fared.

Answers to Review Quiz

1-*d* 2-*a* 3-*b* 4-*d* 5-*a* 6-*c* 7-*c* 8-*d* 9-*b* 10-*b* 11-*c* 12-*d* 13-*a* 14-*b* 15-*c*

12

PARENTS AND CHILDREN

An influential twentieth-century French philosopher recalls in his autobiography the impressions he had of his world at the age of four:

> I have only to give [my character] free play to be showered with praise. . . . I invent. . . . I have the lordly freedom of the actor who holds his audience spellbound. . . . I am adored, hence I am adorable. . . . I am pink and blond, with curls. . . . I know my worth (Sartre, 1975).

Here is a world apart from adults, but at the center of their interest and concern. In our society, though we may be uncertain about defining the boundaries of young adulthood, middle age, and old age, our own memories tell us that childhood is a distinct stage through which everyone passes. However, the very idea of childhood as a biological, psychological, and sociological concept distinct from that of adulthood has developed only over the past three centuries.

Childhood

For a long time, beginning with the Middle Ages, a social awareness of childhood—and of children as members of a special age group—simply did not exist. Unlike the ancient Greeks, who perceived children as belonging to a qualitatively different world, parents in medieval times treated their children like little adults. There was, of course, a period during which the child would be dependent on others for nourishment, protection, and general care. But parents had no sense of policy regarding child rearing—they would not have understood the notion. As soon as he was able, the male child became a member of the larger social community. Commonly he was apprenticed to a master craftsman, if that was the option available to him by class, at the age of seven (Ariès, 1962).

This absence of a concept of childhood as a long and distinct period of life can be related to the fact that there was, for a time, no understanding or system of education. But between the thirteenth and seventeenth centuries this condition of ignorance began to alter. This was due largely to the influence of religious reformers, or moralists, who were deeply concerned not only with the lives and manners of adults but also with the salvation and moral virtue of children. Religious orders, such as the Jesuits, began to assume a major role as teachers of the young, and they conveyed to parents the profoundly affecting notion that they as parents were the shepherds of their children's souls.

> This new concern about education would gradually install itself in the heart of society and transform it from top to bottom. The family ceased to be simply an institution for the transmission of a name and an estate—it assumed a moral and spiritual function, it moulded bodies and souls. The care expended on children inspired new feelings, a new emotional attitude . . . the modern concept of the family (Ariès, 1962, pp. 412–413).

As the cultural historian Philippe Ariès explains, parents began to assume responsibility for the early schooling of, at the very least, their male children, not simply an apprenticeship, or its equivalent, for the eldest child. Parental indifference toward the child—which on one level had probably served as the easiest way of coping with an extremely high infant mortality rate—was being replaced with a deep concern for the child's welfare, a concern which from the seventeenth through the nineteenth centuries was manifested in an increasingly strict code of discipline. The forces of family and school, shaped and guided by centuries of reformers and moralists, together helped to forge the concept and social structure of childhood and separated the child from the world of adult relationships (Ariès, 1962).

Early Child-rearing Theories

As childhood gradually came to be regarded as a special period of life, two distinct theories emerged and were incorporated into family life. The child was viewed either as a charming toy to be coddled and enjoyed, or as a creature of God who must be disciplined and in whom the Christian virtues need to be instilled. The two opposites of coddling and reforming have remained with us, although they have been referred to in other terms, such as permissive child rearing versus restrictive child rearing and progressive methods versus traditional authoritarian methods. The influence of one and then the other has been likened to a pendulum, swinging back and forth even within individual families (Demos and Demos, 1969).

Before the 1920s, parents and teachers advocated mainly the restrictive approach to child rearing. They believed that the child had to be taught to conform to society and that this was best accomplished by the use of punishments and rewards. Behaviorist psychology supported this theory: If properly conditioned to the environment, the child could be expected to develop into a morally responsible adult.

During the 1920s there was an almost complete turnabout. An awareness developed that children have their own world and their own needs and that traumas experienced in childhood can result in a damaged adult. Three men are credited with this revolution in child-rearing practices and educational methods (Dreikurs and Grey, 1968). They are the Frenchman Binet (of the Stanford-Binet IQ test), who demonstrated that intelligence does not depend on class, race, or economic status; Dewey, who laid the groundwork for progressive education; and Freud, who developed the theories on which modern psychoanalysis is based. Since Freud argued that many of the emotional problems of adults are due to a lack of understanding of the special qualities of childhood, many parents and teachers have been persuaded not to use severe and excessive punishment. Dewey stressed the importance of the social and emotional needs of children and of self-determination versus submission to authority. Binet's discoveries and Dewey's philosophy led to the belief that all children, not just the privileged few, are entitled to schooling and a chance to develop into mature human beings.

Thus a great number of educators, parents, and psychologists in the 1920s and 1930s approached child rearing from a "progressive" viewpoint. Emphasis was placed on allowing children freedom of self-expression and on adults' learning about children's needs from children themselves. However, many adults misinterpreted the intentions of Dewey and Freud. The result was laissez faire permissiveness, indulgence, and freedom without responsibility.

Reactions against this approach to child rearing suggested that too much indulgence and an excessive expression of sexual and aggressive

A CHILD invites adoring smiles and comments from passersby and parents alike.

impulses can threaten a child's equilibrium and thus be contrary to his or her needs. For example, in *The Ego and Mechanisms of Defense* (1946), Anna Freud expressed the view that discipline is necessary if a child is to feel secure. There were good reasons, both theoretical and practical, for the existence of the two opposing points of view concerning children. The problem of discipline is not simple; rather, it involves conflicting needs and contradictory solutions. From the standpoint of parents and educators, the arguments in favor of discipline include the idea that allowing children to express themselves in any way and at any time they wish infringes on the freedom and rights of adults.

Those who argue against discipline claim that punishing dependent, vulnerable children may create psychological strain on parents in the form of guilt feelings. Furthermore, they claim that the freedom and responsibilities of adult and child society should be interrelated, not totally segregated, and that this is not possible if parents are strict disciplinarians. From the standpoint of children's needs, those who favor discipline believe that children feel safer, are emotionally more secure, and display more creativity when their freedom is circumscribed within a disciplinary framework. In contrast, others argue that discipline inhibits creativity—that children may lose their individuality if they are not given freedom to express their feelings and to make mistakes (Wolf, 1953).

Recent Approaches to Child Rearing

COMMUNICATION

The theories of Haim Ginott (1969) are representative of the more recent approaches to child rearing. Ginott's emphasis is on the child-parent relationship and the quality of the communication which passes between child and parent. The important thing in child rearing, then, is not what the parent does to the child but how the parent can learn not only to interpret what the child is saying (despite the roundabout way in which the child's feelings may be expressed) but also to have compassion and understanding for those feelings. Ginott says that "conversing with children is a unique art with rules and meanings of its own."

Ginott's code of communication is based on the respect of the parent for the child and on skill in interpreting the child's meaning and responding to his or her feelings. Ginott feels that too often parents either scold or give advice, when what the child really needs is understanding. Communication, according to Ginott, requires that "the message preserve the child's as well as the parent's self-respect" and that "statements of understanding precede statements of advice or instruction." Ginott gives the example of the child who tells his mother that the teacher spanked him. Rather than asking for further details or trying to

ACCEPTANCE AND encouragement contribute to a child's self-esteem and sense of security.

find out what the child did to goad the teacher into the spanking, the mother might draw on her own emotional experiences and show the child that she understands his feelings—feelings, perhaps, of shame, of embarrassment, or of revenge. As Ginott says, "A child's strong feelings do not disappear when the parent tries to convince him that he has no reason to feel that way. Strong feelings do not vanish by being banished; they do diminish and lose their sharp edges when the listener accepts them with sympathy and understanding" (1969, p. 27).

Parents, too, have feelings. Ginott sympathizes with the anger of a parent and with the guilt following a bout with anger. He suggests three steps to survival:

1 We accept the fact that children will make us angry.
2 We are entitled to our anger without guilt or shame.
3 Except for one safeguard, we are entitled to express what we feel. We can express our angry feelings *provided* we do not attack the child's personality or character (1969, pp. 57–58).

Ginott's steps to survival are similar in content and intent to Bach and Wyden's rules for fair fighting (see Chapter 9).

PARENT TRAINING PROGRAMS

Numerous parent training programs, begun in the 1960s and expanded in the 1970s, also emphasize improved communication between parents and children. The four best-known parent training programs at present are (1) the Parent Involvement Program (P.I.P.), (2) the Responsive Parent Training Program, (3) the Challenge Study Groups, and (4) Parent Effectiveness Training (P.E.T.). These programs offer courses consisting of from eight to ten sessions during which parents learn new techniques of handling ordinary problems of child rearing. Parents of children with serious problems are referred elsewhere. Many of these parent training programs are affiliated with schools or churches. Most of those who teach the courses are members of the helping professions, such as teachers, principals, social workers, counselors, psychologists, or ministers, but they also may be parents.

Who are the parents who participate? The great majority are white middle-class women. Recently, however, more low-income minority-group parents have been participating, partly as a result of funding provided through the schools. Another change, according to those in charge of the programs, is that more parents of young children are taking part, for the purpose of preventing problems. Previously the participants had been, for the most part, parents who were already experiencing problems with their children. Most instructors behave toward the parents as they would like the parents to behave toward their children. They teach the techniques by modeling them—that is, by using them in their relationships with the parents in the class. Parents tend to feel that their newly learned skill is making a difference in their families and, in addition, that it is helpful to be able to talk to other parents and realize that one's own child-rearing problems are not unique.

PARENT INVOLVEMENT PROGRAM (P.I.P.) This program, used mostly in the Los Angeles area, is an adaptation of William Glasser's reality therapy. It emphasizes friendly relations between parents and children as a means of changing behavior. Thus children (or anyone) must be convinced that someone else cares about them before they can improve their self-concept or their behavior. Parents are taught techniques for establishing an involvement with their children. Some are familiar techniques, such as talking about topics of mutual interest or stopping everything to sit down with the child when he or she is obviously upset about something. Other techniques use games to encourage talk. (Example: "Now let's both tell about one nice thing that happened to us today.") After a friendship (involvement) has been established, the parent can help the child to evaluate and plan responsible behavior and can ask the child to make a commitment to the plan. If the child succeeds in carrying out the plan, he or she is to be praised; however, failure is not to be punished. Rather, the parent is to help the child reevaluate and revise the plan. The parent is encouraged not to give up or resort to blame and punishment.

RESPONSIVE PARENT TRAINING PROGRAM This program originated in Kansas City. Standard behavior-modification techniques are taught in the courses. Positive reinforcements and mild punishments are advocated. So often in our society, good behavior is taken for granted, and bad behavior is severely punished. For example, when mild punishment is used, it should be paired with a positive reinforcement. Thus, if a boy is isolated briefly after hitting a younger brother, the parent should praise him at another time when he does not engage in such behavior. Parents are encouraged to keep records of the results of their experiments and to note on graphs just when and how their child's behavior changes. The program has been criticized by some on the basis of ethics: Do these techniques lead to the manipulation and control of others? Those in charge of the program say that they do not—that traditional child-rearing procedures use the same positive reinforcements and punishments but without an understanding of what is being done or whether they are effective. They add that, in any case, in a free society a high level of control of others' behavior is not possible.

THE CHALLENGE STUDY GROUPS This program, based in Chicago, follows the ideas of psychologist Alfred Adler as translated into parent-child terms by Rudolf Dreikurs. Dreikurs believes that "a misbehaving child is a discouraged child" and that the goals of misbehavior are attention, power, and revenge (Dreikurs and Grey, 1968). Misbehavior is always related to an attempt to get the better of the parent in some way. The child is discouraged because he or she does not feel secure. In order to establish and encourage constructive behavior, the parent is taught to use encouragement and discipline. Encouragement can take the form of giving the child responsibility, but with realistic standards, and of showing appreciation of effort as well as achievement. Children are allowed to choose what to wear, whom to play with, and how to spend their allowance. In other words, they are encouraged to make many of their own decisions. Weekly family councils are held to discuss problems, assign chores, and make family decisions.

The two major disciplinary techniques used are termed *natural consequences* and *logical consequences*. Natural consequences are those which follow automatically from the child's behavior without parental intervention. For example, the child runs, falls, and hits her head against a table. Since this is an unpleasant experience, it should lead to an avoidance of such acts in the future. Logical consequences are those which are arranged by parents when natural consequences would be dangerous or not forthcoming. For example, a child plays outside and comes home late for dinner. His mother can put his food on his plate and let him eat it whenever he arrives, as long as the rest of the family has not finished. But if the child does not arrive until after the family is finished and the dishes are cleared, he gets no dinner.

Logical consequences are not applicable in all situations. The adult must understand the goal of the child. And the child needs to understand that he or she has a clear and logical choice of behavior and consequences. The adult also is urged to show understanding and sympathy, not anger. According to Dreikurs, "The best formula for the proper attitude toward children is to treat them with kindness and with firmness. Kindness expresses respect for the child and firmness evokes respect from the child" (Dreikurs and Grey, 1968, p. 43).

PARENT EFFECTIVENESS TRAINING (P.E.T.)   Over a quarter of a million parents from every state and some foreign countries have participated in the Parent Effectiveness Training program since its inception in 1962. It is a radical approach to child rearing in that it advocates that parents give up the use of power tactics, both physical and psychological. The founder of the program, Thomas Gordon, has derived much of his philosophy and many of his techniques from the work of Carl Rogers.

In his theory of personality and behavior, Rogers takes the point of view that "the best vantage point for understanding behavior is from the internal frame of reference of the individual himself" (1951). He goes on to explain that psychologists who try to understand, evaluate, and predict a person's behavior on the basis of their own frame of reference are applying their own values or models of behavior to that person. The only way to understand another person's behavior is to understand it as that person perceives it, and this understanding is derived primarily through methods of communication. Rogers admits that communication is at all times imperfect; however, he says that the more freely the individual is able to communicate, unhampered by a need or desire to be defensive, the better his or her frame of reference will be understood. Such communication can best occur in an atmosphere of understanding and acceptance. This is the climate most likely to foster a therapeutic experience and consequent self-acceptance in the person who is exposed to it.

Rogers, of course, is referring to the counselor or therapist in one-to-one client-centered psychotherapy as the person instrumental in creating the proper atmosphere. In Parent Effectiveness Training, Gordon teaches parents to establish this same kind of climate of understanding and acceptance for their children. Gordon (1976) sees the major dilemma of today's parents as being the fact that they perceive only two approaches to handling conflicts between their own needs and those of the child. One he calls the "I win—you lose" approach (the parent wins, and the child loses); the other is the "you win—I lose" approach (the child wins, and the parent loses). These are more or less different names for what previously has been referred to as restrictive versus permissive child rearing. In either method one party ends up feeling hostile and angry as a result of having lost in a power struggle. If the parent wins, the child is denied the opportunity to learn self-discipline and responsibility. If the child continually wins, it may suggest that his or her needs are more important than anyone else's. The child may become self-centered and demanding, making any relationship difficult and leading to a feeling of insecurity (Gordon, 1976).

In place of these two approaches, Gordon suggests that parents learn good communication skills—how to listen to children without judging them, how to communicate their own feelings honestly, and finally how to resolve conflicts through a "no-lose" method of mutual agreement and joint decision making. The skills involved are taught, practiced, and discussed in the P.E.T. classes. But it is also stressed that the effective use of these techniques often requires a fundamental alteration of parental attitudes toward children. Parents must be able to accept their child's feelings no matter how different they may be from their own. They must have trust in the child's ability to handle feelings and to solve problems. And they must be able to see the child as someone separate from themselves—a unique person with an individual identity and life apart from their own (Gordon, 1976).

Chance Factors in Childhood Experience

As we have seen, the issue of discipline is resolved at different times and in different ways within the larger context of general attitudes toward children. But the various disciplinary practices also gain adherents from the larger social and cultural framework. Working-class parents, for example, may hold very different attitudes from those of middle-class parents concerning how children should be reared. Birth order is another factor which affects child-rearing techniques and the parent-child relationship. The only child, the firstborn child, and the later-born child each receive different treatment from parents and undergo different experiences. Such chance factors as birth order and the social class of the family will also make a difference in the way one's early years, and perhaps one's entire life, are experienced.

SOCIAL CLASS

According to M. L. Hoffman and Saltzstein (1967), there are three methods for disciplining children: (1) power-assertion techniques, in which the parent punishes the child physically or deprives the child of a material good; (2) deprivation of love; and (3) induction, the technique in which the parent verbally explains to the child why the child should change some behavior. Although most parents use all three techniques, it has been observed that the principal technique relied upon is related to social class.

Parents in lower socioeconomic groups tend to use power-assertion techniques more than parents in the middle class. Middle-class parents are more likely to threaten a child with the deprivation of love and to use the induction technique, in which they induce desired behavior by means of lengthy explanations. This seems to be changing for the present generation, however. Blue-collar wives who are more exposed to the mass media and have more education are more likely than their husbands to favor withdrawal of love or induction in disciplining children (LeMasters, 1975).

Another important factor in child rearing concerns the transmission of sex roles. The more traditional sex-role teaching, in which boys are not permitted to show emotion and girls are not permitted to be assertive, is also more common in the lower than in the middle classes. This, too, is changing. Blue-collar mothers are increasingly dubious about some aspects of the traditional sex roles which are being imparted to their children (LeMasters, 1975). In general, there is a slow drift toward middle-class values in child rearing among the present-day working class.

BIRTH ORDER

The experience of a child is also affected by his or her birth order (Forer, 1976). For example, the first child has undivided parental attention for awhile. An only child, of course, never loses this position, but in large families the youngest child is summarily "dethroned" from the position of being the "baby" when a new sibling is born. The meaning of this event is difficult to evaluate, but those who emphasize the importance of personality formation in younger years are sure that the trauma has

lifelong effects. Schachter (1959) presented data to show that, as adults, firstborn children are more dependent on contacts with other people than later-born children.

Even after the birth of subsequent children, firstborns continue to receive a greater share of parental interest, enthusiasm, and concern. With their firstborns, parents experience the novelty of watching a child walk and talk for the first time, start school, and learn to read. Family reaction to the first day of school has been captured in an often-repeated Jewish joke:

A young child comes home from his first day at school. He is met by mother, grandmother, and aunt:
MOTHER (enthusiastically): Hello, darling. How did your day go, boobala?
GRANDMOTHER: My shaina tutala! His first day at school!
AUNT: Tell me, faigala. What did you learn today?
CHILD: I learned that my name is Irving.

When the second, third, or subsequent child enters school, enthusiasm may dwindle just because parents have been through the process before.

Parents may be less sure of themselves with the firstborn child. Attention to the child is lavish, but it is more likely to be inconsistent (B. N. Adams, 1972). Later-born children tend to be the subject of less interest on the part of their parents. The result seems to be that firstborns are more likely to turn to adults for standards and guidance, and later-born children are more likely to seek their peers.

One result of greater parental interest in firstborn than in later-born children is related to achievement. In a study of 1450 junior and senior high school students, it was found that significantly higher grades were earned by only children and firstborns. Does this mean that firstborns and only children are smarter than later-born children? The researcher also asked the students to indicate the level of interest their parents had in them. Only children felt that their parents were most interested in them, firstborns experienced less interest, and later-born children indicated that they felt their parents were least interested in them. When firstborns and later-born children reported the same amount of parental interest, no differences in grades existed. Apparently, greater interest and encouragement on the part of parents lead to scholastic advantage for firstborn and only children (E. J. Green, 1970).

Special Parent-Child Relationships

Not all parent-child interactions occur between individuals who have an immediate biological relationship. Tens of thousands of children are adopted each year, and millions of others are stepchildren. All the problems, as well as the joys, of child rearing can be experienced in these relationships. But as stepparents and stepchildren have personally discovered, there can be both special difficulties and pleasures not usually encountered in the typical family situation.

ADOPTION

There are many couples who, for one reason or another, are biologically unable to become parents. Many of these couples, usually from the upper middle class, try to adopt a child. In 1971, some 169,000 children were adopted in the United States, 83,000 by nonrelatives (U.S. Bureau of the Census, 1975). Most couples who try to adopt a child from an agency are of the middle class. The actual process may be frustrating because applicants are screened rigorously by adoption agencies. Not only is the couple's complete background thoroughly investigated, but they also must convince the agency that they are mature and have a positive outlook on life. Naturally, the marriage must be stable (Flanagan, 1974). One of the problems experienced by prospective adoptive parents has been described by a former New York television producer:

First of all, my wife and I are of different religions. I'm Jewish and she comes from a Catholic background. That meant that we couldn't go to a Jewish agency, which would have asked her to convert—aside from the fact that there are almost never any Jewish babies available for adoption. A Catholic agency would have asked me to convert, but it would probably not have accepted my wife anyway, because she has been divorced. So we went to a liberal private agency that was recommended by friends and after a great deal of hassle we agreed to register ourselves as Unitarians. The next thing the social worker wanted to know was how often we were going to church, and whether we'd had the minister over for dinner yet! (Johnson, 1975, p. 63)

Such exasperation has caused some prospective adoptive parents to avoid public and private adoption agencies and go instead to a lawyer or an obstetrician who acts as an intermediary between the couple and an unwed mother. In 1971 one-third of all adoptions were not handled through social agencies (U.S. Bureau of the Census, 1975). Although the great majority of nonagency arrangements are aboveboard and involve only standard professional fees, some fees are exorbitant. There are some lawyers, for example, who charge anywhere from $10,000 to $25,000 for arranging the adoption of an illegitimate but healthy Caucasian baby.

SOMETIMES CHILDREN are raised by grandparents or other relatives when problems or death prevent the biological parents from doing so.

It has been estimated that the traffic in such black-market adoptions involves about 5000 babies a year in the United States (Johnson, 1975).

A growing trend in recent years has been the adoption of children by single men or women who do not wish to marry but do wish to be parents. Said one thirty-six-year-old male teacher who adopted a young boy: "I haven't met anyone I can see being committed to as a husband. But does this have to mean I can't be a father when that's a commitment I feel very able to fulfill? Maybe I'm simply a person who would make a better parent than I would a husband" (C. Klein, 1973).

Not surprisingly, the process of adoption is far more difficult for single parents than for a couple. There are only 500 single adoptive parents in the entire country, and one-fifth of these live in the New York City area. Adopting a healthy white infant is virtually out of the question for single individuals because adoption agencies give priority to married couples. The single person can expect to adopt a school-age child, usually from a racial minority group, who has physical or emotional problems. Still, even under these conditions, the rewards seem to outweigh the disadvantages. For example, the following exchange occurred between a thirty-nine-year-old father and his newly adopted son, Neal, a ten-year-old who had been privately characterized by the adoption agency as a "dumb, hyperactive freakout":

> During one of Neal's worst tantrums, [the father] told his son that he was "hurt, but I didn't do this to you." His response was: "But don't you see? I'm nobody." The adult replied: "But now you're somebody's nobody." To his amazement, the child laughed and threw his arms around his father and said: "Now I'm *your* nobody" (N. Robertson, 1975, p. 16).

STEPCHILDREN

Every year in the United States, one out of three marriages ends in divorce. On the average, 1.22 children are involved in each of these marital dissolutions (U.S. Bureau of the Census, 1975). When a parent remarries, which occurs an average of three years after the divorce, any offspring from the previous marriages are known as *stepchildren* in relation to the new parent. This is also the term used for children whose parents remarry after the death of a spouse. It has been estimated that some 15 million children under eighteen live in families in which there is a stepparent and that another 3 or 4 million youngsters between the ages of eighteen and twenty-two are part of such families (Roosevelt and Lofas, 1976).

All families have problems involving the interrelationships of their members. But the family in which there is a stepparent has special difficulties which can heighten the normal tensions and conflicts that occur in natural families and so raise new problems. Perhaps the major adjustments are those which must be made by the stepchildren. Children, especially young ones, tend to feel hurt, fearful, and insecure after the death or separation of a parent; many feel that somehow the death or divorce was their fault. At times, stepchildren may fear that they will lose their remaining natural parent to the newcomer. The child's stepbrothers and stepsisters often compete with the child for parental attention, affection, and loyalty. When fights break out among the children, the natural parents may not defend their children against the stepchildren because they are afraid of endangering the marriage or because they wish to win or keep the friendship of the stepchildren. In addition to these family relationships, stepchildren frequently find it difficult to adapt to a number of other changes that the new arrangement brings—schools, houses, bedrooms, and even closets and new places at the dinner table may require a special effort of adjustment. Asked to tell what were the best and worst things about being a stepchild, one boy replied: "The worst is you see less of your other parent. The best is that you have somebody extra who cares about you" (Roosevelt and Lofas, 1976, p. 110).

As for the stepmother, frequently she must work to overcome her image as the "wicked witch." Ann Simon (1964) points out that there is some truth in this image. For example, a stepmother can be jealous, hostile, and sometimes cruel toward her husband's children because she may be competing with them for their father's love. However, it can be rough going for the mother, no matter how hard she may try. A stepmother often approaches her husband's family with the idea that love will immediately develop between her and her new children. And, indeed, she often initially showers them with affection. But, as Roosevelt and Lofas point out, stepchildren may recoil from such emotional outpourings because to accept them would seem a disoloyalty to their natural mother. They often fail to notice or appreciate their new mother's nurturing and housekeeping, and frequently they challenge her authority over them. If the stepmother makes a request, the youngster may snap back: "I don't have to obey you; you're not my real mother."

For some stepfathers, their new children are welcome additions. For many other men, however, the role of stepfather can be challenging, to say the least. Often the stepfather is perceived as an intruder and has difficulty establishing and exercising authority. In a classic situation, the stepfather will discipline the child, who then runs to his or her mother for protection. The mother, in turn, becomes angry and vents her feeling on the stepfather. In one instance, a stepdaughter responded to her stepfather's attempt at disciplining by shouting: "You're not my father. You're the person who sleeps with my mother" (Marks, 1976, p. 126).

Adapting to a stepparent situation, then, is a difficult task for all involved. Researchers who have studied families in which there is a stepparent suggest some general guidelines. For example, the stepparent should not attempt to take the place of the child's real parent. Says one stepmother: "I should have accepted the fact that I was not Andrew's mother and never could be. I could never feel towards him the way his mother did; and he could never feel towards me as a son" (Lowe, 1970, p. 53). Another researcher warns that the stepparent should never do or say anything negative concerning the child's real parent or try to compete with the real parent. A stepparent can overcome the jealousy of the child by trying to "share" the spouse with the stepchild. If a stepmother, for example, kisses her husband in the presence of the child, she should also hug or kiss the youngster (Lund, 1975).

What is the effect of a broken home and the subsequent remarriage of a parent on children later in life? Surprisingly, research indicates that such children show little or no difference from those whose families remain intact in terms of adjusting, either socially or psychologically. Lee Burchinal, for example, found that "inimical effects associated with divorce or separation and, for some youths, with the remarriage of their parents with whom they were living, were almost uniformly absent in the population studied" (1964, p. 50). Another study by Kenneth Wilson, Zurcher, McAdams, and Curtis (1975) compared individuals who had experienced stepfather families with those who had been reared in normal families. The researchers found no important differences in certain social and psychological characteristics. Like children in a natural-parent family, these investigators point out, children reared with stepparents can have experiences which are predominantly positive, predominantly negative, or predominantly mixed.

Children's Rights

As we noted earlier, children were not considered separate from adults until the end of the Middle Ages, when the idea of "being a child" emerged. The idea of "having a child," however, is as old as the idea of having any kind of property. Although a concern to meet the special needs of children has been part of family life, religion, and education for three centuries, the notion of the child as property has continued to shape policy in the areas of child rearing, formal education, and treatment under the law.

Legislation such as labor laws aimed at protecting children from abuses began to appear in the nineteenth century when the industrial revolution was well under way. Such legislation was the result of the efforts of social reformers to change the wretched working conditions of young children. They were protected in the physical sense by laws regulating their working hours and preventing them from doing dangerous jobs. Until that time, little boys and girls worked long, hard hours in factories. For example, children contracted cancer of the skin and other diseases while scraping chimneys clean (some of the chimneys in London were only 7 to 9 inches in diameter, and it was commonplace for four- and five-year-old children to crawl inside them in the nude in freezing weather). The new laws, however, "did not interfere with the

rights of parents and gave children somewhat the same status as dogs and
horses, which also were held entitled to protection against 'undue'
cruelty and neglect'' (Coigney, 1975).

Children's rights, as we are beginning to understand them today,
however, entail more than physical protection and go beyond the
responsibility of society for safeguarding children's innocence and instill-
ing in them the values of the larger culture. The United Nations
Declaration of the Rights of the Child (1959) focuses on several special

needs of children. It states, in Principle 8, that "the child shall in all circumstances be among the first to receive protection and relief." The rhetoric is convincing, even inspiring; yet in our own country the child is among the last to receive such aid, it seems. Services are inadequate, and agencies are understaffed and underfunded. Hunger, malnutrition, battering, racial discrimination, sexual abuse, poor health care and education, and delinquency are ongoing problems for "tens of thousands" of American children in this decade (Polier, 1973).

In addition to the obvious problems caused by shortages of social workers and funds are the not-so-obvious problems of interpreting the child's best interests. Procedures we have built up, especially in the area of juvenile justice, to "save the children" have had unforeseen consequences. Child savers in the last century were well-meaning in their efforts to rescue children from a life of crime. Social reformers bent on whisking juveniles from the courtroom and jails set up an informal system whereby children would not have to go through the cumbersome processes involved in getting lawyers and making appeals. However, juveniles thus lost many legal safeguards that adult offenders enjoy.

The "right of the parent" to determine the best interest of the child was assumed by the judge and other agents of the law. Ironically, this policy resulted in procedural injustices for juveniles. Only in 1967 did a case come before the Supreme Court that would restore to juveniles the rights of adult offenders under the legal system. Gerard Gault, aged fifteen, had made a lewd phone call and had been sentenced to remain in a state school until the age of twenty-one. An adult, it turned out, would merely have had to pay a fine for the same offense. The Gault case set a precedent by showing that the juvenile justice system could "throw the book" at young offenders, giving them no recourse to due process. In addition, the Gault case showed that children may sometimes need "protection from protection."

SUMMARY

It is only within the last 200 or 300 years that childhood has been considered a separate status, qualitatively different from adulthood. When Christian reformers began to take an interest in the salvation of children, the education of children became an important vocation. Two attitudes toward children emerged with the clarification of the concept of childhood—the attitude that the innocent child was to be protected and nurtured, and the attitude that the child was born in original sin and was to be disciplined and thereby saved. These two concepts, permissive child rearing and authoritarian child rearing, remain with us to this day.

A more recent approach stresses the relationship between child and parent, with particular emphasis on the process of communication. Haim Ginott encourages the parent to attend to the feelings of the child and to empathize with these feelings rather than to scold, criticize, or instruct the child.

Parents today have access to training programs in which they can learn how to recognize the meanings behind their children's speech and how to help their children handle their feelings. The Parent Involvement Program emphasizes friendship and involvement as a basis for the child-parent relationship. The Responsive Parent Training Program utilizes the methods of experimental psychology, stressing positive reinforcement and mild punishment. In the Challenge Study Groups misbehavior is interpreted as a bid for attention; kindness and firmness are the principal goals. Parent Effectiveness Training (P.E.T.) is based on the client-centered therapy of Carl Rogers, in which the parent-therapist is taught to understand a situation from the child's viewpoint. Conflict is approached as a no-lose proposition.

Child-rearing techniques have been related to social class: Middle-class parents tend to rely on deprivation of love and lengthy explanations to induce desired behavior, and lower-class parents are more likely to use deprivation and punishment. Birth order affects a child's behavior.

Adoption of a child is often a difficult procedure unless a couple are willing to adopt a school-age child from a minority group. Other children who are not reared by both natural parents are children from broken homes, one or both of whose parents remarry. Stepchildren may be fearful after a divorce or the death of a parent, and it takes sensitivity and understanding on the part of the new parent to establish a friendly and loving relationship with a stepchild.

The children's rights movement fosters the belief that each child should be provided with the opportunity to develop into a contributing member of society. Children's rights include the provision of adequate health and social services and protection against physical and legal abuse.

CASE STUDY

The First Child

Rosa Skorios, aged twenty-one, completed her B.S. in sociology in June, three months before her first child, Rachael, was born. She started work toward her M.A. with an intensive course in the first summer session and helped her husband locate and renovate a larger apartment in her spare time. Nicholas, her husband, is twenty-two, works full time, and is taking evening courses toward a B.S. in business. Still, they find the time to visit with Rosa's close-knit Puerto Rican family and Nicholas's Greek parents and sister and to get together with friends on weekends and holidays.

When Rosa became pregnant, she considered the LaMaze method of natural childbirth and other classes for prospective parents, but she and Nicholas felt they did not have time to fit any more classes into their busy schedule. However, Rosa expected to breast-feed her infant, as her mother and cousins had nursed theirs.

Rosa was confident that anything so natural as childbirth was nothing to be afraid of, but a twenty-four-hour labor in the hospital with only unfamiliar medical personnel to attend her was a trying experience. She felt tired, sore, and discouraged during her five-day hospital stay. She was pleased, though, with her red-faced, bright-eyed infant.

Her natural buoyancy reasserted itself when Rosa returned home, and she found herself hanging new draperies in the living room and preparing a special meal for her husband's birthday. However, the stitches from her episiotomy tore, and Rosa became quite ill. She did not feel like nursing Rachael, and so she switched her to bottles of prepared formula. Rachael was fussy, and Rosa found it difficult having Nicholas away from home so much of the time with working and attending classes. When at home, however, he was a willing father, and Rosa believes him to be more patient than she is with Rachael.

Rosa devoted a semester to full-time motherhood and generally enjoyed her active baby. Rachael basked in her parents' attention and demanded, as infants do, a lot of it. Yet Rosa and Nicholas occasionally feel that Rachael has somehow come between them, especially when she insists on staying up past their bedtime. One night they decided to let Rachael cry herself to sleep, but in the end they felt guilty about it.

Rosa was delighted when Rachael began walking at nine months, but she was dismayed at how much mischief Rachael could get into, and how quickly. Rosa's closest girl friend does not have children, and Rosa finds herself constantly fussing at Rachael and apologizing to her girl friend as Rachael's curiosity leads her to explore every magazine, ashtray, and wastebasket in her friend's house.

Nicholas and Rosa bought Rachael a pressed-wood toy box decorated with characters from a popular television program for children, "Sesame Street," for Christmas. Rachael usually heads for the toy box first thing every morning and manages to fairly well empty it in the thirty to forty-five minutes before "Sesame Street" comes on. When she hears the lively tune which announces the beginning of the program, Rachael races for the television set and stands or crouches in front of it for five and ten minutes at a time, alternately running over to the toy box or into the kitchen or bedroom, where her mother is hastily trying to accomplish all her morning chores during this brief period of respite. Rosa serves Rachael's breakfast on a small TV table, hoping in this way to further ensure that her daughter will stay in one place for awhile. Rachael is usually happy to be returned to the living room after her brief forays into the kitchen or bedroom to see where Mommy is.

Rosa is grateful that she can count on these few uninterrupted moments in the morning, but she feels that the rest of her day is often one long series of interruptions, with Rachael opening cupboards here, emptying drawers there, and impishly saying, "No, no!" *before* she pours her midmorning juice on the floor, after which she hastily tries to wipe it up with the same hand that clutches her half-eaten cookie.

Rosa sometimes wonders whether *her* entire vocabulary will degenerate into "No, no!" It sometimes seems to her as though Rachael's every move is designed to undo whatever Rosa has just accomplished. If Rosa sorts the white clothes from the colored laundry for washing, Rachael re-sorts it into her own categories. When Rosa makes the bed, Rachael often insists on pulling on the sheets and bedspread, immediately wrinkling the just-straightened bedding. So Rosa now tries to keep the laundry out of reach and to make the beds when Rachael is not looking.

Rachael seems the most demanding just when Rosa must work at the sink or stove. Dishwashing and cooking are often interrupted, and Rosa often ends up with Rachael wriggling on her hip while she makes some of the dinner preparations. Nicholas's work often looks simple to Rosa by comparison. At times like this Rosa longs for the day when Rachael will be in school and she will have a job, probably as a social worker.

Rosa was almost incredulous recently when she visited one of her former professors and saw his eighteen-month-old daughter busily helping her mother shell peas for the evening meal. Her mother had placed an unbreakable bowl on a low chair in the kitchen, and she opened each pea pod and then handed it to the toddler, who would pick the peas from the pod and put them into the bowl. The baby even crawled after a few that fell on the floor and returned them to the bowl! Rosa noticed that the child's mother did not scold her for dropping a few peas on the floor, and that she praised her, addressing her remarks both to the child and to Rosa, for being "a good helper." She did not fuss even when the toddler finally dumped the whole bowlful of shelled peas onto the floor and then plopped down and picked up a couple of handfuls. The mother just quickly scooped the peas back into the bowl, rinsed them, and poured them into a pan of boiling water on the stove. She then picked up her baby and held her while she talked with Rosa.

From this experience Rosa decided that perhaps praise was better than scolding. The next time Rachael poured her juice out on the floor, she praised her for attempting to wipe up the mess and handed her another small glassful. Rosa was really angry and on the verge of tears when Rachael, delighted by her mother's praise, poured out the second glassful and began wiping it up vigorously too! So Rosa was right back to saying, "No, no!" She wearily asked Nicholas that evening, "Why do you think Rachael is so bad? Is it because she is an only child? Am I spoiling her?"

Interpretation and Questions

Do you think Nicholas and Rosa should have waited another year or so before having a child? If the Skorioses had waited three more years before having their first child, what factors in their family situation would have been different? How might this have affected their feelings about themselves as parents? How might things have been different for their child? Do you think Rachael is hyperactive? Parents, especially mothers, are sometimes accused of wanting to live vicariously through their children. Do you think that is happening in this case?

STUDY GUIDE

Important Terms

childhood
permissive child rearing
restrictive child rearing
Parent Effectiveness Training
   (P.E.T.)
birth order

adoptions
stepparents
Parent Involvement Program (P.I.P.)
Responsive Parent Training Program
Challenge Study Groups

1 There was no conception of childhood as a separate biological, psychological, and social category in:
   a ancient Greece
   b Europe during the Middle Ages
   c the United States during the nineteenth century
   d England during the early twentieth century

2 In the United States, parents and teachers favored the restrictive approach to child rearing:
   a before the 1920s
   b during the 1920s
   c consistently from colonial days to the present
   d in the 1970s after the permissive period of the 1960s

3 Parent training programs presently offered are being attended largely by parents who are:
   a lower-class
   b black
   c middle-class
   d men

For questions 4 through 7 match parent training programs with a brief description. Use the following key:
   a Parent Involvement Program (P.I.P.)
   b Responsive Parent Training Program
   c Challenge Study Groups
   d Parent Effectiveness Training (P.E.T.)

4 Based upon Carl Rogers's philosophy; advocates that parents give up the use of physical and psychological power techniques.

5 Based upon William Glasser's reality therapy; advocates parent-child friendship as a means of improving the child's self-concept and behavior.

6 Based on behavior modification; advocates positive reinforce- ment and mild punishment to inculcate behavioral changes.

7 Based upon the ideas of Alfred Adler; advocates the use of encouragement and discipline to counter the goals of the child's misbehavior, which are attention, power, and revenge.

8 The child-rearing technique in which the parent uses explanations to induce the child to change some behavior is called:
   a power assertion
   b deprivation of love
   c induction
   d behavior modification

9 Parents in lower socioeconomic groups use the technique of _____ in child rearing to a greater extent than those in the middle class.
   a power assertion
   b deprivation of love
   c induction
   d friendship formation

10 In comparison with later-born children, firstborns seem to:
   a have greater affiliation needs
   b have had greater interest expressed in them by parents
   c earn higher grades in high school
   d all the above

11 The number of children adopted in the United States each year is closest to:
   a 10,000
   b 200,000
   c 500,000
   d 1 million

12 Trends in adoptions in recent years show that:
   a the majority of adoptions are arranged through illegitimate markets
   b most adoptions are now being made by single, rather than married, parents
   c most adoptions are now

being made by lower-class couples

d none of the above

13 In the United States, approximately _____ children under the age of eighteen now live in families in which there is a stepparent.

a 100,000
b 1 million
c 5 million
d 15 million

14 Studies of children of divorced parents who became members of families in which there is a stepparent show:

a greater personality problems
b greater difficulty in adjusting to social situations
c greater difficulty in making friends
d no important differences from children raised in natural families

15 The Gault decision, a landmark case in children's rights, found that:

a courts should replace parental control over children under age sixteen
b children and adults should receive the same treatment in court cases
c juveniles should have the same rights to due process as adults
d juveniles should never be sentenced to detention

Opinionnaire

Agree	No opinion	Disagree	
_____	_____	_____	1 Children internalize the values of society more completely under restrictive child-rearing practices.
_____	_____	_____	2 There are no particular skills involved in raising children.
_____	_____	_____	3 "Spare the rod and spoil the child."
_____	_____	_____	4 Parents and children can never really be friends because of the nature of their relationship.
_____	_____	_____	5 A person should have to be licensed by the state before he or she can become a parent.
_____	_____	_____	6 Men should have primary responsibility for their sons' raising, and mothers for their daughters'.
_____	_____	_____	7 It is always a little harder to love an adopted child than to love a natural one.
_____	_____	_____	8 Parents with only one or two children usually can do a more effective job of raising them than those who have larger families.
_____	_____	_____	9 Most parents today do not expect or receive enough obedience from their children.
_____	_____	_____	10 At least half of the responsibility for how a child turns out is the child's, not the parents'.

Exercise

PHOTOANALYSIS

The family photo album is a good source of clues about family relationships. You can use your own family album to test some of the hypotheses discussed in this chapter.

Hypothesis 1: Parents show more interest in firstborn than in later-born children.
Evidence: Count the total number of photographs your family has kept of the firstborn and compare this with the number of photographs of each later-born child.

	First child	Second child	Third child	Fourth child
Total number of photographs	_____	_____	_____	_____

Hypothesis 2: Parents are more anxious and insecure about firstborn than about later-born children.
Evidence: Count the number of photographs showing a parent holding the firstborn child and compare this with the number showing later-born children being held.

	First child	Second child	Third child	Fourth child
Number of photographs showing the child being held	_____	_____	_____	_____

Develop your own hypotheses to test with photoanalysis.
Compare your results with those of other persons in your class.

Projects for Class or Home Study

1 Many libraries keep their older books. Check through a few volumes on child rearing written during the early, middle, and current parts of this century. Are all the older comments irrelevant? Are there similarities among the ideas expressed in the different books?
2 Most urban areas offer several of the types of parent training courses described in this chapter. Call for more information and decide which program seems to fit in best with your own philosophy of child rearing.
3 Adoption-agency requirements provide a statement of what the "ideal" parental situation should be in our society. Call a local agency and ask about their basic qualifications for adopting a child. Do you consider them reasonable?
4 Approximately 11 percent of persons born in the late 1950s grew up as only children, 37 percent grew up as firstborns, and 52 percent grew up as later-born children. Ask your instructor to count and compute birth-order percentages for your class. Generally, a higher proportion of only children and firstborns will enter college and go on to graduate. Does this pattern show up in your class? Can you explain why this happens?

5 The novels of Charles Dickens describe many situations in which children are mistreated, both psychologically and physically. Read some of the descriptions in *Oliver Twist* and then reconsider the issue of children's rights. Do children today have enough protection?

Suggestions for Further Reading

Coles, Robert. *Uprooted children: The early life of migrant farm workers.* New York: Harper & Row, 1970.
   Parents of all social classes can learn from Coles's sensitive portraits of farm workers' children. He lets the children speak for themselves, thereby providing a perspective familiar to few.

Dager, Edward Z. Socialization and personality development in the child. In Harold T. Christenson (Ed.), *Handbook of marriage and the family.* Chicago: Rand McNally, 1964.
   A thorough explanation of how parents and children interact with and influence one another. The article is structured around the concept of identification.

Elkin, Frederick, and Handel, Gerald. *The child and society.* New York: Random House, 1972.
   A well-written, comprehensive manual on socialization.

Hemingway, Ernest. *Islands in the stream.* New York: Scribner, 1970.
   This posthumously published novel is divided into three parts, all concerning an artist who lives in the Caribbean. Part I, Bimini, contains some of the finest prose ever written about what it means to be a parent.

Neill, A. S. *Summerhill: A radical approach to child rearing.* New York: Hart Publishing, 1960.
   The founder of a famous school where children are not compelled to go to class develops his child-rearing theories. The philosophy emphasizes support and approval, with no restrictions on any form of behavior.

Roth, Philip. *Portnoy's complaint.* New York: Random House, 1969.
   A young Jewish boy reacts when his mother tries to pass on outdated values. The parent-child relationship makes the novel transcend the ethnic implications and the pervasive sexual content.

Weisberg, D. Kelly. The Cinderella children. *Psychology Today*, April 1977, **11**, 84–86.
   Children in urban communes are overwhelmed by the number of rules imposed by multiple "parents." Like Cinderella, commune children may also be punished more than once for the same offense.

Answers to Review Quiz

1-*b* 2-*a* 3-*c* 4-*d* 5-*a* 6-*b* 7-*c* 8-*c* 9-*a* 10-*d* 11-*b* 12-*d* 13-*d* 14-*d* 15-*c*

13

THE MATURING FAMILY

Alex Comfort, in *A Good Age* (1976), tells the story of a 104-year-old man who went to a physician complaining of a stiff right knee. "After all," he was told, "you can't expect to be agile at your age." The man replied, "My left knee is 104 too, and it doesn't hurt."

This anecdote illustrates a fairly typical attitude toward what it means to be old in our society. The process of aging itself is assumed to be a sufficient explanation for many of the problems of the elderly. Widespread beliefs about aging persons are stereotyped and often cruel. These attitudes are just as important as the biological process of aging in influencing how the elderly feel. Our centenarian in the first paragraph is actually quite unusual in continuing to resist societal expectations about how his knee is "supposed" to feel.

We have seen in previous chapters that marriage and family relationships are affected by roles outside the family—work roles, friendship patterns, and kin relationships, for example. Husband-wife and parent-child relationships, once established, do not remain static over time. As individuals move through the life cycle, their obligations and commitments to other family members must change. Failure to recognize the inevitability of changing relationships leads to problems; one example is the parent who will not "let go" of a grown child.

Scientists are now beginning to disentangle the actual effects of biological aging from societal beliefs about how persons change as they age. Knowledge of how individuals mature and of how intimate relationships change helps one to understand marriage and family life as a dynamic, changing process. With understanding can come a greater ability to deal with the problems that adjustment to new relationships often brings. First we shall consider what is known about aging, and then we shall discuss the roles of persons in a maturing family.

Aging

What comes to mind when we hear terms like *aging, elderly, old,* and *mature*? William Shakespeare compared youth and age thus:

> Crabbed age and youth cannot live together:
> Youth is full of pleasance, age is full of care;
> Youth like summer morn, age like winter weather;
> Youth like summer brave, age like winter bare.
> Youth is full of sport, age's breath is short;
>   Youth is nimble, age is lame;
> Youth is hot and bold, age is weak and cold;
>   Youth is wild and age is tame.
> Age, I do abhor thee; youth, I do adore thee.
>   —"The Passionate Pilgrim"

Unfortunately, Shakespeare may have helped to perpetuate a number of stereotyped beliefs about the aged and about what aging means. He saw aging as limiting and "abhorrent," a withered reflection of full-blossomed youth. Our modern conceptions have changed very little, as evidenced by the title of a recent *Newsweek* article (Can Aging Be Cured? 1973). As in Shakespeare's time, the belief persists that aging is an unfortunate circumstance to be "cured."

BIOLOGICAL CHANGES

No one really knows why people grow old. Individuals undergo physical, psychological, and sociological changes over time, but aging is not a disease. Some scientists believe that physical decline occurs primarily because the immune capacity breaks down. With the decline in the immune capacity, cancerous cells which earlier were eliminated from the body begin to cause physiological damage. Others suggest that each new cell is coded for a specific number of divisions. As the limit is reached, new cells are no longer produced to replace old ones, and cellular decline in the body becomes more evident. These theories have not been fully evaluated, however. The one absolute certainty is that, barring death at an early age, everyone grows old.

The term that is used to describe changes due to biological aging is *senescence.* The major manifestations of senescence are:

1 The skin becomes rougher and more wrinkled, and heals more slowly when cut; less perspiration occurs.
2 Through changes in the muscular skeletal system, joints stiffen, height is somewhat reduced, and muscular strength declines.
3 Visual acuity declines in many people, and inability to distinguish pitch and intensity of sound may occur. Reflexes decline and reaction time slows.
4 Circulatory capacity gradually diminishes.
5 The total capacity of the lungs decreases with age.
6 The reproductive, temperature control, and kidney filtration systems all show decline with age (Kart, 1976, p. 4).

These changes occur at different rates and therefore at different chronological ages in different individuals. Most studies now indicate that drastic physiological declines should not be expected statistically

until age seventy-five. In fact, acute illnesses become fewer with age, although chronic illnesses increase (Weg, 1975).

In the United States, women may be pictured as "old" by society ten or fifteen years sooner than men. In society's eyes, men may be considered sexually desirable until their late fifties; this is so because male sexuality is more likely to be defined in terms of personality and social roles than female sexuality is. A woman's sexual attractiveness has traditionally been defined in terms of her body. Some women would like to see this double standard changed:

> The middle-aged woman who thickly masks her face with makeup, who submits to surgical face- and breast-lifting, who dyes her hair . . . is as much a victim of socially instilled hatred as the black person who straightens his hair and applies bleaching creams to his skin (I. P. Bell, 1970, p. 76).

Many people may be unable to bolster their partners' flagging egos because they are undergoing problems of their own in middle age. The male climacteric is primarily psychological and not physiological. Early ambitions for economic success and career accomplishment must be tempered with the reality of what has actually been achieved. Reflections on the passing of the years may bring unpleasant reminders of physiological change that the middle-aged male is undergoing, such as prostate problems, perhaps less frequent erections, loss of hair, or expansion of girth. All this combines to make an affair with a younger sexual partner seem an attractive possibility.

While the double standard has defined women's attractiveness in terms of their looks, men have been encouraged to think that work performance is the main criterion of worth, and this comes to form the focus of identity. If you ask a man what he does, he is not likely to answer, "I'm a father" or "I'm a husband." Instead, he will put the answer in occupational terms—"I'm an engineer" or "I'm a postman." The physical changes that occur during the middle years are usually viewed primarily in occupational terms because occupation has long been the center of identity. In *Passages*, Gail Sheehy notes:

> In our society, turning 40 for a man is a marker event in itself. By custom, as if he were merchandise on a rack, he will be looked over by his employers and silently marked up or down, recategorized by his insurers, labeled by his competitors. Pyramids being what they are in the professional world, most men will have to adjust their dream downward to some degree (1976, p. 273).

Furthermore, Sheehy says, even the successful man must face this problem:

> The startling observation here is that the wunderkinder and workaholics who do come close to realizing their dream often have a more rugged transition to make than those who miss the mark. These recognized successes have the

problem of following their own act, an act that rarely brings the sweeping fulfillment they anticipated (1976, p. 273).

After middle age, changes in personality and intellectual functioning are thought to occur but have not been easy to document. There is some evidence that short-term memory declines with age, while long-term memory remains unimpaired. In general, there is no decline in mental ability with age (Birren, 1968). The elderly apparently become more passive and eventually come to show less emotional responsiveness. More impressive than these general findings, however, is the considerable variability among individuals. Many people have remained creative and intellectually vital into very old age—Pablo Picasso, Artur Rubinstein, and Grandma Moses, for example.

A LONG-LIVING PEOPLE

Taking a look at elderly people in another culture may serve to illustrate the truths that biological change does not occur apart from societal attitudes toward it and that individuals may be influenced in several ways by societal attitudes. In the Soviet Republic of Abkhasia, residents enjoy remarkable longevity (Leaf, 1973). Fifteen percent of one village consists of people over ninety-one years of age! A visiting writer remarked: "Not long ago, in the village of Tamish in the Soviet Republic of Abkhasia, I raised my glass of wine to toast a man who looked no more than 70. 'May you live as long as Moses [120 years],' I said. He was not pleased. He was 119" (Benet, 1971).

Why do they live so long? The Abkhasians themselves believe three factors are involved: their work, their sex lives, and their diet. Work is agricultural, and retirement does not exist—even the very old continue to work productively, if slowly, on the farms. Sexual energy is "conserved," and marriage typically occurs at about age thirty. While conservation of sexual energy is an unlikely possibility, the Abkhasian men do seem to retain potency to remarkable ages (doctors obtained sperm from one man who was 119 years old, and another fathered nine children after age 100), and about 14 percent of the women continue to menstruate after age fifty-five. Diets are stable and low in calories and cholesterol.

Sula Benet, who has visited Abkhasia several times, feels that cultural factors are more important than the physical environment:

There is another, broader aspect of their culture that impresses an outsider in their midst: the high degree of integration in their lives, the sense of group identity that gives each individual an unshaken feeling of personal security and continuity, and permits the Abkhasians as a people to adapt themselves—yet preserve themselves—to the changing conditions imposed by the larger society in which they live (1971, p. 3).

THREE GENERATIONS at a birthday celebration.

There is little centralized political authority that is meaningful for rural Abkhasians. Social organization is based on kinship and the extended family. Within a consanguineal system there are no developmental terms such as *adolescence* or *middle age*. The old share values with the young, and thus their advice and opinions are still sought at seventy or 120.

Dismissing genetics as a contributing factor, Benet (1971) lists two reasons why Abkhasians live so long. First, their lives are governed by uniformity and continuity—in work, food, games, and both individual and group behavior. Second, old age brings increasing prestige.

Abkhasians have much that Americans lack as they age, including the feeling that they will always have meaningful work to do and will always enjoy close family relationships. Biological change and the cultural definition of it give meaning to the life cycle, whether one is Abkhasian or American.

Erikson's Stages of Adult Development

How can individuals understand the psychobiological changes of the middle and later years? Erik Erikson has attempted to provide guidance in this. In Chapter 11 we discussed Erikson's view of development through adolescence. Unlike Freud, who believed that personality remained static after the resolution of the oedipal conflict at about age six, Erikson recognizes that development continues throughout life. In addition to the stages already discussed, he posits three adult stages.

Young adulthood follows the identity crisis of adolescence. Here the issue of *intimacy versus isolation* is faced. The developmental task is to enter into relationships involving self-abandonment—friendship, love, and erotic encounters—or to risk increasing isolation.

In full adulthood, *generativity versus stagnation* is the problem. Stagnation is avoided by "establishing and guiding the next generation or whatever in a given case may become the absorbing object of a parental kind of responsibility" (Erikson, 1950, p. 231). Erikson means that developmental progress depends upon becoming a guiding figure, but not necessarily a parent in the literal sense. Men may reorient themselves from striving for personal recognition to teaching younger men occupational roles. Women may become generative through scientific or business endeavors as well as through motherhood. Alice Rossi, among others, has suggested strongly that many women will develop more fully by *not* becoming mothers (1968). However, generativity may pose problems for the woman who has devoted herself to her children, only to find them leaving home during her middle years. This period will be discussed more fully in the next section as a role change.

Integrity versus despair is the final phase of development and confronts the individual with the necessity of making sense out of his or her life. Integrity occurs if the individual is able to find meaning and see

THE DESPAIR of old age in America.

integration in the way his or her life has been lived. The despair of old age comes with futile wishes that life had been different and with an attempt to assess one's own responsibility for this. Integrity gives one "a sense of comradeship with men and women of distant times and of different pursuits who have created orders and objects and sayings conveying human dignity and love" (Erikson, 1950, p. 139).

The Family Life Cycle

The median age at marriage for women in 1975 was about twenty-one years, and the average life expectancy for females was a little over seventy-five years. As an aid to understanding the half century of activity between these two events, a demographer coined the concept of a *family life cycle* (Glick, 1947). There are many variations, however:

> A family comes into being when a couple is married. The family gains in size with the birth of each child. From the time when the last child is born until the first child leaves home, the family remains stable in size. As the children leave home for employment or marriage, the size of the family shrinks gradually back to the original two persons. Eventually one and then the other of the parents die and the family cycle has come to an end (Glick, 1947, p. 164).

The concept of a family life cycle has allowed scientists to identify general changes in families over time. Marital satisfaction, for example, changes in consistent ways. During early periods of the life cycle, marriage typically brings a high level of satisfaction. A straightforward decline in satisfaction was once considered to occur in most marriages, increasing until death or divorce dissolved the marriage. Now, however, it appears that although the early period of high marital satisfaction is followed by a decline, marital satisfaction begins to increase when children start to be "launched" from the family, until finally satisfaction levels reach those of early marriage (Rollins and Cannon, 1974). The same researchers caution, however, that many things other than the family life cycle determine marital satisfaction and that men and women experience different pressures at identical points in the family life cycle.

Robert Atchley (1975), director of the Scripps Foundation for Research in Population Problems, relates the family life cycle to other important events. These events and their meanings can help couples grasp the significance of the inevitable changes that will occur in their lives. Although there is wide variation in the ages at which activities are undertaken or concluded, chronological age is used as the bench mark against which the other cycles are measured. Among the changes that family members inevitably face as they age are the departure of the children, retirement, loss of a spouse, and, finally, preparation for death.

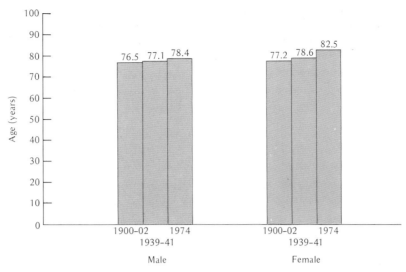

LIFE EXPECTANCY AT AGE SIXTY-FIVE: SELECTED YEARS
A person who is still living at age sixty-five can expect to live until 78.4 if male and until age 82.5 if female. *U.S. Bureau of the Census, 1976c, p. 34.*

THE EMPTY NEST

One family-life-cycle problem which rarely existed in earlier times is that of the prolonged empty-nest period. The fact that people live longer means that husbands and wives may now anticipate spending one to two decades together after their last child leaves home. Launching the last child brings a change to the relationship; whether the change is harmful or beneficial depends upon several factors.

On the one hand, a welcome reduction in supervision of children and in household chores can be expected. There may be opportunities for travel, education, and increased marital intimacy. New roles may be possible. For women, work outside the home may provide new challenges. Yet the empty-nest period can bring depression. Women who were raised to view motherhood as a primary goal often experience a crisis of purposelessness when the role is lost. Confrontation with a competitive job market or an educational system which has changed drastically may add to self-doubts. In a youth-oriented culture, physiological aging may contribute to feelings of depression.

As one researcher points out, society provides few guidelines and little training for the traditional mother who will soon lose the mother role. Suddenly the children are gone. The woman's self-image has been established for a quarter of a century. She is a mother, and now there are no recipients for her mothering. This loss may result in a "mutilated self." As one woman said in an interview: "I don't feel . . . that I'm wanted. I just feel like nothing. I don't feel anybody cares, and nobody's interested, and they don't care whether I do feel good or I don't feel good. I'm pretty useless. . . . I feel like I want somebody to feel for me, but nobody does" (Bart, 1970, p. 71).

In a 1972 Gallup poll, only 8 percent of respondents said they believed that married couples are happiest after the children leave home (Blake, 1974). Actually, studies show that there is a slight increase in marital satisfaction after children leave. Interaction is no doubt different. Money problems lessen. Topics of conversation focus less on children and more on the couple themselves—their interests, experiences, and health (Treas, 1975).

GRANDPARENTHOOD

One of the most eagerly awaited roles in our society is that of grandparent. Everyone is familiar with the grandmother who will produce for even casual acquaintances a purse full of photos of beaming grandchildren. Since they have little responsibility for disciplining or supervising grandchildren, many grandparents see the possibilities for a positive emotional attachment that was not feasible with their own children.

This idyllic picture of grandparenthood is apparently realized infrequently. Many persons become grandparents before their children are married. In 1974, this was true of one out of every eight grandparents (Nye, 1976). One study showed that 52 percent of single teenage mothers who were still in school were receiving financial help from their own mothers (Klerman and Jekel, 1973).

Even among black families, where illegitimacy has fewer negative connotations than among white families, grandmothers may be negative about the role. A researcher reports:

> The mother of a pregnant adolescent may be a young mother still, perhaps just beginning to see some freedom from responsibilities toward her own children. Some are planning to get jobs, to obtain further education, or just to begin enjoying a period of their lives when they might satisfy some of their own needs. Typically, becoming a grandmother—especially when this may mean having to assume at least part of the responsibility for a daughter and her child—is unexpected and unwelcome (E. W. Smith, 1975, p. 2).

Contact between grandparents and grandchildren occurs infrequently in our society, in terms of both visiting and providing mutual assistance (Hill, 1970). In a study of widowhood, Lopata (1973) found that only slightly over half of the widowed grandmothers interviewed felt close to even one of the grandchildren. The percentage feeling close to great-grandchildren was even smaller.

Neugarten and Weinstein distinguished five kinds of grandparents: formal grandparents, fun seekers, distant figures, substitute parents, and reservoirs of family wisdom (1964).

WIDOWS' FEELINGS OF CLOSENESS TO GRANDCHILDREN
AND GREAT-GRANDCHILDREN

Had feelings of closeness	To grandchildren (211 respondents)	To great-grandchildren (229 respondents)
Yes	57%	35%
No	43%	65%

Source: Adapted from Lopata, 1973, p. 170.

Formal grandparents leave all parenting to the parents, but they may do special favors for the grandchild. Fun seekers want to enjoy leisure-time activities with their grandchildren and to exercise a minimal amount of authority and discipline in relation to them. Distant figures lead their own lives and ignore their grandchildren except on special occasions. Some grandparents assume parental responsibility at the invitation of the parents or because a parent is incapacitated. Finally, some grandparents may act as the storehouse of family wisdom, dispensing advice or teaching skills. Most commonly, the relationship allows for expression of concern but rather reserved, infrequent contact. About one-third of the grandparents interviewed expressed disappointment in the role.

These pessimistic findings should not disenchant prospective grandparents, for the role is obviously rewarding to many. Becoming a grandparent probably will not, however, fill voids left by marital, work, or friendship shortcomings. How valuable the role will be depends upon the person's age when he or she becomes a grandparent, on whether being a grandparent interferes with valued or necessary work commitments, and on whether the grandparent has control over the amount of contact with the grandchildren. Being a grandparent can mean doing things for and with grandchildren that were not possible during the busy years with one's own children.

RETIREMENT

Most women have to adjust to a kind of retirement from their role of mother when their children leave home. However, the primary meaning of the word *retirement* is giving up work, a process that affects primarily males in their sixties. Blau (1973) points out that giving up this role affects a man's self-image. Both material and social rewards are lost. After having been trained for years to see his identity in terms of work, a man is suddenly judged by society to be unable to perform a valuable role.

Because the traditional definition of masculinity is job-related, retirement affects working men more than working women. Retirement also affects women who have been full-time homemakers; a husband's retirement may disrupt the normal household routine. The husband, missing the give-and-take of employment relationships, may feel a lack of

ESTABLISHING A schedule of social activities can ease the problem of adjusting to retirement.

purpose, just as his wife did when the children left home. And she, having resolved her crisis many years before, may now be the one to lack sympathy and understanding.

Thus, one functional result of traditional sex roles is that they produce a family life cycle in which men and women undergo meaningful role exits at different points. If men were more involved with child rearing and women gained more of a sense of identity from work, each spouse could better understand the meanings of the other's loss of role. A clear indication of the importance of sex roles comes from a comparison of blue-collar and white-collar workers. The blue-collar worker, who holds more traditional sex-role attitudes, has greater difficulty making the transition from worker to retiree (Loether, 1967). The lower average income of the blue-collar worker may also contribute significantly to retirement dissatisfaction. The most important factor in determining whether a couple will enjoy retirement is financial security (McCary, 1975). Formerly, older family members had to depend upon their children to finance this stage of the family life cycle. Now social security and pension plans have made economic independence a reality for many older couples.

If a couple have financial security, the retirement period can have certain advantages over earlier periods. Increased leisure time makes it possible to travel or pursue hobbies. New experiences and new friends can prove invigorating. If the couple have maintained a close relationship, the energy that they formerly devoted to children and work can be channeled into a rekindling of sexual activity. A more equal sharing of household chores may provide a basis for a more egalitarian relationship.

LOSS OF A SPOUSE

This last stage in the family life cycle is experienced more by women than by men. Of those over age sixty-five who lost a spouse in 1975, four times as many were female as were male. Loss of a spouse was studied extensively by Helena Lopata in a sample of Chicago-area widows (1973). Symptoms of grief and depression, including weight loss, insomnia, and irritability, usually last for a few months after the spouse's death, but one in five widows in Lopata's study reported never having recovered from grief (Lopata, 1973, p. 51). The widow often misses the familiar roles played by the deceased husband, such as sex partner, nurturant caretaker, and companion, and she may have to undertake unfamiliar tasks such as making minor repairs on the house, paying the bills, or putting out the garbage. Customary supports may be withdrawn. Only one-fourth of the widows in Lopata's study saw the deceased husband's relatives with any frequency (Lopata, 1973, p. 57).

Lopata suggests five major needs that widows will experience:

1 "grief" work
2 companionship
3 solution of immediate problems
4 building of competence and self-confidence
5 help in reengagement (1973, p. 271).

Surviving children may assist their widowed mothers in three major ways. First, they may directly assume some of the father's responsibilities. Second, the children may serve as objects of the mother's attention.

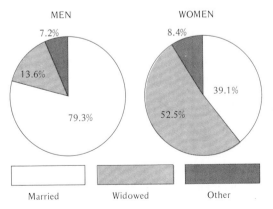

THE MARITAL STATUS OF OLDER PERSONS (SIXTY-FIVE AND OVER), 1975
Most older men are married; most older women are widowed. *U.S. Department of Health, Education, and Welfare, 1976.*

Third, they can maintain close interpersonal relations with her (Lopata, 1973, p. 101).

There may be a limit to the assistance children can provide, however. Greg Arling concluded from a recent study that family members actually do little to elevate widows' morale (1976). More important, he feels, are contacts of friends and neighbors because they are based on common interests and lifestyles. Furthermore, data from a comparative study of five countries indicate that widows have lower morale and are less affiliated than their married counterparts simply because they are poorer (Harvey and Bahr, 1974). As longevity increases, widowhood will become an increasingly important phenomenon. At present, there are no agencies that provide a systematic "socialization" to widowhood, but they are sorely needed.

Government Support of the Elderly

Many people picture the elderly as being ill, existing in a state of impoverishment, and/or living in institutions. Although there are some people over sixty-five in each of these categories, such a picture is grossly inaccurate. Fewer than one in twenty older people are institutionalized. Family settings are the homes of 80 percent of older men and 60 percent of longer-living older women. While only 14 percent of older people are without chronic health conditions, diseases, or impairments, 82 percent get along well independently (U.S. Department of Health, Education, and Welfare, 1975). Apparently persons who live alone are still staying in contact with family members. In one study, 90 percent of respondents aged sixty-five and over reported having seen one of their children in the last month (Shanas et al., 1968).

Largely as a result of increasing government benefits, the income situation of the elderly has been improving. In 1967 nearly one in three older persons had an income below the poverty level. By 1974, the ratio had been cut in half, and one out of every six older Americans is now counted as poor. Even the poor have an improved lifestyle as a result of federal health supplements through Medicare and Medicaid programs.

The fact remains, however, that approximately 1 million elderly persons are institutionalized at any one time, mainly in nursing homes. Nursing homes vary, but almost all are twenty-four-hour, full-care facilities. They are a relatively new phenomenon—as recently as the 1930s, only a handful existed. There are a number of reasons for their growth, as one writer understands it:

> The children of old people frequently will not pay for them. In addition, many old people have no responsible relatives: half the people in nursing homes

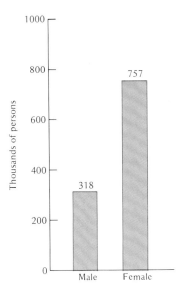

NURSING-HOME RESIDENTS, BY SEX, 1973–1974
Because of the greater longevity of the female population, more than seven out of ten nursing-home residents are women. And, on the average, more than 75 percent of nursing-home residents are seventy-five years of age or older. *U.S. Bureau of the Census, 1976c, p. 30.*

have no immediate family at all. Other old people have drifted apart from their families; the children are living far away, or are indifferent, or both. Many families do care but cannot afford the cost of a nursing home for the parent—the bill now averages around $14 a day. Finally, even if they can pay, society no longer holds the children responsible for their parents. This change, in effect the end of the family unit, is now recognized by law, for, when the resources of the old are calculated, the income of their children is not included. The son may be making $100,000 a year and own a winter home in Florida, but if his mother has no income she qualifies for public housing or Medicaid or other forms of assistance to the poor. That seems to be the way we Americans want it to be. . . . Americans have turned over the responsibility for older people, when they are sick and poor, to the state (Mendelson, 1974, p. 35).

The government pays for upkeep of the elderly through two programs, both adopted in 1965. Medicare provides money for most forms of health care for people over sixty-five years of age, regardless of income, and includes financing up to 100 days in a nursing home. After that, Medicaid, a joint federal and state program, pays for an unlimited nursing-home stay.

Payment is made directly to nursing homes. A flat rate may be paid (say, $14 per day), or payment may be on a cost-plus basis—that is, the home's cost of maintaining a patient plus a reasonable profit. Several types of abuse of the programs have been reported. Under flat-rate plans, the nursing home may try to minimize its costs by hiring unqualified help or furnishing an inadequate diet. One way to maximize profit when payment is on a cost-plus basis is to inflate costs artificially. Illegal kickback ties may be formed with pharmacies, doctors, and even funeral homes (Mendelson, 1974). Several recent congressional actions have been directed toward tightening controls on payments to nursing homes to assure that payments are actually used for the elderly.

Theories of Aging

Two contrasting theories attempt to provide guidance on what to do about advancing age. Unfortunately, neither explains adequately all we need to know about aging. Some of the evidence seems to support one theory, and some another.

Activity theory stems from an early statement by Havighurst and Albrecht (1953) that life satisfaction depends on maintaining a high level of social activity. The reasoning behind this theory is that, except for biological changes, the elderly remain the same as middle-aged persons. Social and psychological needs do not diminish; thus the need for activity remains constant. Optimal aging occurs when one remains active and does not allow social contacts to diminish. Participation in the economic sphere should continue as long as possible, and substitute activities should be found when declining health forces retirement. As old friends die, new networks of friends should be substituted.

THIS COUPLE keep a hardware store in a small town in New England. Working together, they seem active and happy with themselves and each other.

Many thinkers believe that continued activity into later years is inappropriate. The psychologist Carl Jung wrote:

Aging people should know that their lives are not mounting and expanding, but that an inexorable inner process enforces the contraction of life. For a young person it is almost a sin, or at least a danger, to be preoccupied with himself; but for the aging person it is a duty and a necessity to devote serious attention to himself. After having lavished its light upon the world, the sun withdraws its rays in order to illuminate itself (1960, p. 25).

Social scientists have recently stated this thesis more formally. *Disengagement theory* views a gradual decrease of social interaction as inevitable and mutually desirable by both society and the individual. The individual is seen as developing a natural preoccupation with self and a decreasing emotional involvement with others. The person with greater psychological well-being is seen as one who has reached a new equilibrium characterized by fewer relationships, greater psychological distance from others, and less social interaction (Cumming, 1963).

Studies designed to test these theories furnish unclear evidence. Lemon, Bengston, and Peterson (1972), in a test of activity theory, found only social activity with friends to be related to life satisfaction. Havighurst and Albrecht (1953) found that continued activity suited some elderly people, whereas disengagement seemed to keep others happy.

Although both theories are stated in an understandable and straightforward manner, it seems unlikely that either is the final answer to successful aging. Any theory must ultimately explain the conditions under which it will predict behavior. In physics, laws concerning the speed at which an object will fall specify the condition of a vacuum. Social theories likewise must specify such fundamental conditions as whether the individual chooses to become disengaged or whether this decision is made by others. Such conditions concerning the elderly are so numerous or so unknown that we cannot at present specify a general principle of successful aging.

Myths about aging are beginning to succumb to scientific study, however. As we learn about aging and the potential for understanding and adapting to change, it seems that the pessimism of a Shakespeare might be replaced by the optimism of a Tennyson:

The lights begin to twinkle from the rocks:
The long day wanes: the slow moon climbs: the deep
Moans round with many voices.
Come my friends.
'Tis not too late to seek a newer world.

—"Ulysses"

As individuals move through life, the nature of their relationships with other family members changes. Knowledge of biological aging, as distinct from attitudes toward the aged, is helpful to an understanding of these changes. Senescence, biological aging, is manifested by wrinkles and a general slowing down of the body. Change occurs at different rates and at different ages in different individuals. In American society the standards for a youthful appearance for women are higher than those for men.

A cross-cultural examination shows that there are societies, such as that of the Abkhasians, in which a more venerating attitude toward the aged is associated with much greater longevity and a much more youthful appearance among older people than are found in our own society. Such old people maintain a high degree of self-esteem and continue to make important contributions to their communities. Erik Erikson views adulthood as an unending development, rather than a final, static stage. In old age, Erikson sees the problem to be that of integrating into oneself and accepting the life one has lived.

The process in which a nuclear family is formed, increases in membership, and then disappears with the deaths of the original members is the family life cycle. Almost half of one's life as a founding member of a family is lived after the children leave, years often referred to as the "empty-nest" period. Often the children have been the main concern of family life, and a serious readjustment must take place after they are gone. The next stage for many couples is that of becoming grandparents. Reactions to this role are mixed. For many, grandchildren provide enjoyment without responsibility; others may have little contact with their grandchildren or derive little satisfaction from them.

Retirement usually requires a more difficult role change for men than for women. An important factor in satisfaction with this stage in the family life cycle is financial security. A final stage is that of loss of a spouse, which is experienced mostly by women. Widows, according to Helena Lopata, need a time for grief, companionship, a rebuilding of self-confidence, and help in making a new life. For the needy aged there is support from the government in the form of nursing homes, Medicaid and Medicare, and social security. Few people contribute to the support of their elderly parents.

There are two opposing theories concerning the best way to cope with old age: activity theory and disengagement theory. The first theory suggests that optimal aging occurs when one remains active and maintains social contacts. According to the second theory, it is a duty and a necessity for an aging person to gradually and gracefully withdraw from society.

CASE STUDY

An Older Woman Views Her Life

Lelia Smith married Richard Ladley forty-four years ago. At the time, she wanted to continue with her career, psychiatric social work, since she felt that it was important for her to work outside the home. But she greatly desired marriage and babies, too. When she had a miscarriage after several years of being frustrated at not becoming pregnant, she felt as if insult had been added to injury. Then she bore three sons in five years, adored them, and found mothering as rewarding as she had imagined it to be. During the early years she kept busy outside the family with volunteer work at the YMCA and the League of Women Voters. By the time her youngest was three, she had completed a master's degree in elementary education and was interested in teaching full time.

However, when her children started to suck their thumbs and stutter, she realized there was too much pressure in the family and sought help through counseling. With the help of her therapist, Lelia gained greater confidence in herself and was more able to think of herself as a separate person and to plan her career to benefit herself without causing harm to her family. It took a long time for Lelia to be convinced that she could make a career for herself on her own merits. At first she worked at an adoption agency three days a week. When her youngest son entered fifth grade, she became a supervisor with an urban welfare bureau.

At the time the children were having difficulties, Lelia's father was dying of cancer. She turned to her minister for emotional support, but instead she had an affair with him and immediately informed her husband. Rich was so furious that he hit her. He felt betrayed and hurt, and not only did he want the minister punished, but he even insisted that Lelia tell the minister's wife. For the next ten or eleven years Rich would remind Lelia of her infidelity at least once a week. But she never thought of leaving him until about three years ago. Lelia noticed that when they disagree Rich always views himself as being right, whereas she can see some fault in herself, and so she really has to get up her courage to say, "Look, I'm tired of being the bad one." She felt miserable when Rich told her that she was guilty and worthless for having an affair. Finally, twenty years later, she told him, "Shut up, I'm tired of hearing about it. If we're going to be married, let's forget it."

Lelia "retired" from social work seven years ago at the age of fifty-nine and began training as a psychotherapist. She completed her program in individual psychotherapy in three years. As she studied, she began seeing clients at her training institute and located an agency where she works mostly with couples two evenings a week. She is presently enrolled in a two-year training program in family therapy. She says of her work, "It took me a long time to realize it, but it is all right for me to mean something; I'm entitled to respect. I am a marriage counselor and know how to do it. There are personal benefits, too. We have a lot of love and communication in our family. With all the talk and reading on sex therapy, Rich and I are almost majoring in sex in our old age."

At sixty-six, Lelia believes she is living on borrowed time, since her mother died at sixty, and her father at sixty-seven. She used to fear death both because she saw her burly father reduced to a self-pitying grouch by illness and because Rich cannot stand being around ill people. However, she trusts that her sons and daughters-in-law will give support and comfort when the time comes, and she knows that people who love her will remember and mourn her.

Her Husband's View

Rich still remembers the first time he met Lelia on a blind double date for dinner at a fashionable seaside club. He had gotten hungry and was eating graham crackers with a glass of milk when she arrived in a Cadillac. He bounded out of the house and offered her a graham cracker. He found their early years together uneventful but not boring. He thought of himself as a loving father, but not the appropriate kind of person to raise children. He says that a bit of the anger over Lelia's affair remains with him, although it has not drastically affected his view of the marriage. Rich holds no grudge against the clergy since the minister is only a person too, and he has worked with some members of the clergy whose views on civil rights he respects.

Rich still looks with pride on the schools, libraries, and office buildings he designed as an architect. When he inherited substantial amounts from his parents and an aunt fourteen years ago, he took advantage of the opportunity. He sold his architectural business to his black partner, became an activist, and devoted himself to the fair housing movement and welfare rights.

He gradually got into his third career in the human potential movement. He explains, "For many years I was out to lunch, not into feelings, and very unaware of myself. When Lelia was a social worker and invited me to a weekend encounter group, I was angry. I was a private and respected person and felt I had to strip naked emotionally. Then I got into groups, and my children said I changed." He began conducting groups six years ago and coleads two or three a week with a forty-year-old woman. He finds that he is too competitive with Lelia to facilitate groups with her.

Rich resents Lelia's criticizing him for "getting into her act," since he was concerned with welfare rights when she was a social worker and then because he became interested in encounter groups when she was engaged in counseling. He feels that he chose his own paths logically. He supports her full-time professional growth but would like more togetherness. He feels cut off when she comes home tired and relaxes by devouring a novel or watching television. Sex is still exciting, and he thinks that their sexual functioning has abated very little since their thirties and forties. But he would like increased nonsexual intimacy between them. He wishes that they could sit hand in hand while watching TV or that they could touch spontaneously, just as he pets Tiffin, his big, shaggy dog. He senses an embarrassment between them about nonsexual touching. He also would like more companionship with Lelia. Sometimes he feels he has to make a date to talk to her, and he wishes that there was more spontaneous humor between them and that each was more interested in what the other was doing.

Rich wants to be needed. For Rich marriage means someone to come home to and a feeling of security. He disdains the kind of gut loneliness that arises from having no one to love. At seventy-one, Rich feels vigorous. He often tells inquirers he is sixty-five so that he will not be stereotyped as being over the hill. He still plays singles tennis with his son and enjoys sailing. Rich expects to live at least as long as his father, who died at eighty-four.

Interpretation and Questions

What have been the turning points in the Ladleys' relationship? Do you regard Lelia and Rich as having a successful marriage? How have their careers affected their marriage? Would you like to have Rich and Lelia for parents? For friends? Is their attitude toward sex typical? Do Lelia and Rich have anything worthwhile to tell us about aging?

Important Terms

family life cycle
senescence
empty nest
retirement
widowhood

Medicare
Medicaid
activity theory
disengagement theory

Review Quiz

1 People grow old because of:
  a a breakdown in the immune capacity of the body
  b the cessation of cellular reproduction after a finite number of reproductions
  c the stresses of social life
  d reasons at present unknown

2 The term used to describe changes due to biological aging is:
  a senility
  b senile psychosis
  c senescence
  d gerontology

3 Sula Benet, who has studied the longevity of residents in Abkhasia, believes that the people there are so long-lived primarily because:
  a they conserve their sexual energy
  b they eat a well-balanced diet
  c they retire from work at an early age
  d old people have meaningful work to do and are highly regarded

4 According to Erik Erikson, the issue of the last stage of development which must be resolved is:
  a trust versus mistrust
  b intimacy versus isolation
  c generativity versus stagnation
  d integrity versus despair

5 Marital satisfaction, over the course of the family life cycle, follows a pattern in which:
  a there is high satisfaction during the early period of marriage
  b after an initial high level of satisfaction there is a decline in the middle period
  c marital satisfaction increases again when children go off on their own
  d all the above

6 For an average couple, the "empty-nest" period lasts for:
  a five years
  b ten years
  c twenty years
  d forty years

7 The effects of sexual equality and the Women's Liberation movement should mean that the satisfaction of women with their lives during the empty-nest period will:
  a increase
  b decrease
  c remain the same
  d be unpredictable

8 The role of grandparent in this society has many advantages, but it may be marred by the fact that one in _____ persons becomes a grandparent before the grandchild is married.

   a two
   b eight
   c twenty
   d fifty

9 The most common grandparent role today is that of the:
   a formal grandparent
   b fun seeker
   c substitute parent
   d reservoir of family wisdom

10 Men's retirement from work in their mid-sixties may have serious consequences because:
   a in the United States work is an important source of identity for men
   b material and social rewards may be lost
   c their wives may have little understanding of, or sympathy for, the problems they face
   d all the above

11 The transition from worker to retiree generally will be easier for:
   a blue-collar workers than white-collar workers
   b women than men
   c persons who have no financial security
   d those who have unsatisfactory marital lives

12 Recent studies of adjustment to a spouse's death show that:
   a family members may have less impact on morale than friends and neighbors because the latter have more in common with the bereaved person in terms of interests and lifestyle
   b how much money the bereaved person has does not affect his or her level of morale
   c men are now more likely to lose a spouse than women are
   d all the above

13 In the United States, about _____ of the elderly (over sixty-five) are institutionalized.
   a 5 percent
   b 20 percent
   c 50 percent
   d 75 percent

14 The joint state and federal program which pays for an unlimited nursing-home stay for persons over sixty-five is called:
   a Medicare
   b Medicaid
   c social security
   d the old-age pension

15 The activity theory of aging contends that:
   a optimal aging occurs when one remains active and does not allow social contacts to diminish
   b one should increase the amount of attention devoted to oneself as aging continues
   c the number of relationships should be systematically decreased as one ages
   d disengagement from activity should occur gradually as one ages

Opinionnaire

Agree	No opinion	Disagree	
_____	_____	_____	1 People who use cosmetics to hide the fact that they are aging are vain and silly.
_____	_____	_____	2 There is no reason for frequency of sexual relations to decrease as couples become older.

——— ——— ———

——— ——— ———

——— ——— ———

——— ——— ———

——— ——— ———

——— ——— ———

——— ——— ———

——— ——— ———

3 It is natural for an old person to look back and wish that his or her life had been lived differently.

4 The happiest time of married life is when all the children are at home and the house is always active.

5 Grandparents usually will be closer to their grandchildren than to their own children.

6 No one should be forced to retire from any job by law or company policy.

7 Women who feel that there is no longer any purpose or meaning to their lives after their children have left home have only themselves to blame.

8 Women should not marry older men because to do so increases their chance of being lonely in later life.

9 The government is already contributing too much to the support of older citizens.

10 Anyone who puts a relative into a nursing home is not meeting his or her family obligations.

Exercise

CHARACTERIZING OLDER PEOPLE

The exercise below asks you to rate a social object on several bipolar adjectives. Decide which of the opposite terms best describes the stimulus object and check the space which best indicates how closely the word describes the stimulus. Reserve the middle blank for completely neutral, or irrelevant descriptions. Do not try to figure out logically what the descriptions mean; rather, place the checks according to your first emotional reaction.

The first stimulus term, to be written in the appropriate blank, is *a seventy-seven-year-old man.*

Social object: _____

Wise	___	___	___	___	___	Dull
Fast	___	___	___	___	___	Slow
Rich	___	___	___	___	___	Poor
Big	___	___	___	___	___	Little
Clean	___	___	___	___	___	Dirty
Sexy	___	___	___	___	___	Unsexy
Bright	___	___	___	___	___	Dull
Strong	___	___	___	___	___	Weak
Aware	___	___	___	___	___	Unaware
Liberal	___	___	___	___	___	Conservative

Now change the social object to *a twenty-seven-year-old man* and make the same ratings. Compare the two by numbering the five blanks (in either direction: 1 to 5 or 5 to 1), adding the total ratings, and dividing by 10.

Which social object had ratings closest to the left-hand side? Do the ratings reflect actual differences or societal stereotypes?

Try this scale on other people. The social objects can be changed to an old woman and a young woman.

Projects for Class or Home Study

1   Engage an elderly person in conversation about some events which took place a long time ago and some which occurred recently. Does the person seem to have a sharper awareness of earlier events?

2   Since women now have a life expectancy about eight years longer than that of men and since, on the average, they marry men two years older than themselves, an average woman may have to spend the last ten years of her life without a partner. A simple solution to this problem would be for women to marry men several years younger than themselves. Is this a realistic possibility? Explain.

3   Estimate the average ages of some of the male and female romantic leads currently starring in movies. At what age do women stop being cast in romantic roles? What about men? What effect does this have on societal attitudes?

4   Many retirement communities indicate their philosophy of retirement in illustrated brochures. Send for some brochures and see whether the philosophies seem to be based on the activity theory or the disengagement theory of aging.

5   Take a tour through a nursing home during open-house hours. (Many homes are seeking volunteers to spend time with the elderly. If your career goals are in one of the helping professions, this could be a valuable experience.) Compare the nursing-home environment with that of the family. What are the differences?

Suggestions for Further Reading

de Beauvoir, Simone. *The coming of age.* New York: Putnam, 1972.
    A novelist and social critic comments on the problems being endured by the aged. Her point of view is passionate and critical.
Jury, Mark, and Jury, Dan. Gramp. *Psychology Today,* February 1976, **9**, 57–63.
    This is the moving story, told partly in pictures, of an eighty-one-year-old man who chose to die. His loving family recognized his choice and supported him through his last weeks.
Maas, Henry S., and Kuypers, Joseph A. *From thirty to seventy.* San Francisco, Jossey-Bass, 1974.
    A report of a longitudinal study covering a forty-year period in the lives of 142 subjects. The authors are concerned with lifestyle and personality.
Pirandello, Luigi. The soft touch of grass. In Luigi Pirandello, *Short stories.* New York: Simon and Schuster, 1959.

An old man, in despair after losing his wife, attempts to behave in a concerned, fatherly manner toward a young girl in a park. His actions are misinterpreted as lewdness.

Robertson, Joan F. Grandmotherhood: A study of role conceptions. *Journal of Marriage and the Family,* February 1977, **39**, 165–174.

In the most complete study yet done on the role of grandmother, the author describes what grandmothers do and how happy they are in doing it. Most feel that being a grandparent is far more satisfying than being a parent in every way.

Updike, John. *The poorhouse fair.* New York: Knopf, 1958.

This book marked Updike's debut as a novelist. Relationships in an old-age home are developed through a portrait of a ninety-six-year-old man named Hook. This is a sensitive account of a lifestyle which has now been adopted by almost 1 million institutionalized older Americans.

Answers to Review Quiz

1-*d* 2-*c* 3-*d* 4-*d* 5-*d* 6-*c* 7-*a* 8-*b* 9-*a* 10-*d* 11-*b* 12-*a* 13-*a* 14-*b* 15-*a*

14

STRESS

Trouble for a couple or family can stem from many different causes and can have an even wider variety of effects. For example, prolonged unemployment of the father may cause one family to move to a slum neighborhood, trigger the father's drinking problem, and expose the children to criminal activities; it may stimulate the members of another family to work together to discover a source of income and find ingenious ways to cut expenses, bringing greater mutual respect all around.

Troubles create changes, and it is changes—routines that no longer work—that cause stress. Birth and death, marriage and divorce, sudden success or failure—are all to a greater or lesser degree life events that are stressful. The Social Readjustment Rating Scale ranks the life events which cause stress for the individual, from the greatest stressors to the lesser ones. Even the changes in daily routine caused by Christmas or a vacation are causes of stress.

In her recent book, entitled *Passages*, writer Gail Sheehy explains how the different stages of adult development in men and women conflict, placing stress on a marriage. One woman described her husband to Sheehy:

> "He started from nothing and built his own company, which now has worldwide offices," recounted Nora, the puzzled wife of a young president, "but in the past year he's been in some kind of personal agony. More and more he thinks less and less of himself and what his work means. He needs to know he matters to the children. I think he's feeling that all his past absences have to be made up for" (Sheehy, 1976, p. 292).

Sheehy also describes the development of a dream that provides purpose to one's life. The realization that the dream will not come true (or, if it does come true, that it is not as good as the fantasy) can also bring stress to a marriage. Sheehy quotes a forty-three-year-old writer, talking about his situation:

> I was absolutely horrified to discover that in the back of June's head—she admitted it one night—she had always expected I would become Scott Fitzgerald or Gay Talese, that at some point I would have the half-million-dollar book. . . . I realized that what she'd had all these years was the white, middle-class dream that you marry the romantic writer. It threw me into deep depression. I didn't write for six months. . . . I felt rotten, and I began to shove off some blame on her . . . and it was horrible for June. She let herself go physically (Sheehy, 1976, p. 288).

In the accompanying table, life events are ranked according to the degree of stress they evoke. Highest values require greatest adaptation and are most likely to trigger disease.

Some individuals and families react to stressors in an unpredictable fashion. "It has always puzzled observers," writes social worker Reuben Hill, "that some families ride out the vicissitudes of floods and disasters without apparent disorganization, whereas most families are at least temporarily paralyzed." The difference, Hill believes, lies partly in the *meaning* that a family attaches to an event. "Stressors become crises in line with the definition the family makes of the event" (1958, p. 141). And the family's definition may follow that of the community: a boy caught shoplifting may be a disgrace in one community and a hero in another.

Families also differ in the resources they have to meet stress. A loss of income may be taken in stride by a family with substantial savings and investments in stocks and real estate, but may be disastrous for a family without reserves of health, energy, or ideas for coping with crisis, much less of cash. Families devoid of such resources are perilously crisis-prone, vulnerable to crippling disorganization from every strain that comes along. Other families, by contrast, seem to be almost crisis-*proof*—but they have more going for them than just savings accounts and real estate. In Hill's words, a crisis-proof family has "agreement in its role

SOCIAL READJUSTMENT RATING SCALE

Rank	Life event	Mean value
1	Death of spouse	100
2	Divorce	73
3	Marital separation	65
4	Jail term	63
5	Death of close family member	63
6	Personal injury or illness	53
7	Marriage	50
8	Fired at work	47
9	Marital reconciliation	45
10	Retirement	45
11	Change in health of family member	44
12	Pregnancy	40
13	Sex difficulties	39
14	Gain of new family member	39
15	Business readjustment	39
16	Change in financial state	38
17	Death of close friend	37
18	Change to different line of work	36
19	Change in number of arguments with spouse	35
20	Mortgage over $10,000	31
21	Foreclosure of mortgage or loan	30
22	Change in responsibilities at work	29
23	Son or daughter leaving home	29
24	Trouble with in-laws	29
25	Outstanding personal achievement	28
26	Wife begins or stops work	26
27	Begin or end school	26
28	Change in living conditions	25
29	Revision of personal habits	24
30	Trouble with boss	23
31	Change in work hours or conditions	20
32	Change in residence	20
33	Change in schools	20
34	Change in recreation	19
35	Change in church activities	19
36	Change in social activities	18
37	Mortgage or loan less than $10,000	17
38	Change in sleeping habits	16
39	Change in number of family get-togethers	15
40	Change in eating habits	15
41	Vacation	13
42	Christmas	12
43	Minor violations of the law	11

Source: Solomon, 1971, p. 29.

structure [and] subordination of personal ambitions to family goals"
(1958, p. 144). Members of a crisis-proof family find satisfaction in
group-shared goals, and, as a group, they support and care for one
another physically as well as emotionally.

Although crisis-proof families have their fair share of troubles, they

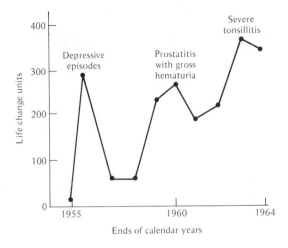

Life change units (y-axis): 0, 100, 200, 300, 400
Ends of calendar years (x-axis): 1955, 1960, 1964

Depressive episodes

Prostatitis with gross hematuria

Severe tonsillitis

RELATIONSHIP OF LIFE CRISES AND HEALTH CHANGES Life changes are often closely linked to sickness. This chart shows life and health changes during a nine-year period in the life of a young physician. *After Solomon, November 1971, p. 28.*

manage to keep them from developing into full-blown crises. But what kinds of trouble force the family to mobilize its resources? What stresses and strains plunge a less resourceful family into disorganization?

In this chapter we have space to examine only three causes of family stress: alcoholism, which affects millions of families and is always difficult to cope with; infidelity, which also affects millions but is not always a threat to the family; and death, which eventually strikes every family that has not already dissolved through some other cause.

Death

There are still some people who, to twist a phrase, never say "die," only "pass away," and in general avoid all thought of death. Our culture has just gone through a phase of shunning the subject both in books and in everyday conversation. Not that people were any more squeamish or fearful a few years ago than they are today. They only believed that to dwell on death was morbid or pathological and far from helpful to a person getting over a bereavement.

Recently, however, that belief has been challenged by investigators who have studied terminally ill patients, the mourning process experienced by surviving spouses and parents, and children's reactions to death in the family. In most cases these investigators have found that people deal with death best by facing it frankly and expressing all their emotional reactions to it. When we want to help others who are dying or bereaved, we no longer try to deceive them or to ignore death. Instead, we tell the truth, accept their feelings, and above all stick with them to the end. But this can be very difficult. The findings of recent research have proved quite helpful in such circumstances.

INANIMATE OBJECTS, like this old rocking chair, can evoke poignant memories of a loved one who has died.

DYING

Death comes unexpectedly to many of us, but there have always been people who knew from the way they felt that the end was near. Today, with degenerative diseases (cancer, heart trouble, and others) on the rise and techniques for diagnosing them almost foolproof, people can learn that their illness is fatal several months before they die. Psychiatrist Elisabeth Kübler-Ross has studied terminally ill patients and has found that dying is easier for those who are allowed to hope, are reassured that they will never be deserted, and have someone to talk to freely about the consequences of their death.

Kübler-Ross and her colleagues (1969) have noticed that people pass through five stages after learning that death is inevitable:

1 *Disbelief.* Unable to believe the diagnosis, the person searches frantically for a more favorable opinion. Families can help by being understanding of this apparently futile behavior, by keeping themselves open, and by being willing to talk.

2 *Anger.* "Why me?" The person bitterly envies those who will survive. He or she may complain about everything at this stage, but the family, instead of returning the anger, should try to treat the person with continued respect.

3 *Bargaining.* The person promises good behavior to the physician or to God in exchange for more time or freedom from pain. This is usually a short stage. If the bargain is revealed to family members, it should be listened to and not brushed off.

4 *Mourning.* The person mourns his or her approaching death. Attempts to cheer the person up are misguided; family members should allow the grief to be expressed fully.

5 *Acceptance.* A quiet acceptance replaces anger and depression. The person loses interest in news of the outside world. Only the presence of one or two close family members is required, and little talk is necessary.

MOURNING

Adults helping a terminally ill family member may pass through the same five stages themselves, thus preparing for their own mourning process. But when death comes without warning, they can mourn only afterward. The characteristics of mourning depend on many different factors: on whether the deceased was wife, husband, or child; on the personal relationships between the deceased and other family members; and on individual psychological backgrounds. In no circumstances, however, can mourning be escaped altogether. It can be postponed with drugs, frantic activity, or other strategems, but sooner or later the person will go through some form of mourning—or will seem to lose all capacity for feeling.

Mrs. Dean's husband, for example, got sick with no previous warning. A few days later he was diagnosed as having an incurable cancer, and a week after that he was dead.

> Mrs. Dean was stunned, overcome by shock. She could not grasp that this was real, that she had lost her husband forever. She felt empty and utterly bereft. It was as if all the goodness her husband had put into her had gone with him. . . .
>
> She wanted to be alone with her grief and drown herself in her sorrow, but this was not allowed. Everybody around her—her family, doctor, priest—expected her to pull herself together, not to make an exhibition of herself, not to upset her children; not to endanger her job by moping; not to worry others with her depression (Pincus, 1974, p. 165).

Mrs. Dean did what was expected of her. Several years went by during which she never talked with her two sons about their father. She even felt it a strain to have them around, though she always took good care of them. It was just that she could not show any feeling in front of them. She was terrified to get close to them because this might "open the floodgates of feeling," and all three might be swept away (Pincus, 1974, pp. 156–157).

Then, soon after she started to explore her feelings with a family therapist, Mrs. Dean underwent severe hemorrhaging, "as if an old wound had opened," and had to have a hysterectomy. She gave in to the illness, and for the first time since her husband's death she allowed herself to be pampered and cared for. Her family, friends, and colleagues showed much concern, prompting her to take a new look at herself. When she recovered, she found that she could acknowledge the appreciation given to her in her work and could respond to her sons with feeling. In turn, her sons became more accessible to her (Pincus, 1974, pp. 167–168).

Giving way to mourning is a necessity for every bereaved person. Anyone who represses or postpones it for any length of time risks becoming, like James Boswell, a "solitary wanderer": "I have ever since seemed to myself broken off from mankind; a kind of solitary wanderer in the wild of life, without any direction, or fixed point of view; a gloomy gazer on the world to which I have little relation" (1953, p. 196).

But no one should imagine that mourning is anything but a terribly disrupting and miserable alternative to the stable state of being a "solitary wanderer." There is little to say in its favor except that it does eventually run its course, leaving the person able to grow again. The course, moreover, may be quite prolonged. A mourning period of two years or more is not abnormal, although after the first months mourning usually takes the form of relapses that come less and less frequently and last for shorter spells.

English social worker Lily Pincus doubts that mourning proceeds in a typical series of stages like those found by Kübler-Ross in terminally ill patients. Mournings seem to be as various as the individuals who mourn. In one way or another, however, most mournings do involve certain typical responses: depression, grief, anger, searching for the lost person, and regression (Pincus, 1974, p. 88).

Yvonne was inconsolable, Pincus writes, when her husband died. "She cried and sobbed for days, unable to accept her loss. Her sons and daughters-in-law tried to comfort her, . . . but Yvonne felt that 'nobody helped, no one understood' " (1974, p. 62). It is worse than useless to try to cheer up a person who is feeling such grief. Any such attempt may be interpreted as disapproval for giving in to one's feelings. All a sympathetic person can do is to look after the mourner (who may neglect himself or herself and who is probably quite accident-prone) and be indulgent of the mourner's thoughts and behavior.

Though helpless with grief, mourners may feel a raging fury at having been so monstrously hurt. A wave of irrational anger may sweep over them at unpredictable moments. This can seem so different from their usual behavior that they wonder whether they are going crazy. Anger may even be directed against the deceased, the person who has caused so much pain.

Any loss evokes the behavior of searching. Although mourners know the lost person can never be found, during unguarded moments and in dreams they keep on searching. One man told Pincus that "again and again in his dreams he tried, with great urgency, to get to a place where he might find his lost wife" (1974, p. 116). Often searching is expressed not in such obvious images but in restless behavior, tension, and loss of interest in all that does not concern the deceased.

The myth of Orpheus and Eurydice illustrates the search for a dead lover. Orpheus travels to Hades, makes a bargain with the god of the underworld for the return of Eurydice, and then loses her again at the last moment.

Regression—the return to a less mature way of behaving—can be triggered by any major change in one's life situation, especially the death of a family member, since this requires mobilization of all one's forces to cope with the anguish and guilt, leaving no reserves to maintain one's usual standards. Of a bereaved friend, Pincus wrote: "In one of the moments of greatest despair after her husband's death, when she just did not know what to do or where to turn, she wrapped herself, head to foot, in a soaking hot bath towel and curled up in her favorite chair, as in her mother's womb" (1974, p. 42). Unfortunately, too many mourners have inhibitions that keep them from indulging in such regressions to infantility. But regressing in private may be frightening to mourners who do not understand their childish impulses. They may feel that they are losing control of themselves or are going insane, for they do not know that regression is common among people in mourning and will pass. Friends and other family members can help the mourner by not demanding mature behavior. Instead, they can show sympathy and loving acceptance of regressive behavior, in this way giving support and the assurance that the mourner has not been abandoned.

Think what this advice means in practice to people who would like to help a mourner. It means spending weeks taking care of and indulging the infantile behavior of someone who is inconsolable and incompetent. No wonder most people would rather believe it is better to say, "Be brave" or "Act your age." And indeed, if the function of mourning were simply to allow one to get used to the fact that a loved one is lost forever, such extravagances of behavior, such lavish wastes of time, would be hard to justify. Would it not be easier for the bereaved to face reality at once, rather than bit by excruciating bit?

One researcher, Melanie Klein, believes that the function of mourning is more than just that of making it possible to face reality and withdraw love from the dead person. Mourning is also, she says, an effort "to rebuild with anguish the inner world, which is felt to be in danger of deteriorating and collapsing" (1940, p. 125). In other words, the deceased must be taken into oneself and made part of one's inner self. But this takes time, since for quite awhile the bereaved is still in touch with external manifestations of the lost person. Eventually, however, the bereaved becomes less dependent on these external presences and draws more and more on memories. Sharing these memories with others makes it possible to talk, think, and feel about the deceased. At this point, internalization of the dead, perhaps the most important task in mourning, has been accomplished.

CHILDREN AND DEATH

A child's reaction to the death of a mother or father usually depends more on the behavior of the surviving parent and on the new circumstances of life than it does on the child's own feelings of loss. The death of a mother, for example, may lead to the breakup of the whole family, and the child may go to live with relatives—a change that will obviously have many profound consequences for the child. The death of a father may leave a son in the hands of a mother who cannot manage independently and clings to him in an effort to put him in her dead husband's place. Instead of forcing the child to grow up faster, this often slows his maturation.

While changed conditions may have the most important effects on them, children certainly do have their own feelings toward the loss. Even infants between six months and three years of age react strongly to the loss of their mother. At first they cry loudly in grief and anger, demanding their mother's return and expecting her to appear at any moment. Then they stop wailing, stop looking for her, and indeed lose interest in everything else as well. Apathetic, grieving inwardly now, they barely react to other people and may spend the day rocking back and forth sucking their thumb. Finally they cheer up, become responsive again to other people, and appear to have forgotten their mother (Bowlby, 1961).

Between the ages of three and five, children are so terrified of being abandoned altogether that they may not grieve the loss of one parent very much if the surviving parent reassures them and keeps their lives from changing drastically. Children over five, however, become interested in death itself, ask questions about it, and may be deeply affected by a death in the family.

Sula Wolff recounts the story of Allan, aged five, who lived on a farm with his little stepbrother, aged two. One day, while Allan was running to join his stepfather in the lambing shed, he was followed by the little toddler. Allan shouted at his brother to stay behind, but the child climbed over a low wall, fell into a well, and drowned.

> Allan's behavior now changed completely. He became a very aggressive child, frequently in fights with other children at school and unable to concentrate on his lessons. He climbed dangerously and sustained several bad falls so that his mother was constantly afraid he would seriously injure

AT AN early age, children are capable of responding to death in much the same way as adults.

himself. [When he was ten years old he could still remember his brother's death in great detail], and the steady conviction that he had been responsible . . . never left him (Wolff, 1969, pp. 107–108).

Beginning at about age nine, children begin to mourn a death in the family as adults do. They have crying spells, become depressed and apathetic, and feel hostile not only toward the doctors who failed to save the loved one but also toward everyone who has not been stricken by such a loss.

When children talk about death, their conceptions are vague and erroneous until the age of four or five. After age five, they mix up death in their magical thinking with aggressive feelings and fears of punishment for wrongdoing. A more realistic understanding of death does not come until about age nine (Wolff, 1969, p. 97). However, the knowledge that children will not fully understand is no excuse for hiding the death of a family member from them. Although children may not know what is actually going on around them, they can perceive that they are being lied to. Parents who lie to their children about a death in the family are reacting to their own needs, rather than understanding those of their children.

The best course for outsiders wishing to help a bereaved child is to help the surviving parent mourn without interrupting the parent-child relations, since it is, as we have seen, the parent's behavior toward the child that is the most important factor in the child's final acceptance of the loss. Outsiders also can keep in mind that the death of a parent almost invariably brings financial restrictions to a family, whether the deceased is the breadwinner or the homemaker, whose work must be replaced by a paid helper.

Alcoholism

For every skid-row derelict in the United States there are fifteen other alcoholics trying to maintain some semblance of a normal life. Most of them are family members, as the derelict himself once was. Learning to cope with alcoholism is not a problem for the alcoholic alone. It is a problem for every member of the family and can be met only by the whole family.

Since there are an estimated 10 to 12 million alcoholics in the United States, when all the members of the alcoholic's family are counted, the number of people involved in alcoholism rises to at least three times that figure. This figure amounts to one in every six Americans.

WHAT IS ALCOHOLISM?

Traditionally people have ascribed drunkenness either to wanton disregard of responsibilities or to personal inadequacy and weakness. Either way the alcoholic has been condemned, and his or her family disgraced. In recent years, however, Alcoholics Anonymous and the American Medical Association have propounded the view—the medical model— that alcoholism is an illness similar to an incurable disease and that it is caused, ultimately, by unknown factors. The implication of this view is

that the alcoholic is powerless over the disease. You can no more blame a person for being an alcoholic than you can blame a diabetic for lacking insulin. As an incurable disease, alcoholism can be arrested but never cured. The alcoholic can learn to refrain from drinking but will always be an alcoholic (Jellinèk, 1960).

Some psychologists, most notably Claude M. Steiner (1971), have been critical of the disease analogy. The Alcoholics Anonymous program, however, has been the most successful program for coping with alcoholism, and it is likely that the disease analogy they advocate, which removes the alcoholic's overwhelming feelings of guilt about his or her drinking, will remain a cornerstone for the treatment of alcoholics for some time to come.

Just why one person becomes an alcoholic and another does not is unknown. Psychologists have noted certain behavioral traits commonly found among alcoholics, but they are by no means universal and certainly

ALCOHOLISM IS a common problem among young people in our society.

cannot be regarded as causing alcoholism. They do suggest, however, some of the problems faced by the alcoholic family. According to these studies, alcoholics tend to:

1 Experience intense, though often brief, enthusiasms
2 Be perfectionists who demand too much of themselves and others and who try to do too much, too fast
3 Have high ideals which they are unable to live up to in their own lives
4 Be indifferent to the destruction they may cause themselves and others
5 Be self-destructive
6 Be dependent on others and willing to lean, rather than stand on their own (Al-Anon, 1976).

In short, alcoholics are unable to be the people they would like to be. They find life with its limitations painful, and they drink to regain a childlike freedom from adult responsibility.

An alcoholic can be identified by any of these typical behavior patterns: drinking before noon, skipping meals in favor of drinking, failing to remember actions that were taken when drunk, needing a drink before making a difficult decision, remaining intoxicated for several days at a time, drinking on the job or at any time when responsible behavior is required, being unable to stop drinking until thoroughly intoxicated, hiding bottles, and vehemently denying the role alcohol has assumed in his or her life (Hornik, 1974). As a generalization, it can be said that an alcoholic is a person whose health, interpersonal relations, or work has begun to be affected in a persistent manner by drinking.

PATTERNS OF THE ALCOHOLIC FAMILY

Paradoxically, however, it may not be the alcoholic who betrays the drinking problem in a family. "A drinking problem in the home," argues one woman who spent many painful years with an alcoholic husband, "can often be more easily recognized *by the wife's* (or husband's) behavior than by that of the drinker" (Al-Anon, 1966, p. 2). This statement makes sense when we view the alcoholic not as an isolated individual but as part of an alcoholic family.

In an alcoholic family, as in a nonalcoholic one, each action by one member and the subsequent responses by the others shape all future interactions. Patterns developed between husband and wife or between parent and child are followed again and again in the course of family life. The alcoholic's first acts of excessive drinking, accordingly, are met by certain responses on the part of other members of the family in their attempt to resolve the crisis brought on by the drinking. Each success or failure influences future interactions and helps to determine the form the crisis will take in later stages.

By his drinking and the harm he inevitably causes, the alcoholic man typically provokes his wife and children into anger and loss of temper. At first they may try to discuss the problem reasonably, but soon they begin to nag, cry, scream, plead, and threaten. This diffuses their ability to help. At the same time, the drinker's behavior arouses strong anxiety; the family feels the need to cover up for him and to protect him from the consequences of his drinking.

Unfortunately, both responses only intensify the alcoholic's motivation to drink. On the one hand, he drinks to escape the pain of failure and to deny his dependency on others; the anger of loved ones serves to remind him of the failure he is all too acutely aware of. The guilt he already feels because of his inadequacy is now compounded by his drunkenness. On the other hand, shielding him from the consequences of his alcoholism teaches him a dangerous lesson: that he can drink and behave badly with impunity, for others will take care of him. They will bear his burden, pick him up when he falls, and protect him from serious harm. This lesson results in deeper dependency as the drinking continues.

As psychiatrist Joan K. Jackson has pointed out, family members attempt to deal with alcoholism within the boundaries of their cultural experience. The wife of an alcoholic seeking to stabilize her disrupted family, for example, may be bound by several conceptual limitations—a definition of alcoholism as weakness, inadequacy, or sinfulness; a prescribed role as devoted wife; and a set of values that call for family solidarity and self-sufficiency at all times. Such definitions, roles, and values, Jackson argues, leave the wife with no idea of what to do that is appropriate to the crisis. In fact, these roles and values suggest steps that, as we have just seen, only serve to worsen the situation (Jackson, 1954).

From her research on the wives of alcoholics, Jackson has identified seven stages of family adjustment during an alcoholic crisis. The later stages are reached when family members and others have played out their responses to the alcoholic's drinking. Each stage tends to set a pattern of action and response for the following stages.

STAGE 1. ATTEMPTS TO DENY THE PROBLEM Excessive drinking begins. The alcoholic's wife confronts him with her concern, and he promises to stop. Both feel shame—he for his drinking and she for what she now thinks was excessive concern. As the drinking continues, usually sporadically, she searches unsuccessfully for the right formula to control it. Because American society tolerates frequent drinking among males, she finds little support for her concern and fear.

STAGE 2. ATTEMPTS TO ELIMINATE THE PROBLEM The family begins to become socially isolated. Guided by the cultural value that a family ought to resolve its own problems, members retreat from contact with other people and cover up when the alcoholic's actions threaten exposure of the problem. The family becomes desperate in its attempt to control the alcoholic. All its actions revolve around the problem. The children often develop emotional disorders at this stage, while the parents try to maintain the traditional husband-wife-children roles. The wife, half believing his accusations that she is driving him to drink, assumes the blame and berates herself for failing to find a solution.

STAGE 3. DISORGANIZATION Family relations become marked by chaos. The drinking continues, and family members live in fear of the future. By this time they have ceased trying to control the drinking and now seek only to relieve their own tensions. The alcoholic can no longer perform his roles as husband and father, and the wife and children feel the frustration of unsatisfied needs.

STAGE 4. ATTEMPTS TO REORGANIZE IN SPITE OF THE PROBLEM The wife has now taken over complete control of the family, and some semblance of stability emerges. She begins to view her husband as a recalcitrant child, and she treats him more with pity than with hostility. As she enlarges her control of the family, the husband may attempt to reassert himself. These first efforts are often unsuccessful, adding to his feelings of inadequacy.

STAGE 5. EFFORTS TO ESCAPE THE PROBLEM Separation is a painful decision because the wife must overcome the feeling that her husband is her responsibility and should not be abandoned. She must also resist both the social pressures that call for her to stay with him and his own strong efforts to keep her near. Eventually, however, she decides that the welfare of her children and herself requires a separation.

STAGE 6. REORGANIZATION OF PART OF THE FAMILY The family reorganizes without the husband.

STAGE 7. RECOVERY AND REORGANIZATION OF THE WHOLE FAMILY The husband achieves sobriety, and attempts are made to reinstate him in the family. These efforts do not run smoothly. The long period during which the wife has directed the family makes it difficult for normal husband-wife-child roles to be reestablished (Jackson, 1954).

COPING WITH ALCOHOLISM

Alcoholism is a family process. It depends as much on the responses of other family members as it does on the problems of the alcoholic. Only when alcoholics are allowed to stand on their own and accept full responsibility for their actions can they regain their self-respect and develop the strength to control their drinking. Unfortunately, few alcoholics go outside the family for help until they have done something so frightening that the pattern of denial with which they have shielded themselves is shattered (Kellermann, 1969).

Most alcoholics can be helped by physicians, psychiatrists, or community organizations such as Alcoholics Anonymous. Just as important, perhaps, is the help available to the families of alcoholics. For example, Al-Anon, the companion organization to Alcoholics Anonymous, serves alcoholics' spouses. Many of Al-Anon's members are men, for although in this chapter we have discussed the alcoholic husband, women suffer from alcoholism too. In Al-Anon, spouses learn that they could not have done anything to make their partner stop drinking. This relieves their feelings of guilt and responsibility. They give each other mutual support and share their anxieties and experiences, thus strengthening their efforts to cope.

For some spouses, coping means coexistence, living with the alcoholic but throwing off all sense of personal responsibility for the alcoholic's actions. For others it means separation, divorce, and an attempt to reconstruct the family by themselves. In either case, the spouse must come to understand how he or she played a role compatible with the other's drinking and must gain the courage to face life alone and allow the alcoholic to do the same (Coudert, 1972).

Infidelity

A man discovers that his wife has been having an affair with another man. This form of stress requires no change in his daily routine. The stress arises from the changes he must make in his thinking to accommodate the fact that his wife has been unfaithful—reinterpreting a thousand and one remarks, smiles, glances, disappearances, phone calls. What is the meaning of infidelity in our society? How do people cope with the unfaithfulness of a spouse or lover?

There are some couples who put their relationship on an "open" basis. They mutually agree that both may have sex on the outside. No one needs to lie or conceal anything; both can be adulterous without being unfaithful (O'Neill and O'Neill, 1972). In this chapter, however, our concern is not just with extramarital sex, but with infidelity (stemming from the Latin word for "unfaithfulness"). We are talking here about sexual behavior that one's mate would not tolerate; thus we are talking about behavior that obliges one to deceive.

ATTITUDES TOWARD INFIDELITY

The law is traditionally hostile to infidelity. In many states adultery is—or was until recently—a criminal offense, punishable by fine or imprisonment. It has also been recognized in many courts as grounds for divorce. If law reflects the attitudes of people in a democracy, we must conclude that Americans regard infidelity as a grave transgression. And indeed, many Americans do take exactly this attitude and govern their lives accordingly. Others, however, feel differently. Morton Hunt (1969) believes there are two distinct attitudes toward infidelity in the United States, each with millions of adherents. (Other millions, Hunt admits, may have mixed-up feelings that include elements of both.)

The dominant attitude, the one that dictates our laws, stems from the newer tradition—the Judeo-Christian. According to this tradition, the marriage relationship transcends the roles of husband and wife and should be the most intense, most meaningful of human relationships. "In our fragmented and anomic culture," Hunt writes, "romantic and faithful marriage partners are an island of emotional security for each other" (1969, p. 23).

The longer-established but publicly disapproved tradition, which Hunt calls the "pagan-courtly model," offers novelty, excitement, and the continued experience of personal discovery. For most people the new and different is more exciting sexually than the old and familiar. How can sex still be ecstatic with the same partner and no one else for thirty or forty years?

> The southern European [marriage] pattern . . . sets limits to the interaction of husband and wife, and seeks supplemental but measured doses of intimacy and love outside of marriage. . . . Those who choose this alternative may have to pay for it: Infidelity is expensive and time-consuming, it conflicts with the home-based habits of middle-class society, it is socially and professionally hazardous, it may be psychologically traumatic to one's self, wife, and children if discovered—and even if not discovered (Hunt, 1969, pp. 22–24).

The pagan-courtly tradition has usually been associated with the double standard: discreet infidelity for men and strict fidelity for women. The apparent collapse of the double standard which is taking place now, however, does not seem to have brought the pagan-courtly tradition down with it. Linda Wolfe, who interviewed sixty-six women for her book *Playing Around*, found that even when extramarital sex was not entirely pleasurable, many women were still pleased with themselves for having had the experience. Partly, they liked to feel daring. "But it was also because they seemed to come away from their experiences reassured of the wisdom of their marital choices" (Wolfe, 1975, p. 99). A woman usually starts an affair, Wolfe observes, not to disrupt her marriage but to preserve it (1975, p. 129). And certainly women get as much sexual pleasure and as much of an ego boost out of their affairs as men do. One woman said:

> I felt all the things an affair makes you feel. Beautiful again. Less afraid of growing old. I'd visit this boyfriend in his apartment. In reality it was a dirty actor's pad in the Village, but I'd come out of there feeling glowing all over, like we'd just been to the beach (Wolfe, 1975, p. 127).

Regardless of which tradition a person subscribes to, there may be mixed motives for being unfaithful or for remaining faithful. For example,

361

STRESS

a person might pass up an opportunity for extramarital sex merely out of a sense of inadequacy or fear of failure. Nor is it certain that guilt will inevitably sour every marriage in which one partner is unfaithful. Some people are simply incapable of feeling guilty. They are inhibited, if at all, only by shame—what others think of them—never by the inward feeling of self-revulsion that most people know as guilt. Indeed, for the majority of couples in one study, guilt never even entered the picture. And the wronged partner felt far from offended. Instead, he or she was relieved to be free of a relationship that was stifling growth (Cuber, 1969). A young business executive whose infidelity was discovered by his wife reveals his utter lack of conscience and, conversely, his great fear of public disgrace, in this little scene:

> I came home late. The lights were on, and she was lying in the middle of the living-room floor, out cold and snoring, with a whisky decanter and a half-empty bottle of sleeping pills nearby where I couldn't miss them. "Good God," I thought, "couldn't she have tried something less drastic?" I pulled her to her feet . . . walked her around outside in the cold air for awhile . . . then sat her down in the kitchen and made her drink a lot of coffee. She was crying and blubbering. . . . Finally I said I would go into psychotherapy. . . . The implication was that I was deeply neurotic. I didn't believe that, but I had to do something. Suppose she tried again and succeeded, or suppose somebody else found her before I did? How could one live with that kind of thing on the record for everyone to see? How could I face my son and daughter . . . if they ever found out . . . why their mother killed herself? (Hunt, 1969, p. 116).

But what if this man's wife had never discovered his infidelity? It is quite possible that he could have continued with his affairs and loved his wife just as much as he would ever have been capable of loving her. In general, it seems that for some persons and in some circumstances, infidelity in itself need not be a threat to the family (Ellis, 1969).

PERILS OF INFIDELITY

Many people do, however, feel guilty about being unfaithful. In some cases, in fact, their guilt is so intense that they cannot eat or sleep. Others weep hysterically, vomit, or suffer migraine headaches. One of the most common consequences is impotence or unresponsiveness with one's spouse. Guilt can also be unconscious: After using three methods of contraception in extramarital sex—diaphragm, foam, and rhythm—one woman still developed a phantom pregnancy that tormented her for two months. Some people fear exposure at any moment; they freeze with terror whenever their spouse answers the phone or gets the mail. Many of these disorders are a form of self-punishment, a substitute for the punishment that the person feels he or she should receive from society or the spouse (Hunt, 1969, p. 136).

About half the people interviewed by Hunt said their affairs had not changed their marriages much, for either the better or the worse, but about half the men and a third of the women said that even without any important changes, they personally found their marriages more tolerable thanks to their affairs.

This finding naturally leads to the question, "What is the relationship, if any, between infidelity and one's satisfaction with one's marriage?" Robert Bell, Turner, and Rosen (1975) studied more than 2200 married women who reported having had at least one extramarital sexual experience. Not unexpectedly, they found that women who are not satisfied with their marriages tend to be unfaithful to their husbands more than other wives. However, many women who had happy marriages reported having affairs. This finding suggests that it is not the stress of marital dissatisfaction that drives a married person into the arms of a lover, but other personal and social factors. Singh, Walton, and Williams (1976), for example, found that an individual's liberality was an important factor in extramarital relationships: By and large, those who approve of extramarital affairs also approve of premarital sex.

Not to be overlooked is the possibility that infidelity itself may be a symptom, or at least a concomitant of other, more basic stressors. One study of upper-middle-class couples revealed that those who reported feelings of alienation—characterized by powerlessness, meaningless lives, and social isolation—tended to seek release and fulfillment by having an affair (Whitehurst, 1969).

Often the unfaithful spouse makes desperate efforts to save his or her marriage. A husband may talk with his wife about the differences that have arisen between them and may try hard to change his ways so that they can get along better together. Sometimes such leveling can help to patch things up and may even lead to the guilty party's breaking off the affair (J. Edwards, 1973). But these efforts may have the opposite effect, as the unfaithful person may unconsciously want them to. Instead of thinking things through to find the reasons for his marital dissatisfaction, the unfaithful husband may actually be comparing his new love with his marriage and finding his marriage less desirable in every way. The discussions between him and his wife, instead of clearing up misunderstandings, may actually give him a chance to air his hostility. In these and other ways he may provoke his mate to do things that offend him, thus giving him more justification for leaving her (Hunt, 1969, pp. 195–196).

Not all spouses who find out that their mates are unfaithful react violently. Some are tolerant, understanding, or even happy. But most fight the infidelity by weeping, throwing tantrums, or threatening to kill themselves (in the case of wives) or by withholding money, smashing furniture, or threatening to kill the faithless wife or her lover (in the case of husbands). And sometimes the wronged spouse wins. The unfaithful one ends the affair feeling ennobled by tragedy: "Of course I'll cry. But I wouldn't have missed you for anything" (Hunt, 1969, p. 229).

Sometimes it is the marriage that ends, making way for the lovers to wed. But some of the divorced women Wolfe interviewed "had never become even temporarily attached to their lovers. They had casual affairs while hoping to preserve their marriages," seeking "adventure, self-exploration, sexual variety or temporary balm for a husband's neglect or his own extramarital adventuring," just as many other women did whose marriages remained intact (Wolfe, 1975, p. 168). Yet their husbands divorced them. In one case the husband complained that the wife's infidelity was only one symptom of her general neglect and loss of interest in him. Another husband who had tolerated his wife's brief affairs for years finally tried one himself—and promptly fell in love, divorced his wife, and married his mistress (Wolfe, 1975, pp. 169–177).

Obviously, the lesson of these and countless other cases is that infidelity can be tricky, even dangerous. But that, for many people, has always been just another of its attractions. That an affair is kept secret constitutes a risk of change—perhaps stressful, but minor compared with the greater changes that a divorce might bring. Discovering infidelity is a shock—stressful to the degree that it is destructive of the ideals of the marriage relationship held by the couple. Certain changes in each partner's conceptions of the other are irreversible. After an affair there is a loss of trust that can never be regained.

SUMMARY

Stress may be defined as a change in routine that brings about a physiological reaction in an individual. People and families react differently to similar stressful conditions—some cope successfully, and some are ill prepared for any crisis. Life events, such as birth, death, marriage, and loss of a job, can be causes of stress, as can conflict in a marriage.

The death of a spouse or a close family member causes more stress than any other life event. Acknowledging rather than suppressing grief, according to recent research, is the best way to cope with the shock. Kübler-Ross has named five stages experienced by a dying person: disbelief, anger, bargaining, mourning, and acceptance. The bereaved, too, may pass through similar stages of mourning before the final acceptance of death. Pincus suggests that those close to the bereaved should be sympathetic, take care of the bereaved, and not disapprove of expressions of grief, even when they seem infantile. Melanie Klein suggests that a mourning period is necessary so that the deceased can be absorbed into, and made a part of, the bereaved person.

Children's reactions to death depend to a great extent on the behavior and attitudes of the people around them. The changes are hard for children. Even babies have a strong reaction to the death of a mother. Parents should not try to pretend to their children that there has been no death; children may not have a clear conception of death, but they do know when they are being lied to.

Alcoholism causes stress and anguish for all members of an alcoholic's family. The medical model, that alcoholism is an incurable disease, protects both the alcoholic and the members of his or her family from guilt. Alcoholics tend to find life's limitations painful, and they drink to escape from adult responsibilities.

An alcoholic's family usually tries to shield the drinker from the consequences of the drinking. Joan Jackson has identified seven stages in the adjustment of the family to the alcoholism of one of its members: (1) denial, (2) attempts to eliminate the problem themselves, (3) disorganization, (4) attempts to organize in spite of the problem, (5) efforts to escape, (6) reorganization of part of the family, and (7) recovery and reorganization of the whole family. The most successful programs for alcoholism, those of Alcoholics Anonymous and Al-Anon, utilize mutual support and helping others to understand alcoholism.

Infidelity is a cause of stress in many marriages. Infidelity—adultery—is illegal as well as grounds for divorce in many states. Morton Hunt identifies two attitudes toward adultery: that stemming from the Judeo-Christian tradition, which advocates romantic love and faithfulness in marriage, and that stemming from the pagan-courtly tradition, associated with the double standard, according to which the wife is faithful and the husband may break his marriage vows with discretion. The double standard is breaking down, and there is a rise of infidelity among women.

CASE STUDY

Her View

When Anne Macchi, who was eight years younger than her brother, was conceived, her fifty-two-year-old father refused to sleep with his wife any longer and had a series of sexual affairs. Both her parents were heavy drinkers. Anne recalls bringing hot compresses to her mother, who suffered from frequent migraine headaches that lasted for a couple of days.

Anne was a timid child. When she began school, her parents had to push her out the door in the morning as she cried and resisted. Although she skipped two grades in grammar school, her parents thought college appropriate only for her brother, who flunked out, married, and turned to his parents for support. Anne excelled in two years of art school and worked for three months before her marriage to Mike Macchi.

Anne's parents had raised her strictly. After the wedding ceremony, her mother, with whom she had slept since childhood, explained sexual relations to her for the first time. On the first day of her honeymoon trip, Anne felt so anxious about the sexual aspects of her marriage that she obtained some tranquilizers from the emergency room of a hospital. She finally agreed to consummate the marriage four months later.

A month after Anne's wedding, her parents began visiting every weekend. At first they came on Sunday and then on Saturday and Sunday, until finally they were staying regularly from Thursday to Sunday evenings. Anne felt torn between loyalty to her husband and respect for her parents. After a year of these frequent visits she acceded to Mike's demand that they move to a house off the bus route. Then her mother came only one Saturday a month.

Cyndy, their first child, was born after fifteen months of marriage. Anne then became so severely depressed that she required hospitalization for postpartum depression in a psychiatric unit for four months. Upon release she felt like an outcast. She felt as if she had "crazy" inscribed on her forehead, especially since Mike's parents were caring for Cyndy. She sat in the house feeling dejected day after day with the shades drawn, never talking with friends or neighbors. Then five weeks after being released from the hospital, she locked herself in the bathroom and cut her wrist. Mike came home, broke down the bathroom door, and called an ambulance.

The next week, on her birthday, she packed her bags and returned to her parents' apartment. Her father gave her the money to see an attorney to file for divorce. She also consulted with the priest who had witnessed their marriage and began marriage counseling. Within two months she had enrolled in a journalism course and was working as a newspaper illustrator.

Five months later she gave in to Mike's importunings, and after consultation with her pastor she returned to live with Mike and Cyndy. In eighteen months Edward was born. Anne says that by this time "the dust was settling," and Anne stayed at home and took care of her family.

When Cathy was born four years later, Anne's mother was terminally ill. After her mother's funeral, Anne's father, almost entirely deaf and physically rather feeble, needed a place to live, and they took him in. Two years later Anne bore a second son, Paul. Since Paul's birth Anne has feared becoming pregnant again and has resisted Mike's sexual advances or felt guilty about using contraceptives; five months ago she prevented further pregnancy by having a tubal ligation.

Three months before Paul's birth, Mike insisted that Anne ask her father to move out. He did, but he refused to speak to her again. A month later he had a stroke and never regained the use of his speech until he died six weeks later. She regrets to this day that they were not reconciled.

Anne feels that in many ways her marriage began after her parents were deceased. She saw herself, Mike, and their children settling down as a family after that. She found security and satisfaction in knowing that her husband was expanding the family business, in living in a commodious suburban home, and in raising their four children. For about ten years she perceived no major problems, and she was satisfied to fulfill her role as a suburban housewife and raise her children as she considered a proper mother should.

Four years ago Anne sensed a change when Cyndy was a high school junior. Anne would become upset by Cyndy when Cyndy did not come home for dinner, when she did the dishes in between TV shows or did not make her bed, or on the occasions when she stayed out until 2 A.M. At the same time, Edward was doing poorly in the parochial high school. When Mike contended he was wasting money on the boy, Anne defended her son's performance as being about the best he could do. She also defended his being on the wrestling team after Mike objected because he thought Edward was too puny. Anne became depressed when she noticed Mike staying at the office later and yelling at both Cyndy and Edward. She was afraid of what the neighbors might say if their children did not turn out right.

Anne would like Mike to compliment her on what she does well. She feels she receives criticism for any mistakes but only silence for good performances. She is angry at Mike for not praising the children, but she is fearful of making any demands lest he leave them before the children are raised. Sometimes when Mike teases her or when the children are acting up, she finds it impossible to eat her meals. Anne feels off balance because she and her husband never really sit down and plan or solve problems together; events just seem to happen in their house. She is also upset because when she asks Mike to share his feelings with her, he jokes around. When she feels really blue, she sits down at the piano and plays beautifully for an hour or two. Two years ago she considered taking an enrichment course at the local community college. When she told Mike she wanted to return to college, he said, "You can't return to something you didn't start," and she did not go. Three months ago, when Mike's bookkeeper became ill, Mike volunteered to train Anne to do the job, and she agreed. She is also learning to handle the family's finances.

His View

Mike is a burly, heavyset, generally jovial forty-four-year-old who thinks of himself as willing to protect his family and provide security for them. Over the years he has perceived Anne as irresponsible because she leaves lights on all over the house, does not turn off the TV when she has finished watching, and spends the rather lavish amount of money he gives her without keeping any account of where it goes. When she suggests that he compliment her occasionally, he replies, "Nobody praises me; I don't give out report cards." He wants his children to succeed and regards them as failures when they do not excel. When asked about Edward's school performance, he answers, "He's no Einstein; I don't know why I waste my money on him." Mike likes to give his family expensive items and expects them to live up to his standards, which he does not see the need to express. When his children fail to meet his unspecified expectations (for example, carry the garbage out with a smile, come home by 11 P.M. on Friday and Saturday nights without even discussing it, or mow the lawn every two weeks, summer and winter), he becomes aggravated and considers them failures. Mike feels that Anne does not back him up on the principles he considers correct for the children. He bought Cyndy and Edward each a car and later regretted it because they have both done poorly in school. Last summer Edward worked for the family business, doing heavy work and enjoying it. Mike was disappointed that Edward liked the physical labor; he would prefer his son to be more management-oriented. Mike wavers between wanting his son to have nothing to do with the family business and planning on allowing him to take over in about ten years so that he himself can start an allied business.

Mike likes to socialize. He enjoys dining out and dancing at least once a week. For the past four years he has worked actively at his church, and he is president of the lay council in the parish. In this capacity he has organized several social functions each year. He often takes business customers out to lunch and frequently orders a bottle of wine. A couple of nights a week he likes to visit the neighbors and sit around talking or watching television while sipping cocktails. When he has time before dinner, and on Sundays, he breaks out a bottle of Scotch or bourbon, mixes a drink, and offers Anne one. Mike complains that Anne does not want to mingle with people and that she often gets high on two drinks and then becomes morosely silent. He blames her for breaking up every friendship he initiates once they start to get close to the other couple.

Mike's mother is terminally ill now. Mike and Anne go to visit his parents almost every Sunday. His mother is bedridden, but she manages to eat her dinner at a card table a few feet from their bed. They often find his father tenderly helping his wife hobble to the table for a dinner he has prepared. After dinner, Mike's folks sit side by side, holding hands and watching television. Both Mike and Anne are touched that his parents are still in love during their last days together.

Interpretation and Questions

In what different ways did Anne respond to the changes in her life? Why should her children become a cause for stress? Is her husband's behavior stressful to her, and in what way could she behave differently? How does Mike respond to the stress in his life? How did Anne's parents respond to stress? How do Mike's parents seem to respond to stress?

STUDY GUIDE

Important Terms

stressor
life-change units
crisis-prone family
crisis-proof family

regression
alcoholism
infidelity

Review Quiz

Questions 1 through 5 ask you to rank the five stressor events according to their potential disruptiveness for most people. Place an *a* next to the life event with the greatest disruptiveness, a *b* beside the next most serious event, and so on, down to *e*.

1 _____ Sex difficulties
2 _____ Unemployment of husband as a result of firing
3 _____ Death of spouse
4 _____ Retirement
5 _____ Divorce

6 Families which seem to be crisis-proof:
   a manage to cope even with no resources

b subordinate personal ambitions to family goals
c are made up of members who are independent and do not support one another physically or emotionally
d all the above

7 Elisabeth Kübler-Ross has identified five stages through which persons pass after they learn that they are dying. The first stage is:
   a anger
   b disbelief
   c mourning
   d acceptance

8 Therapists now believe that the most helpful approach to the mourning of another is to:

a advise the mourner to "be brave"

b help the person avoid facing reality for a long time

c tolerate regression to infantile behavior

d avoid referring to the death which has occurred

9 Children mourn a death in the family in the same fashion as adults at about age:

a three

b six

c nine

d twelve

10 The medical model of alcoholism implies that:

a alcoholism is a disease

b alcoholism may be arrested but never cured

c an alcoholic is powerless to control his or her drinking

d all the above

11 The behavioral traits of alcoholics are not universal but may include:

a a lethargic and depressed personality

b perfectionism

c a realistic self-concept

d a high nurturance need, that is, a need to care for others

12 After family problems due to alcoholism are confronted and the whole family attempts to reorganize:

a efforts may not run smoothly because of past failures

b problems may arise because the family has been restructured by the nonalcoholic spouse

c organizations such as Al-Anon continue to help the partners alleviate their anxiety and feelings of guilt

d all the above

13 The difference between infidelity and adultery is that:

a adultery is a legal term; infidelity refers to unfaithfulness

b a woman can be an adulteress but not an infidel; a man may be both an adulterer and an infidel

c adultery may cause a marriage to terminate; infidelity is usually expected in marriage

d none of the above

14 According to the women in Linda Wolfe's sample, extramarital affairs are often begun:

a out of boredom

b for sexual pleasure

c to preserve a marriage

d out of fear of growing old

15 About _____ of the people interviewed by writer Morton Hunt said that their affairs had not changed their marriages much for better or worse.

a 90 percent

b half

c one-fourth

d 10 percent

Opinionnaire

Agree	No opinion	Disagree		
_____	_____	_____	1	Families can do a lot to make themselves more able to cope with environmental stress.
_____	_____	_____	2	The stress involved with natural growth stages, such as becoming forty, is almost entirely imaginary.
_____	_____	_____	3	Discussion of death when it is not necessary is morbid.

_____ _____ _____ 4 A strong person will be pretty much recovered from the loss of a family member within a few months.

_____ _____ _____ 5 The hardest kinds of stress to cope with are those of an indefinite duration, such as caring for a mentally retarded or chronically ill family member.

_____ _____ _____ 6 No individual has control over whether he or she will become an alcoholic.

_____ _____ _____ 7 A spouse is morally obligated to remain with an alcoholic partner.

_____ _____ _____ 8 The problems posed by extramarital sex will always outweigh any positive factors.

_____ _____ _____ 9 The discovery that a spouse has been unfaithful is not a sufficient reason for divorce.

_____ _____ _____ 10 A partnership can never be the same after one of the partners has been unfaithful.

Exercise

THE CRISIS-PRONE FAMILY

Below are listed resources that can insulate a family against many crises. Assume that you want to provide maximum protection for your family. Since no family can be totally safe, you may have only four of the six resources (A through F) listed. Which four do you choose?

One characteristic of stressor events is that they are difficult to predict. Choose a number between 1 and 5 at random and turn the page upside down to find out which crisis will occur and what the effects will be. Was your family vulnerable in that area?

A family also must undergo many crises, not just one, during its existence. Realign your resources if you feel it is necessary and then choose another number at random. Continue until all five crises have occurred. Would your family have been able to withstand the stresses and remain intact?

A Good interpersonal relations among all members
B Members who place the good of the family above their individual welfare
C Good neighbors and strong community support for the family
D Good income and a solid economic foundation
E Members who have realized most of their aspirations and goals
F Good physical health of members

Stress	Main resources needed
1 War forces separation	A D B C
2 Flood destroys home	D C F B
3 Parents are divorced	D B A F
4 Breadwinner loses job	D B A F
5 Child is adjudged delinquent	A B C E

Projects for Class or Home Study

1 Look again at the Social Readjustment Rating Scale. Richard Nixon's resignation from the Presidency combined several types of stress. What would you guess the mean value of this event to be on the scale?

2 Al-Anon and Alcoholics Anonymous disseminate literature discussing the problems encountered by a family affected by alcoholism. Send for some of this literature and read it to gain a more thorough understanding of the involvement of such a family.

3 Some writers have proposed that hospitals establish a policy of sustaining life artificially in individuals who are beyond recovery. This would create a pool of resources for organ transplants to save the lives of other patients who might otherwise die. How do you think a person would cope with the knowledge that the life of a family member was being sustained in order to provide an organ bank for some stranger?

4 One-fourth of all students attending college are married. Are these campus marriages more or less stressful than others involving similar age groups?

5 A large number of television programs, movies, and novels deal with infidelity as a theme or an event in the plot. How often are adulterous characters portrayed sympathetically? Is the answer equally true for women and men?

Suggestions for Further Reading

Baldwin, James. *If Beale Street could talk.* New York: Signet Books, New American Library, 1974.
> In this novel Baldwin contrasts the different reactions of two families to the stress produced when a young man is accused of rape and imprisoned.

Fitzgerald, F. Scott. *The crack-up.* New York: New Directions, 1945.
> The famous novelist describes the stresses that led to his "crack-up."

Go ask Alice. New York: Avon, 1971.
> A diary left by a sensitive adolescent girl. She describes her experiences with drugs and the pressure this creates in her family relationships. With the help of a close, supportive family she almost survives.

Green, Betty R., and Irish, Donald P. (Eds.). *Death education: Preparation for living.* Cambridge, Mass.: Schenkman, 1971.
> The editors have collected papers presented in a symposium on death education. Collectively they are an excellent practical guide to knowledge about the impact of death.

Haley, Jay. The family of the schizophrenic: A model system. In Gerald Handel (Ed.), *The psychosocial interior of the family.* Chicago: Aldine, 1967.
> This brief article links the family to mental illness as part of the same network. The model could be extended to other forms of stress as well.

Laing, R. D. *The politics of the family and other essays.* New York: Vintage Books, Random House, 1972.
> Laing places the blame for mental illness squarely on the family. The complete power parents have over their children can create the perfectly reasonable response of madness, according to Laing.

Lifton, Robert J. *Home from the war.* New York: Simon and Schuster, 1973.
A psychologist who did an earlier study of Chinese brainwashing during the Korean war writes about the effects of the war in Vietnam on veterans and their families.

Answers to Review Quiz

1-*e* 2-*c* 3-*a* 4-*d* 5-*b* 6-*b* 7-*b* 8-*c* 9-*c* 10-*d* 11-*b* 12-*d* 13-*a* 14-*c* 15-*b*

15

BREAKING UP

> I didn't know anything was really wrong. It was like a bomb dropping. Oh, we had been married a lot of years, and I knew we had a couple of problems, but I would say, "I feel sorry for all these people who are married and the marriage gets very dull. We still love each other." And we did, you know, in terms of sex. That is why it was such a bomb falling on me. Now I see it was there all the time, but our way of communicating was so poor that it just never got to me (Weiss, 1975, p. 5).

These words were spoken to a marriage counselor by a man in his late thirties. The "bomb" he referred to was his wife's announcement that she wanted to terminate their marriage. The morning after this confrontation, the wife packed her bag and left.

Such scenes are being played out with increasing frequency in America. The number of divorces granted in a single year passed the 1-million mark in the United States for the first time in 1975. That is twice the number of divorces granted in 1966, and almost triple the number granted in 1950 (Divorce Epidemic, 1976, p. 36). This increase is reflected in a rising divorce rate. In 1965, for example, there were 2.5 divorces for every 1000 people in America; by 1976, this figure had risen to 4.6 per 1000 population (U.S. Bureau of the Census, 1976a). The United States has one of the highest divorce rates in the world.

Paul Glick, senior demographer with the U.S. Bureau of the Census, estimates that one marriage in every three ends in divorce. Actually, there were almost half as many divorces as weddings in 1975, but Glick says, "The fact that there were a million divorces in 1975 and little more than two million marriages does not mean that half of America's marriages end in divorce. People usually do not get divorced the same year they get married, so the figures have to be adjusted to produce a reliable percentage. We think it will be more like a third when the current figures have been adjusted" (quoted in Love, 1976).

There are a number of limitations to these statistics. First, they are incomplete and hence may be too low. They do not take into account those marriages in which one or the other partner simply packs up and leaves, without going through the legal process of divorce. Moreover, as J. Lynn England and Phillip Kunz (1975) point out, the sample upon which the statistics are based—the total American population—includes individuals who are not "at risk" to divorce. Children who are too young to marry and single older people who have elected not to marry cannot, for obvious reasons, be included as candidates for divorce. Had the sample been based on the number of married people in the population or on specific age groups within the population, the rate undoubtedly would be different.

Although these figures may be inaccurate, they do reflect the fact

DIVORCE RATES FOR THE UNITED STATES, 1910 TO 1974
Divorce rates have risen rapidly since 1960, but they have been rising constantly all during the twentieth century. *Adapted from U.S. Bureau of the Census, 1975, p. 51.*

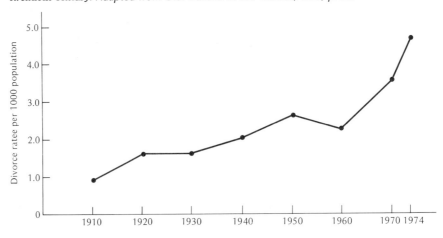

that the trend toward divorce is increasing. How do these statistics apply to the average person? When and if we marry, must we resign ourselves to having only two chances in three of keeping the marriage intact? Not at all. Statistics confirm that the odds may be better or worse, depending on certain vital statistics of the married couple.

Factors Affecting the Divorce Rate

By reading the paper and watching the news, it is easy to get the impression that divorce happens only to "other people." The divorce of superstars like Elizabeth Taylor and Richard Burton makes good copy for the media—much better than that of cousin Cecilia in Toledo. Perhaps it allays our envy of the rich and the famous to hear about divorces in the penthouse rather than in a street-floor apartment and makes us think that our marriages will last longer than theirs. But there are a million divorces a year; those people cannot all be superstars. Some of them are our friends, our neighbors, our relatives, ourselves. What do these million people have in common? What can we learn from their experience?

AGE AT MARRIAGE

Although we have never heard of most of the people who get divorced each year, demographers have statistics on some of their characteristics. Several studies show, for example, that teenage marriages are likelier to break up than marriages begun at any other age (Glick and Norton, 1971; Schoen, 1975). In fact, people who marry in their teens are more than twice as likely to end up divorced than those who marry in their late twenties, which is the best time to marry for beating the odds on divorce. The next best time is in one's thirties. The odds for divorce for those marrying in their twenties are high, but for marriage between people in their teens they are highest of all. As shown in the accompanying table, however, the proportion of people in their twenties who divorced increased from 1960 to 1970, but so did the remarriage rates.

Why are teenage marriages so divorce-prone? Teenagers often get

PERCENTAGE DECLINE IN YOUNG MARRIEDS, 1960–1970

	Ages 20–29	
	1960	1970
Total number (millions)	21.7	29.5
Percent single of persons aged 20–29	28	32
Percent married of persons aged 20–29	70	65
Percent divorced of persons aged 20–29	2	3
Percent remarried of all married persons	5.8	6.6

Source: Adapted from U.S. Bureau of the Census, 1972, pp. 5, 9.

married for inappropriate reasons, such as the desire to escape from unhappiness at home or the need to feel wanted. Early marriage frequently means that the partners will not finish their education, giving them a poor chance of finding a satisfying job with a good future. With relatively little experience of the world, of each other, or of themselves, couples in their teens may have unpleasant discoveries in store for them. The outcome of these various pressures is that sooner or later one or both partners come to regret and then resent the marriage.

This all sounds as if people who marry young have only themselves to blame, since they ought to have known better. But Margaret Mead, the anthropologist, is not so sure. A mother herself and an astute observer of several generations of marriages, she writes: "We all too often use marriage as the means of getting young people to settle down. . . . Since they are married, we expect them to behave as adults. But at the same time, because they are so young and inexperienced, we expect them to fail" (1974a, p. 72). Indeed, some parents may be delighted to get the children out of the house and to have the financial burden of their upkeep come to an end.

In the recent past, a principal reason why many people married young was that all their friends were getting married. Those who waited feared they would be left out. But this is no longer true. The U.S. Bureau of the Census reports that the number of people between twenty-five and thirty-four years of age who have never married went up 50 percent between 1970 and 1975. And in the twenty- to twenty-four-year age bracket, 60 percent of the men and 40 percent of the women were unmarried in 1975 (U.S. Bureau of the Census, 1976a). In fact, today the opposite is more likely to be true. People who marry much before the age of twenty-five are likely to have to explain to their friends and even their families why they feel it necessary to get married. So, those who decide to wait have plenty of company.

INCOME AND MARRIAGE

We have all heard of couples who loved each other in adversity only to break up as soon as they became prosperous. The wife worked at a low-paying job, for example, to help the husband through school; for years they lived in a dingy little apartment eating pinto beans and rice. Then the husband graduated and began his career, while the wife had a baby, and things still were not much better. The husband's income was not very high, but the baby's expenses were. Through all these struggles the husband and wife loved each other dearly. But then the husband began to earn more money. At last things were becoming easier, and the couple could enjoy all they had worked so hard for. Instead, they got a divorce.

Statistically, however, the number of marriages spoiled by prosperity is negligible compared with the number of marriages blighted by poverty.

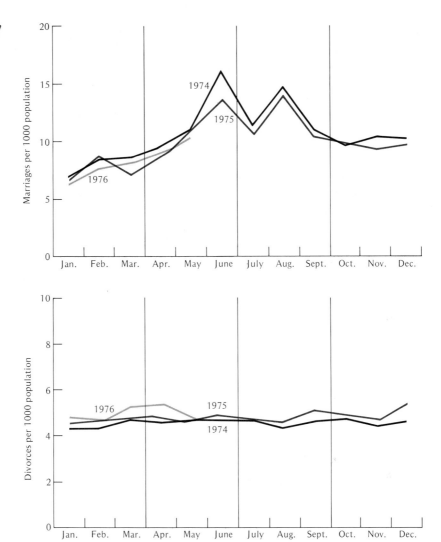

MARRIAGE AND DIVORCE RATES, 1974 TO MAY 1976
June is still the most popular month for weddings, but there are proportionally fewer of them each year. Meanwhile, the divorce rate continues to rise through the mid-1970s. *U.S. Bureau of the Census, 1976c, p. 4.*

For every doctor who works hard through his twenties and begins to make good money in his thirties, there are thousands of people who hammer out car fenders for a fair wage in their twenties, then again in their thirties, and again in their forties, fifties, and sixties, never getting ahead. Census figures show that the lower a couple's income, the likelier they are to break up (Glick and Norton, 1971). In 1966, couples who made less than $3,000 a year were three times as likely as couples making $8,000 or more to get divorced in the first four years of marriage and four times as likely to get divorced in the fifth through the ninth years. (These incomes are in 1966 dollars; double them to approximate a comparable income today.) People in their late twenties generally make more money than people in their teens. Thus, the two factors of age and income work together in their influence on marital stability.

OTHER FACTORS LEADING TO DIVORCE

Some couples have children to save their marriage. Unfortunately, there is no evidence that having children helps to bring a couple together again. To the contrary, it may actually drive them farther apart (Chester, 1972). According to one study, the more children a couple had per years of marriage, the less satisfactory they felt their marriage to be (Hurley and Palonen, 1967). However, people in the lower socioeconomic groups are likely to have more children, and so money is again important.

What are a person's chances of keeping a new marriage intact after an unsuccessful marriage experience? Once again, a huge majority of second divorces or abandonments occur among couples with low incomes. Second marriages are only very slightly more likely to end in divorce than first marriages. On the basis of current rates, the Census Bureau projects that about 36 percent of all first marriages and 40 percent of all second marriages will end in divorce (U.S. Bureau of the Census, 1976a).

Other factors that can improve an individual's chances somewhat are having religious beliefs which oppose divorce, growing up on a farm, and living with both parents until the teen years. Marrying someone whose age or education is markedly different from one's own, on the other hand, reduces the chances of staying together for life (Bumpass and Sweet, 1972).

The Divorce Experience

There is more to a divorce than a court decree. Divorce usually starts years before that datable event, and it can be many years after a divorce before a person feels the marriage is completely over.

How do marriages become so unhappy that people are willing to end them by an almost equally agonizing divorce? In many cases, the intolerable behavior is quite specific: the husband loses his job, the wife drinks to the point of alcoholism, or one of the partners finds a new romance, for example. In other cases, neither spouse can say just what it is that he or she cannot accept any longer.

But whether or not the cause can be specified, the marriage was entered into with high hopes. Most marital problems come on gradually;

the marriage falls apart bit by bit. It is often said that the leading cause of divorce is marriage.

FALLING APART

Couples usually go through certain stages of coming together. We saw in Chapter 2 how the two partners learn more about each other at each stage. As they gain trust in each other, they reveal more of themselves and begin to act more naturally. Then they become more intimate and are an increasingly important part of each other's lives. Finally they are proud and happy to accept the congratulations of friends and relatives, as well as the larger community, at the wedding ceremony.

Many marriages go through the same stages when they fall apart, only in reverse. As Jessie Bernard has observed, emotions have a snowballing effect. Show someone you like her, and she may indicate she likes you in return. If this makes you feel good, you may do something to make her feel good, and so on. It can also work the other way: "A disagreement may begin with only a moderate amount of hostility present; but each parry or thrust adds to the hostility of the other and leads him, in turn, to increase his own hostility" (Bernard, 1964, p. 724).

Married people know where to hit each other if they want to wound. As the marriage falls apart, they tear each other down, engage in intimacies less often and less warmly, and become wary where once they were trustful. At some point, the marriage becomes more of a torment than a comfort and delight. But even if both spouses recognize that this point has been passed, the worst is still to come: the divorce and its aftermath. "One of the reasons it feels so good to be engaged and newly married," writes anthropologist Paul Bohannan, "is the rewarding sensation that, out of the whole world, you have been selected. One of the reasons that divorce feels so awful is that you have been de-selected. It punishes almost as much as the engagement and the wedding are rewarding" (1970, p. 33). Another reason it feels so bad is that like the wedding, it is a legal ceremony, but this time friends, relatives, and the larger community may denounce the participants. The state may even consider one of the partners to be legally "guilty" of causing the breakup.

THE LEGAL PROCESS

The state regulates the marital life of its citizens, certifying marriages and granting or withholding divorces. Why should the state have the power to interfere with private lives in this manner? One important reason is that the state bears the responsibility of seeing to it that dependent children have some support. When two people marry, they officially commit themselves to support any children they may have. If they do have children and then want a divorce, the state will use its powers to make sure that they continue to support the children, for if they do not, the state is responsible for this support. The same reasoning can apply to a wife who has sacrificed her earning power to the marriage. For example, if a woman spends thirty years of her life rearing children and keeping house and then finds herself without a husband, she might not have the skills required to get a job and support herself. In this case the state may force the husband to contribute toward her support through alimony payments. There are even a few cases in which the situation is reversed, and the wife must pay alimony to the husband.

In other words, the state not only assumes that people have certain obligations to their spouses and their children but also tries to make them meet those obligations. Because a person who has only one spouse and one set of children is more likely to be able to meet his or her obligations—and because bigamy is morally offensive to most citizens—the state prohibits having more than one spouse at a time. That is why no one can legally remarry until his or her previous marriage has been legally dissolved.

Suppose a woman separates from her husband. If she has a good job and they have no children, he will have no continuing financial responsibility toward her. If he moves in with another woman, the state probably will not trouble him. But if he remarries without divorcing his previous spouse, he is liable to prosecution for bigamy, a felony in most states.

If, on the other hand, he does not marry his new partner, on his death his estate may go to his legal spouse. Even though he might have children with his new partner, he may not be able to leave them his money and property because they are illegitimate. For this reason, most people who want to establish a new family first get a divorce from their previous spouse and then marry their new partner legally.

Recently, many states have begun changing their divorce laws. The old laws empowered a court to grant a divorce only if the spouse bringing suit (the plaintiff) could prove that the other spouse (the defendant) was guilty of a specific fault. In some states, such as New York, the only fault admitted as grounds for divorce was adultery. Other states would grant a divorce for desertion, nonsupport, or other faults. Whatever one's reason for wanting a divorce, he or she had to persuade the judge that the spouse was guilty of a fault recognized by the state as grounds for divorce. The trouble with this process was that the case was usually a fabrication. Only seldom was the fault argued in court the real reason for the divorce. And it was expensive for both parties. Lawyers spent their time working up fictitious cases, and private detectives and psychiatrists were often employed to give evidence. The trial was a travesty of justice that made perjurers of those who testified. Moreover, everyone was aware of these perjuries, even the judge.

Under the old laws, when the plaintiff brought suit against the defendant to sever the marriage bond, the state assumed that the defendant would deny that he or she was guilty of the fault. The court procedure thus enabled the judge to decide whether the defendant was really guilty of the alleged fault and whether the marriage should be dissolved despite the objections of the defendant.

Today's laws recognize that not many people who are party to a divorce suit honestly want to preserve the marriage. They may be deeply hurt and they may feel wronged, but they realize that the marriage has already fallen apart if their spouse wants to sever the marriage bond. Unfortunately, the old laws made no provision for this situation. Technically, it was a crime known as *collusion* for both parties to be seeking a divorce, and so the defendant had to pretend that he or she opposed it. Much of this pretense has been eliminated by the new divorce laws that have been enacted by some states and are under consideration in others.

NO-FAULT DIVORCE By January 1974, twenty-three states had adopted some form of no-fault divorce legislation. Moreover, legislators in nearly all other states are considering ways of incorporating the no-fault feature into existing laws. The new divorce laws still empower the courts to force parents to continue to support their children. They still provide for alimony awards, prohibit bigamy, and declare children born out of wedlock to be illegitimate. But in cases where both husband and wife want the divorce, agree on arrangements for child support, and agree on how their joint property should be divided, the new laws do not require them to face each other as adversaries in court. No longer need one spouse, acting as plaintiff, bring suit against the other as defendant and go through the charade of fighting it out. The court does try to make sure that neither spouse has been intimidated into accepting a settlement that he or she does not really think is fair. But once the judge is satisfied that both parties agree freely, the court will hear a joint petition for divorce.

Another substantial legal change is the addition of new grounds for divorce. The old grounds were faults of which one or the other spouse was allegedly guilty—adultery, cruelty, or nonsupport, for example. The new ground added by most of the new laws is one which does not place blame on anyone—hence the name "no-fault" laws. In California, which began granting divorces under a new law in 1970, the ground is called "irreconcilable differences." Both partners affirm the following statement to the court: "In the course of our marriage, there arose irreconcilable differences which led to the irremediable breakdown of our marriage. There is no chance for reconciliation." The court's only job is to approve the settlement—or to adjudicate it, if the partners have not been able to agree on all its provisions. In New York, the couple sign an agreement to separate for one year; this constitutes a ground for divorce, which is made final in court at the end of the separation year.

Although there are many variations in the new laws from state to state, most of them enable people to get divorced with much less trouble and at much less expense than under the old laws. Some counselors and lawyers believe, however, that easy-to-get divorce is tempting people to end their marriages unnecessarily. One lawyer says: "Many people divorce before giving a potentially good marriage a chance, and many people divorce without looking at their personal problems that could be solved by counseling—so they are back in court for second and third divorces without learning anything" (The Surge in Easy Divorces, 1974, p. 43).

The truth of such a statement would be difficult to establish scientifically. For example, Dorothy Stetson and Gerald Wright (1975) have shown that there is a strong relationship between the relative ease of obtaining a divorce in a state and the rate of divorce. These investigators studied the divorce laws and the rates of divorce in fifty states. After statistically adjusting for the effects of economic development and social norms on divorce rates, they found that those states with the most permissive divorce laws had the highest divorce rates. Conversely, they found a correlation between restrictive laws and a lower divorce rate. Does such a finding indicate that the more permissive laws are allowing people to divorce who might be able to salvage their marriages? Or does it merely show that people are taking advantage of the new divorce laws where they exist and are finding alternative, though not necessarily better, solutions in states where divorce is not only difficult but also expensive?

Some critics argue that many no-fault divorce laws leave the wife with no bargaining power and thus make her vulnerable to an unfair settlement. However, this inequity would not necessarily be remedied by going back to the old laws. Other provisions for further new legislation have been suggested:

1 Automatic fifty-fifty division of all assets . . . acquired during marriage, no matter in whose name they were held.
2 Alimony based on one partner's need and the other's ability to pay, regardless of their sex.
3 Mutually shared child support based on the actual income and earning power of each partner (No-Fault Divorce Has Some Faults, 1974, p. 53).

Even these provisions do not necessarily mean that there will be an equitable distribution of assets and responsibilities. It is unlikely that any formal legal provisions can treat fairly both partners in a marriage who are unable to reach a divorce agreement.

LEGAL ARRANGEMENTS In California, Oregon, Alabama, and some other states, a couple may be able to get a divorce without a lawyer, depending on whether they have children and on how good they are at filling out forms and dealing with courthouse clerks. Kits containing instructions and the necessary forms are available in California bookstores for anywhere from $20 to $75. Before an individual can start on such a divorce, however, his or her spouse must consent to the divorce. Moreover, the two must agree on all the terms of the settlement, including custody, visitation rights, child support, alimony, and the division of property.

Who should attempt to obtain a divorce without a lawyer? A person who is poor and childless might find it the best choice (Moffett and Scherer, 1976). But if there are children or substantial property, the person may later regret saving a lawyer's fee at the expense of a favorable settlement.

Those who seek to engage a lawyer will find that fees vary with the amount of work involved. Some states allow one lawyer to serve both husband and wife; in this case, the simplest possible divorce might cost a minimum of $350. But more complicated cases will naturally be more expensive. For example, if both partners consented to the divorce but could not agree on all the terms of the settlement, two lawyers would be needed. Each would probably charge around $500 to $1000. Legal fees are highest when the divorce is contested—that is, when one of the spouses does not want the divorce and is prepared to fight it in court. Then lawyers' fees could amount to $5000 or more for each spouse.

In complicated cases the choice of a lawyer is very important. Divorce is a legal specialty, and a person is best represented by a specialist in the field. Personal and emotional factors also can make a difference. If a wife is trying to win a large alimony settlement, for example, a lawyer who himself is paying alimony to three wives might not be the most sympathetic representative. To find the best lawyer, ask an attorney you already know, for although he or she may not be a specialist in divorce, some friends and colleagues probably are. Or contact the local lawyers' referral service or legal aid office for names of attorneys in your area that specialize in divorce cases.

REVENGE OR FORGIVENESS?

Adversary divorce or no-fault divorce, good lawyers, bad lawyers, or no lawyers—obviously the legal apparatus has much influence on how a divorce will turn out. What can affect the final result even more, however, are the attitudes of the parties themselves. A divorcing woman, for example, may try to make her friends and even her children take sides against her husband; a wealthy husband may try to hide his wealth from the court to cheat his wife of a fair settlement. Other divorcing partners, on the other hand, seem to part in amity and mutual respect.

One divorced woman, Judith Viorst, thinks a cordial divorce would be impossible for her:

> I do not know from graceful resignation. What I know from is getting even. . . . This thirst for revenge . . . is certainly immature. And self-defeating. And bad for the soul, besides. Nevertheless, it thrives—with equal vigor in both sexes. And sometimes it can be slaked only if the bad guy (the husband, let's say) is completely wiped out.
>
> In other words, he should be reduced to penury, and his kids should recoil from his touch, and his boss should fire him for moral turpitude, and his mother should say, "You aren't my son any more." He should also get fat,

lose his hair and develop such a terrible case of B.O. that he never ever finds true love again. He should, in addition, be impotent. He should . . . be miserably unhappy all his life. Now, I've actually known women who have wished every one of these fates on their once-treasured husbands, just as I have known men with similar feelings of tenderness toward their wives. These are the people who call up a lawyer and whisper one word in his or her ear. That word is: "Destroy" (1974, p. 29).

Another divorcée, Mary McDermott Shideler (1971), describes a couple whose attitude toward each other at the time of their divorce was the very opposite of vengeful. Although both knew they could no longer remain married, they continued to like and respect each other. They also saw their divorce as the beginning of a new condition of their lives, just as their wedding had been, and therefore they decided to mark it with a religious ceremony, as marriage and other important occasions—birth, graduation, death—are marked. Mrs. Shideler wrote a liturgy for the dissolution of a marriage. At the start of the ceremony, Matthew and Anne Surrey, the divorcing couple, gathered in a circle with the officiant and a few friends in a private home. Here, in part, is the liturgy:

OFFICIANT: Matthew Surrey, do you now relinquish your status as husband of Anne, freeing her from all claims upon and responsibilities to you except those that you willingly give to all other children of God?
MATTHEW: I do.
OFFICIANT: Do you forgive her any sins she has committed against you, and do you accept her forgiveness, thus freeing her from the burdens of guilt and sterile remorse?
MATTHEW: I do.
OFFICIANT: Do you release her with your love and blessing, in gratitude for the part she has played in your life, in knowledge that her part in you will never be forgotten or despised, and in faith that in separation as in union, you both are held in the grace and unity of God?
MATTHEW: I do.
   [The same questions were asked of Anne, and she replied in the same way.]
OFFICIANT: Matthew, what sign do you give to Anne as a token of your forgiveness and your release of her?
MATTHEW: Her wedding ring reconsecrated to her freedom. [He placed it on the third finger of her right hand.]
OFFICIANT: Anne, what sign do you give to Matthew as a token of your forgiveness and your release of him?
ANNE: His wedding ring reconsecrated to his freedom. [She placed it on the third finger of his right hand.]
OFFICIANT: Let us pray. Almighty and loving God, who has ordered that seasons shall change and that human lives shall proceed by change, we ask thy blessing upon thy children who now, in their commitment to thee, have severed their commitment to each other. Send them forth in the bond of peace. When they meet, sustain them in their liberty. Keep them both reminded that thy love flows upon and through them both. Sanctify them in

their lives, deaths, and resurrections, by the power of thy Holy Spirit, and for the sake of thy Son, Jesus Christ our Lord (Shideler, 1971, p. 555).

Single Again

Perhaps the divorce ceremony helped Anne and Matthew become single again both in their own eyes and in the eyes of their friends. Clearly they anticipated that to become single again is a problem, and they did all they could do to ease the process for themselves and their friends. But they had been married a long time. Morton Hunt (1966), in his study of divorced people, found that a person who divorces young and has no children soon rejoins the never-married crowd and largely forgets both marriage and spouse. But a person with children who divorces after many years of marriage never truly becomes single again. Hunt describes such people as a group apart, and he calls them "the formerly married."

Almost no one escapes feeling depressed immediately after a divorce. Much as the recently divorced person may have longed to be rid of a hated spouse and an oppressive relationship, there is inevitably a sense of loss, the same sort of grief that he or she would feel if a loved one had died. Whether reasonably or not, most people also feel guilty about a divorce. And a sense of failure is practically inevitable. People feel they have botched one of the most important responsibilities in their life.

There is little that is cheering about the practical matters that must be handled after a divorce. Husbands may have to find living quarters; mothers may have to spend all their waking hours with their children, for there is no one else to look after them. Both spouses may have to live on a sharply reduced income. Men may suddenly have to learn how to take care of their laundry and prepare their meals; women may have to find a job. Small wonder that the suicide rate for divorced women is three times as high as that for married women. Divorce seems to have an even greater effect on men: Four times as many divorced men as married men commit suicide (Moffett and Scherer, 1976).

For awhile the postdivorce period may seem to be the worst time of all. The ego was battered for months or years as the marriage disintegrated, hostility has been aroused by the legal process, and now one's domestic and social life is in shambles—a person wonders whether the misery will ever end. But one day, surprisingly, the pain is gone. Somehow the divorced person has managed to become accustomed to his or her new life.

According to Hunt, the first date, the first kiss, and the first sexual experience after divorce are all terribly hard for most formerly married people. Several years of monogamy leave one unsure of how to do these things with different people. When one has been out of the sexual marketplace for many years, during which time a few pounds and a few gray hairs may have been added, one tends to lack confidence in one's ability to attract another person. However, most formerly married people are amazed to find that they do very well, especially with other formerly married people. Among them there are no forbidden subjects of conversation; people often reveal their most painful, personal feelings at the first meeting. Nor are there any conventions governing the ways they meet and spend time together. The standard date consisting of drinks, dinner, and dancing or a show is modified at will to suit the two people's schedules, pocketbooks, and inclinations.

Remarriage

Formerly married people may fall in love and have affairs, but they are wary of marrying the wrong person again. If it is too soon after the divorce and the formerly married person does not yet feel psychologically ready for marriage, he or she may break off an attachment despite a fondness for the other person. Normally, however, the period of just not being ready for another marriage comes to an end before long.

Four out of five divorced people eventually remarry. On the average, in fact, they do it three years after the divorce, and often with another divorced person. Women wait just slightly longer than men (3.2 versus 3.1 years, on the average), and more women than men never remarry at all (U.S. Bureau of the Census, 1976a, pp. 20, 15). One reason for this is that women seldom marry younger men, as we saw in Chapter 5. For the divorced woman, the pool of eligible mates her own age or older is smaller than the pool for a divorced man, who may marry a younger woman.

Young couples have always had higher divorce rates than older couples. But the remarriage rates of young couples are also high. These two rates are not independent of each other, but part of the same trend (Feldberg and Kohen, 1976). About one-fourth of all weddings solemnized in the United States today are remarriages for one or both partners. When the previously married spouse has children by the former marriage, the new family, known as a *blended* or *reconstituted family*, must absorb the complications of relationships already formed—complications that do not exist in families formed by first marriages. Each spouse may have to relate to the other ex-spouse and children. And the children may have to relate not only to a stepmother, a stepfather, and stepbrothers and stepsisters but eventually also to half brothers and half sisters in both the reconstituted families of their parents. (See Chapter 12 for a discussion of stepchildren.)

Not to be forgotten are the in-laws of the former spouse. Divorcées with children are more likely to maintain their relationships with their in-laws than are divorcées who do not have children (Spicer and Hampe, 1975).

Children of Divorce

The children go through it all: the breakup of their parents' marriage, the legal process, the loneliness and grief and tight budget of a single-parent home, the reconstituted family. Perhaps a young child's worst fear is the fear of abandonment. Though children may seem to understand their parents' sympathetic explanations, they cannot help but feel half abandoned when one parent leaves the home. And if one parent can leave them, it suddenly becomes conceivable that the other one might do the same.

Parents who cannot agree on alimony and the division of property in the legal process of divorce are often equally unable to agree on who should have legal custody of the children. And the battle for the children is not always confined to the courts. It is the children who suffer most as the father or mother attempts to persuade the child to remain with him or her.

It also increases the hardship for children if they have to move to a new residence when their parents divorce, for then not only is their family in pieces, but their school life and friendships are disrupted as well. Another hardship affecting children is a reduction in the family's standard of living. Unfortunately, a great many single-parent families

soon find themselves short of money. In a study of broken homes in Wisconsin, it was found that after one year, over 40 percent of the fathers were no longer making any support payments at all, and 20 percent more were behind in their payments (The Surge in Easy Divorces, 1974, p. 45). Alarmed at these figures, Margaret Mead (1974b) has suggested that life insurance companies add a divorce provision to the policies they sell fathers. As now written, most life insurance policies provide for the support of children in the event of the father's death. Mead suggests that they also pay in case the father and mother are divorced.

Children often feel resentful when their parents begin to date other people. They tend to remain loyal to the excluded parent and to regard the interloper as an obstacle to their parents' reconciliation. They also now have their parents' affection all to themselves and have no wish to share it with a stranger.

Family counselors Thomas Hozman and Donald Froiland (1976), using the ideas of Elisabeth Kübler-Ross (1969) on loss (see Chapter 14), have proposed that children of divorced parents may progress through five stages. The first stage is denial, in which they refuse to accept the situation and eliminate all thoughts of the parents' separation from their minds. During this stage, children isolate themselves from parents, peers, and teachers, often showing a lack of interpersonal skills.

If and when children finally accept the reality of the situation, they enter the second phase. They become extremely angry and attempt to attack all those involved in the divorce. It they progress through the denial and anger stages, they enter the bargaining phase. During this period, children will attempt to reunite the parents, sometimes by overpleasing them whenever they make a request.

When children are unable to negotiate a reconciliation, they may become extremely depressed. Frequently, children in the depression stage will throw temper tantrums. Finally, they may pass into the acceptance stage. They begin to understand that the parents' reconciliation is not possible and that they will have to learn to live their daily lives with only one parent.

It should be pointed out that not all children will progress through all five stages, nor will they go through them in the same order. However, most children will go through most of the stages.

As Hozman and Froiland point out, an experienced counselor can diagnose each stage and offer therapy to help the child cope with the turmoil being experienced. During the anger stage, for example, the counselor must induce the child to recognize what is happening in his or her family life. "The important concept at this point," write the investigators, "is to enable the children to legitimize their feelings. Feelings, good or bad, warm or hostile, are real. These feelings must be properly channeled and understood so that the child may come to express them" (Hozman and Froiland, 1976, p. 272).

As the five-stage theory of Hozman and Froiland suggests, most children relent toward their parents and even resign themselves to the eventuality of remarriage. Children and stepparents may become quite fond of one another in the atmosphere of happiness and optimism that accompanies the founding of a new family. The exception may call for professional help.

For children who do not have help during the period of the divorce, problems may become acute. A common example is that of young sons of broken homes. As the number of fatherless families with inadequate incomes has increased, mental health workers have observed an influx into their clinics of physically aggressive, defiant, unmanageable young boys. Though only four to seven years old, these boys set fires, hit other children over the head with lunch boxes, steal food and money, and punch strange adults passing on the street. Many of them sleep poorly at night and wet the bed. When interviewed by a mental health worker, a boy of this type gives the illusion that "he is neither very afraid nor very interested in the interviewer. . . . He usually responds to the interviewer's opening gambit by calmly ignoring questions or statements about his problems or worries, or by just as calmly informing the interviewer that he can take care of his own problems" (Tooley, 1976, p. 34).

The boys' mothers are just the opposite. They are exhausted, overworked, and overwhelmed. With the departure of their husbands, the women are trying to manage a household on an average of only 50 percent of the income they had before the divorce. They are sometimes hysterical, and sometimes despairing and depressed. In contrast to their aggressive little boys, the mothers seem helplessly confused and hopelessly incompetent. Gas-station attendants, repairmen, and even married friends advise, berate, and bully them, as they fail to assert their rights.

The approach taken by many mental health workers with such families is to help the mother gain a sense of strength and competence and convey more certainty to her children. This is not easy when she holds a full-time job. She must spend every evening cooking, cleaning, breaking up fights, and seeing to baths, leaving the laundry and shopping for weekends. Nevertheless, many of the mothers manage, and as they do, the violent behavior of their boys subsides considerably, in some cases disappearing altogether.

SUMMARY

Despite the difficulty in establishing accurate statistics on divorce, there is no doubt that the divorce rate is rapidly increasing. However, certain demographic characteristics of the couple will increase the likelihood of divorce. People are more likely to divorce if they marry when they are younger than twenty-one, if they are poor, if they have a lot of children, if they have been married once before, or if they differ in terms of religion, social class, or educational background.

Divorce is usually the end product of a process of growing apart. The legality of divorce always used to involve an adversary proceeding in which one of the parties was held culpable, and the other blameless. Today no-fault divorces are the rule in many states. No-fault divorce tends to equalize the blame, decrease the cost of divorce, and make it unnecessary to lie or trump up false charges in the courtroom. The final separation is an occasion deeply unsettling to the divorced pair but unmarked by any social formality.

Most people find divorce and the adjustment to single life painful emotionally and difficult in regard to the practical matters of everyday living. The tasks of arranging for child care, for employment, for a new domicile, and for a social life as a single person are all problematic. However, the chances of remarriage are excellent. Four out of five divorced people eventually remarry.

For children, the initial adjustment to the divorce of their parents is difficult. Contested divorces are likely to be particularly difficult for children. After their initial stages of denial and then anger, most children become reconciled. Counseling services are recommended for children and their parents who have difficulty coming to terms with their new arrangements.

CASE STUDY

Carolyn was stunned when Joe, her husband of eight years, announced one morning at breakfast that he wanted a divorce. She was aware, however, that things were not going as smoothly as they once had. There had recently been an increasing number of arguments, and these were becoming more intense. In one fight, triggered by a trivial incident, Carolyn hit Joe with her purse. In another, Joe, in a rage, punched in the refrigerator door. But Carolyn's eagerness to talk about any problems and to work on them, and Joe's usual reticence in dealing with emotional issues had masked the depths of his dissatisfaction from her.

Her View

Carolyn married Joe "because he always had everything under control. He never seemed to get upset over little things, like I do. I always thought of Joe as being very strong. He has a way of making people feel comfortable, though I have learned that you can't always tell what is on *his* mind. Maybe that is why he's a good salesman."

Carolyn sees Joe, a business graduate, as very bright but bored with his work in automotive sales. His mother supports Carolyn's belief, saying, "Things always came easy for Joe, but he never liked to apply himself." Carolyn, a graduate of secretarial school, is earning a small salary in a part-time job and has no plans for her own advancement.

Carolyn wants children and felt it was unfair when Joe insisted that she wait and work now to help pay for their new house. Carolyn accused Joe of not assuming enough responsibility for the care and upkeep of the house and lawn. She often asked her father to make small household repairs or to do lawn chores when Joe, in her opinion, had let them fall behind. She was genuinely puzzled when Joe saw her father's work as meddling rather than helpful. Carolyn had been the initiator in sexual activity for some time, but she attributed Joe's decreasing interest in sex to what she felt to be general dissatisfaction with his work and his lack of advancement.

Carolyn's family does everything together. When Joe entered the service a few weeks after their marriage, he and Carolyn moved to a naval base across the country from her parents. Carolyn's mother immediately indicated that their tightly knit family circle was not to be broken by the marriage of her older daughter. She came with Carolyn's younger sister, Jane, to stay for a month. Carolyn feels that Joe was excessively cool to her mother and sister then and that he has always been standoffish with both his own family and hers.

Carolyn thinks that Joe's war experiences may have contributed to their drifting apart. Soon after he entered the service, Joe was sent on a two-year tour of active duty, and Carolyn returned to live with her parents and sister. During those two years she saw Joe only once for a ten-day holiday in Hawaii. When Joe returned home, Carolyn felt he had changed from the happy-go-lucky person she once knew into a quiet loner. She pleaded with him to share his experiences with her and was pleased when Joe told her about some of the pranks he and his buddies had played to relieve the tensions of life under wartime conditions. She was disappointed when he indicated that other experiences were unpleasant and confidential and that anyway she would not want to hear about them.

Carolyn was especially confused when, after Joe indicated that he wanted a divorce, he still treated her kindly most of the time. She made several attempts at reconciliation, including visits to a marriage counselor. But when Joe refused to reconcile, it was Carolyn who filed for divorce, and it was she who moved out of their house, at Joe's insistence, and into a separate apartment.

Carolyn's parents were as involved in her divorce as they had been in her marriage. When she located an apartment for herself, her father contributed money and labor toward fixing it up. Her mother wanted to know every detail of what furnishings and other material goods Joe was keeping and which ones Carolyn was getting. She encouraged Carolyn to push for more. Her parents' constant unannounced visits deprived Carolyn of much of the time and privacy she needed to sort out her own emotions and made it difficult for her to find new male and female friends outside the family setting.

Carolyn's active, outgoing nature stood her in good stead. People were there for her when she needed them. She stayed with an aunt and uncle until she found her apartment. She joined, and soon left, a women's discussion group because she felt she was working through her own problems more rapidly than the rest of the women in the group. She decided to take a course at a nearby university and began considering the possibility of further education for herself. And she began dating.

His View

Joe says he married Carolyn because she was so vivacious—"She was always good for conversation, whether we were alone or with another couple"—and because she really made him feel important and needed. "She was always asking me whether the eggs were done just right and tried to do everything to please me." He is not sure just where the relationship began to go sour.

He thinks he should have paid more attention to the "temper tantrum" Carolyn threw on the eve of their wedding when he returned from a bachelor party given in his honor to find his bride-to-be in his apartment packing his clothing for their wedding trip, having already packed her own. Carolyn began angrily throwing Joe's clothing at him, crying uncontrollably and accusing him of not wanting to marry her or to take a wedding trip, since he so obviously was not preparing for it. Joe thought at the time that she was simply overwrought from anxiety and fatigue because of the wedding preparations, but he now sees Carolyn as "an emotional person who cries whenever she is upset about anything, which is pretty often."

Joe sees himself as a pretty average kind of guy, although he hints that he was given a great deal of responsibility while he was in the service and admits to close friends that he has turned down the opportunity to become an area sales manager "since that would mean more paperwork and office work and put me directly under the scrutiny of the state director. I prefer keeping my own schedule and going out to companies at their convenience and mine. I don't like having to report in all the time."

Joe likes his own family because "they don't interfere." He has not discussed his divorce with them; he simply told his father that he and Carolyn were not able to keep the marriage together. He intensely dislikes Carolyn's family. He sees them as intrusive and interfering. "Carolyn was on the telephone most of the time, talking to either her mother or her sister. Or, worse, they were over at our house. She always made me feel more like she was theirs than mine."

Joe describes himself as not liking to rush at things, like buying a house or having children. "Those are things you take some time planning for." He thinks he would eventually have liked to have children, had his relationship with Carolyn been more satisfactory.

Joe's rational approach to life has helped him to expedite the many details involved in the business of divorcing, such as the division of the material goods and the termination of joint insurance policies. He assisted Carolyn with these details to the end.

Joe has faced the difficulties of divorcing alone, without the advice or support of family or close friends. He thinks he would like to remarry, but he is hesitant about dating seriously, fearing that he might again get caught up in an unsatisfactory relationship.

Interpretation and Questions

Why are Joe and Carolyn getting a divorce? What do you think are the sources of Joe's and Carolyn's marital difficulties? How are Carolyn and Joe different from each other? Is one more impulsive than the other? Is one more controlling? Is either, or are both, too dependent or too independent? Is one more ambitious? More outgoing? Are differences always a source of conflict? If Joe and Carolyn should decide to remarry, would you advise them to choose a different kind of mate, to make changes in themselves, or both?

STUDY GUIDE

Important Terms

divorce rate
alimony
divorce court
no-fault divorce

adversary divorce
the formerly married
reconstituted family

Review Quiz

1 The divorce rate in the United States today is approximately _____ that of a decade ago.
   a one-half
   b equal to
   c double
   d five times

2 The probability of divorce is higher for:
   a older couples, as opposed to those in their teens
   b those with higher rather than lower incomes
   c those in a second or subsequent marriage, as opposed to a first marriage
   d none of the above

3 Which of the following would have the greatest likelihood of divorce, all else being equal?
   a a couple with religious beliefs opposing divorce
   b a couple who had both grown up on a farm
   c a couple whose parents have been divorced
   d a couple whose age and education are almost identical

4 The state has the power to grant or withhold divorces because:
   a the state also has the responsibility for seeing to it that dependent children have some support
   b one spouse may have sacrificed earning power to the marriage and may need alimony for support
   c bigamy would make the network of obligations and commitments among spouses and children unclear
   d all the above

5 Divorce laws which do not require that one of the couple be "guilty" are called:
   a collusion laws
   b no-fault divorce laws
   c adversary laws
   d none of the above

6 Long-standing divorce laws do not permit _____ as grounds for divorce, but no-fault divorce laws do.
   a adultery
   b cruelty
   c nonsupport
   d irreconcilable differences

CHAPTER 15

7 The total legal costs of a divorce in the United States, using attorneys, now range from:
   - a $25 to $500
   - b $50 to $750
   - c $100 to $1000
   - d $350 to $5000

8 Adjustment to life after divorce depends upon:
   - a whether the couple have children
   - b how long the couple were married
   - c how old the divorcing persons are
   - d all the above

9 The problems that one should anticipate following a divorce include:
   - a an almost inevitable sense of guilt
   - b living on a reduced income
   - c a sense of loss and grief
   - d all the above

10 Studies of the relationship between divorce and suicide show that:
   - a married men commit suicide more often than divorced men
   - b married women commit suicide more often than divorced women
   - c divorced men commit suicide more often than divorced women
   - d none of the above

11 When formerly married people begin dating:
   - a they are much more restrictive in their conversation than never-married persons
   - b they may initially lack confidence in their ability to attract another person
   - c they must observe more conventions concerning how their dates will be structured than never-married people
   - d all the above

12 The statistics on divorce and remarriage show that:
   - a both men and women remarry, on the average, about three years after the divorce
   - b about 80 percent of divorced people eventually remarry
   - c more women than men never remarry at all
   - d all the above

13 The divorce rate is highest for:
   - a first and second marriages
   - b third marriages
   - c fourth marriages
   - d first and third marriages

14 Children may adjust better to their parents' divorce if:
   - a both parents communicate a concern for the children's well-being
   - b the residence of the children can be changed to give them a new start
   - c the parent with custody over the children begins to date immediately
   - d all the above

15 The initial stage that children seem to undergo when they are informed of their parents' impending divorce is:
   - a anger
   - b denial
   - c depression
   - d bargaining and trying to reunite the parents

395
BREAKING UP

Opinionnaire

Agree	No opinion	Disagree		
_____	_____	_____	1	The high divorce rate in this country is an alarming indication of the coming death of the family.
_____	_____	_____	2	No matter what the specific reason, people who have to get a divorce must be considered failures.
_____	_____	_____	3	Individuals should not marry until they are out of their teens in order to avoid the high risk of divorce
_____	_____	_____	4	One of the two marriage partners is always more responsible for the divorce than the other.
_____	_____	_____	5	All divorces should be no-fault divorces.
_____	_____	_____	6	The easier it is to obtain a divorce, the more people will seek divorces to avoid having to solve marital problems.
_____	_____	_____	7	If both parents are capable of raising the children after divorce, fathers should receive equal consideration along with mothers for custody.
_____	_____	_____	8	The process of divorce is so painful that there is practically no chance that a couple can remain friends.
_____	_____	_____	9	If two people gave more consideration to the adverse effects of divorce on children, there would be fewer divorces.
_____	_____	_____	10	A person who has been divorced once is a poor prospect as a marriage partner.

Exercise

This exercise will help you to understand better the formulation and logic of statistics. (All statistics are from U.S. Bureau of the Census, 1975.)

THE DIVORCE RATE

This statistic is the one usually cited when divorce trends are discussed. It refers to the number of divorces in a year per 1000 population. The divorce rate is computed from a formula as follows:

$$\text{Divorce rate} = \frac{\text{no. of divorces in one year}}{\text{midyear population}} \times 1000$$

Problem: Compute the United States divorce rate for 1974. There were 970,000 divorces that year, and the population at midyear was 211,894,000.

Answer: _____

DIVORCE PRONENESS

One way to compute divorce proneness is to compute the divorce rate, using the formula above, and then compare rates from two or more different groups. For example, if persons with less than a high school education have a rate higher than the overall rate, we conclude that their marriages are *more* prone to divorce.

Problem: States vary widely in conditions which either promote or inhibit divorce. Which of the states below would you guess has the highest rate? Why? Using the population figures below, compute a divorce rate for each state. How good was your guess? Can you explain any of the results? Now compare the rates in these states with the overall United States rate. Are the people in these states more or less prone to divorce than the population as a whole?

	Population (1974)	Divorces (1974)	Rate	Divorce proneness
New York	18,111,000	47,500	_____	_____
Ohio	10,737,000	48,900	_____	_____
Minnesota	3,917,000	11,000	_____	_____
Maryland	4,094,000	14,200	_____	_____
Alabama	3,577,000	21,300	_____	_____
Oklahoma	2,709,000	20,500	_____	_____
Nevada	573,000	8,600	_____	_____
California	20,907,000	117,700	_____	_____

ANSWERS TO EXERCISE

1 United States divorce rate (1974) = 4.6
2 Divorce rates and divorce proneness in individual states:

New York = 2.6 (less)   Alabama = 6.0 (more)
Ohio = 4.6 (the same)   Oklahoma = 7.6 (more)
Minnesota = 2.8 (less)   Nevada = 15.0 (more)
Maryland = 3.5 (less)   California = 5.7 (more)

Projects for Class or Home Study

1 Divorce is often hard to face, but sometimes the alternative is much worse. Many divorce-court proceedings are open, and sitting through a few cases can be an educational experience. Often the experience of seeing divorce proceedings changes the viewer's attitudes.

2 Loss of a spouse through divorce does not seem to entitle one to the same emotional support from friends and relatives as loss through death. Ask someone who has been divorced how much support he or she received from others.

3 Some countries, such as the Soviet Union in the 1920s, have experimented with making divorce merely a matter of filing written notification with the state. Do you think this would be a good idea in the United States? What do you think might be the result?

4 With the number of older women living alone after the death of a spouse increasing, some analysts have suggested that bigamy may be a viable alternative to monogamy. Do you think legalized bigamy for older Americans is a good idea?

5 Of course, no one goes into marriage expecting to get a divorce, but many marriages end that way. Check your own socioeconomic characteristics against the "proneness" statistics in the text to see how divorce-prone you are (if you are married) or would be if you married someone with similar characteristics. Would a high degree of divorce proneness stop you from marrying someone you loved?

Suggestions for Further Reading

Epstein, Joseph. *Divorce in America.* New York: Dutton, 1974.
   A New York editor describes the personal anguish of his own divorce. The negative view of divorce contrasts with that of Krantzler (see below).

Grollman, Earl A. *Talking about divorce: A dialogue between parent and child.* Boston: Beacon Press, 1975.
   Many parents need help in explaining divorce to their children. This book does just that in a simple, straightforward fashion.

Gunter, B. G. Notes on divorce filing as role behavior. *Journal of Marriage and the Family,* February 1977, **39**, 95–98.
   Evidence is continuing to accumulate about the effects of divorce laws on divorce. The author suggests that legal changes have made it much more likely that women will initiate divorce proceedings.

Hetherington, E. Mavis, Cox, M., and Cox, R. Divorced fathers. *Psychology Today,* April 1977, **11**, 42–46.
   A research report covering the lives of seventy-two divorced fathers. The first two years after divorce were very difficult ones for almost all the fathers.

Ibsen, Henrik. *A doll's house.* (First published in 1879) New York: Dutton, 1970.
   Ibsen's play, written in the nineteenth century, has gained a new audience since the women's liberation movement. The heroine finally walks out on her husband with a "door slam heard 'round the world."

Krantzler, Mel. *Creative divorce.* New York: New American Library, 1973.
   Divorce can be a growth experience if approached creatively. The author, who went through the divorce experience himself, writes from a personal viewpoint.

Updike, John. Dear Alexandros. In John Updike, *Pigeon feathers.* Greenwich, Conn.: Fawcett, 1962.
   In this brief classic, Updike telescopes a family breakup in a letter written to an adopted child overseas by his American "parent."

Answers to Review Quiz

1-*c* 2-*c* 3-*c* 4-*d* 5-*b* 6-*d* 7-*d* 8-*d* 9-*d* 10-*c* 11-*b* 12-*d* 13-*c* 14-*a* 15-*b*

16

LIVING SINGLE

To begin with, I wasn't raised to be single. In addition to good training in homemaking, the tacit lesson of such things . . . as mother-daughter dresses (and brooms, and pots and aprons) was that, naturally, you'd grow into the role as well as the wardrobe (Calvert, 1975, p. 144).

—A single woman

I've gotten a lot of headaches from my family because I'm not married. A nice Jewish boy is supposed to get married as soon as he's out of college and started in business. I think there was always the unspoken thought lurking around: "Could my baby boy be a homosexual?" (Jacoby, 1974, p. 48).

—A single man

As in Noah's ark, all cultural signposts in American life point to the notion that living in pairs is the natural and necessary state of affairs—necessary not just for procreation but for personal fulfillment as well. Any other lifestyle is a lesser alternative, an exception to be pitied or maligned. From earliest childhood we are taught to assume that, like our parents and the vast majority of adults we see around us, we will someday marry and have children.

The negative social stigma attached to being single only helps reinforce the positive pressures to marry. "Old maid" and "spinster" are not coveted labels. They signify a woman who is either too unattractive or too aggressive to succeed in the marriage market (M. Adams, 1971). The man who stays single much past the age of thirty-five is verging on becoming a "confirmed bachelor." While this is a less derogatory term than "old maid" or "spinster," an unmarried man is still regarded with some mistrust in a society that places a high value on marriage and the family. At best, a bachelor is an immature playboy who is unwilling to accept responsibility for a wife and family; at worst, he is suspected of being homosexual (Gilder, 1974).

The Single Life

Despite social pressures, a significant number of American men and women are single—in 1975, over 43 million people aged eighteen and over. Included in this number were those who had been married and were single as a result of divorce or the death of a spouse. Living single seems to be on the increase. In 1960, for example, 17 percent of the men in the United States were single (had never been married), while in 1975, 21 percent fell into this category. The comparable figures for women were 22 percent and 30 percent (U.S. Bureau of the Census, 1976a).

It is unclear whether the larger proportion of singles is due to a trend away from marriage or whether many Americans are marrying when they are older. However, the high visibility and large concentrations of young singles of marrying age have given rise to a new "singles" image. Particularly noticeable in large urban centers, the "swinging single" is pictured as flaunting traditional mating patterns in favor of independence and casual no-strings-attached sexual liaisons. "Swingles," as these affluent singles are referred to in the media, are responsible for the proliferation of singles' bars, singles' apartment complexes, and a whole host of travel and recreational opportunities designed exclusively for the new single lifestyle.

The evidence suggests that neither the image of "lonely loser" nor that of "free and independent pleasure seeker" is typical of most single adults. Studies based on interviews with hundreds of singles in metropolitan areas indicate that singles' life goals and lifestyles are not so different from those of their married counterparts (Starr and Carns, 1973). They seek many of the same satisfactions but are not convinced that marriage is a necessary choice for them. Instead, they are beginning to explore other options. Serial marriage—that is, several marriages and divorces— as well as communal living and single parenthood are some of the options they have chosen. They think of their single status as neither a terrible accident of fate nor a whirlwind of romantic adventures, but rather as a choice and a challenge (M. Edwards and Hoover, 1974).

CHOOSING TO BE SINGLE

Judith is twenty-nine and a member of the Boston Women's Health Book Collective. Like all the other members of the Collective, she has never been married. Discouraged from going to graduate school by a male professor who convinced her that she would "become too much like a man—and never get married," Judith moved to New York, where she spent a lot of time "looking for an exciting job and ways of meeting exciting people." Her evenings were spent talking to her three roommates about men, waiting for someone to call for a date, or finding someone to be with. She says she knew even then that she was not ready to get married: "There were so many things I wanted to do—travel, meet people, find exciting work." But she was not sure how long she could continue. Marriage seemed the only way out. "The horror of not being married was the loneliness, the lack of intimacy and honesty."

Now twenty-nine and no longer "on the make" for a potential husband, or even a mate for the night, she looks back on her earlier years this way:

> In retrospect I realize that I chose to be single. I wanted independence and excitement more than marriage but at the time I couldn't see it as a choice. It must be my fault. There must [have been] something wrong with me that I didn't have a permanent and lasting relationship with a man (Boston Women's Health Book Collective, 1971, p. 9).

Such a premium has been placed on marriage (intimacy, security, freedom from loneliness), that not much credence has been given to the notion that a person might choose to be single. The decision that most men and women must make is not whether to marry but whom to marry. Even when there is no real desire to marry, as in Judith's case, there is the nagging suspicion that either something is wrong or something is being missed. Some authorities agree. Psychotherapist Allan Fromme says:

> Even if the marriage turns out to be a mistake, it is more of a mistake not to make this mistake. The longer an individual remains unmarried, the longer he is avoiding a commitment, detaching himself, unrelating himself to other people. And the more he is courting that permanent detachment that we call loneliness (quoted in E. M. Edwards and Hoover, 1974, p. 27).

Influenced by the prevailing notion that being married is better than being single, many singles think of their status as temporary. They may prefer to be single for the moment, but they intend, of course, to marry eventually. The result of always thinking that one's future will be different, however, can have a ruinous effect on the present. Women who are ambivalent about marriage find that they do not think in terms of a career, that they fail to plan ahead financially, and that they live an altogether too transient life.

Karen, a never-married thirty-eight-year-old, always worked as a secretary because she assumed that someday she would get married and would not need to work. The results of a self-inventory test showed that what she really wanted was to work in merchandising and that she really had no overwhelming desire to marry at all. The knowledge that her single status was not temporary, but rather what she wanted, freed her to make plans for her own growth. She began studying merchandising in the evening and subsequently became assistant buyer in a New York City department store (E. M. Edwards and Hoover, 1974).

For some singles the notion that marriage "should" be their ultimate goal is changing. They are beginning to think of their status as representing a perfectly valid choice. According to Columbia University anthropologist Herbert Passin, "For the first time in human history the single condition is being recognized as an acceptable adult lifestyle for anyone. It is finally possible to be both single and a whole person" (quoted in E. M. Edwards and Hoover, 1974).

Ellen Sudo, a researcher for the Democratic study group in the United States House of Representatives, is typical of the new "single-by-choice" adult:

> Until very recently I've always thought of the single state as something impermanent. Now I feel that I want a home and I want it now—I don't want to wait for someone else to come along and make it for me. . . . I'd like to plant flower bulbs—it's a small thing but, damn it, I want to know whether I can have flowers next spring or not (Jacoby, 1974, p. 43).

Choosing to be single is made easier by the fact that many of the traditional reasons for marrying no longer exist. The sexual revolution, for one thing, has removed much of the moral opprobrium against sex outside marriage. As long as there are strict taboos about premarital sex, sex is bartered in exchange for security and commitment, and many marriages take place that would not otherwise. Furthermore, effective methods of birth control and legalized abortion in some states have removed the fear of unwanted pregnancies and eliminated the need for many hasty marriages that used to occur because the woman was pregnant. In addition, the elimination of some of the barriers that kept women from pursuing careers has made it unnecessary for many of them to marry in order to find a means of support (M. Adams, 1971). There is also evidence of a declining interest in children and families. In the decade between 1960 and 1970 the birthrate among women of childbearing age declined by nearly half. As a thirty-nine-year-old never-married male high school teacher told a workshop of single adults:

I've had some long-lasting, good relationships with women, but they always ended up wanting to get married and I didn't feel the need. Maybe if I wanted kids of my own it would be different, but I don't. And if you don't want children, I think marriage is unnecessary (M. Edwards and Hoover, 1974, p. 28).

Many singles report that their attitudes toward marriage become more positive as they get older. And many choose to marry after experiencing the advantages gained from being single. Jerry Zweig, a forty-three-year-old divorced male from Jersey City, New Jersey, remembers that for a year after his divorce he was embarrassed to talk about it:

Now there are so many people like me that I don't feel ashamed. I'm not opposed to marriage. I'd like to get married again, but I want to take some time to learn some things about myself. I see this as a perfectly legitimate desire now. When I was in my 20's and early 30's, the idea would have been unthinkable (Jacoby, 1974, p. 49).

For many persons, then, the decision not to marry is a deliberate one, made by those who decide that one's life should be neither left to blind chance nor determined by blind tradition. The decision to remain single is usually made because a person wants the freedom to experience and do things that a married person cannot. It is not made without the awareness that being single also has its limitations, especially in a society that gives so much preference to marriage. As another member of the Boston Women's Health Book Collective expressed it:

At times we feel excited that single women seem freest to change their lives. At other times we feel burdened and saddened by the insecurity of being single. We want to find new ways of relating to men but we have to forge our own models. . . . In short, there is still fear but also joy and relief about the roles we have grown out of and the possibilities we see ahead of us (1971, p. 7).

THE SINGLE LIFESTYLE

Who are the 43 million single men and women in the United States? How do they live? What do they want out of life? And how are their lives different from those of Americans who are married? Singles include everyone from recent college graduates who are savoring their first taste of independence to senior citizens who are living together in order to collect two social security checks. In between are millions of single parents coping with the problems and pleasures attendant on a combination of family life and the single state.

One stereotype created by the media in the late 1960s and early 1970s is that of singles whose lives revolve around bars, parties, and sexual adventures. The swinging-single image is typified by such housing arrangements as Woodway Square Apartments in Houston, Texas. Just one of twenty or thirty similar complexes in the northern end of Houston, Woodway houses 1200 single men and women in a luxurious setting of tennis courts, swimming pools, putting greens, and recreational lounges. A highlight of the year is the annual Superman Contest, when Woodway residents crown the male who can prove he has bedded the most Woodway women in one year. The winner of the 1971 Superman Contest, Charley Hazzard, expressed the sentiments of many Woodway males this way: "All that bein' a one-woman man seems like it must have happened to somebody else. I'm into playin' and lovin' and not givin' a damn for the rest of my life" (Proulx, 1973).

In most large cities without singles' housing complexes, ample opportunities to socialize are provided for the liberated new young single generation. Singles' bars, singles' magazines, guides to places and events for meeting sexually compatible partners, singles' weekend excursions and resorts, and even singles' magazines form the freewheeling urban singles scene in most American cities.

Sociologists and psychologists offer a number of explanations for the swinging-singles phenomenon. Eric Margenau explains it in terms of singles' pain: "They anesthetize themselves with a lifestyle that consists of ritually getting drunk, getting stoned, getting laid. The very nature of their interaction is one of *not* dealing with anything real or intense, of not dealing with their own feelings" (quoted in Proulx, 1973, p. 65). Salomon Rettig has another, more pragmatic explanation: affluence. He says that young people in their early twenties have never had so much money. Money buys the freedom to live alone and go where one pleases. Rettig also sees the singles scene as a response to the shortage of meaningful labor in our society. By and large, he says, the singles who participate in the "swingles" scene are men and women whose jobs do not offer them an opportunity to be creative, to make decisions and see the results, or to contribute to society (Proulx, 1973).

The Charley Hazzards of Woodway are not uncommon, but their lifestyles are not typical of those of most singles. The evidence suggests that when singles do participate in the "scene," they readily tire of what it has to offer. There is always a waiting list to get into Woodway, according to the manager, but the turnover rate is extremely high compared with that in most adult apartment houses (Proulx, 1973). Personal interviews with singles in the Chicago area revealed that it was a rare woman who continued to look for social contacts in singles' bars after six months in the city. Men, it was discovered, continued to frequent the bars a little longer than women, but they, too, spoke of the bar scene as a "meat market" and the clientele as "plastic." When comparing it with the social experiences they had had in college, Chicago singles said they found "the requirements for survival and success in the swinging-singles scene totally repugnant." The Chicago study concluded that most Chicago singles do not lead lives of wild sexual abandon, and that singles' apartments are not co-ed dormitories without housemothers (Starr and

Carns, 1973). A thirty-four-year-old executive with the Coca-Cola Company in Atlanta summed it up:

> Five years ago I was used to hearing sorrowful comments about my "loneliness." Now I get lecherous envy. From reading the press, you'd think that every girl is 36-24-36 like the blonde on the cover of *Newsweek*, and every guy lounges by a poolside and waits for the beautiful blondes to admire his rippling muscles. The truth just isn't very glamorous—some single people are happy and some aren't, just like married people (Jacoby, 1974, p. 13).

One fact of life that all singles face is economics. Susan Jacoby concluded from her interviews with singles of all income levels that middle- and upper-middle-class singles have a definite advantage over those who are less affluent. Without money it is hard to translate the theoretical freedoms of the single life into reality. Most singles in the city cope with the high cost of urban living by having roommates. In addition to the fact that urban living is more expensive than suburban or rural living, singles, on the whole, make less money than their married counterparts. The median income for college-educated single men is $10,500, compared with nearly twice that amount for college-educated married men in the same age bracket (Gilder, 1974). While single women fare better, on the average, than single men, women, by and large, do not take advantage of their higher incomes. Even when they make substantial salaries, single women are less likely than single men to make the kinds of investments that would assure their continued independence. If they have money, singles can partially compensate for some of the disadvantages of being single. "The most satisfying single lives are dotted with unhappy love affairs and sexual droughts," says a thirty-year-old Washington journalist. "If you have money you can go to New York for a weekend or Europe for a month" (Jacoby, 1974, p. 41).

Loneliness is another real factor in the lives of single men and women. The fear of loneliness is sometimes so great that people are propelled into marriage without realizing what is motivating them. The experience of intimacy in a good partnership is fulfilling and satisfying, but heterosexual relationships are not the only ones that can provide that experience. Some women are finding that being close and intimate with other women is a satisfying experience which they had not considered before. Whereas ten or fifteen years ago many women considered a date for dinner and a movie with a woman friend second best—a date to be broken if a man extended an invitation to either of them—today women are discovering the pleasures of the companionship of women friends.

As Luther Baker points out, "Love can have many partners. It can come in connection with some soul-satisfying endeavor, or the sense of belonging which comes from participating with one or more other persons in some significant and creative endeavor" (1971). Many women have found this kind of fulfillment in the women's movement. The

combined sentiments of the single women in the Boston Women's Health Book Collective are recorded in the following words:

> We are a group of single women in our twenties. We have all had relationships with men that have been important to us, but none of us has ever been married. For the past few years we have all been deeply, personally involved in the Women's Liberation Movement, and our lives have changed drastically. All of us have varying degrees of intimacy with people now, primarily with women. None of us has a primary relationship that defines who we are. Together we are trying to explore our independence and find positive identities for ourselves—not in isolation from other people but outside relationships that feel limiting or defining (1971, p. 2).

Then, too, there is a difference between being lonely and being alone. Spending time alone can be a richly rewarding experience, one that married persons are sometimes denied because of the close proximities of the family relationship. Karen Durbin (1975) recalls a sense of freedom that came with being alone as a child. On days when she did not have to go to school—when she did not have to go anywhere and had the whole day to do just as she pleased—she would stand at the window of her room while everyone else in the house was asleep and think about what she wanted to do:

> I was claiming the day . . . claiming myself and my part in the day . . . Being alone is no longer a lesser alternative to being in love; they simply offer different sorts of pleasures, and, for that matter, pains. The singular pleasure of the first is a sense of freedom . . . (Durbin, 1975, pp. 77, 122).

In *Final Analysis*, Lois Gould writes of her struggles, as a writer, with loneliness and of how, with the help of her analyst, she was able to turn her time of loneliness and isolation into a time of productivity and creativity:

TO DR. FOXX: UTTERLY CONFIDENTIAL
TOPIC: ALONE VS. LONELY
I am learning that alone is different from lonely. Not always, but at its best, very different. Alone can be nicer than together, if you know how. Remember the song, "Me and My Shadow"?: "At 12 o'clock we climb the stair, we never knock 'cause there's nobody there"? Nonsense; I'm there. And aren't I terrific to be with? . . . After a long time alone I'm learning to smile at myself. I'm beginning to appreciate this person. I even like playing with her. . . . I can work at this window for hours at a time, writing in longhand on lined paper, and either I am happy here or else I am at peace, now. I am alone. I have never felt less lonely.
Hey, you know what? I'm functioning! (1974, p. 72).

One of the biggest advantages of being single is the opportunity it affords for personal growth. Because single people are under no pressure to accommodate to a spouse and children, they have more time to explore avenues for growth and enrichment. They can try new career options, travel more, have a wider variety of experiences, and expose themselves to the opportunities which lead to personal growth. A married woman's quest for identity and fulfillment can be stifled by the notion that her primary responsibility is not to herself but to her husband and children. A married man can become fearful of losing the job that provides support for his family and fail to risk a change that might prove beneficial.

While men and women share many of the problems and pleasures attached to being single, in some ways the experience is not the same for both sexes. The evidence suggests that in many ways women fare better and have an easier time adapting to the single life than men do.

THE SINGLE WOMAN

Unlike that of a man, whose primary source of identification or sense of personal worth has been tied to his work or career, a woman's fulfillment has traditionally been associated with her domestic role. However, studies comparing the personal and social adjustment of never-married women with that of happily married women have found that never-married women are as fulfilled as those who are married. In such areas as self-reliance, a sense of personal worth, and freedom from nervous symptoms, never-married women scored as high as, if not higher than, married women. There are no scientific data to support the notion that women who never marry lead less satisfying lives (Baker, 1968).

If anything, according to Jessie Bernard, the evidence suggests that never-married women have a better chance than married women of achieving a sense of personal fulfillment. In a survey of the literature, Bernard (1972) found that among women over the age of thirty, married women are more likely than single women to suffer from depression, severe neurotic symptoms and phobic tendencies, and a whole host of symptoms of psychological distress. Similarly, in his discussions with married women, especially young women who embraced the roles of wife and mother, Baker (1968) noted the frequent use of such words as "trapped," "boxed in," or "at a dead end."

A feeling of fulfillment, Baker suggests, does not depend on whether a woman has given birth to children. Fetal development, he reminds us, is a function of the body, not of the person. Maternal fulfillment comes from the contribution a woman makes to the needs of her child—from watching her child develop as a result of her caring and creative efforts. The same experience can be had in other ways. The experience of being a mother can be a joyful one, but a joyous devotion can also characterize women who devote themselves to other forms of creative endeavor (Baker, 1968).

THE SINGLE MAN

Single women fare better than single men, according to a survey conducted by Angus Campbell. "The truth is that there are more carefree spinsters and anxious bachelors" (A. Wilson, 1975). However, unlike the single woman, who is stereotyped as being only half a woman, the single man can enjoy a positive stereotype—that of a man who is free of emotional attachments and uses women primarily for his pleasure. He may admire women, but he is never committed to any one woman for any length of time. In the eyes of his married peers he may appear to "have it made," to be free of the demands of a wife or the burden of supporting a family (Balswick and Peek, 1971). He appears to be able to enjoy all the women he likes without any of the hassles of commitment.

The swinging single man may try to cultivate a playboy image, but the literature on single men suggests that the gulf between image and reality is very wide. Referring to them as "naked nomads," George Gilder (1974) says that financially, emotionally, and physically single males suffer in comparison with both single females and, particularly, their married counterparts.

According to Gilder, the median income for college-educated single men, as noted earlier, is $10,500, not much higher than the median income for all black males and single women. The median income for college-educated married men in the same age bracket is almost double that amount. In terms of emotional adjustment, Gilder claims that 12 percent more single men than married men exhibit some signs of depression and that 16 percent more single than married men are victims of inertia and passivity. In the health category Gilder claims that 27 percent of all single men have some chronic physical disability, compared with 20 percent of all married men. And of more consequence, Gilder asserts, single men are four times more likely than married men, and twice as likely as single women, to commit suicide. Moreover, when they do kill themselves, he says, they do it coolly, thoroughly, and with little bid for attention. Some 60 percent of convicted criminals are single men, who commit 90 percent of all crimes. Gilder concludes that the life of the single man is "nasty, brutish, and violent." The solution, claims Gilder, is marriage. Love, sex, and marriage, he believes, are the best cure for the single male's violence and disease (Gilder, 1974).

Not all single men lead lives as depressing as these statistics would lead us to believe. One handicap that afflicts almost all single men, however, is the popular notion that they are not married because they are immature and irresponsible. A thirty-four-year-old Michigan State University professor found, for example, that it was almost impossible for a single man to rent an apartment in a university town. "People just have this image of a single man as an irresponsible person who has beer busts and will probably break up the joint" (Jacoby, 1974, p. 48). A survey of fifty major American corporations found that although most corporations claimed they had no hiring or promotion bias against single men, 80 percent had single men in only 2 percent of their management positions. Sixty percent of the corporate respondents said they thought that single men tended to make snap judgments and were less stable than married men (Jacoby, 1974).

In their study of single men in Chicago, Starr and Carns divided single men into three groups in terms of work incentive and work interests—groups nearly identical to those found among married men. The second largest grouping was made up of single men in conventional careers who were striving for success in traditional terms of prestige and financial gain. The smallest group consisted of those who consciously rejected traditional work options and wanted to work at temporary jobs such as driving a cab or doing construction work. The largest group, as in the case of married men, was made up of those who straddled both worlds and claimed they wanted material success but lacked the talent, skill, or motivation to achieve it (Starr and Carns, 1973).

Alternative Lifestyles

When adults choose not to marry, they do not give up the need, or the desire, to love and be loved. Warm and loving relationships are among the benefits that accrue to members of a family. Part of the single's challenge is to discover alternative ways of meeting those needs—the need to feel secure and loved in a relationship, for example, or the need to belong to a contained unit of caring and connected persons. Some may adopt or have children of their own, or they may share responsibility for the children of friends. Others forge new models for loving relationships with members of their own sex. Still others live communally with like-minded adults. However, not all communes are composed of single men and women. Many include married couples and children—men and women searching for an alternate lifestyle to that of the nuclear family in a competitive, mass society.

THE COMMUNAL LIFESTYLE

The commune is by no means a new experiment in living. Rosabeth Kanter refers to the experimentation with communal living in the late 1960s and early 1970s as a revival of the search for utopia that has gone on in America since 1680. The earliest American communes were founded by European religious sects whose members rejected established theology and moved to the wilderness to live out their shared religious beliefs in harmony and close association with their fellow believers (Kanter, 1972).

The Oneida Community is an example of a successful attempt to develop a communal lifestyle on the basis of shared religious beliefs. The group grew out of a Bible class taught by John Noyes, a "Perfectionist" Christian minister who believed that heaven was already here on earth and that human beings could now live without sin and achieve perfection (Kephart, 1966). With twelve members of his class, Noyes moved to a small farm outside Oneida, New York, and set about establishing a heavenly order in this world. Members were required to sign a document on joining which transferred ownership of all possessions to the community. Even clothes were community property. The person who happened to be wearing them was only "using" them for the day.

Oneidans practiced *complex marriage*, a system in which every man was permitted to have sexual relations with every woman in the group, providing she consented. Noyes believed that "we need love as much as we need food and clothing, and God knows it; and if we trust Him for those things, why not for love?" (quoted in Kephart, 1966, p. 172) However, Noyes did not believe in romantic love; it encouraged jealousy and possessiveness, he thought. Indeed, as Kanter has pointed out, each commune, in order to survive, must solve the problem of maintaining the primary loyalty of each member to the group as a whole, rather than to a family or a lover. A romantic attachment or a child would, for the couple involved, be a threat to group interests. Another option open to communes is celibacy. The Shaker communities of New England practiced celibacy, as, of course, do the oldest and most successful communes of all—the religious orders of the various Christian churches.

As of 1971, there were several thousand communes of recent vintage located in many different areas in the United States. Not unlike the members of early American communes, who were motivated by the desire to reject or challenge established religious or political practices, the members of today's communes are often motivated by a reaction against the alienation which they believe is fostered by the institutions and mores of present-day society.

The counterculture communes of the 1960s were attempts to re-create environments of love that could heal both the social isolation and the inner fragmentation which the youth of that decade blamed on "the establishment." Usually loosely structured, these communes were intent on giving members the freedom to "do their own thing." Many did not survive what Kanter terms the "anarchic" stage of commune development. Some did, however, and, in a more highly structured form, have continued into the 1970s (Kanter, 1972).

Located on 1700 acres of Tennessee farmland, for example, The Farm, now America's largest working commune, had its origins in San Francisco when Haight Street was a haven for members of the counterculture from all over the United States. Unlike the Oneida Community, The Farm encourages monogamous marriages. Children are reared by their natural parents, and the birth of a child is regarded as a spiritual occasion of renewal for the entire community. Midwifery is a highly valued occupation among The Farm's women. Like the Oneida Community, The Farm has one spiritual leader who teaches a simple Christian ethic based on the dictum, "Love thy neighbor." Organization is provided by a board made up of heads of each of fifteen work crews. Board decisions are restricted to matters affecting the planting and harvesting of crops, the purchase and maintenance of farming equipment, and the provision of basic services, such as education, medicine, and housing for

MEMBERS OF The Farm, currently the largest working commune in the United States

the community's members. The only strict Farm rules are those governing diet, drugs, and violence. All forms of violence, whether physical or mental, are strictly forbidden. If, in the opinion of The Farm's spiritual leader, members are creating violence by their presence, they are asked to leave. All members adhere to a strict vegetarian diet, and drugs of any form are forbidden (Johnston, 1977).

The Elm Lane Eight is a suburban, middle-class group who call themselves an experimental, nontraditional family. The group consists of three couples, two singles, and three children. In a style of communal living that has emerged in the 1970s, the Elm Lane Eight live together in a large suburban house which they purchased jointly and saved from deterioration. Those who live in *evolutionary communes*, as these newest experiments in communal living are called, are usually motivated by the high costs of modern family living, problems in managing home-care and child-care responsibilities when both partners in a traditional marriage want to work, and a desire to recapture a sense of community.

Although each of the marriages was healthy, the group members felt a restlessness to "do better what we were [already] doing well: caring, enjoying involvement, sorrowing, rejoicing, and sharing. . . . Our ideal is to live and feel as a single family, in which there are naturally special intimacies but in which each person responds to every other with the commitment of a spouse or sibling" (Elm Lane Eight, 1973). Structurally, the Elm Lane Eight have a contract which specifies the eight partners' joint ownership of all physical property, as well as insurance policies on each member's life payable to the Elm Lane Eight savings account. There are no written rules, and problems as well as job assignments are handled at weekly meetings. All major decisions must be unanimous. When there is no unanimity, discussions continue, with members voicing their opinions and listening to one another until a solution emerges.

THE GAY LIFESTYLE

A lifestyle which is not new to American culture but which has only recently surfaced in the light of public attention is that of the homosexual. Homosexuals live most often as singles. As such, they must confront the same problems faced by heterosexual singles, especially that of living in a culture which still places a premium on marriage and the family and which is most often structured to accommodate the couple. Homosexuals, however, also must deal with a long tradition of ridicule and discriminatory practices and laws, whether they live independently or as monogamous couples. Indeed, because of repressive public attitudes toward, and legal sanctions against, homosexual acts, most homosexuals are still forced to hide their orientation. Many even have felt compelled by social pressure to conform to heterosexual patterns by marrying and having children, while maintaining covert homosexual friendships.

But in the wake of the sexual revolution and the women's liberation movement, some homosexuals have openly declared their orientation and are working actively to acquire the same rights and privileges taken for granted by heterosexual members of our society. Such activism has brought some changes. The American Psychiatric Association, for example, reversed its long-held stance on the pathology of homosexuality and, in 1973, in a majority decision, removed homosexuality from its list of "emotional disturbances." Employment practices also have altered somewhat, with a few major corporations issuing public policies of nondiscrimination in relation to homosexuals in hiring and promotion. But a price continues to be paid for being open about being different. As one lesbian explains:

> You can be laughed at in public for advocating civil rights for white women, black women, for all women, but we can be fired and blackballed out of our jobs for life. We can be ostracized in a way that you cannot even be touched. We can be put in jail for our sexual preferences. Even the most respectable among us, who advocate nothing wilder than social and civil rights with the same obligations now granted automatically to heterosexuals, live with the daily danger of job loss. It is this fear that has most crippled the homophile community, both male and female—the constant fear of losing economic viability (Damon, 1970, p. 33).

Even if discrimination in employment and housing were to be immediately abolished, general attitudes probably would continue to militate against homosexuals for some time, partly as a result of misunderstandings and distortions about who homosexuals are and what they do. Contradicting one of the erroneous notions which persists about gay men and women is the fact that they are represented in every occupation and every social class. A common impression of the homosexual lifestyle is that it consists of a series of short-term relationships or promiscuous sexual rituals initiated in gay bars. This may be more a stereotype than a general truth, and, where it exists, it is probably more related to situational and normative factors than to a "homosexual psyche" (Mileski and Black, 1972). In other words, it would seem that if homosexual relationships functioned within a tradition of legitimacy and social acceptance, homosexual couples would find themselves more willing to make lasting commitments to each other.

Like members of other minority groups who have been radicalized by their experiences within an essentially hostile social environment, a number of homosexuals are helping to form their own support groups. In some metropolitan areas, for example, there are gay churches and synagogues, counseling centers run by and for gays, and referral centers for gays which provide information about medical and legal services. There are also periodicals and organizations which publicize gay social activities and which function as a dating service for singles in the homosexual community.

Encouraged by the gay liberation movement, several prominent people have chosen to disclose publicly their homosexual lifestyle. By "coming out" in the mass media, these people have, in turn, provided support and encouragement for others in the homosexual community and may be helping to weaken stereotypes and modify negative social attitudes. Some are also helping to create a better understanding of the commonality of human experience, whether one is homosexual or heterosexual. Merle Miller, a successful journalist, revealed his own homosexuality and commented on the gay lifestyle in his book entitled *On Being Different*: "It has been my observation, and I have done considerable looking into the matter, that relationships are very much the same, no matter what the sex of the people involved. It's never easy" (1971).

The Single-Parent Experience

Single parents are by no means new to American culture. Prior to World War I, most single parents were women whose husbands had died early deaths or been killed in action. Public attitude toward the "heroic" mother left with responsibility for rearing a family was sympathetic and supportive. In more recent years, however, with a change in divorce customs and the high incidence of unwed mothers among the lower socioeconomic classes, public sentiment toward the single parent has changed somewhat. Generally, it has been assumed that two parents are better than one, and the deliberate choice to have children out of wedlock or to "divorce despite the children" has not been looked upon with much public favor (LeMasters, 1970).

Despite the social criticism that awaits their decision, some singles, both men and women, are choosing parenthood without the benefit of a

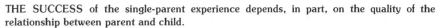

THE SUCCESS of the single-parent experience depends, in part, on the quality of the relationship between parent and child.

marriage partner. Singles who make such a choice generally say that they feel competent to rear a child and desire to do so, but that they do not want to enter into a traditional marriage arrangement. Nor do they necessarily desire help with child-rearing responsibilities. There is some controversy surrounding such decisions, but the general consensus seems to favor the single parent's choice.

Some sociologists warn that the demands are so great (when combined with making a living) that some parental tasks are inevitably shortchanged when one person attempts to be both parent and single head of a household. "The areas of communications, family power structures, and affectional relationships are often the areas that become strained when one parent attempts to maintain the family alone" (Glasser and Navarre, 1965). A still more persistent theme in the literature on single parenthood, however, is that relations are so strained in marriages in general today that growing up with any set of parents has built-in hazards. "Research has shown that having a good relationship with one parent is healthier soil for emotional growth than growing up with two discontented parents" (C. Klein, 1973). In her book devoted to the subject of single parenthood, Klein concludes that any realistic, hard-headed assessment of the state of marital affairs today encourages the growth of the single-parent family (C. Klein, 1973). LeMasters (1970) reminds us that a review of the literature on the one-parent family did not produce sufficient data to support the hypothesis that the one-parent family is inherently pathological or dysfunctional.

The single most important factor contributing to the success of the single-parent experience, according to Klein, is the absence of parental guilt. "The ability to break free of guilt associated with old ideas of parental responsibility affects how a single parent will manage his or her role" (C. Klein, 1973). She recommends that if the decision is made to become a single parent, it should at least be made positively and without any guilt.

No one has suggested that the single-parent experience does not have its own set of problems. Chief among them is the financial problem. "While households headed by women comprise only about 10 percent of all U.S. households, they constitute 25 percent of the families in the so-called poverty group in America" (LeMasters, 1970). Many single parents have to depend on Aid to Dependent Children programs to supplement their own incomes, while others depend on the help of family and friends. "Despite the constant struggle, many women function amazingly well to provide decent food, clothing, and to make a home for their families" (Billingsley, 1968).

Another problem faced by single parents has to do with role conflict. "Single parents tend to be in conflict with themselves over which roles, that of father or mother, or both, they should or want to fill. They also have a tendency to become overloaded with role commitments, such as breadwinner, nurse, or disciplinarian" (LeMasters, 1970).

A more pragmatic problem is created by a variety of schedules that sometimes conflict, such as work schedules that do not mesh with school or school vacation schedules. And there is always the problem of what to do in case of illness. Who stays home to take care of the sick child? In the words of one close observer of single-parent families, " . . . being the head of a household is, for most women, an eighteen-hour-a-day, seven-days-a-week, and 365-days-a-year job. It would seem that only the most capable and the most fortunate can perform all of the roles involved effectively" (LeMasters, 1970).

SUMMARY

The prevalent, almost pervasive lifestyle in the United States is that of the married couple. Yet despite social pressure to marry, as of 1975 over 43 million adults were living as singles. Although media coverage exploits the sensationalism of "swinging" lifestyles, single people have goals similar to those of married people, and they live their daily lives in a way that is remarkably similar to the way their married counterparts live theirs.

For the first time, remaining single is being considered as an option—chosen over that of marriage. Living single is recognized as acceptable because (1) the sexual revolution has eased the moral sanctions against sex outside marriage, (2) birth control and legalized abortion have removed the fear of unwanted pregnancy, (3) childlessness has become a growing trend, and (4) some of the barriers which have kept women out of good jobs have been removed, making work outside the home as a means of self-support a more attractive prospect for many women.

In order to achieve the theoretical freedom of the single lifestyle, a middle- or upper-middle-class income is preferable, as it is, indeed, for most lifestyles. However, the ability to pay for amusements and travel may be especially important to single people, who often feel a need to compensate for the lonely times. Good friends of the same sex are another hedge against loneliness. Loneliness can also be regarded as a challenge to be met by the discovery of inner resources to turn aloneness to advantage.

Studies which compare the single and the married woman tend to show that the relative quality of life of the single woman is equal to, if not better than, that of her married counterpart. She is in much better shape than the single man. Statistics show that the single man, contrary to his "swinging" image, makes half as much money as the married man and is more likely to commit suicide, go to jail, and suffer mental or physical illness than either the married man or the single woman.

The communal lifestyle is another alternative to the nuclear family. Utopian communes have been a feature of American life since the seventeenth century. Recently revived as a lifestyle in the 1960s, communes must solve the problem of primary commitment to the group on the part of members, if they are to survive. Another alternative is the gay lifestyle. Homosexuals, in the wake of the women's and the black liberation movements, have organized politically in order to gain acceptance for, and to combat prejudice and discrimination against, gay men and women. Single parenthood is another family form on the increase for those who do not wish to commit themselves to a lifetime with a partner.

CASE STUDY

A Single Woman's View

Lynne Weiss's memories of the first four years of her life as a child in prewar Germany are all associated with her parents' preparations for fleeing the country. Her father, a well-known physician, and his wife considered themselves fortunate to get out of the country with their child, and very little money, just before the invasion of the Low Countries.

With the generous assistance of family and friends, the Weiss family was able to live decently in a section of New York where rents were modest while Dr. Weiss spent several months preparing for the state board examinations which would enable him to practice in their new homeland.

Lynne made friends easily. When they were seven or eight years old, she and a girl friend, Hannah, would make up games to entertain the three- and four-year-old children of a family in their apartment building. They would write original stories and read them to the younger children, take the children out, make paper dolls for them, and include them in their own play.

Lynne liked to read, both comic books and regular books, and she frequently checked out four or five books at a time from the public library. Her parents were strict with Lynne, fearing that she might grow to be like a "wild American kid." Her father had very clear and firm expectations of his child, and Mrs. Weiss stuck by her husband on almost every decision. Lynne recalls, "I felt that nobody was on my side, and I showed my resentment to my parents. I would yell at my mother, but not at my father, of course. I remember my mother asking me every day at lunch, 'What did you do at school today?' And I would always say, 'Nothing!' But I liked school. I liked being with my friends. And I liked doing my schoolwork. It gave me a feeling of accomplishment. I was generally an A or a B student, but I once got a C in math. My parents thought that was awful!"

Lynne describes her father as a bright man who was well known and well liked, but somewhat conceited. He was first in his medical school class and a leader in the synagogue. He spent a lot of time with Lynne and told her about many things. He would quiz her to see whether she understood what he had been saying. This intimidated Lynne, and she learned to pay close attention because she feared being unable to measure up to his expectations.

Dr. Weiss died when Lynne was twenty-two. Lynne has two distinct, but very different, feelings about her mother. "As a child I saw my mother as a shadow of my father, never as a person. She always agreed with him. They never had arguments. She would ask for my father's opinion on everything, and I didn't respect her because of that. But she was more on my level. She was kind and sweet and would stroke my forehead. And she was selfless. But during the last thirteen years of her life, after my father died, my mother became a person.

Although she had been a secretary for an uncle of mine before she married and worked as a secretary-receptionist for my father, she had no professional training. But she was willing to learn and wanted to stand on her own two feet. She went to school to learn an adaptation of shorthand and worked for a time as a secretary. She was working for an insurance company for the last few years and worked right up to the end, even after she knew she had cancer. I really grew to admire her."

Lynne majored in elementary education and was working as a substitute teacher. She interrupted her work and studies to follow the man she was dating to the West Coast, where he had accepted a position teaching art history at a state university. She worked there during the fall semester as a translating secretary for a chemical corporation, but she returned to New York in the spring to work on her M.A. and to ponder the question of marriage. The relationship was off and on, but Lynne broke it off definitely a year later. She decided not to complete her M.A. and accepted a position as full-time substitute teacher with a slow third grade. Lynne has been working full time in the schools ever since.

Lynne feels that she did not distinguish herself during her first two years of teaching. But during her third year she felt more relaxed with herself and with the children. She was in a new school with an idealistic principal who liked her work and asked Lynne to take the top third-grade class. Although she felt she was not ready for that, Lynne reluctantly accepted his offer and entered an exciting period, during which she feels she excelled as a teacher. "My classroom always had a noncompetitive atmosphere. There was a lot of structure, but a lot of freedom. When the children finished their work, I had a lot of things for them to explore. I had what I called 'clubs' in art and creative writing and an individualized reading program. All the kids had jobs. It was terrific, very demanding of my time and energy, but very rewarding. Some of my kids still write and come to visit me."

After five years in the new school, Lynne felt that she knew the children better than anyone else there, but she felt that as a classroom teacher she did not have enough clout. For a year or so she had been allowing children to come up individually and sit beside her at milk-and-cookie time to discuss with her anything about which they were concerned. She had begun to feel that "each child is a universe." She began taking counseling courses during the summers. When she eventually took the counselors' examination, Lynne was seventh out of the 500 people who took the exam.

Today, as an elementary school counselor, Lynne describes herself as a "child advocate" vis-à-vis parents and teachers. She works with children both individually and in small groups and often uses their artwork or creative writing as a means of helping them to understand themselves. She also runs therapeutic parents' groups and does volunteer telephone counseling one evening a week.

Still, Lynne finds time for entertaining and keeping up with a number of close friends, both single and married, and for spending time with one man in particular with whom she has shared meaningful sexual experiences for the past five years. She frequently travels abroad in the summer and is an active member of a number of professional organizations. She was recently on a panel that discussed the use of art in therapy. With a friend, she occasionally gives workshops on career guidance. Lynne also finds time for herself. She practices yoga each morning and still enjoys reading. When asked whether she is lonely, Lynne replies, "No. Although my parents are deceased, I still have a lot of aunts, uncles, and cousins, and we are close. And I feel as if there are many people in my orbit whom I can count on in a crisis.''

Interpretation and Questions

How is Lynne like her mother? How is she like her father? How is she different? Do you think Lynne should have married her friend on the West Coast? Single women past a certain age used to be stereotyped as sexless social failures who were thought to lead rather dull lives. How does Lynne challenge this stereotype?

STUDY GUIDE

Important Terms

serial marriage
single lifestyles
communes

complex marriage
gay lifestyles
single parents

Review Quiz

1 During the decade 1960–1970, the proportion of single young persons (between twenty and twenty-four):
   a increased
   b decreased
   c remained about the same
   d has not been measured
2 The term "swingle," a combination of "swinging" and "single," is applied to:
   a single persons in urban areas
   b those who reject the traditional mating and dating patterns
   c singles who see themselves primarily as independent pleasure seekers
   d all the above
3 In the United States it is difficult to remain single by choice because:
   a one may be labeled with a derogatory term such as "spinster," "old maid," or "queer"
   b there is a pervasive belief that it is better to be married than single
   c many institutions still systematically discriminate against those who remain single
   d all the above
4 Surveys of persons leading the lifestyle of an urban single indicate that:
   a most urban singles are of the lower class, rather than the middle or upper middle class
   b few singles have roommates
   c on the whole, singles make less money than their married counterparts
   d few singles ever experience loneliness
5 Evidence suggests that in adapting to single life:

    a women have an easier time than men

    b men have an easier time than women

    c neither men nor women encounter much difficulty

    d women and men have an equally difficult time

6 Overall comparisons of single and married women seem to indicate that:

    a single women over thirty have fewer depressions and neurotic symptoms than married women

    b married women are much more self-reliant than single women

    c women who never marry have less satisfying lives than those who marry

    d there is no true fulfillment for a woman unless she gives birth to a child

7 In comparing single men and married men, indications are that:

    a single men seem to exhibit more behavioral disorders

    b single men are more likely to be thought immature and irresponsible

    c corporations apparently favor married men for management positions

    d all the above

8 The nineteenth-century Oneida Community practiced _____ to regulate sexual relationships.

    a monogamy

    b abstinence

    c complex, or group, marriage

    d none of the above

9 The counterculture communes of the 1960s were generally based upon:

    a a loose structure with little organization

    b religion

    c tightly structured bureaucracies

    d free love

10 The Tennessee commune known as The Farm is based upon a policy of:

    a sexual promiscuity

    b lack of work structure

    c religious convictions and cooperative labor

    d complete freedom of choice in diet and behavior

11 The urban commune called the Elm Lane Eight, as a prototype of many urban communes in the 1970s:

    a is called an *evolutionary commune*

    b is composed of both singles and married couples

    c was begun partially because of the high cost of living and partially because of the members' desire for a sense of community

    d all the above

12 Homosexuals face the same problems as heterosexual singles, and in addition they:

    a are still considered emotionally disturbed by the American Psychiatric Association

    b face discrimination in hiring practices and in their personal lives

    c have no national organizations to speak for their rights

    d none of the above

13 Common myths about homosexuals which have been shown to be false include the idea that:

    a homosexuals are concentrated in a few occupations

    b homosexuals almost always have sex lives characterized by promiscuous relationships in gay bars

    c relationships between homosexuals are different in character from those between heterosexuals

d all the above

14 Research into the single-parent family shows that:

 a it is declining in number

 b it is *not* inherently pathological or dysfunctional

 c it is almost never deliberately chosen

 d all the above

15 The single-parent experience may pose more problems than

are encountered in a two-parent family because:

 a many households headed by women have incomes below the poverty level

 b the parent often becomes overloaded with commitments and responsibilities

 c schedule conflicts between work and school create continuing difficulties

 d all the above

Opinionnaire

Agree	No opinion	Disagree		
———	———	———	1	The time is near when remaining single will become more common than marrying.
———	———	———	2	The people called "swinging singles" are usually very unhappy and lonely underneath.
———	———	———	3	Marriage is the natural state of affairs.
———	———	———	4	The principal reason people are single is that they cannot find a marriage partner.
———	———	———	5	People who join communes are generally looking for variety in sexual relationships.
———	———	———	6	A commune can be a better environment for life than the nuclear family.
———	———	———	7	Communes should be available for adults, but no children should have to be raised in them.
———	———	———	8	There is no reason for any state to have laws prohibiting homosexual behavior.
———	———	———	9	Homosexuality is as natural a way of life as heterosexuality.
———	———	———	10	Most children would be better off with a foster family than in a single-parent home.

Exercise

THE COMMUNE MANIFESTO

This exercise will allow you to construct a set of guidelines for the operation of a modern commune. The manifesto is intended to provide a unified philosophy, which you will furnish by completing the blanks. If any statement seems inappropriate, cross it out.

The name of this commune will be _____.
Membership in the commune will be limited to _____ persons. Applicants for membership will be selected by _____. Upon entry, each member will be required to _____ his or her private property.

The commune will be governed by _____. All decisions regarding policy will be made _____. Work necessary to maintain the living quarters and provide meals will be assigned by _____. The leadership structure will be in office for _____.

The economic support of the commune will be based upon _____. Each member's responsibility for economic support will be to _____. Money will be distributed to each member of the commune by _____. If there is a surplus, the money will be _____.

Children may be brought into the commune when _____. Responsibility for nursing and physically caring for a newborn child will lie with _____. The child will be reared by _____.

Sexual relations will be a matter of _____.

The overall philosophy of this commune will be based upon _____. If questions arise which are not covered by this manifesto, they will be answered by _____. Any member who refuses to obey the rules and spirit of this manifesto will be _____.

Were you able to specify an answer for each blank? Are important aspects of communal living not covered by the manifesto?

Projects for Class or Home Study

1   The publicity given to singles' bars is often distorted. They are, however, much different from family bars, transient bars, or others. Drop by a few of the bars (they usually advertise as singles' bars) and note the patterns of involvement which occur.
2   Many clubs exist in urban areas to promote relationships among singles. Almost all provide free literature for prospective members. Send for some of this material and read it to gain an understanding of the motivations underlying singles' clubs.
3   There are a few thousand communes in the United States today, and most people are near at least one. College newspapers often run ads of communalists seeking new members. Make arrangements to visit a commune. Ask the members to explain their motivations and operating philosophy. If you are sincerely interested, most members will be happy to talk with you.
4   One, Incorporated, and the Mattachine Society are organizations which promote the cause of homosexuals. Their literature is free and describes the contributions of famous past and present homosexuals. Read some of this literature to gain an understanding of the problems with which homosexuals must contend.

5   If you are using this text in a course in marriage and the family, the probability is high that there is a single parent in your class. If so, ask this person to describe some of the rewards and problems of being a single parent.

Suggestions for Further Reading

Campbell, Angus. The American way of mating: Marriage sí, children only maybe. *Psychology Today*, May 1975, **9**, 37–40.

   A survey of 2,146 adults reports that married people are happier than singles. Also, women get along without men better than men get along without women.

Edwards, Mari, and Hoover, Eleanor. *The challenge of being single.* Los Angeles: Tarcher, 1974.

   A collection of papers from singles' workshops. The material covers the problems and prospects of those who have chosen to remain single.

Kinkade, Kathleen. *A Walden Two experiment.* New York: Morrow, 1973.

   A book reporting on a utopian experiment in communal living based upon psychological learning theory (behaviorism). Marriage is permitted and child rearing is collective, but most participants are living a singles lifestyle.

Lopata, Helena Z. *Widowhood in an American city.* Cambridge, Mass.: Schenkman, 1973.

   A sociological study of adjustment and aloneness at the end of life.

Mendes, Helen A. Single fathers. *Family Coordinator*, October 1976, **25**, 439–444.

   Most single-parent homes involve women, but one-half million single American men are now raising children. This study is the first to explore the problems, the needs, and the common experiences of single fathers.

Shapiro, Joan H. *Communities of the alone.* New York: Association Press, 1971.

   One of the most frequently mentioned problems of being single is loneliness. The author presents a sensitive, informative account of the effects of loneliness.

Welty, Eudora. *The optimist's daughter.* New York: Random House, 1972.

   A Southern novelist explores the reasons why a single woman cut herself off from family, roots, and heritage. Her father's death helps her find a new involvement with people.

Answers to Review Quiz

1-*a* 2-*d* 3-*d* 4-*c* 5-*a* 6-*a* 7-*d* 8-*c* 9-*a* 10-*c* 11-*d* 12-*b* 13-*d* 14-*b* 15-*d*

GLOSSARY

Abortion Induced termination of pregnancy before the fetus is capable of surviving independently.

Abstinence As a method of family planning, a total avoidance of sexual intercourse except when a child is desired.

Acceptance A deep regard for the inherent worthiness and value of a person as distinct from the feelings and behavior of that person.

Activity theory of aging According to Havighurst and Albrecht (1953), the theory that life satisfaction depends on maintaining a high level of social activity into old age and that the needs of the elderly remain substantially the same as those of middle-aged persons.

Adversary divorce Divorce granted by a court only if the spouse bringing suit can prove that the other spouse is guilty of a specific fault.

Agape Altruism, or a concern for the welfare of the other person.

Al-Anon A companion program to Alcoholics Anonymous whose members are the spouses of alcoholics.

Alcoholics Anonymous A nationwide democratically structured program for enabling alcoholics to cope with the absence of alcohol.

Alcoholism The excessive consumption of alcohol to the extent that it interferes with functioning as an adult in society. In terms of the medical model, an illness similar to an incurable disease and caused, ultimately, by unknown factors.

Alimony Payment made for support of a spouse following a legal separation or divorce.

Anal stage The second psychosexual stage of child development, according to Freud, during which pleasure is focused on the sensations of the sphincter and urethral muscles.

Androgens Male hormones which determine the development of sexual characteristics.

Androgyny Masculine and feminine behavior which is free of stereotyped differences based on sex alone.

Assets Possessions such as cash and savings and the monetary value of physical belongings.

Authentic love According to Rollo May, a combination of sex, eros, philia, and agape.

Authoritarian child rearing See *Restrictive child rearing.*

Birth control Any method of preventing childbirth or spacing the birth of children. Thus abortion is considered a method of birth control.

Birthrate The number of births per 1000 population.

Body language See *Tacit communication.*

Budget A plan or guideline for spending money in order to distribute income according to needs.

Cash-flow record An accounting of how and where money is spent during a given period of time.

Cash-value insurance Insurance that combines a savings account with life insurance. The rate usually does not change over the life of the policy.

Centration According to Piaget, the tendency of a small child to focus on

one aspect of an object or situation and make cause-and-effect associations which are not necessarily reasonable.

Cervix A narrow passageway between the vagina and the uterus in the human female.

Children's rights A recognition that children are entitled to protection and support.

Chronic conflict A characteristic of a marriage in which small incidents constantly lead to major disruptions.

Clitoris A highly sensitive part of the female genitalia, homologous to the penis.

Cognitive process Intellectual functions such as reasoning, thinking, and problem solving. Often contrasted to emotional or physical functions.

Cohabitation As defined by Eleanor Macklin, a practice in which two people of the opposite sex share a bedroom or bed for a minimum of four nights a week and three consecutive months without being married to each other.

Coitus interruptus See *Withdrawal.*

Common stocks Shares in a corporation.

Commune A group, often with utopian goals, whose members share their lives and property as if they were a family.

Communication Various means, verbal and nonverbal, by which messages and meanings are transmitted from one person to another.

Companionate marriage A marriage based on equality, intimacy, and personal interactions between the partners.

Complementarity A characteristic of a relationship in which the two people have different, but complementary, personality traits.

Complex marriage A system of marriage practiced by members of the Oneida Community, in which every man was permitted to have sexual relations with every woman in the group, providing she consented.

Condom A birth control device used by men. It consists of a thin rubber sheath which can be pulled over the erect penis. The condom also provides protection against venereal disease.

Confidentiality The secret knowledge which two close friends have of each other and which they conceal from the outside world.

Conflict Struggle between two people, having the potential of being either a positive or a negative force.

Conflict-habituated marriage Cuber and Harroff's term for the kind of marriage which thrives on tension and conflict, much of which is controlled.

Consensual union An alternative term for cohabitation.

Contraception Techniques to prevent conception.

Cunnilingus The oral manipulation and stimulation of the female genitalia.

Dating A planned event involving an activity to be shared by two or more single persons.

Devitalized marriage Cuber and Harroff's term for the kind of marriage in which the partners have lost much of their interest in each other and in sharing their activities.

Diaphragm A birth control device used by women. The diaphragm is a thin, circular rubber membrane supported by a flexible wire rim. When inserted into the vagina to cover the cervix properly, it is the least dangerous and most effective contraceptive method.

Disengagement theory of aging The belief that a general decrease of social interaction and an increase in preoccupation with self are inevita-

ble and desirable as an individual grows older.

Division of labor A system of work roles and specializations within a society or within any economic unit of that society, such as the family.

Douching A washing out of the vagina, especially as a method of birth control to wash out any sperm that may be present.

Ejaculation The discharge of semen and other fluids from the penis as a result of muscular contractions during orgasm.

Electra complex Analogous to the oedipal complex except that, according to Freud, the actors in the drama are daughter and father.

Empty-nest period The period in the family life cycle that begins when the last child has left home and the couple are alone again.

Endogamy Marriage between two people who are in the same general social-class, religious, or racial group, for example.

Epididymis The long, coiled tube connected to each testis in which sperm collects.

Eros Rollo May's term for the drive to create; the drive toward union with one's own potential and the people with and through whom that potential is realized.

Evolutionary commune A group, usually made up of couples, their children, and unrelated individuals, who live together and share expenses.

Fallopian tubes Passageways between the ovaries and the uterus.

Familiarity The public knowledge that two acquaintances acquire about each other as they interact over time.

Family life cycle The changes in membership and focus of a family from its formation with a marriage until its dissolution as a result of the death of the last member or divorce.

Family planning The use of effective contraceptive techniques to prevent unwanted pregnancies and to plan for a child when the couple desire one.

Feedback An important term in communication theory which involves a check to be sure that one has understood correctly the meaning conveyed by another person.

Fellatio Oral manipulation and stimulation of the male genitalia.

Feminine mystique Betty Friedan's term for the role dissatisfactions and identity problems of American women in a sexist culture.

Fertilization The successful penetration of an egg of the female by a sperm from the male. The moment of conception.

Fixed expenses Necessities which cost roughly the same amount of money during a given period, such as rent, utilities, and insurance.

Gay liberation The movement among homosexuals aimed at gaining recognition of homosexuality as a way of life and at combating discrimination in housing, in employment, and among the community at large.

Gemeinschaft Tönnies's term for social relations in the small, relatively isolated and intimate community.

General sexual dysfunction Helen Singer Kaplan's term for the female experience of a general lack of erotic feelings and a lack of vasocongestion in response to sexual stimulation.

Generativity versus stagnation According to Erikson, the crisis of adulthood during which the individual decides whether to establish and guide the next generation. The alternative to such development is stagnation.

Gesellschaft Tönnies's term for the impersonal social relations in the organized life of the city.

Group insurance Insurance which can be bought by a group at a cheaper rate than if bought by individuals.

Hedonism The doctrine that pleasure or happiness is the chief good in life.

Hermaphrodite A human being whose sexual identity cannot be readily determined on the basis of physical characteristics.

Humanism A philosophical viewpoint which asserts the primacy of human values, the fundamental worthiness of every human being, and the capacity of humans to realize their individual potential.

Impotence The inability of a man to achieve or maintain an erection to the point of successful coitus.

Induction According to M. L. Hoffman and Saltzstein (1967), a method of disciplining children by giving them a verbal explanation of why they should change their behavior.

Infidelity Marital unfaithfulness in the form of extramarital sexual relationships which are deliberately concealed from one's spouse.

In loco parentis Literally, "in the place of parents." A term often applied to an institution such as a college or a summer camp which assumes parental responsibilities.

Institutional marriage A rigid hierarchical structure that focuses on the marital roles of the partners.

Integrity versus despair According to Erikson, the final phase of development, during which the individual either finds the meaning of his or her life or succumbs to feelings of despair and futility in old age.

Intimacy versus isolation According to Erikson, the crisis of young adulthood during which the individual either enters into intimate relationships that involve self-abandonment or risks increasing isolation.

Investment The use of money to make more money—for example, by purchasing stocks, bonds, or real estate.

IUD (intrauterine device) A contraceptive device consisting of a small plastic or metal object which is inserted into the uterus by a trained medical worker. Once the device is properly in place, no further attention need be paid to contraception.

Labia majora Elongated folds of skin which form the outermost boundaries in the adult female genitalia.

Labia minora Highly sensitive folds of skin which unite in the upper part of the female genital area to form a hood over the clitoris.

Laparoscopic sterilization A method of sterilization of women in which the fallopian tubes are cauterized or permanently closed by means of a safe and simple procedure.

Leveling A process, described by Bach and Wyden in *The Intimate Enemy*, in which two partners communicate clearly and simply their complaints and what they would like done about them.

Liabilities Items owed, such as debts, unpaid bills, and mortgages.

Linguist A student of the development, structure, and processes of language.

Macho A term connoting an extreme of the masculine role, such as arrogance, stubbornness, and aggressiveness. Used to describe cultures and individuals reflecting these characteristics.

Major medical insurance Insurance that covers long-term illnesses or serious accidents. It usually takes over when initial health insurance runs out.

Marital adjustment According to Jessie Bernard, all those actions that tend to bring about functional changes in the relationship between spouses.

Marital bargaining or *reciprocity* An ongoing process of give-and-take exchanges in marriage.

Marriage enrichment A common term for interpersonal techniques which are designed to improve and enhance the marital relationship.

Masturbation Manipulation and stimulation of one's own genitals, usually to the point of orgasm.

Modeling A method of teaching by example, with an emphasis on social learning.

Mons veneris The part of the external female genitalia which becomes covered with hair during puberty.

Mutual mirroring A phenomenon which enables both partners in an intimate relationship to see themselves as others see them.

Nature and nurture Terms referring to biology and culture, respectively, as they influence one's development.

Net income Income after income taxes have been deducted.

No-fault divorce A term for legislation which provides for mutual desire and consent to divorce, rather than placing blame on either partner.

Oedipal complex A conflict, according to Freud, in which a son makes futile attempts to win the mother. The conflict finds resolution in emulation of the father.

Openness A willingness to confront and explore one's own thoughts and feelings as well as those of other people.

Oral contraception The prevention of conception by means of a potent drug in the form of a pill which prevents ovulation by changing the hormonal balance in a woman's body.

Oral stage The first psychosexual stage of child development, according to Freud, during which most sensation and satisfaction center in the mouth.

Orgasm A series of muscle contractions in the pelvic region and surrounding the anal sphincter which occur toward the end of coitus, accompanied by intense pleasurable sensations.

Orientations Initial meetings between people, characterized by comparatively superficial exchanges.

Ovaries The organs which produce female reproductive cells and sex hormones.

Ovum or *egg* A single female reproductive cell.

Parent Effectiveness Training (P.E.T.) A program for parents which emphasizes an understanding of a child's behavior from the reference point of the child. P.E.T. is based on Carl Rogers's client-centered therapy.

Parent Involvement Program (P.I.P.) A parent training program which emphasizes friendly relations between parents and children and involvement of parents with their children.

Parent training Programs to improve communication between parents and children.

Passive-congenial marriage Cuber and Harroff's term for a marriage in which the partners have never experienced a genuinely deep interest in each other or their relationship but, rather, have always been more interested in such things as their careers.

Peer groups Groups whose members are alike in terms of age, status, and accomplishments.

Penis The male genital structure consisting of masses of tissue in the form of a shaft, which swells at the tip to form a highly sensitive head, or glans.

Permissive child rearing An attitude toward child rearing that emphasizes self-expression and the special qualities of each child. The goal is the fulfillment of each child's potential.

Sometimes called *progressive child rearing* or *coddling.*

Phallic stage According to Freud, the stage in child development during which pleasure is focused on stimulation of the genital area.

Philia Friendship, or brotherly love.

The pill See *Oral contraception.*

Polarization In communication, an oversimplification of reality in which choices are limited to only two alternatives which are seen as either black or white.

Power-assertion techniques The use of physical punishment or deprivation of a material good for the purpose of changing a child's behavior.

Premature ejaculation The absence of voluntary control over ejaculation once a certain level of arousal has been reached.

Prime interest rate The rate of interest paid by larger banks to the Federal Reserve Bank for borrowing money.

Progressive child rearing See *Permissive child rearing.*

Propinquity The factor of nearness in place and time which facilitates meeting, dating, and mating.

Psychosexual A Freudian term describing the stages of human development. Freud's term emphasizes the influences of sexual drives on behavior.

Puberty A two- to four-year-period in adolescence during which the body attains sexual maturity.

Reconstituted family The new family which is formed when a divorced spouse with children remarries.

Regression A return to a less mature way of behaving, often triggered by a major change in one's life situation.

Responsive Parent Training Program A program emphasizing conditioning and training of children by means of standard behavior-modification techniques.

Restrictive child rearing A theory of

child rearing in which discipline and responsibility are emphasized. These goals are to be achieved by training and conditioning.

Rhythm method A method of birth control in which sexual intercourse is engaged in only during the infertile periods of the menstrual cycle—from the onset of menstruation until the middle of the cycle, when ovulation takes place.

Scripting The playing out of behavior solely on the basis of role expectations rather than personal identity.

Scrotum The saclike part of the external male genitalia which covers and protects the testes.

Secondary sexual characteristics After puberty, those physical differences which are determined by sex: for girls, breasts and hips; for boys, facial hair, a deeper voice, and musculature.

Selectivity In communication, the process by which we choose to focus on only some of the ideas to which we are exposed, according to our own interests and values.

Self-actualization Maslow's term for a continual process of growth which is directed toward the satisfaction of personal and interpersonal needs and desires and the development of one's potential self.

Semen A milky substance which is a mixture of sperm and fluids and which is ejaculated by the male during orgasm.

Senescence Changes in an individual due to biological aging.

Sensorimotor stage A term used by Piaget to describe the earliest stage of child development.

Serial marriage A series of marriages, as entered into by a person who marries, divorces, remarries, etc.

Sexism Actions and attitudes which reflect opposition to the concept of equality between the sexes and which specifically militate against the rights and opportunities of women.

Sex role Behavior that is socially assigned and expected on the basis of gender.

Sexual response cycle According to Masters and Johnson, an invariable sequence of bodily changes which can result from sexual stimulation and which can be divided into four phases: the excitement phase, the plateau phase, the refractory period, and the resolution phase.

Sexual stereotype A set of biased, exaggerated, and inaccurate generalizations about people based on their gender.

Significant others A term coined by George H. Mead to refer to family members and intimate friends whom a person uses to validate his or her identity and whose values and standards become important reference points in that person's own value system.

Single parenthood Parenthood without a marriage partner, often, but not always, resulting from divorce or the death of a spouse.

Social class A grouping of people whose educational background, income level, and occupational status are similar and who often share values and attitudes.

Socialization The process of learning to behave in a way that is expected by the particular society in which one grows up.

Sperm or spermatozoon A single male reproductive cell.

Spermicides A chemical means of contraception used by women. Spermicides are designed to destroy sperm after ejaculation.

Sterilization A contraceptive technique which is usually permanent and irreversible. See *Vasectomy* and *Tubal ligation.*

Stressors Life events, such as death or divorce, which can have a critical, even if transitory, effect on an individual's development or well-being.

Swinging single The stereotyped image of a single person as one whose life revolves around bars, parties, and sexual adventures.

Tacit communication Unspoken messages in which meaning is carried by symbolic gestures (body language). Tacit communication is particularly subject to misinterpretation.

Term insurance An inexpensive form of life insurance in which cash value does not accrue. The policy pays off only in the event of death.

Testes Glands within the scrotum which produce sperm and male sex hormones.

Total marriage According to Cuber and Harroff, the kind of marriage in which partners share in numerous aspects of each other's lives, are open about their differences, and consistently maintain a vital interest in each other.

Transduction According to Piaget, a child's faulty reasoning in which cause-and-effect relationships are made on the basis of memory and association. For example, a child may believe that sitting in a high chair will cause dinner to be served.

Trial marriage An outdated term referring to a situation in which two people of the opposite sex cohabit for the purpose of determining whether they would be suitable marital partners.

Tubal ligation A method of sterilization of women requiring major surgery during which both fallopian tubes are severed or cauterized. Tubal ligation is being supplanted by laparoscopic sterilization.

Understanding The ability to see things from another person's viewpoint.

Unmarried liaison An alternative term for cohabitation.

Urethra A single duct which runs the length of the penis.

Uterus The part of the female reproductive anatomy in which the fertilized egg becomes implanted and develops into a human fetus.

Vagina The muscular cavity in the female sexual anatomy which runs upward and back from the external genitalia.

Vaginismus An involuntary spastic contraction of the muscular opening to the vagina.

Value conflict A situation that develops when a couple discover they have basic disagreements about ideals and standards.

Value differences Differences between a couple concerning ideals and standards.

Variable expenses Discretionary items of expense, such as food, clothing, and entertainment, on which greater or lesser amounts of money can be spent.

Vas deferens In the male reproductive system, the ducts which carry sperm from the epididymis to the prostate gland, where they merge with the urinary tract from the bladder.

Vasectomy A method of sterilizing men which consists of a minor operation. The vas deferens is either cut or tied off, preventing sperm from reaching the urethra.

Vasocongestion The engorgement of body tissues with an increased supply of blood, usually resulting in changes in the size and color of the affected tissues.

Vestibule The funnel-shaped area of the female genitalia in which the vaginal opening is located.

Vital marriage According to Cuber and Harroff, a marriage in which sharing and being together are the most important things in the lives of both partners.

Vulva The area of the female anatomy which includes all external genitalia.

Withdrawal (coitus interruptus) A method of birth control which involves a withdrawal of the penis from the vagina by the male before ejaculation.

Work An activity from which the participant derives certain benefits, including a salary, a feeling of social significance, personal status, and an opportunity to establish relationships outside the family structure.

REFERENCES

Adams, Bert N. Birth order: A critical review. *Sociometry*, 1972, **35**, 411–439.

Adams, Margaret. The single woman in today's society. *American Journal of Orthopsychiatry*, 1971, **41**(5), 776–786.

Adams, Wesley J. The use of humor in teaching human sexuality at the university level. *Family Coordinator*, 1974, **23**, 365–368.

Al-Anon. *What do you do about the alcoholic's drinking?* New York: Al-Anon Family Group Headquarters, 1966.

Al-Anon. *Living with an alcoholic with the help of Al-Anon.* New York: Al-Anon Family Group Headquarters, 1976.

Aldous, Joan. Occupational characteristics and males' role performance in the family. *Journal of Marriage and the Family*, November 1969, **31**(4), 707–712.

Allport, Gordon W., Vernon, Philip E., and Lindzey, Gerald. *Study of values.* Boston: Houghton Mifflin, 1951.

Altman, Irwin, and Taylor, Dalmas. *Social penetration.* New York: Holt, 1973.

Anderson, Sherwood. *Winesburg, Ohio.* New York: Viking Press, 1919.

Ariès, Philippe. *Centuries of child-*

436

REFERENCES

hood: *A social history of family life.* (Robert Baldick, Trans.) New York: Vintage Books, Random House, 1962.

Arling, Greg. The elderly widow and her family, neighbors and friends. *Journal of Marriage and the Family,* November 1976, **38**, 757–768.

Atchley, Robert C. The life course, age grading, and age-linked demands for decision making. In Nancy Datan and Leon H. Ginsberg (Eds.), *Life span developmental psychology: Normative life crises.* New York: Academic Press, 1975.

Audran, Stephane, quoted in Women and love. *Mademoiselle,* July 1976, **82**, 64–75.

Austen, Jane. *Pride and prejudice.* (First published in 1813) New York: Dell, 1959.

Bach, George R., and Goldberg, H. *Creative aggression.* New York: Avon, 1974.

Bach, George R., and Wyden, Peter. *The intimate enemy.* New York: Morrow, 1968.

Back, Kurt W., et al. *Social psychology.* New York: Wiley, 1977.

Bahr, Stephen J., Chadwick, Bruce A., and Strauss, Joseph H. The effect of relative economic status on fertility. *Journal of Marriage and the Family,* May 1975, **37**, 335–343.

Bailey, R., Finney, P., and Helm, B. Self-concept support and friendship duration. *Journal of Social Psychology,* 1975, **96**, 237–243.

Baker, Luther G., Jr. The personal and social adjustment of the never-married woman. *Journal of Marriage and the Family,* 1968, **30**, 473–479.

Baker, Luther G., Jr. Sex, society and the single woman. In Lester A. Kirkendall and Robert N. Whitehurst (Eds.), *The new sexual revolution.* New York: Donald W. Brown, 1971.

Baldwin, James. *If Beale Street could talk.* New York: Signet Books, New American Library, 1974.

Balswick, Jack O., and Peek, Charles W. The inexpressive male: A tragedy of American society. *Family Coordinator,* October 1971, **20**, 363–368.

Bart, Pauline. Mother Portnoy's complaints. *Trans-action,* November–December 1970, **8**, 69–74.

Bell, Inge P. The double standard. *Trans-action,* November–December 1970, **8**, 75–80.

Bell, Robert. *Marriage and family interaction.* (4th ed.) Homewood, Ill.: Dorsey Press, 1975.

Bell, R., Turner, S., and Rosen, L. A multivariate analysis of female extramarital coitus. *Journal of Marriage and the Family,* May 1975, **37**, 375–384.

Benet, Sula. Why they live to be 100, or even older, in Abkhasia. *The New York Times Magazine,* Dec. 26, 1971, p. 3.

Berger, Bennett M. *Working-class suburb.* Berkeley: University of California Press, 1960.

Berkowitz, Leonard. The case for bottling up rage. *Psychology Today,* July 1973, **7**, 24–31.

Bernard, Jessie. The adjustments of married mates. In Harold T. Christensen (Ed.), *Handbook of marriage and the family.* Chicago: Rand McNally, 1964.

Bernard, Jessie. *The future of marriage.* Tarrytown-on-Hudson, N.Y.: World, 1972.

Bettelheim, Bruno. Joey: A "mechanical boy." *Scientific American,* March 1959, **200**, 116–127.

Billingsley, Andrew. *Black families in white America.* Englewood Cliffs, N.J.: Prentice-Hall, 1968.

Bird, Caroline. Is money the root of all freedom? *Ms.,* December 1972, **1**(6), 82.

Birren, James. Psychological aspects of aging: Intellectual functioning. *Gerontologist,* 1968, **8**, 16–19.

Blake, Judith. Can we believe recent data on birth expectations in the

437

REFERENCES

United States? *Demography*, February 1974, **11**(1), 25–44.

Blau, Zena S. *Old age in a changing society.* New York: New Viewpoints, 1973.

Blood, Robert O., Jr. *Love match and arranged marriage.* New York: Free Press, 1969.

Bohannan, Paul. The six stations of divorce. In Paul Bohannan (Ed.), *Divorce and after.* Garden City, N.Y.: Doubleday, 1970.

Bostock, J., and Shackleton, Marjorie. Enuresis and toilet training. *Medical Journal of Australia*, 1951, 110–113.

Boston Women's Health Book Collective. *Our bodies, ourselves: A book by and for women.* New York: Simon and Schuster, 1971.

Boswell, James. *Life of Johnson.* (First published in 1791) New York: Oxford University Press, 1953.

Bowlby, John. Childhood mourning and its implications for psychiatry. *American Journal of Psychiatry*, December 1961, **118**, 481–498.

Brickman, Philip. *Social conflict.* Lexington, Mass.: Heath, 1974.

Brittain, Clay V. Adolescent choices and parent-peer cross-pressures. *American Sociological Review*, June 1963, **28**, 385–391.

Brody, Jane. So couples can handle explosive issues—without exploding. *The New York Times*, Sept. 20, 1976, p. 36.

Brownmiller, Susan. *Against our will.* New York: Simon and Schuster, 1975.

Buber, Martin. (Collected writings) In N. N. Glatzer (Ed.), *The way of response: Martin Buber.* New York: Schocken Books, 1966.

Bumpass, Larry L., and Sweet, James A. Differentials in marital instability. *American Sociological Review*, 1972, **37**, 754–766.

Burchinal, Lee G. Characteristics of adolescents from unbroken, broken, and reconstituted families. *Journal of*

Marriage and the Family, February 1964, **26**, 31–44.

Burgoon, Michael. *Approaching speech communication.* New York: Holt, 1974.

Burke, Ronald J., and Weir, Tamara. Relationship of wives' employment status to husband, wife and pair satisfaction and performance. *Journal of Marriage and the Family*, May 1976, **38**, 279–287.

Byczek, Roger. In my opinion. *Seventeen*, May 1973, **32**, 106.

Cadwallader, Mervyn. Marriage as a wretched institution. In J. Gipson Wells (Ed.), *Current issues in marriage and the family.* New York: Macmillan, 1975.

Calvert, Catherine, in Women! Four very personal reports on hating or loving being single. *Mademoiselle*, July 1975, **81**, 76.

Cameron, C., Oskamp, S., and Sparks, W. Courtship American style: Newspaper ads. *Family Coordinator*, January 1977, **26**, 27–30.

Campbell, Angus. The American way of mating: Marriage sí, children only maybe. *Psychology Today*, May 1975, **9**, 37–40.

Can aging be cured? *Newsweek*, Apr. 16, 1973, **81**, 56–58.

Cannon, Poppy. *A gentle knight: My husband Walter White.* New York: Rinehart, 1956.

Carter, Hugh, and Glick, Paul C. *Marriage and divorce: A social and economic study.* Cambridge, Mass.: Harvard University Press, 1970.

Catlin, N., Croake, J., and Keller, J. MMPI profiles of cohabiting college students. *Psychological Reports*, 1976, **38**, 407–410.

Chester, Robert. Is there a relationship between childlessness and marriage breakdown? In Ellen Peck and Judith Senderowitz (Eds.), *Pronatalism: The myth of mom and apple pie.* New York: Thomas Y. Crowell, 1972.

Clanton, Gordon, and Smith, Lynn G.

438
REFERENCES

The self-inflicted pain of jealousy. *Psychology Today*, March 1977, **11**, 44–49.

Clarke, Alfred. An examination of the operation of residential propinquity as a factor in mate selection. *American Sociological Review*, 1952, **17**, 17–22.

Clayton, Richard R. *The family, marriage, and social change.* Lexington, Mass.: Heath, 1975.

Cochrane, Susan H., and Bean, Frank D. Husband-wife differences in the demand for children. *Journal of Marriage and the Family*, May 1976, **38**, 297–307.

Coigney, Virginia. *Children are people too: How we fail our children and how we can love them.* New York: Morrow, 1975.

Cole, M., Gay, J., Glick, J. A., and Sharp, D. W. *The cultural context of learning and thinking.* New York: Basic Books, 1971.

Coles, Robert. *Uprooted children: The early life of migrant farm workers.* New York: Harper & Row, 1970.

Coles, Robert. The cold, tough world of the affluent family. *Psychology Today*, November 1975, **9**, 67–77.

Comfort, Alex. *The joy of sex: A Cordon Bleu guide to lovemaking.* New York: Crown, 1972.

Comfort, Alex. *A good age.* New York: Crown, 1976.

Cookerly, J. Richard. The outcome of six major forms of marriage counseling compared: A pilot study. *Journal of Marriage and the Family*, November 1973, **35**, 608–611.

Corman, Louise, and Schaefer, Judith B. Population growth and family planning. *Journal of Marriage and the Family*, February 1973, **35**, 89–92.

The costs of having a baby today. *Changing Times*, July 1976, **30**, 13–16.

Cottle, Thomas J. Men's consciousness-raising groups. *Win*, Nov. 21, 1974, **10**(39), 4–9.

Cottle, Thomas J. *A family album: Portraits of intimacy and kinship.* New York: Harper & Row, 1975.

Coudert, Jo. *The alcoholic in your life.* New York: Stein and Day, 1972.

Cox, Frank D. *Youth, marriage and the seductive society.* Dubuque, Iowa: Wm. C. Brown, 1967.

Crane, Stephen. The pace of youth. In Stephen Crane, *Maggie and other stories.* New York: Airmont, 1968.

Cuber, John. Adultery: Reality versus stereotype. In Gerhard Neubeck (Ed.), *Extramarital relations.* Englewood Cliffs, N.J.: Prentice-Hall, 1969.

Cuber, John F., and Harroff, Peggy B. *The significant Americans.* New York: Appleton-Century-Crofts, 1965.

Cumming, Elaine. Further thoughts on the theory of disengagement. *International Social Science Journal*, 1963, **15**, 377–393.

Cutler, Beverly, and Dyer, William. Initial adjustment processes of young married couples. In Jacqueline Wiseman (Ed.), *People as partners.* San Francisco: Canfield Press, 1971.

Cutright, Phillips. Income and family events: Family income, family size and consumption. *Journal of Marriage and the Family*, February 1971, **33**, 161–173.

Dager, Edward Z. Socialization and personality development in the child. In Harold T. Christensen (Ed.), *Handbook of marriage and the family.* Chicago: Rand McNally, 1964.

Damon, Gene. The least of these: The minority whose screams haven't yet been heard. In Robin Morgan (Ed.), *Sisterhood is powerful.* New York: Vintage Books, Random House, 1970.

Dankman, Linda, and Cooley, Candace. Ask him out? *Seventeen*, December 1971, **30**, 94.

Davis, Murray. *Intimate relations.* New York: Free Press, 1973.

de Beauvoir, Simone. *The second sex.* New York: Knopf, 1953.

439

REFERENCES

de Beauvoir, Simone. *The coming of age.* New York: Putnam, 1972.

Demos, John, and Demos, Virginia. Adolescence in historical perspective. *Journal of Marriage and the Family*, November, 1969, **31**, 632–638.

Deutsch, Morton. Conflicts: Productive and destructive. *Journal of Social Issues*, 1969, **25**, 7–41.

Dickinson, George E. Dating patterns of black and white adolescents in a Southern community. *Adolescence*, 1971, **6**, 285–298.

Divorce epidemic. Editorial. *The New York Times*, June 15, 1976, p. 36.

Dixon, Ruth B. Hallelujah the pill. *Trans-action*, November–December 1970, **7**, 44–49.

Dodson, Fitzhugh. *How to parent.* Los Angeles: Nash Publishing, 1970.

Don't let the credit pushers trap you. *Changing Times*, April 1976, **30**, 15–16.

Dowd, Merle E. *How to get out of debt and stay out of debt.* Chicago: Regnery, 1971.

Dreikurs, Rudolf, and Grey, Loren. *Logical consequences: A new approach to discipline.* New York: Hawthorn, 1968.

Durbin, Karen, in Women! Four very personal reports on hating or loving being single. *Mademoiselle*, July 1975, **81**, 77.

Dyer, Everett D. Parenthood as crisis: A re-study. *Marriage and Family Living*, May 1963, **25**, 196–201.

Edwards, John. Extramarital involvement: Fact and theory. *Journal of Sex Research*, August 1973, **9**, 210–224.

Edwards, Marie, and Hoover, Eleanor. *The challenge of being single.* Los Angeles: Tarcher, 1974.

Eisner, Betty Grover. *The unused potential of marriage and sex.* Boston: Little, Brown, 1970.

Elkin, Frederick, and Handel, Gerald. *The child and society.* New York: Random House, 1972.

Elkind, David. *Children and adolescents: Interpretive essays on Jean Piaget.* New York: Oxford University Press, 1974.

Ellis, Albert. *Sex without guilt.* New York: Grove Press, 1965.

Ellis, Albert. Healthy and disturbed reasons for having extramarital relations. In Gerhard Neubeck (Ed.), *Extramarital relations.* Englewood Cliffs, N.J.: Prentice-Hall, 1969.

Elm Lane Eight. Commune in disguise flourishes in suburbs. *The New York Times*, Dec. 7, 1973, sec. 8, p. 1.

England, J. Lynn, and Kunz, Phillip. The application of age-specific rates to divorce. *Journal of Marriage and the Family*, February 1975, **37**, 40–46.

Epstein, Cynthia Fuchs. Bringing women in: Rewards, punishments, and the structure of achievement. In Ruth B. Kundsin (Ed.), *Women & success: The anatomy of achievement.* New York: Morrow, 1974.

Epstein, Joseph. *Divorce in America.* New York: Dutton, 1974.

Erikson, Erik H. *Childhood and society.* New York: Norton, 1950.

Erikson, Erik H. *Childhood and society.* (2nd ed.) New York: Norton, 1963.

Erikson, Erik H. *Identity: Youth and crisis.* New York: Norton: 1968.

Fasteau, Marc Feigen. *The male machine.* New York: McGraw-Hill, 1974.

Feldberg, Roslyn, and Kohen, Janet. Family life in an anti-family setting: A critique of marriage and divorce. *Family Coordinator*, April 1976, **25**, 151–159.

Fensterheim, Herbert, and Baer, Jean. *Don't say yes when you want to say no.* New York: Dell, 1975.

Filene, Peter Gabriel. *Him her self: Sex roles in modern America.* New York: New American Library, 1976.

Fitzgerald, F. Scott. *The crack-up.* New York: New Directions, 1945.

Flanagan, William. Personal business. *Business Week*, May 4, 1974, pp. 89–90.

Ford, C. S., and Beach, F. A. *Patterns of sexual behavior.* New York: Harper & Row, 1951.

Forer, Lucille. *The birth-order factor.* New York: McKay, 1976.

Fowler, Elizabeth M. Management: Managers' damaging competitiveness. *The New York Times*, Mar. 2, 1977, p. D1.

Freeman, Jo. The social construction of the second sex. In Helena Z. Lopata (Ed.), *Marriages and families.* New York: Van Nostrand, 1973.

Freud, Anna. *The ego and mechanisms of defense.* London: Hogarth Press, 1946.

Freud, Sigmund. *An outline of psychoanalysis.* New York: Norton, 1949.

Friedan, Betty. *The feminine mystique.* New York: Dell, 1963.

Fromm, Erich. *Psychoanalysis and religion.* New Haven, Conn.: Yale University Press, 1950.

Fromm, Erich. *The sane society.* New York: Holt, 1955.

Fromm, Erich. *The art of loving.* New York: Perennial Library, Harper & Row, 1956.

Fromme, Allan. *The ability to love.* New York: Farrar, Straus and Giroux, 1965.

Gaylin, Jody. Those sexy Victorians. *Psychology Today*, December 1976, **9**, 137–143.

Gelles, Richard. *The violent home: A study of conjugal violence.* Beverly Hills, Calif.: Sage Publications, 1974.

Gilder, George. *Naked nomads: Unmarried men in America.* New York: Quadrangle, 1974.

Gilliam, Ellen. Is dating outdated? *Seventeen*, March 1973, **32**, 106.

Gillies, Jerry. *My needs, your needs, our needs.* Garden City, N.Y.: Doubleday, 1974.

Ginott, Haim G. *Between parent and child: New solutions to old problems.* (First published in 1965) New York: Avon, 1969.

Glasser, Paul, and Navarre, Elizabeth. Structural problems of the one-parent family. *Journal of Social Issues*, January 1965, **21**, 98–109.

Glick, Paul C. The family cycle. *American Sociological Review*, April 1947, **12**, 164–174.

Glick, Paul C., and Norton, Arthur J. Frequency, duration, and probability of marriage and divorce. *Journal of Marriage and the Family*, 1971, **33**, 307–317.

Go ask Alice. New York: Avon, 1971.

Golantry, Eric. *Human reproduction.* New York: Holt, 1975.

Goldsby, Richard. *Biology.* New York: Harper & Row, 1976.

Goodwin, Hilda, and Mudd, Emily. Marriage counseling: Methods and goals. In Ben Ard, Jr., and Constance Ard (Eds.), *Handbook of marriage counseling.* Palo Alto, Calif.: Science and Behavior Books, 1969.

Gordon, Thomas. *P.E.T. in action.* New York: Wyden, 1976.

Gould, Lois. *Final analysis.* New York: Random House, 1974.

Greely, Andrew M. Catholics prosper while the church crumbles. *Psychology Today*, June 1976, **10**, 44–51.

Green, Betty R., and Irish, Donald P. (Eds.). *Death education: Preparation for living.* Cambridge, Mass.: Schenkman, 1971.

Green, Ernest J. Birth order, parental interest and academic performance. Paper presented at the meeting of the Southern Sociological Association, Atlanta, April 1970.

Green, Ernest J. The illusion of performance grading. *Community and Junior College Journal*, October 1973, **44**, 35–36.

Green, Ernest J. *Marriage and family: A basic self-instructional guide.* New York: McGraw-Hill, 1977.

Grollman, Earl A. *Talking about divorce: A dialogue between parent and child.* Boston: Beacon Press, 1975.

Gross, Paul. A run for your money.

House and Garden, August 1976, p. 42.

Guidelines for equal treatment of the sexes. New York: McGraw-Hill, 1974.

Gunter, B. G. Notes on divorce filing as role behavior. *Journal of Marriage and the Family*, February 1977, **39**, 95–98.

Gurin, G., Veroff, J., and Feld, S. *Americans view their mental health.* New York: Basic Books, 1960.

Hacker, Helen M. Women as a minority group. *Social Forces*, October 1951, **30**, 60–69.

Hacker, Helen M. The new burdens of masculinity. *Marriage and Family Living*, August 1957, **19**, 227–233.

Hacker, Helen M. *The social roles of women and men: A sociological approach.* New York: Harper & Row, 1975.

Haley, Jay. The family of the schizophrenic: A model system. In Gerald Handel (Ed.), *The psychosocial interior of the family.* Chicago: Aldine, 1967.

Hardy, Thomas. *Tess of the d'Urbervilles.* (First published in 1891) New York: Airmont, 1965.

Harvey, Carol D., and Bahr, Howard M. Widowhood, morale, and affiliation. *Journal of Marriage and the Family*, February 1974, **36**, 97–106.

Havighurst, Robert J., and Albrecht, R. *Older people.* New York: Longmans, 1953.

Haviland, William. *Anthropology.* New York: Holt, 1974.

Heer, D. M. The prevalence of black-white marriage in the United States. *Journal of Marriage and the Family*, May 1974, **36**, 246–258.

Heiman, Julia R. The physiology of erotica: Women's sexual arousal. *Psychology Today*, April 1975, **9**, 90.

Hemingway, Ernest. *Islands in the stream.* New York: Scribner, 1970.

Hemingway, Ernest. *The Nick Adams stories.* New York: Scribner, 1972.

Hemming, James, and Maxwell, Zena. *Sex and love.* New York: Praeger, 1974.

Henze, Lura, and Hudson, John. Personal and family characteristics of cohabiting and noncohabiting college students. *Journal of Marriage and the Family*, November 1974, **36**, 722–727.

Herrigan, Jackie, and Herrigan, Jeff. *Loving free.* New York: Grosset & Dunlap, 1973.

Herschberger, Ruth. *Adam's rib.* (First published in 1948) New York: Har/Row Books, Harper & Row, 1970.

Hetherington, E. M., Cox, M., and Cox, R. Divorced fathers. Psychology Today, April 1977, **11**, 42–46.

Hill, Reuben. Social stresses on the family. 1. Generic features of families under stress. *Social Casework*, 1958, **39**, 139–156.

Hill, Reuben. *Family development in three generations.* Cambridge, Mass.: Schenkman, 1970.

Hite, Shere. *The Hite report.* New York: Macmillan, 1976.

Hoffman, Lois Wladis. The professional woman as mother. In Ruth B. Kundsin (ed.), *Women & success: The anatomy of achievement.* New York: Morrow, 1974.

Hoffman, Lois Wladis, and Nye, F. Ivan. *Working mothers.* San Francisco: Jossey-Bass, 1974.

Hoffman, M. L., and Saltzstein, H. D. Parent discipline and the child's moral development. *Journal of Personality and Social Psychology*, 1967, **5**, 45–57.

Hofmann, Hans. *Sex incorporated.* Boston: Beacon Press, 1967.

Holmstrom, Lynda L. *The two-career family.* Cambridge, Mass.: Schenkman, 1972.

Horn, Patrice. How to enhance healthy sexuality. *Psychology Today*, November 1975, **9**, 94–95.

Horner, Matina. Fail: Bright women. *Psychology Today*, November 1969, **3**(6), 36–38.

Hornik, Edith Lynn. *You and your alcoholic parent.* New York: Association Press, 1974.

How much are you worth? *Changing Times*, February 1976, **30**, 9.

Hozman, Thomas L., and Froiland, Donald J. Families in divorce: A proposed model for counseling the children. *Family Coordinator*, July 1976, **25**, 271–276.

Hubley, Season, quoted in Women and love. *Mademoiselle*, July 1976, **82**, 64–75.

Hunt, Morton M. *The natural history of love.* New York: Knopf, 1959.

Hunt, Morton M. *The world of the formerly married.* New York: McGraw-Hill, 1966.

Hunt, Morton M. *The affair.* Tarrytown-on-Hudson, N.Y.: World, 1969.

Hunt, Morton M. *Sexual behavior in the 1970s.* Chicago: Playboy Press, 1974.

Hunt, Morton M. Learning to love. *Seventeen*, February 1976, **35**, 87.

Hunter, Marjorie. A fresh start for Betty Ford. *The New York Times*, Jan. 25, 1977, p. 1.

Hurley, John R., and Palonen, Donna P. Marital satisfaction and child density among university student parents. *Journal of Marriage and the Family*, 1967, **29**(3), 483–484.

Ibsen, Henrik. *A doll's house.* (First published in 1879) New York: Dutton, 1970.

Ilg, Frances L., and Ames, Louise Bates. *Child behavior from birth to ten.* New York: Harper & Row, 1955.

Illegitimate rate of births 14.2%, setting a record. *The New York Times*, Jan. 1, 1977, p. 4.

Irwin, Orvis C. Infant speech. *Scientific American*, September 1949, **181**(3), 22–32.

Jackson, Joan K. The adjustment of the family to the crisis of alcoholism. *Quarterly Journal of Studies on Alcohol*, December 1954, **15**(4), 562–586.

Jacoby, Susan. 49 million singles can't all be right. *The New York Times Magazine*, Feb. 17, 1974, p. 13.

Jacoby, Susan. The mystery of the happy marriage (or, who has the key to contentment?). *Redbook*, August 1975, **145**, 65.

Jellinèk, E. M. *The disease concept of alcoholism.* New Haven, Conn.: Hillhouse Press, 1960.

Johnson, David W. *Reaching out: Interpersonal effectiveness and self-actualization.* Englewood Cliffs, N. J.: Prentice-Hall, 1972.

Johnson, Sheila K. The business in babies. *The New York Times Magazine*, Aug. 17, 1975, p. 63.

Johnston, Jill. The Farm: The friendliest place in America. *The Village Voice*, Jan. 3, 1977, p. 17.

Jourard, Sidney. Some dimensions of the loving experience. In Herbert Otto (Ed.), *Love today.* New York: Association Press, 1972.

Jung, Carl G. The stages of life. In Carl G. Jung (collected works), *The structure and dynamics of the psyche.* Vol. 8. London: Routledge, 1960.

Jury, Mark, and Jury, Dan. Gramp. *Psychology Today*, February 1976, **9**, 57–63.

Kagan, Jerome. Do infants think? *Scientific American*, March 1972, **226**(3), 74–82.

Kagan, J., and Moss, H. A. *Birth to maturity: A study in psychological development.* New York: Wiley, 1962.

Kanin, Eugene J. Selected dyadic aspects of male sex aggression. *Journal of Sex Research*, February 1969, **5**, 12–28.

Kanter, Rosabeth Moss. "Getting it all together": Some group issues in communes. *American Journal of Orthopsychiatry*, July 1972, **42**(4), 632–643.

Kaplan, Helen Singer. *The new sex therapy: Active treatment of sexual dysfunctions.* New York: Quadrangle, 1974.

Kart, Cary S. Some biological aspects of aging. In Cary S. Kart and Barbara B. Manard (Eds.), *Aging in America.* Port Washington, N.Y.: Alfred Publishing, 1976.

Katchadourian, Herant A., and Lunde, Donald T. *Fundamentals of human sexuality.* (2nd ed.) New York: Holt, 1972.

Keller, Helen. *The story of my life.* New York: Airmont, 1965.

Kellermann, Joseph L. *A guide for the family of the alcoholic.* New York: Al-Anon Family Group Headquarters, 1969.

Kelley, Robert. *Courtship, marriage and family.* (2nd ed.) New York: Harcourt Brace Jovanovich, 1974.

Kephart, William M. *The family, society, and the individual.* (2nd ed.) Boston: Houghton Mifflin, 1966.

Kerckhoff, A. C., and Davis, K. E. Value consensus and need complementarity in mate selection. *American Sociological Review*, February 1962, **27**, 295–303.

Kinkade, Kathleen. *A Walden Two experiment.* New York: Morrow, 1973.

Kinsey, Alfred C., Pomeroy, Wardell B., and Martin, Clyde E. *Sexual behavior in the human male.* Philadelphia: Saunders, 1948.

Kinsey, Alfred C., Pomeroy, Wardell B., Martin, Clyde E., and Gebhard, Paul H. *Sexual behavior in the human female.* Philadelphia: Saunders, 1953.

Klein, Carole. *The single-parent experience.* New York: Avon, 1973.

Klein, Melanie. Mourning and its relationship to manic-depressive states. *International Journal of Psycho-Analysis, 1940,* **21**, 112–116.

Klerman, Lorraine V., and Jekel, James. *School-age mothers: Problems, programs and policy.* Hamden, Conn.: Shoe String Press, 1973.

Komarovsky, Mirra. Cultural contradictions and sex roles. *American Journal of Sociology*, 1946, **52**, 182–189.

Komarovsky, Mirra. *Blue-collar marriage.* New York: Random House, 1962.

Komarovsky, Mirra. Cultural contradictions and sex roles: The masculine case. In Joan Huber (Ed.), *Changing women in a changing society.* Chicago: University of Chicago Press, 1973.

Kopecky, Gini. The dating scene. *Seventeen*, January 1976, **35**, 25.

Kramer, Roslyn. Federal credit regulations. In Kathryn Paulsen (Ed.), *Woman's almanac.* Philadelphia: Lippincott, 1976.

Krantzler, Mel. *Creative divorce.* New York: New American Library, 1973.

Kron, Joan. The dual-career dilemma. *New York*, Oct. 25, 1976, **9**(43), 49.

Krupinski, J., Marshall, E., and Yule, V. Patterns of marital problems in marriage guidance clients. *Journal of Marriage and the Family*, February 1970, **32**, 138–143.

Kübler-Ross, Elisabeth. *On death and dying.* New York: Macmillan, 1969.

Laing, R. D. *The politics of the family and other essays.* New York, Vintage Books, Random House, 1972.

Landis, Judson T. *Your marriage and family living.* (3rd ed.) New York: McGraw-Hill, 1969.

Landis, Judson T., and Landis, Mary G. *Building a successful marriage.* (6th ed.) Englewood Cliffs, N.J.: Prentice-Hall, 1973.

Lantz, Herman, and Snyder, Elaine. *Marriage.* (2nd ed.) New York: Wiley, 1969.

Lasser, J. K., and Porter, Sylvia F. *Managing your money.* New York: Holt, 1961.

Lasswell, Marcia, and Lobsenz, Norman. *No-fault marriage.* Garden City, N.Y.: Doubleday, 1976.

Leaf, A. Growing old. *Scientific American*, 1973, **229**(3), 44–53.

Lederer, William J., and Jackson, Don. The quid pro quo, or the marital bargaining table. In Lloyd Saxton

444

REFERENCES

(Ed.), *The individual, marriage, and the family: Current perspectives.* Belmont, Calif.: Wadsworth, 1970.

LeMasters, E. E. Parenthood as crisis. *Marriage and Family Living,* 1957, **19**, 352–355.

LeMasters, E. E. *Parents in modern America.* Homewood, Ill.: Dorsey Press, 1970.

LeMasters, E. E. *Blue-collar aristocrats: Lifestyles at a working-class tavern.* Madison: University of Wisconsin Press, 1975.

Lemon, Bruce W., Bengston, Vern L., and Peterson, James A. An exploration of the activity theory of aging: Activity types and life satisfaction among in-movers to a retirement community. *Journal of Gerontology,* 1972, **27**, 511–523.

Lessing, Doris. *The golden notebook.* New York: Simon and Schuster, 1962.

Levinger, George. Sources of marital dissatisfaction among applicants for divorce. *American Journal of Orthopsychiatry,* 1966, **36**, 803–807.

Lewis, Emma. How to be married and free. *Harper's Bazaar,* February 1976, **109**, 76.

Lewis, Michael. The busy, purposeful world of a baby. *Psychology Today,* February 1977, **11**, 53–56.

Liebow, Elliott. *Tally's corner.* Boston: Little, Brown, 1967.

Lifton, Robert J. *Home from the war.* New York: Simon and Schuster, 1973.

Lobsenz, Norman. Living together. *Redbook,* June 1974, **143**, 86.

Lobsenz, Norman M., and Blackburn, Clark W. *How to stay married.* New York: Family Service Association of America, 1969.

Loether, Herman. *Problems of aging.* Belmont, Calif.: Dickenson, 1967.

Lopata, Helena Z. *Widowhood in an American city.* Cambridge, Mass.: Schenkman, 1973.

Love, Keith. For first time in U.S., divorces pass 1 million. *The New York Times,* Feb. 18, 1976, p. 49.

Lowe, Patricia T. *The cruel stepmother.* Englewood Cliffs, N.J.: Prentice-Hall, 1970.

Lowen, Alexander. The spiral of growth. In Herbert Otto (Ed.), *Love today.* New York: Association Press, 1972.

Lund, Dorothy. Stepparents on trial. *Parents' Magazine,* January 1975, **50**, 38.

Maas, Henry S., and Kuypers, Joseph A. *From thirty to seventy.* San Francisco: Jossey-Bass, 1974.

McCary, James L. *Freedom and growth in marriage.* New York: Wiley, 1975.

McClintock, Jack. The Edith Project. *Harper's Magazine,* March 1977, 21–24.

Maccoby, Eleanor E. Woman's intellect. In S. M. Farber and R. H. L. Wilson (Eds.), *The potential of women.* New York: McGraw-Hill, 1963.

Maccoby, Eleanor E., and Jacklin, Carol N. *The psychology of sex differences.* Stanford, Calif.: Stanford University Press, 1974.

Maccoby, Michael. The corporate climber has to find his heart. *Fortune,* December 1976, **94**, 98–101.

Mace, David R. *Getting ready for marriage.* Nashville, Tenn.: Abingdon Press, 1972.

Mace, David R., and Mace, Vera C. Marriage enrichment: Wave of the future? *Family Coordinator,* April 1975, **24**(2), 131–135.

McGrady, Mike. *The kitchen sink papers: My life as a house husband.* Garden City, N.Y.: Doubleday, 1975.

Macklin, Eleanor D. Heterosexual cohabitation among unmarried college students. *Family Coordinator,* October 1972, **21**, 463–472.

Macklin, Eleanor D. Cohabitation in college: Going very steady. *Psychology Today,* November 1974, **8**, 53–59.

Malinowski, Bronislaw. *Sex and repression in savage society.* Cleveland: World Publishing, 1927.

Mancini, Anthony. Living together and the law. *New York Post,* Jan. 8, 1977, p. 25.

Marches, Joseph R., and Turbeville, Gus. The effect of residential propinquity on marriage selection. *American Journal of Sociology,* May 1953, **58**, 592–595.

Marks, Jane. Adjusting to a stepparent. *Seventeen,* June 1976, **35**, 126–127.

Maslow, Abraham H. *Motivation and personality.* New York: Harper & Row, 1954.

Maslow, Abraham H. *Toward a psychology of being.* (2nd ed.) New York: Van Nostrand, 1968.

Masters, William H., and Johnson, Virginia E. *Human sexual response.* Boston: Little, Brown, 1966.

Masters, William H., and Johnson, Virginia E. *Human sexual inadequacy.* Boston: Little, Brown, 1970.

Masters, William H., and Johnson, Virginia E. The role of religion in sexual dysfunction. In Mary S. Calderone (Ed.), *Sexuality and human values.* New York: SIECUS/Association Press, 1974.

Masters, William H., and Johnson, Virginia E. *The pleasure bond.* Boston: Little, Brown, 1975.

Mathes, Eugene. The effects of physical attractiveness and anxiety on heterosexual adjustment over a series of five encounters. *Journal of Marriage and the Family,* 1975, **37**, 769–773.

May, Rollo. *Love and will.* New York: Norton, 1969.

Maykovich, Minako K. Attitudes versus behavior in extramarital sexual relations. *Journal of Marriage and the Family,* November 1976, **38**(3), 693–699.

Mead, G. H. *Mind, self and society.* Chicago: University of Chicago Press, 1934.

Mead, Margaret. *Coming of age in Samoa.* New York: Morrow, 1928.

Mead, Margaret. *Sex and temperament in three primitive societies.* (First published in 1935) New York: Morrow, 1963.

Mead, Margaret. Too many divorces, too soon. *Redbook,* February 1974, **142**, 72. (a)

Mead, Margaret. Divorce Insurance: A new idea. *Redbook,* March 1974, **142**, 38. (b)

Medley, Morris L. Marital adjustment in the post-retirement years. *Family Coordinator,* January 1977, **26**, 5–11.

Mendelson, Mary A. *Tender loving greed.* New York: Random House, 1974.

Mendes, Helen A. Single fathers. *Family Coordinator,* October 1976, **25**, 439–444.

Mileski, Maureen, and Black, Donald. The social organization of homosexuality. *Urban Life and Culture,* July 1972, **1**(3), 187–199.

Miller, Howard, and Siegel, Paul. *Loving: A psychological approach.* New York: Wiley, 1972.

Miller, Mary Susan. Living together. *Ladies' Home Journal,* May 1976, **93**, 44.

Miller, Merle. *On being different: What it means to be a homosexual.* New York: Random House, 1971.

Miller, S., Corrales, R., and Wackman, D. Recent progress in understanding and facilitating marital communication. *Family Coordinator,* April 1975, **24**(2), 143–152.

Moffett, Robert K., and Scherer, Jack F. *Dealing with divorce.* Boston: Little, Brown, 1976.

Money, J., and Ehrhardt, A. *Man and woman, boy and girl.* Baltimore: Johns Hopkins Press, 1972.

More children have mothers who work. *The New York Times,* March 1, 1977, p. 27.

Morgan, Robin (Ed.). *Sisterhood is*

powerful. New York: Vintage Books, Random House, 1970.

Mousseau, Jacques. The family, prison of love. *Psychology Today*, August 1975, **9**, 52–53.

Mussen, P. H., Conger, J. J., and Kagen, J. *Child development and personality.* (3rd ed.) New York: Harper & Row, 1969.

National Organization of Women. Report on sex bias in the public schools. New York: NOW, 1972.

Neill, A. S. *Summerhill: A radical approach to child rearing.* New York: Hart Publishing, 1960.

Neugarten, Bernice, and Weinstein, Karol. The changing American grandparent. *Journal of Marriage and the Family*, 1964, **26**, 199–204.

No-fault divorce has some faults. *McCall's*, February 1974, **101**(5), 53.

Nuccio, Sal. *The New York Times guide to personal finance.* New York: Harper & Row, 1967.

Nye, Ivan F. *School-age parenthood: Consequences for babies, mothers, fathers, grandparents and others.* Extension Bulletin 667. Pullman: Washington State University Cooperative Extension Service, 1976.

Oates, Joyce Carol. *Marriages and infidelities.* Greenwich, Conn.: Fawcett, 1972.

Olsen, Tillie. *Tell me a riddle.* New York: Dell, 1971.

O'Neill, Nena, and O'Neill, George. *Open marriage: A new life style for couples.* New York: M. Evans, 1972.

Osofsky, Joy D., and Osofsky, Howard J. Androgyny as a lifestyle. *Family Coordinator*, October 1972, **21**(4), 411–418.

Otto, Herbert A. (Ed.). *Love today: A new exploration.* New York: Association Press, 1972.

Parten, M. L. Social participation among pre-school children. *Journal of Abnormal and Social Psychology*, 1932, **27**, 243–269.

Paul, Jordan, and Paul, Margaret. *Free to love: Creating and sustaining intimacy in marriage.* Los Angeles: Tarcher, 1975.

Peele, Stanton, and Brodsky, Archie. Interpersonal heroin: Love can be an addiction. *Psychology Today*, August 1974, **8**, 22–26.

Peterman, D., Ridley, C., and Anderson, S. A comparison of cohabiting and noncohabiting college students. *Journal of Marriage and the Family*, May 1974, **36**, 344–354.

Piaget, Jean. *The origins of intelligence in children.* (First published in 1936) New York: International Universities Press, 1952.

Piaget, Jean. *The psychology of intelligence.* Totowa, N.J.: Littlefield, Adams, 1960.

Piercy, Marge. *Small changes.* Garden City, N.Y.: Doubleday, 1973.

Pincus, Lily. *Death and the family: The importance of mourning.* New York: Pantheon, 1974.

Pirandello, Luigi. The soft touch of grass. In Luigi Pirandello, *Short stories.* New York: Simon and Schuster, 1959.

Place, Dorothy M. The dating experience for adolescent girls. *Adolescence*, 1975, **10**, 157–173.

Planned Parenthood Federation of America. *Eleven million teenagers.* New York: PPFA, 1976.

Polier, Justine Wise. Introduction. In Albert E. Wilkerson (Ed.), *The rights of children: Emergent concepts in law and society.* Philadelphia: Temple University Press, 1973.

Powell, John. *The secret of staying in love.* Niles, Ill.: Argus Communications, 1974.

Proulx, Cynthia. Sex as athletics in the singles complex. *Saturday Review/ Society*, May 1973, pp. 61–66.

Putney, Snell, and Putney, Gail. *The adjusted American.* New York: Harper & Row, 1964.

Quinn, Jane Bryant. Where and how to borrow money. *The Reader's Digest*, August 1976, pp. 96–99.

Rainwater, Lee. *And the poor get children.* Chicago: Quadrangle, 1960.

Regula, Ronald R. Marriage encounter: What makes it work? *Family Coordinator*, April 1975, **24**(2), 153–159.

Reik, Theodore. *Of love and lust.* New York: Farrar, Straus & Giroux, 1949.

Renne, Karen S. Correlates of dissatisfaction in marriage. In Robert Winch and Graham Spanier (Eds.), *Selected studies in marriage and the family.* (4th ed.) New York: Holt, 1974.

Robertson, Joan F. Grandmotherhood: A study of role conceptions. *Journal of Marriage and the Family*, February 1977, **39**, 165–174.

Robertson, Nan. Those single-parent adoptions: Still rare, but growing rapidly. *The New York Times*, Sept. 1, 1975, p. 16.

Rogers, Carl R. *Client-centered therapy.* Boston: Houghton Mifflin, 1951.

Rogers, Carl R. *On becoming a person: A therapist's view of psychotherapy.* Boston: Houghton Mifflin, 1961.

Rogers, Carl R. *Becoming partners: Marriage and its alternatives.* New York: Delacorte Press, 1972.

Roiphe, Anne. Keeping and carrying the house together. *New York*, Oct. 25, 1976, **9**(43), 54.

Rolfe, David J. The financial priorities inventory. *Family Coordinator*, April 1974, **23**(2), 139–144.

Rollins, Boyd C., and Cannon, Kenneth L. Marital satisfaction over the family life cycle: A reevaluation. *Journal of Marriage and the Family*, May 1974, **36**, 271–282.

Roosevelt, Ruth, and Lofas, Jeannette. *Living in step.* New York: Stein and Day, 1976.

Roper, Brent S., and Labeff, Emily. Sex roles and feminism revisited: An intergenerational attitude comparison. *Journal of Marriage and the Family*, February 1977, **39**, 113–119.

Rosenberg, Morris. *Society and the adolescent self-image.* Princeton, N.J.: Princeton University Press, 1965.

Rossi, Alice S. Transition to parenthood. *Journal of Marriage and the Family*, February 1968, **30**, 26–39.

Roth, Philip. *Goodbye, Columbus.* New York, Bantam, 1959.

Roth, Philip. *Portnoy's complaint.* New York: Random House, 1969.

Rubin, Theodore. Your questions answered. *Ladies Home Journal*, May 1975, **92**, 40.

Sartre, Jean-Paul. *The words.* (First published in 1964). New York: Fawcett, 1975.

Saxton, Lloyd. *The individual, marriage, and the family.* (2nd ed.) Belmont, Calif.: Wadsworth, 1972.

Scanzoni, Letha, and Scanzoni, John. *Men, women and change: A sociology of marriage and family.* New York: McGraw-Hill, 1976.

Schachter, Stanley. *The psychology of affiliation.* Stanford: University of California Press, 1959.

Schaffer, H. R., and Emerson, P. E. The development of social attachments in infancy. *Monographs of the Society for Research in Child Development*, 1964, **29**(3).

Schoen, Robert. California divorce rates by age at first marriage and duration of first marriage. *Journal of Marriage and the Family*, 1975, **37**, 548–555.

Schulder, Diane. Does the law oppress women? In Robin Morgan (Ed.), *Sisterhood is powerful.* New York: Vintage Books, Random House, 1970.

Schwartz, Pepper, and Lever, Janet. Fear and loathing at a college mixer. *Urban life*, January 1976, **4**(4), 413–430.

Scott, John F. Sororities and the husband game. *Trans-action*, September–October 1965, **2**, 10–14.

Sears, R. R., Maccoby, E. E., and Levin, H. *Patterns of child rearing.* New York: Harper & Row, 1957.

Segal, Julius. Choosing a best friend. *Seventeen*, December 1975, **34**, 102.

Sex counseling over the telephone. *Sexual Behavior*, August 1972, **2**(8), 22–25.

Shanas, Ethel, et al. *Old people in three industrial societies.* New York: Atherton Press, 1968.

Shapiro, Joan H. *Communities of the alone.* New York: Association Press, 1971.

Sheehy, Gail. *Passages: Predictable crises of adult life.* New York: Dutton, 1976.

Shideler, Mary McDermott. An amicable divorce. *The Christian Century*, May 5, 1971, **88**, 553–555.

Shorter, Edward. *The making of the modern family.* New York: Basic Books, 1975.

Simon, Ann. *Stepchild in the family.* New York: Odyssey Press, 1964.

Singh, B., Walton, B., and Williams, J. Extramarital sexual permissiveness: Conditions and contingencies. *Journal of Marriage and the Family*, November 1976, **38**, 701–712.

Slater, Philip. *The pursuit of loneliness.* Boston: Beacon Press, 1971.

Smith, Carlton, and Pratt, Richard P. *The Time-Life book of family finance.* New York: Time-Life, 1969.

Smith, Eleanor W. The role of the grandmother in adolescent pregnancy and parenting. *Journal of School Health*, May 1975 **45**(5), 278–283.

Solomon, Joan. The price of change. *The Sciences*, November 1971, **11**(9), 28–31.

Spanier, Graham. Perceived sexual knowledge, exposure to eroticism, and premarital sexual behavior: The impact on dating. *Sociological Quarterly, 1976*, **17**, 247–261

Spicer, Jerry W., and Hampe, Gary D. Kinship interaction after divorce. *Journal of Marriage and the Family*, February 1975, **37**, 113–119.

Spitz, René. Hospitalism. *The Psychoanalytic Study of the Child*, 1945, **1**, 53–72.

Spitz, René. The smiling response. *Genetic Psychology Monographs*, 1946, **34**, 57–125.

Srole, L., Langer, T. S., Michael, S. T., Opler, M. K., and Rennie, T. A. C. *Mental health in the metropolis.* New York: McGraw-Hill, 1962.

Stack, Carol B. *All our kin: Strategies for survival in a black community.* New York: Harper & Row, 1974.

Stafford, R., Backman, E., and Dibona, P. The division of labor among cohabiting and married couples. *Journal of Marriage and the Family*, February 1977, **39**, 43–57.

Starr, Joyce R., and Carns, Donald E. Singles in the city. In Helena Z. Lopata (Ed.), *Marriages and families.* New York: Van Nostrand, 1973.

Stein, Edward V. MARDILAB: An experiment in marriage enrichment. *Family Coordinator*, April 1975, **24**(2), 167–170.

Steinbeck, John. *The grapes of wrath.* New York: Viking Press, 1939.

Steiner, Claude. *Games alcoholics play: The analysis of life scripts.* New York: Grove Press, 1971.

Steinmetz, Suzanne K., and Straus, Murray A. (Eds.). *Violence in the family.* New York: Harper & Row, 1974.

Stephens, William N. Marriage defined. In Lloyd Saxton (Ed.), *The individual, marriage and the family: Current perspectives.* Belmont, Calif.: Wadsworth, 1970. (a)

Stephens, William N. Predictors of marital adjustment. In Lloyd Saxton (Ed.), *The individual, marriage and the family: Current perspectives.* Belmont, Calif.: Wadsworth, 1970. (b)

Stetson, Dorothy M., and Wright, Gerald C., Jr. The effects of laws on divorce in American states. *Journal of Marriage and the Family*, August 1975, **37**, 537–546.

Stevens, Evelyn P. Machismo and marianismo. *Society*, September–October 1973, **10**(6), 57–63.

Stolte-Heiskanen, Veronica. Family needs and societal institutions: Potential empirical linkage mechanisms. *Journal of Marriage and the Family*, November 1975, **37**, 903–916.

Strong, John R. A marital conflict-resolution model: Redefining conflict to achieve intimacy. *Journal of Marriage and the Family*, July 1975, **37**, 269–276.

Suelzle, Marijean. Women in labor. In Helena Z. Lopata (Ed.), *Marriages and families*. New York: Van Nostrand, 1973.

The surge in easy divorces—and the problems they bring. *U. S. News & World Report*, Apr. 22, 1974, p. 243.

Swensen, Clifford. The behavior of love. In Herbert Otto (Ed.), *Love today*. New York: Association Press, 1972.

Swerdloff, Peter, and the Editors of Time-Life. *Men and women*. Human Behavior Series. New York: Time-Life, 1975.

Tavris, Carol. Good news about sex. *New York*, December 1976, **9**(49), 51–57.

Tavris, Carol. Men and women report their views on masculinity. *Psychology Today*, January 1977, **10**(8), 34.

Tepperman, Jean. Two jobs: Women who work in factories. In Robin Morgan (Ed.), Sisterhood is powerful. New York: Vintage Books, Random House, 1970.

Terkel, Studs. *Working*. New York: Pantheon, 1972.

Theodore, Athena (Ed.). *The professional woman*. Cambridge, Mass.: Schenkman, 1971.

Thompson, Jean. *The house of tomorrow*. New York: Harper & Row, 1967.

Thorman, George. Cohabitation: A report on the married-unmarried life style. *The Futurist*, December, 1973, pp. 250–253.

Tiffany, Donald W., Cowan, James R., and Tiffany, Phyllis M. *The unemployed: A social-psychological portrait*. Englewood Cliffs, N.J.: Prentice-Hall, 1970.

Toffler, Alvin. *Future shock*. New York: Random House, 1970.

Toman, Walter. *Family constellation: Its effects on personality and social behavior*. (3rd ed.) New York: Springer, 1976.

Tooley, Kay. Antisocial behavior and social alienation post divorce: The "man of the house" and his mother. *American Journal of Orthopsychiatry*, 1976, **46**(1), 33–42.

Travis, Robert, and Travis, Patricia. The pairing and enrichment program: Actualizing the marriage. *Family Coordinator*, April 1975, **24**(2), 161–165.

Treas, Judith. Aging and the family. In Diana S. Woodruff and James E. Birren (Eds.), *Aging: Scientific perspectives and social issues*. New York: Van Nostrand, 1975.

U.S. Bureau of the Census. *We, the young marrieds*. Report No. 11. Washington: GPO, 1972.

U.S. Bureau of the Census. *Current population reports*. Ser. T-60-101. Washington: GPO, 1974.

U.S. Bureau of the Census. *Statistical abstracts of the United States:1975*. Washington: GPO, 1975.

U.S. Bureau of the Census. Number, timing, and duration of marriages and divorces in the United States. *Current Population Reports*, Ser. P-20, No. 297, June 1975. Washington: GPO, 1976. (a)

U.S. Bureau of the Census. *Statistical abstracts of the United States: 1976*. Washington: GPO, 1976. (b)

U.S. Bureau of the Census. *Status: A monthly chartbook of social and economic trends*. Washington: GPO, August 1976. (c)

U.S. Department of Health, Education, and Welfare. Office of Human Development. Statistical Memo No. 31. Publication No. OHD-75-20013. Washington: GPO, 1975.

U.S. Department of Health, Education, and Welfare. Office of Human Development. *Facts about older Americans.* Publication No. OHD-77-20006. Washington: GPO, 1976.

Updike, John. *The poorhouse fair.* New York: Knopf, 1958.

Updike, John. Dear Alexandros. In John Updike, *Pigeon feathers.* Greenwich, Conn.: Fawcett, 1962.

Updike, John. *Of the farm.* New York: Knopf, 1965.

Veroff, Joseph, and Feld, Sheila. *Marriage and work in America: A study of motives and roles.* New York: Van Nostrand Reinhold, 1970.

Vessey, M., Doll, R., Peto, R., Johnson, B., and Wiggins, P. A long-term follow-up study of women using different methods of contraception: An interim report. *Journal of Biosocial Science,* October 1976, **8**(4), 373–427.

Viorst, Judith. It's never a nice divorce. *Redbook,* January 1974, **142**, 29.

Viorst, Judith. What is this thing called love? *Redbook,* February 1975, **144**, 12.

Vreeland, Rebecca. Is it true what they say about Harvard boys? *Psychology Today,* January 1972, **5**, 65.

Wahlroos, Sven. *Family communication: A guide to emotional health.* New York: Signet Books, New American Library, 1974.

Waller, Willard. The dating and rating complex. *American Sociological Review,* 1937, **2**, 727–734.

Walmsley, John. *Neill and Summerhill: A man and his work.* Baltimore: Penguin, 1969.

Walster, E., Aronson, V., Abrahams, D., and Rottmann, L. Importance of physical attractiveness in dating behavior. *Journal of Personality and Social Psychology,* 1966, **4**, 508–516.

Watzlawick, P. *An anthology of human communication.* Palo Alto, Calif.: Science and Behavior Books, 1964.

Webber, M. Order in diversity: Community without propinquity. In L.

Winger (Ed.), *Cities and space.* Baltimore: Johns Hopkins Press, 1963.

Weg, Ruth B. Changing physiology of aging: Normal and pathological. In Diana S. Woodruff and James E. Birren (Eds.), *Aging: Scientific perspectives and social issues.* New York: Van Nostrand, 1975.

Weinstein, Grace W. *Children and money.* New York: Charterhouse, 1975.

Weisberg, D. Kelly. The Cinderella children. *Psychology Today,* April 1977, **11**, 84–86.

Weiss, Robert S. *Marital separation.* New York: Basic Books, 1975.

Welty, Eudora. *The optimist's daughter.* New York: Random House, 1972.

Whitehurst, Robert. Extramarital sex: Alienation or extension of normal behavior. In Gerhard Neubeck (Ed.), *Extramarital relations.* Englewood Cliffs, N.J.: Prentice-Hall, 1969.

Wilkinson, Melvin. Romantic love: The great equalizer? Sexism in popular music. *Family Coordinator,* April 1976, **25**, 161–166.

Wilson, Angus. The American way of mating. *Psychology Today,* May 1975, **8**(12), 37.

Wilson, K., Zurcher, L., McAdams, D., and Curtis, R. Stepfathers and stepchildren: An exploratory analysis from two national surveys. *Journal of Marriage and the Family,* 1975, **37**, 526–536.

Winch, Robert F. *Mate selection.* New York: Harper, 1958.

Winch, Robert F. The functions of dating. In Robert Winch and Graham Spanier (Eds.), *Selected studies in marriage and the family.* (4th ed.) New York: Holt, 1974.

Winter, Gibson. *Love and conflict.* Garden City, N.Y.: Doubleday, 1961.

Winter, Ruth. Lonely America: Looking for a friend. *Science Digest,* January 1975, **77**, 60–66.

Winthrop, Henry. Love and companionship. In Herbert Otto (Ed.), *Love today.* New York: Association Press, 1972.

Wittman, James S., Jr. Dating patterns of rural and urban Kentucky teenagers. *Family Coordinator,* January 1971, **20**, 63–66.

Wolf, Katherine M. *The controversial problem of discipline.* New York: Child Study Association of America, 1953.

Wolfe, Linda. *Playing around.* New York: Morrow, 1975.

Wolff, Sula. *Children under stress.* Baltimore: Penguin, 1969.

Wolfgang, Marvin E. Husband-wife homicides. *Corrective Psychiatry and Journal of Social Therapy,* 1956, **2**, 263–271.

Women on Words and Images. *Dick and Jane as victims: Sex stereotyping in children's readers.* Princeton, N.J.: WWI, 1972.

Women's Caucus, University of Chicago. The halls of academe. In Robin Morgan (Ed.), *Sisterhood is powerful.* New York: Vintage Books, Random House, 1970.

Women's lib: The case against chauvinism. A 20-year bill of particulars. *Human Behavior,* May–June 1972, **1**, 46–49.

Yankelovich, Daniel. The meaning of work. In Jerome M. Rosow (Ed.), *The worker and the job: Coping with change.* Englewood Cliffs, N.J.: Prentice-Hall, 1974.

ACKNOWL-EDGMENTS

Literary Sources

Extracts from *Becoming Partners*, by Carl R. Rogers, copyright © 1972 by Carl R. Rogers. Reprinted by permission of Delacorte Press.

Extracts from Julius Segal, "Choosing a Best Friend," *Seventeen*, December 1975. Reprinted from SEVENTEEN® Magazine. Copyright © 1975 by Triangle Communications, Inc. All right reserved.

Extract from Season Hubley, quoted in "Women and Love," *Mademoiselle*, July 1976, copyright © 1976 by The Condé Nast Publications, Inc. Reprinted by permission of the author and the publisher.

Extract, Are You a Sexist? from "Women's Lib: The Case against Chauvinism. A 20-year Bill of Particulars." Reprinted by permission. © 1972 Human Behavior Magazine.

Extracts from Mirra Komarovsky, "Cultural Contradictions and Sex Roles," *American Journal of Sociology*, 1946, **52**, 182–189. Copyright 1946 by The University of Chicago Press. All rights reserved. Reprinted by permission.

Extracts from Thomas J. Cottle, "Men's Consciousness-raising Groups," *Win*, Nov. 21, 1974, **10**(39), 4–9.

455

**ACKNOWL-
EDGMENTS**

April 1947. Copyright 1947 by American Sociological Association. Reprinted by permission.

Extract from Eleanor W. Smith, "The Role of the Grandmother in Adolescent Pregnancy and Parenting," *Journal of School Health*, May 1975. Copyright Charles B. Slack, Inc. Reprinted by permission.

Two figures from Joan Solomon, "The Price of Change," *The Sciences*, November 1971. Copyright 1971 The New York Academy of Sciences. Reprinted by permission.

Extract from Judith Viorst, "It's Never a Nice Divorce," *Redbook*, January 1974. Copyright © 1974 by Judith Viorst. Reprinted by permission.

Extract from "An Amicable Divorce," by Mary McDermott Shideler, copyright 1971 by Christian Century Foundation. Reprinted by permission from the May 5, 1971, issue of *The Christian Century.*

Extract from Catherine Calvert, in "Women! Four Very Personal Reports on Hating or Loving Being Single," *Mademoiselle*, July 1975. Copyright © 1975 by The Condé Nast Publications Inc. Reprinted by permission.

Extracts from Susan Jacoby, "49 Million Singles Can't All Be Right," *The New York Times Magazine*, Feb. 17, 1974, © 1974 by The New York Times Company. Reprinted by permission.

Extract from Karen Durbin, in "Women! Four Very Personal Reports on Hating or Loving Being Single," *Mademoiselle*, July 1975. Copyright © 1975 by The Condé Nast Publications Inc. Reprinted by permission.

Photo Sources

Chapter 1   Page   2   Charles Gatewood
           Page   9   Peter Krupenye

Chapter 2   Page 22   Serge Honinow
           Page 24   Jack Daly
           Page 27   David Linsell
           Page 29   Peter Krupenye
           Page 33   Charles Gatewood

Chapter 3   Page 46   Charles Gatewood
           Page 49   Charles Gatewood
           Page 52   Gloria Karlson
           Page 54   Charles Gatewood
           Page 61   Charles Gatewood
           Page 65   Charles Gatewood

Chapter 4   Page 74   Susan Hajjar
           Page 77   Jack Daly
           Page 90   Jack Daly

Chapter 5   Page 104   Charles Gatewood
           Page 108   Charles Gatewood
           Page 112   Carrie Boretz
           Page 115   Carrie Boretz
           Page 118   Jack Daly
           Page 120   Jack Daly

Chapter 6   Page 130   Gloria Karlson
           Page 133   Jean Shapiro

456

ACKNOWL-
EDGMENTS

INDEX